The Birds of the Nebraska Sandhills

Paul A. Johnsgard

School of Biological Sciences
University of Nebraska–Lincoln
Lincoln, Nebraska

Josef Kren

Department of Biomedical Sciences
Bryan College of Health Sciences
Lincoln, Nebraska

Zea Books
Lincoln, Nebraska: 2020

Abstract

This book provides basic information on all the species of birds that have been reliably reported from the Nebraska Sandhills region as of 2020. They include 46 permanent residents, 125 summer breeders, 125 migrants, and 102 rare or accidental species, totaling 398 species. Information on status, migration, and habitats is provided for all but the very rare and accidental species. There are also descriptions of 46 refuges, preserves, and other public-access natural areas in the region and seven suggested birding routes. The text contains more than 90,000 words and over 250 literature references along with more than 20 drawings, 9 maps, and 32 photographs by the authors.

Copyright © 2020 Paul A. Johnsgard and Josef Kren

ISBN: 978-1-60962-178-0   paperback (b&w)

doi:10.32873/unl.dc.zea.1272

Composed in Merriweather and Merriweather Sans types.

Zea Books are published by the University of Nebraska–Lincoln Libraries

Electronic (pdf) edition published online at
https://digitalcommons.unl.edu/zeabook/

Print editions sold at
http://www.lulu.com/spotlight/unllib

UNL does not discriminate based upon any protected status.
Please go to http://www.unl.edu/equity/notice-nondiscrimination

Color versions of the black and white photographs are available online at
https://digitalcommons.unl.edu/zeabook/96/

Contents

List of Maps 4
List of Tables 4
List of Figures 5
List of Photographs 5

Preface 7

The Nebraska Sandhills and Their Unique
    Wetlands 9
The Drums of April and the Dances of Life . . . 11
Biological Profiles of Some Typical Sandhills
    Birds 15

Introduction

Natural History of the Nebraska Sandhills . .22
    Geography 22
    Lakes and Rivers 24
    Wetlands 26
    Landscape Ecology 28
    Climate 29
    Birds and Humans in the Nebraska
        Sandhills 30
    Human Impacts on Birds 30
    Ornithological Research and Regional
        Birding 30

Species Accounts

Terms and Inclusion Criteria for Species
    Accounts 34
Family Anatidae (Swans, Geese, and
    Ducks) 35
Family Odontophoridae (New World
    Quails) 50
Family Phasianidae (Pheasants, Grouse,
    and Turkeys) 50
Family Podicipedidae (Grebes) 57
Family Columbidae (Pigeons and
    Doves) 59
Family Cuculidae (Cuckoos) 62
Family Caprimulgidae (Goatsuckers) . . .62
Family Apodidae (Swifts) 63
Family Trochilidae (Hummingbirds) . . . 64
Family Rallidae (Rails, Gallinules,
    and Coots) 65
Family Gruidae (Cranes) 69
Family Recurvirostridae (Stilts and
    Avocets) 71
Family Charadriidae (Plovers) 73
Family Scolopacidae (Sandpipers and
    Snipes) 75
Family Laridae (Gulls and Terns) 87
Family Stercorariidae (Jaegers) 92
Family Gaviidae (Loons) 92
Family Phalacrocoracidae (Cormorants) . . .93
Family Pelecanidae (Pelicans) 93
Family Ardeidae (Herons and Egrets) . . . 94
Family Threskiornithidae (Ibises and
    Spoonbills) 98
Family Cathartidae (New World Vultures) . 100
Family Pandionidae (Ospreys) 100
Family Accipitridae (Hawks, Eagles,
    and Kites) 101
Family Tytonidae (Barn Owls) 106
Family Strigidae (Typical Owls) 108
Family Alcedinidae (Kingfishers) 113
Family Picidae (Woodpeckers) 113
Family Falconidae (Falcons and
    Caracaras) 115
Family Tyrannidae (Tyrant Flycatchers) . . 118
Family Laniidae (Shrikes) 122
Family Vireonidae (Vireos) 123
Family Corvidae (Crows, Jays, and
    Magpies) 126
Family Alaudidae (Larks) 127
Family Hirundinidae (Swallows) 129
Family Paridae (Chickadees and Titmice) . 132

Family Sittidae (Nuthatches) 132
Family Certhiidae (Creepers) 133
Family Troglodytidae (Wrens). 133
Family Cinclidae (Dippers) 135
Family Polioptilidae (Gnatcatchers) 135
Family Regulidae (Kinglets). 135
Family Turdidae (Thrushes). 136
Family Mimidae (Mockingbirds, Thrashers, and Catbirds) 138
Family Bombycillidae (Waxwings). 139
Family Sturnidae (Starlings) 140
Family Passeridae (Old World Sparrows) . 140
Family Motacillidae (Pipits) 141
Family Fringillidae (Boreal Finches). . . . 141
Family Calcariidae (Longspurs and Snow Buntings). 143
Family Passerellidae (New World Sparrows and Towhees) 144
Family Icteriidae (Chats) 155
Family Icteridae (Blackbirds, Orioles, and Meadowlarks) 155
Family Parulidae (New World Warblers) . . 164
Family Cardinalidae (Cardinals, Tanagers, and Grosbeaks) 172

Refuges, Preserves, and Other Natural Areas in the Sandhills Region 175

Suggested Birding Routes in the Western and Central Nebraska Sandhills 184

References
General Surveys 189
Geology, Physiography, and Wetlands . . . 189
Botany, Zoology, and Ecology 190
Birds 192

Index to Bird Species and Families. 198

Maps

1. Location of the Nebraska Sandhills, Ogallala aquifer, and other features 22
2. Distribution of wetlands in the Nebraska Sandhills. 24
3. Rivers and counties in the Nebraska Sandhills. 25
4. The extent of surface sand and associated counties in the Nebraska Sandhills 26
5. Wetlands and roads in the western Sandhills of Garden County and southern Sheridan County 27
6. Major roads and highways in the Nebraska Sandhills. 176
7. Locations of counties, wildlife refuges, and other protected areas in the Nebraska Sandhills. 177
8. Crescent Lake National Wildlife Refuge and northern approaches. 185
9. Vicinities of Antioch and Lakeside, showing suggested birding routes 186

Tables

1. Sandhills County Codes, Areas, and Human Populations 23
2. Geographic and Ornithological Aspects of the Nebraska Sandhills Counties 31
3. Relative Spring and Summer Abundance Indices of Mostly Wetland Bird Species in Three Sandhills National Wildlife Refuges . 33

Contents

Figures

Greater prairie-chicken. 12
Burrowing owl 15
Northern harrier 17
Long-billed curlew, in flight 21
Upland sandpiper. 33
Snow geese 36
Sharp-tailed grouse, male display postures . . 52
Greater prairie-chicken, male display
    postures 55
American bittern, pied-billed grebe,
    double-crested cormorant, American
    white pelican, sandhill crane, and
    whooping crane 68
Long-billed curlew and piping plover 74
Forster's terns, mating 91
Ferruginous hawk 107
Burrowing owl 110
Prairie falcon and green-winged teal 117
Loggerhead shrike 123
Grasshopper sparrow 145
Savannah sparrow, clay-colored sparrow,
    lark bunting, grasshopper sparrow,
    and horned lark 153
Eastern and western meadowarks and
    bobolink. 158
Baltimore oriole, Bullock's oriole, and
    hybrid phenotypes. 160

Photographs

Long-billed curlew, adult female flying. . . . 6
Trumpeter swan 8
Trumpeter swan family 38
Wood duck, male 40
Northern pintail, males 44
Sharp-tailed grouse, male 51
Greater prairie-chicken, male. 54
Pied-billed grebe, adult. 56
Eared grebe, adults 58
Clark's and western grebe, adults 60
Sora, adult 67
Black-necked stilt, adult 70
American avocet, adult 72
Upland sandpiper, adult 76
Long-billed curlew, adult female 78
Short-billed dowitcher, adults 82
Wilson's snipe, adult 84
Wilson's phalarope, adults 86
American bittern, adult male 95
Great blue heron, adult 97
Black-crowned night-heron, adult 99
Swainson's hawk, adult. 105
Great horned owl, adult 109
Burrowing owl, adult 111
Loggerhead shrike, adult 124
Horned lark, adult 128
Cliff swallow, adults 131
Grasshopper sparrow, male. 146
Lark sparrow, adult. 148
Yellow-headed blackbird, male 156
Red-winged blackbird, male 162
Common yellowthroat, male 167

Preface

One summer day, after returning from a two-year postdoctoral fellowship in England in 1961, and with a contract in hand to begin a teaching job at the University of Nebraska in Lincoln that autumn, I decided to take a detailed look at a Nebraska state map. I had never visited the state and knew little about it. However, I remembered that I had once been told by Al Hochbaum, then director of the Delta Waterfowl Research Station in southern Manitoba that, other than my home state of North Dakota, Nebraska might be the most important state south of Canada having a nationally important waterfowl breeding region. He specifically said that the Sandhills region of Nebraska is probably the heart of the state's waterfowl breeding habitats.

With that I mind, I started searching on the map for a place called "Sandhills" and was disappointed to find that only a small indefinite area of north-central Nebraska south of Valentine was identified as "sand hills."

Nevertheless, after finishing my first year of teaching, I packed up our Volkswagen microbus and, with my wife and two small children, started across Nebraska on Highway 2 in mid-June in search of natural Nebraska and a seemingly near-mythical place called the Sandhills.

I specifically wanted to see a spot called Crescent Lake National Wildlife Refuge prior to taking a family camping trip into the Pine Ridge region and South Dakota's Black Hills. I turned south onto a sandy road when we approached a small roadside village called Lakeside, where a map showed a crooked secondary road heading south to the refuge. I soon found us on what was essentially a sandy trail without road markers, fences, or billboards and instead an endless panorama of pastures. It was a hot day, and our microbus lacked both a gas gauge and air-conditioning. Our children were soon complaining of the heat, dust, and lack of cold drinks, and after driving about 15 miles without seeing any road signs or waterfowl, I lost my courage and sadly turned back north toward Lakeside.

It was not until the following May, after leaving my family behind, that I drove north from Oshkosh in search of the Sandhills and its reputed waterfowl paradise. After a 25-mile trip over increasingly deteriorating roads, I suddenly encountered the first of many shallow marshes decorated like gigantic Christmas trees by flocks of white pelicans, western and eared grebes, and at least a dozen species of ducks, including my favorite of all duck species, the ruddy duck. There were also long-billed curlews calling from the hillsides, burrowing owls staring at me warily from rustic wooden fenceposts, several species of shorebirds, and countless cliff and barn swallows coursing overhead. I suddenly felt as if I were back among my beloved glacial-formed marshes of eastern North Dakota and knew that I had finally found a new spiritual home in Nebraska.

During my 40-year teaching career at the University of Nebraska, including a 17-year stint at the university's Cedar Point Biological Station in Keith County, I returned repeatedly to the heart of the Sandhills and never tired of its beauty and biological riches. In 1995 I finally published a comprehensive book on the biology of the Sandhills. At that time I thought I was "written-out" on the Sandhills, but I continued after my retirement in 2001 to return to them nearly every year for birding and photographing wildlife. An ex-doctoral student, Josef Kren, was my most frequent companion, and in 2019 he asked me if I would collaborate with him on a book on the Sandhills' birds. I initially declined, inasmuch as I had five book projects going on already. Yet, he promised to assume most of the drudgery of data collection, and I finally relented. This present book is the result, and I hope readers will find it of enough interest to stimulate them to visit the Sandhills. Some of the maps have been reprinted from *This Fragile Land*, and unless otherwise indicated are in my copyright, as are all the drawings. Likewise, I have quoted short pieces of text from various of my books that describe the Sandhills, sometimes with minor changes.

Although this book's cover suggests that it was produced by only Josef and me, the real brains behind all of my Digital Commons books have always been Paul Royster and his ultra-competent editorial colleague, Linnea Fredrickson. In a sense they have been my personal literary angels for more than a decade and have allowed me to turn my ideas and hopes into some 30 books and nearly 5,000 pages of text and illustrations. It is these two invaluable colleagues to whom I dedicate this book.

Paul A. Johnsgard
September 2020

Long-billed curlew, adult female in flight. *Photo by P. Johnsgard.*

The Nebraska Sandhills and Their Unique Wetlands

Paul A. Johnsgard

> Imagine a place in the Great Plains where the nights are so dark that almost every star in the visible universe can be seen, and the evenings are so quiet that coyotes can be heard yipping from miles away. Visualize a land where the nearest grocery store or filling station may be 50 miles or more distant, and where the sight of a billboard is sufficiently rare that one actually notices and reads it. Think of a locality where the presence of old, discarded cowboy boots stuck upside down on a fencepost may be the only sign of human influence, and where a line shown as a road on a state highway map may represent nothing more than two narrow tracks in bare sand that disappear over the far hills without so much as the slightest hint that anything or anyone might exist at the other end. It is not a land for the fainthearted, for those in a hurry to be somewhere else, or those unwilling to feel totally alone and self-reliant. It is a land, however, of gracefully bending horizons, of waving grass and shifting late afternoon shadows, of stunning sunsets, and of inner peace. It is called the Nebraska Sandhills.
>
> Over time I have come to realize that the true heart and spirit of Nebraska is not to be found in our eastern cities, our vastly overrated athletic programs, or even in the historic and now dying Platte River that whispers sad dirges to times past as it glides eastward to meet an equally altered and degraded Missouri River. Rather, the state's pioneer spirit persists in the quiet recesses of our Sandhills, particularly in the fortitude of the people whose ancestors once homesteaded them, and whose descendants sometimes still live there.
>
> —*This Fragile Land*

The Sandhills region is by far the largest of Nebraska's major ecosystems, covering more than 19,000 square miles and consisting of dunes that on the basis of recent evidence were probably first formed at the end of the region's final glacial period, less than 15,000 years ago.

The Sandhills support the largest number of the state's wetlands, totaling more than 1 million acres. Estimates of the number of lakes in the Sandhills have varied widely, but there are probably well over 1,000, 95 percent of which are no deeper than eight feet and none deeper than 20 feet. Sandhills lakes have been defined as those wetlands in which the water table is at the land surface or above it for most of the year, wet meadows are those wetlands in which the water table is at the land surface or below it for most of the year, and marshes are a transitional wetland type connecting the two. By this definition, a wetland may be defined as a lake in the spring but not in the fall when the water table declines. These between-season and between-year variations make conclusive lake inventories and areas impossible.

Sandhills lakes also vary as to their relative connections with groundwater. Groundwater lakes may have a direct groundwater flow in and out of the lakes through local underground flow systems, while others may have only poor connections to the groundwater reservoir. Still others may have no connection with groundwater. Additionally, the Sandhills lakes vary greatly in their alkalinity. Most of the lakes that are west of a geological uplift extending from Sheridan County southeast to Hooker County are much more highly alkaline than those east of the uplift.

The relative wealth of water in the Sandhills results from the fact that the Ogallala aquifer lies directly below the dunes, storing nearly 1 billion acre-feet of water. Besides covering an area of about a quarter of Nebraska's total area, the Sandhills have extremely low human population densities and very few improved roads. They thus represent the nearest thing to a true wilderness area anywhere east of the Rockies, in addition to supporting the largest intact area of mixed-grass prairie that still exists anywhere south of Canada.

The region's other superlatives include the remarkable fact that, although desertlike by some measures, more than 80 percent of the state's 463

Trumpeter swan. *Photo by P. Johnsgard.*

documented bird species have been reported there, and it rather inexplicably contains the most important waterfowl and shorebird breeding area south of the Dakotas' glaciated wetlands. Thousands of shallow, often small and unnamed, wetlands are present that range from being some of the most alkaline waters in the western hemisphere to highly productive lakes and marshes that have an amazing diversity of plant and animal life.

In spite of the great variety of water-dependent plants and animals that exist in the region, total precipitation in the Sandhills is no different from that supporting mixed-grass prairie to the north and south. The rain that falls is immediately drawn down through the sand to join the waters of the Ogallala aquifer, which in some places almost reaches the land surface. In such places the low interdune depressions are subirrigated, and hundreds of permanent marshy wetlands are present as a result of this high water table. In still other locations artesian springs emerge from the bases of sand dunes to form small streams that eventually join others and flow generally eastwardly out of the Sandhills in the form of a half dozen rivers and many permanent creeks.

At least 105 bird species breed in the Sandhills, which represents almost half of the state's total breeding avifauna. The Sandhills are easily the most important breeding and migratory habitat for water-, marsh-, and shoreline-dependent birds in the state. The western Sandhills are the state's primary breeding area for the western and Clark's grebes, canvasback, long-billed curlew, willet, Wilson's phalarope, American avocet, and black-necked stilt. The Sandhills generally are also the major or only Nebraska breeding grounds for additional species such as the trumpeter swan, American wigeon, cinnamon teal, ruddy duck, eared grebe, American bittern, black-crowned night-heron, white-faced ibis, marbled godwit, black tern, and Forster's tern. The wetlands are also of national and international importance to more than 10 million migrating waterfowl and shorebirds.

Many wetland plants are also endemic, or nearly endemic, to the Sandhills. They include several fen-adapted wetland species that are post-Pleistocene survivors now often hundreds of miles south of the species' other surviving populations. In the western Sandhills, alkaline lakes and wetlands support a limited but unique biota of salt-tolerant species, while those in the central and eastern parts of the Sandhills exhibit a greater overall diversity of wetland flora.

The Sandhills region contains three major national wildlife refuges (NWR) entirely within Nebraska—Crescent Lake NWR, Fort Niobrara NWR, and Valentine NWR—as well as one—LaCreek NWR—that is located just north of the Nebraska–South Dakota border in Bennett County. Nearly all of the Sandhills land, other than these national wildlife refuges and state parks and other state properties, is in private ownership, primarily by ranchers who are used to living out of sight and sound of all other humanity, and whose ears are attuned to the conversations of cattle rather than those of next-door neighbors. There are thus probably far more miles of two-track sandy trails leading to isolated ranches as there are improved roads connecting the region's widely scattered Sandhills towns and villages.

> Most roads in the Sandhills lead nowhere, and that is one of their primary attractions. They tend to become more and more indecisive the farther one goes, and finally disappear in sandy confusion, often at a fence or rancher's gate. Thus, traveling on unfamiliar Sandhills roads is always a kind of adventure that frequently has an unknowable ending. Probably the best treat of all in the Sandhills comes shortly before sundown. Then the shadows of the dunes play carelessly over their still-lighted slopes, creating endless yin-yang patterns to remind the viewer that light without darkness is incomplete, just as life and death are inextricably locked companions in the weft and warp of nature's rich tapestry.
>
> —*This Fragile Land*

The Drums of April and the Dances of Life

Paul A. Johnsgard

As each March in Nebraska slips into April, I know I will soon be hearing a rare chorus, a sunrise serenade of grassland dancers, an event that is just as memorable and magical as watching flocks of sandhill cranes revolving in great mandala-like circles as they rise to find invisible thermals and forsake the Platte River valley for their Arctic nesting grounds. To hear and see prairie grouse dancing at dawn requires more planning and far more patience than is needed for watching the spring exodus of sandhill cranes.

To see greater prairie-chickens display, Nebraskans must either drive to the southeastern corner of the state, where in a few counties native prairie grasses still grow thickly over glacially shaped hills, or travel to the Sandhills. Then a person must find the right county road and locate the best stopping point for setting up a viewing blind, based on prior advice or personal experience. Almost always the best place for a blind's location is atop a hill covered with low prairie grasses, located at least several hundred yards away from tall trees or thick shrubbery and a quarter mile or more away from any occupied dwellings.

Advance scouting the day before, with critical odometer information recorded, and the setting out of a few flag markers to show the best predawn walking route, often makes the difference between finding the exact site or an entire morning's efforts wasted. Scattered bird droppings and grouse feathers provide the best clues for judging the center of mating activity.

If all goes well, one is settled in the blind at least a half hour or more before sunrise, before the eastern sky begins to brighten and the surrounding landscape features begin to take shape. If there is a full moon, an even earlier predawn arrival is needed, whereas a cloudy sky will mean that the curtain rising for the dawn serenade will be somewhat delayed. Then, one must quietly wait, listening for early-rising coyotes or perhaps the last great horned owl duet of the night. This is a time to be thankful for the preservation of these native prairie relicts—nowhere else in North America are there still so many locations where, without making reservations or paying a hefty viewing fee, a person can watch and hear the dawn drumming and dancing of greater prairie-chickens.

I have often described the greater prairie-chicken as the spirit of the prairie; few other birds are so closely associated with native prairies or are so sensitive to their destruction. It is a bird the color of autumn grasses, its feathers disruptively patterned in vertical stripes of switchgrass buff and Indiangrass brown, so that a motionless prairie-chicken simply melts visually into its background.

Also completely hidden beneath the elongated lance-shaped neck feathers of adult males are two patches of bright orange-red skin. Like secret codes, these areas are exposed only during the dawn and dusk mating ceremonies of prairie-chickens, when the males fill their throats with air, inflating these skin "air sacs" on each side of the throat, causing each side of their necks to resemble half tangerines. As the esophagus is inflated, the male utters a mellow and low-pitched cooing. The resulting eerie sound resembles that produced by blowing across the top of an empty bottle, but it is uttered in a three-part cadence somewhat resembling "Old-Mul-Doooon." Although this low-pitched "booming" vocalization is not loud, the combined chorus of many birds calling can be heard for a great distance under ideal conditions.

While booming, the male also simultaneously stamps his feet rapidly, producing a soft drumming sound, and quickly fans and closes his tail feathers during each call sequence. While displaying, the male erects his long neck feathers so that two ear-like feather groups are exposed on the sides of his head. He also tilts his tail vertically, exposing otherwise hidden white under-tail feathers. This dramatic transformation of the bird's appearance, movements, and sounds produces a hypnotic effect on humans and also, it would seem, on the female prairie-chickens for whom it is intended.

When the females arrive on the mating grounds, usually at about sunrise, they begin to inspect each male carefully, moving around the group like housewives searching for the best Thanksgiving turkey but giving no outward indication of their possible preferences. The males in turn ratchet up the speed and

Greater prairie-chicken

intensity of their displays as each female approaches, and it is probably the relative vigor and perfection of an individual male's display behavior that helps females make their final mating choices. Not only are the males' minor display variations a possible basis for female choice but of equal or greater importance is each male's relative position among the other males, as a reflection of his ability to defend and maintain a desirable territory.

Socially dominant and centrally positioned male grouse ("master cocks") are often at least four years old and are the most effective at attracting and successfully mating with females. Indeed, even among a lek of 20 or more interacting males, a single highly experienced and socially dominant male is likely to obtain at least 80 percent of all matings. Clearly, mate selection works most rapidly and effectively in nonmonogamous species such as most grouse, in which most or all of a female's potential mates are gathered at a single place and time, allowing easy comparisons.

Sharp-tailed grouse perform similar communal courtship ceremonies, sometimes at the same locations as prairie-chickens but usually on drier and more open terrain. These highly localized and strongly competitive congregations of displaying males are called "leks," and their territorial courtship behavior is called "lekking." Lekking behavior appears to function biologically as a means of making certain that only the fittest males are able to attract mates and propagate the species' genetic line. Such a highly selective function requires an unfailing ability by females to assess all the males rapidly and accurately, and likewise favors those individual males able to develop ever more effective ways of competing with other males and attracting females.

This selective mating process, which gradually improves the genetic effectiveness of individual birds in selectively attracting and mating with those of the other sex, is called sexual selection. Sexual selection thus accounts for the evolution of such male grouse features as the presence and exhibition of conspicuous feathers or colorful skin, the utterance of complex vocalizations, and performance of extravagant postural displays, by which breeding females might identify and choose specific males for mating. It also explains the comparable presence of such male traits as intense aggressive behavior among males, especially in nonmonogamous species in which a single male might dominate mating in an entire local flock. Charles Darwin realized that, to be effective, this "sexual selection" must work reciprocally, with females being able to accurately detect and choose the most virile males on the basis of their differing anatomical and behavioral traits.

Over time, successful males thus evolve increasingly unique traits that facilitate matings by only the fittest individuals, outcompeting other competing males, through intimidation and physical dominance, or by attracting females more effectively than other males. Over time, these interacting mating attributes that improve both differential male-to-male dominance and varied male-to-female attractiveness result in ever more apparent sexual differences in the social behavior and physical appearance of both sexes.

When watching lek activities carefully, one can often detect spatial and behavioral differences among the males, as the size and positions of their territorial boundaries become apparent, and realize that some males are more self-assured, more aggressive, and more active than others. Thus, it becomes easier to realize that females are indeed able to choose their most desirable mating partner rapidly, even during the half-light of dawn and among the melee of intensely competing males.

Mating itself is brief and might be easily overlooked if one is not paying close attention. The female then quickly leaves the lekking ground and begins to search for a nest site, which may be as far as a mile or so away. Only a single successful mating is needed for a female to lay a clutch of 12 or more fertile eggs. She will not interact again with males or other females until her brood is grown and autumn flock formation begins.

In Nebraska, the males continue their daily display activities with diminishing enthusiasm until well into May. Some of the late matings probably are the result of females having lost their original clutch and attempting a second mating. The males play no roles in chick-rearing or other familial duties. After a summer of molting and foraging, the older males usually return to the lek in early fall, apparently to reclaim possession of their spring territories, or perhaps to try expanding into space made available by the deaths of others.

This renewed autumnal display activity also attracts the attention of young males, who may become peripheral viewers or even minor participants.

As each male grows older and more experienced, he is likely to move his territory ever closer to the middle of the lek, with the potential for eventually becoming a master cock if he lives long enough and competes intensively enough.

There are several possible options for visiting a prairie-chicken lek in Nebraska. Prairie-chickens are most common in the eastern and central Sandhills, where optimum survival conditions are provided by a combination of native Sandhills prairie and access to corn and other grain crops that supplement winter foods. Sharp-tailed grouse leks can be found throughout the entire Sandhills region.

Some commercial businesses in the Sandhills offer guided lek viewing from preestablished viewing blinds, which are often converted school buses. Some facilities offer the choice of viewing a lek of greater prairie-chickens or sharp-tailed grouse. Free public-access permanent blinds at grouse leks are also available at a few locations, such as the Bessey Ranger District of the Nebraska National Forest in Thomas County, or the three Nebraska national wildlife refuges, where viewing blinds are also usually available on a first-come-first-serve basis.

No Nebraska naturalist should consider his or her life complete without experiencing the unique sights and sounds of a Sandhills spring on a prairie grouse lek. Like seeing the first long-billed curlews arriving at their breeding grounds on a Sandhills meadow, gazing in awe at a star-rich Sandhills sky unhindered by city lights, or seeing and hearing sandhill cranes migrating so high above the sand dunes that they are almost lost from view among the clouds, watching prairie grouse performing their ancient annual dances at sunrise is a defining experience of life in natural Nebraska.

We have far too few sacred natural sites in the eastern Great Plains; most of the holy sites of the Native Americans that once ruled the plains have since been "developed," or their exact locations have been long forgotten. But we must not forget the locations of prairie-chicken leks; they whisper to us of secret places where grama-grasses and bluestems grow thick on the ground, and where flint arrowheads are likely to lie buried beneath the thatch and loess. They tell us of meadowlark and dickcissel song-perches, and of traditional coyote hunting grounds. They are as much a connection to our past as are the ruts left in the soil by immigrants' wagons, or the preserved costumes of Native American cultures carefully stored in museums.

—*Grassland Grouse and Their Conservation*

Biological Profiles of Some Typical Sandhills Birds

Paul A. Johnsgard

Burrowing Owl

Among all the grassland birds probably the most charismatic is the burrowing owl. Few birds will have birders screeching their cars to a halt faster than a burrowing owl perched quietly on a fence post or peering quizzically out of a prairie dog hole. Whether standing solemnly beside a burrow or atop a low fence post, a miniature owl standing erect and in plain view during the middle of the day is such an unlikely apparition that it requires prolonged and extensive study. Something in the animal's intense yellowish green eyes demands to be watched with equal intensity, and the burrowing owl's comical, not-quite-erect stance might remind birdwatchers of a feather-clad leprechaun still trying to recover from last night's hangover. The seemingly curious, if not actually friendly, manner of the burrowing owl when approached by humans is probably the reason that in some parts of the American West the species is known as the "howdy" owl.

The usual rules of owl decorum are not obeyed by burrowing owls. First, they are not as highly nocturnal as most other owls but instead are active mainly during broad daylight. In fact, their retinas lack the reflective surface that increases nocturnal visual sensitivity and produces the "eye shine" typical of most owls. Second, unlike the larger owls of the grasslands, burrowing owls are surprisingly insectivorous, at least during the summer months when large, slow-moving insects, such as dung beetles and ground beetles, are abundant around prairie dog towns and easily captured.

Third, burrowing owls seem to lack the acute binaural hearing and precise sound-source localization abilities that owls as a group are primarily noted for, and instead they appear to rely on their keen daytime vision for finding prey. In correlation, their faces have only poorly developed facial disk feathers surrounding their ears, which help funnel extremely faint sounds into the ear canals of the most highly nocturnal owls. When a burrowing owl is confronted by an approaching human, it is more likely to stay put than to immediately fly away. Often, after a few slight horizontal or vertical head movements

Burrowing owl

by the bird, as if it is trying to shake its head clear of a foggy memory, but which are probably designed to get a better distance-estimating fix on the new intruder into its personal space, the owl will probably duck back into its hole. Or, if perched on a post, it may take silent flight over the prairie dog town and land near its burrow entrance.

When cornered in its burrow, a burrowing owl will produce a sound that mimics a rattlesnake's rattle, and at such times it may also spread and tilt its wings vertically, apparently to make itself appear larger and more dangerous. The male's courtship call is usually soft and owl-like, but adults of both sexes also utter a rapid chatter when alarmed or while defending the nest.

Although a burrowing owl is perfectly content to take over a prairie dog burrow without making major structural changes or other renovations, it is likely to gather fragments of dried bison or cattle dung, break them into small pieces, and line the entrance area in front of its burrow with these bits of debris. The biological function of the scattered ungulate droppings is uncertain, but they may help mask the odors of an active owl burrow, for burrowing owls are highly vulnerable to badgers. Such markings can help a birder recognize an active burrowing owl burrow, as can nearby dried owl pellets, which are usually rich in chitinous insect fragments such as the undigested skeletal remnants of grasshoppers and scarab and carabid beetles.

In Nebraska, it is primarily the black-tailed prairie dog that offers the owls housing. Besides being able to exploit inactive dog burrows for escape and nesting, the owls favor the combination of low shrub coverage, short vegetation, and the high percentage of bare ground that is typically present in prairie dog colonies. When their ground-level vision is variously obstructed, the birds find suitable nearby observation posts to use, such as fence posts or boulders.

Within prairie dog towns, burrowing owls favor larger and active colonies; typically a town that has been abandoned by prairie dogs will also be abandoned by burrowing owls within three years, perhaps largely as a result of vegetation encroachment. No proof has been found that prairie dogs directly benefit from the presence of burrowing owls, and the ever-alert rodents sometimes utter alarm notes when the owls fly overhead, suggesting that prairie dogs are at least somewhat wary of the owls.

As for seeing burrowing owls, Nebraska's Fort Niobrara National Wildlife Refuge usually has a few burrowing owls visible in the prairie dog colony near the refuge headquarters. However, to placate ranchers, prairie dogs are still being poisoned on most state and federal lands in Nebraska, including at the Oglala National Grasslands in the northwestern corner of the state's panhandle (Johnsgard, 2004, 2006).

In western Nebraska, one population study (Desmond, Savidge, and Eskridge, 2000) found that a 58 percent population decline of burrowing owls occurred between 1990 and 1996, during a period of intensive prairie dog poisoning and their associated rapid population declines. Across the owl's North American range, the greatest population declines have occurred in the northern Great Plains. Sadly, the familiar "howdy owl" of the plains is in increasing danger of having to say "adios" to much of western North America.

> Probably no single grassland bird species is as fascinating to observe for hours on end as is the burrowing owl. It is an owl that doesn't seem to accept the fact that owls should sleep during the day and hunt at night. Instead it sits interminably on fenceposts or large boulders, carefully surveying its daytime surroundings with all the solemnity of a spindly-legged Bible-belt preacher on his pulpit, constantly scanning his flock to make certain they are all paying proper attention. Also, like many such self-righteous preachers, burrowing owls typically produce a large, unmanageable brood of youngsters in progressive stair-step sizes, who seem too prone to leave the confines of their burrow prematurely and wander away at the earliest opportunity, thereby often encountering trouble enough on their own.
> —*Great Wildlife of the Great Plains*

Northern Harrier

It seems not quite fair to claim the northern harrier as a North American wetland bird; I have seen this species coursing gracefully over the lowlands and upland moors of Scotland and northern England, where it is called the hen harrier. A similar species of harrier, confusingly called the marsh harrier, also occurs in Britain. It was probably for such reasons

Northern harrier

that the common English name "northern harrier" was adopted a few decades ago in North America in preference to "marsh hawk," its traditional North American name. Somehow "marsh hawk" seems most appropriately descriptive of this bird. Its current name "harrier" refers not to the birds' unlikely preying on hares but to the harrying behavior these birds exhibit toward their prey.

Probably the happiest choice for this hawk's name is its Latin one. *Circus* refers to the undulating or almost looping (thus "circular") flights of territorial males in early spring as they define their territories, and *hudsonicus* refers to Hudson Bay, an older generic name for northern Canada. The species is generally distinctly northern in its North American breeding distribution, but there are local breeding records south as far as the Gulf Coast. The now outdated but more descriptive species name *cyaneus* describes the somewhat bluish tint to the adult male's gray plumage, which contrasts with its darker "dipped-in-ink" wingtips.

More than any other large hawk of the central plains, the adult northern harrier exhibits strong plumage dimorphism of the sexes as well as moderate dimorphism in body mass. Females are not only larger than males by about 40 to 50 percent but are also a rich chocolate brown on their upperparts, perhaps allowing them to blend in with their dead-grass nesting environment. Juveniles are basically the same color as females for their first year but are a much richer cinnamon-rufous on their underparts. Both juveniles and adults of both sexes have white rump patches that, together with their long tails and wings, provide for easy field identification.

The long wings of harriers allow them to glide at rather slow speeds. They maintain their aerial stability by adopting a distinct upward tilt in their wing positioning, much like gliding turkey vultures. Another feature of harriers is their evolution of somewhat owl-like facial disks. These feathers, together with unusually well-developed hearing, allow the birds to detect the movements of even small rodents, such as mice, as well as other rodents and ground-dwelling songbirds such as horned larks and meadowlarks.

Unlike prairie falcons, which also often capture meadowlarks, harriers do not subdue such birds during prolonged chases but are more likely to grab them unawares while they are perched or hiding among grasses. During summer, harriers' prey spectrum broadens and especially is likely to include older nestlings and recently fledged birds. A typical prey item is tiny relative to the harrier's body mass, on average weighing only about two ounces, which is closer in mass to a northern cardinal than a meadowlark. Rarely, mammalian prey as large as about two pounds may be taken. The success rates of attacks on birds is lower than those on mammals, and vole hunting over snow cover is more successful than hunts done in the absence of snow.

Harriers have unusually long tarsi, somewhat like those of barn owls, but have fairly weak toes and talons, at least as compared to those of buteo hawks. Like those of barn owls, their long tarsi might be useful for reaching down into tall grass to grab prey. Prey is located using varied strategies, including gliding or powered low-altitude flights over fairly long distances, shorter quartering flights, and flights that follow vegetational edges, such as fencerows. Pounces may be preceded by hovering, quick turns, or direct attacks without change of speed or direction. Early morning and evening hunts are commonplace, but no true nocturnal hunting in the manner of owls seems to have been reported. Under favorable foraging conditions the birds may cache excess prey for later consumption, at least during the breeding season. Not surprisingly, females tend to take larger prey than do males during the breeding season.

Peak numbers of harriers occur during winter in various parts of the southern plains. Many of these concentrations are located near wildlife refuges, and there the birds are prone to specialize on wounded waterfowl. During winter, foraging individuals may cover about 100 miles per day, mostly within localized hunting territories up to a square mile in area. Females exclude the smaller males from such territories. It seems likely that young birds winter farther south than do adults, and females perhaps winter north of males, based on their relative body masses and consequent probable cold tolerance. Yet, in spring males precede females in their arrival times on northern nesting grounds, probably because of the importance of establishing good breeding territories as early as possible.

By March or April, birds will have arrived on their breeding areas of the northern plains, and males soon begin advertising their territories. The birds seek out relatively large areas of thick grasslands, especially low prairies, lightly grazed meadows, and nearly dry marshes with thick edges of emergent vegetation. Less often they choose drier upland prairies or even croplands, but wetter environments are more frequently used than dryland habitats. With the arrival of females on the breeding grounds, usually a week or more after the males, territorial and courtship interactions begin. Little or no mate retention seems to occur from year to year, and at least in some areas there is a slight predominance of females in the adult population.

Males begin territorial advertising and female attraction by performing "sky-dancing," which consists of a series of frequently repeated U-shaped aerial maneuvers, ascending and descending 30 to 300 feet above the ground, tracking over a course of up to a half mile in linear distance. At the end of the flight, the male may descend to earth and disappear at a point that may serve to indicate a potential nest location. Interested females will follow the male and perhaps investigate the site themselves.

Evidently those males that perform aerial displays most vigorously are able to attract females most effectively, and such birds may acquire a harem of from two to five females. However, many males acquire just one mate, and some evidence shows that subadult yearling males are likely to attract only subadult females. Breeding territory sizes seem to be highly variable in area, and such variation is probably a reflection of the relative food resources within the territories as well as a presumable indication of variations in individual male fitness.

Forster's Tern

The marshy lakes of the western Sandhills are Nebraska's only nesting areas for the beautiful Forster's tern. During the 1990s I saw it nesting most often at Crescent Lake National Wildlife Refuge in Garden County, but there are also confirmed breedings in Cherry and Grant Counties (Mollhoff, 2001) and reported breeding in Arthur County (Brown et al., 1996). Unlike the insectivorous black tern, Forster's terns are almost exclusively fish-eating birds, which means that the generally fish-poor Sandhills lakes are probably not ideal breeding habitat.

Observations in Minnesota have indicated that fishes presented to prospective mates during courtship include, in descending frequency, yellow perch, shiners, sunfish, and northern pike, whereas among those given to chicks the corresponding frequencies were yellow perch, shiners, and sticklebacks, showing some apparent judgment of relative suitability of species as food for chicks. Those fish fed to mates averaged larger than those seined nearby, and those fed to chicks increased in size as the chicks grew (McNicholl, Lowther, and Hall, 2001).

Courtship in this tern begins or is already underway upon arrival at the breeding grounds, typically between mid-April and mid-May. In one common display, two terns, one carrying a fish, perform a "high flight" with rapid wingbeats and the wings angled backward. After reaching a high point, the leading bird then begins a gliding descent, and on landing the fish-carrying individual feeds the other bird. During so-called "low flights," the wings are beat quickly but with low amplitude while being held high above the back. Often a second bird will join in this flight and may land with the first, when terrestrial courtship occurs.

Land courtship includes the parading of the fish-carrying bird around a presumed female, followed by an exchange of the fish. Incipient nest-building (scraping behavior) may occur during parading. Courtship feeding is not only a part of courtship and precopulatory behavior but continues through incubation.

Nesting is done colonially, often in groups of from 2 to about 100 nests; the nests are sometimes placed within a few meters of one another. The simple nest may be placed on a raft of floating vegetation or on a muskrat house, and at times the nest material may be soggy, or the eggs may even touch the water. Two or three eggs constitute the usual clutch, and incubation begins with the first egg. Incubation is performed by both sexes, with frequent nest changeovers. It lasts 24 to 25 days, with the last egg in two- or three-egg clutches typically hatching two days after the first. The chicks leave the nest at about four days of age when they are called away by the adults, but they are not able to fly until they are about four to five weeks old. The age of sexual maturity is still not known with certainty, but it is probably at least two years, with breeding thereafter done yearly. The maximum reported longevity of banded birds is 12 years.

Wilson's Phalarope

The presence of wet meadows apparently is the major habitat criterion for the Wilson's phalarope, which is found near fresh to highly saline water and is associated with watery environments ranging from ditches or river edges to seasonal, semipermanent, or permanent ponds and lakes. Its nests are well hidden in wet meadows or sometimes in grassy swales or on hummocky areas of shallow marshy habitats. They are shallow scrapes in the ground, lined with dead grass built up into a cup about two inches thick. When placed over water they may be built up to a level about six inches above the water.

The clutch size is normally four eggs, occasionally three. The eggs are buffy with a varying amount of darker spotting. The incubation period is 16 to 22 days, probably averaging about 20 days. Incubation is normally by the male; there is no proof that females produce more than one clutch, in contrast to most bird species that have reversed sexual dimorphism. Although female Wilson's phalaropes are appreciably larger and more brightly colored than males, recent studies have cast doubt on the idea that they are regularly polyandrous, unlike the typically polyandrous mating patterns of most sex-reversed birds.

Pair bonds apparently are formed after the birds arrive at breeding areas during a period of behavior that is intensely aggressive but not very indicative of typical territoriality. The female probably makes the nest scrape after the pair is formed, but the male adds the nest lining. Eggs are laid about 48 hours apart, and presumably the female plays no further role in parental care. The male incubates, and he leads his brood from the nest to foraging areas only a few hours after they hatch. The fledging period is probably less than three weeks. Like other phalaropes, the Wilson's has a long migration to South American wintering areas. Up to a half million Wilson's phalaropes stop over for a few weeks in Utah and at Mono Lake, California, before undertaking their long flights southward to winter on some high-altitude Andean salt lakes of Argentina.

Yellow-headed Blackbird

The yellow-headed blackbird has a broad breeding distribution that is centered in the Sandhills and extends west locally into the Nebraska panhandle counties. It also breeds south into the Rainwater Basin, at least during years of plentiful water. This blackbird needs water of sufficient depth to provide open water adjacent to beds of cattails, bulrushes, or other emergent plants, with cattails being the highly preferred substrate for nest supports (Mollhoff, 2001).

More generally, this species is associated with prairie wetlands, but it prefers deeper water than the red-winged blackbird does, where there are stands of cattails, bulrushes, or reeds interspersed with open water. Primarily aquatic prey—mainly insects obtained within the territory, if they are abundant—are eaten during the breeding season. These include emerging dragonflies and damselflies, and a variety of beetles, lepidopteran larvae, and dipterans. Males are prone to forage more widely than females, often on terrestrial weed or crop seeds.

Territorial males are both visually and acoustically conspicuous. They produce two different song types. One is a "buzzing" and distinctly nasal song that lasts up to four seconds and is directed to other nearby individuals. It is usually accompanied by an asymmetrical song-spread display, with the head turned sideways and tilted somewhat and the wings slightly spread. The second, an accenting song, is more musical, with several fluid introductory notes sometimes followed by a variable trill. It is directed toward more distant birds and is usually accompanied by a symmetrical song-spread display. The buzzing song is similar among males, but the accented song varies greatly among males as to its length, phrasing, and timing (Twedt and Crawford, 1995).

Territory sizes vary according to habitat quality and may range in size from less than a hundred to several thousand square yards, with emergent vegetation covering 35 to 77 percent of the area. Females maintain small "territories" surrounding the nest site but ignore male boundaries. In contrast to some earlier findings on red-winged blackbirds, female mating choices are evidently not significantly influenced by the male's sexually distinctive yellow head plumage, as those males whose heads had been experimentally blackened were able to attract females, defend their boundaries, and sometimes were even able to usurp the territories of others.

Typically the number of females in a single "harem" are from one to six. Marshes with higher rates of dragonfly emergence have been reported to have higher female densities and more females per male than less productive marshes. In one study, the number of females within a territory was found to be directly related to the amount of edge present but inversely proportional to territory size. Yellow-headed blackbirds are larger than red-winged blackbirds and dominate them in territorial conflicts. They are also highly aggressive toward marsh wrens, although their territories are not mutually exclusive (Twedt and Crawford, 1995).

Males arrive first on breeding areas, and their territories have been established by the time the females arrive. The females' nesting sites are located within the territories of the males. Evidently females will perform precopulatory crouching in response to any males and will copulate with them when the territory owner is absent.

Nesting begins as soon as the females arrive at the breeding grounds, with some nests initiated within three days; in one study the majority of nests had an egg present only one day after the nest was completed. The usual clutch size is three to four eggs, and the incubation period is 12 to 13 days. Only a single brood is raised per season, but renesting will occur if the first nest is destroyed. During fall migration, yellow-headed blackbirds evidently do not join to form massive mixed-species flocks; females migrate farther south than males, often to southern Mexico. Once at their wintering grounds, they roost in wetlands with other blackbirds in groups that might number in the millions.

Long-billed Curlew

Easily the most impressive and largest of North America's shorebirds, and the proclaimed favorite bird of Sandhills ranchers, the long-billed curlew is mostly limited to the wet meadows and upland prairies of the western Sandhills and, in decreasing numbers, the shortgrass plains of the Nebraska panhandle (Mollhoff, 2001).

Long-billed curlews are especially evident shortly after they arrive in April, when unpaired males perform advertisement flights above their territories. During these so-called soft "*kerr, kerr* flights," the males rise almost perpendicularly, then set their wings in an umbrella-like manner and glide down, uttering a series of rapid and melodious *kerr* notes. They may almost reach the ground before rising to start another calling and gliding sequence.

A quite different aerial display called the "arc flight" is performed when human or other mammalian intruders come near a nest or brood. The threatening bird flies directly toward the intruder, only to veer away at the last moment and begin a high arcing flight that precedes the next approach. A wing-lifting display that exposes the beautiful cinnamon-colored underwing surface is used by adults during intense threat display, and a similar upright wing-fluttering is performed by males just before copulation. Ritualized nest-scraping behavior by the male is used during courtship and may result in the choosing of an actual nest site.

Females hide their nests in low cover on the upland Sandhills prairies, often in a clump of grass less than a foot high, or barely enough to cover the incubating bird. Yet they are virtually invisible under those conditions. I have been in a blind within ten feet of an incubating female and aware almost exactly of where the nest was located yet was usually unable to see the bird before it lifted its head, when I could see a huge brown eye through the grass. Often the nest is situated near a shrub, rock, or mound of soil, providing a landmark that perhaps helps the female locate her nest.

During late May and early June, it is rare to spend a day in the western Sandhills without seeing and hearing curlews. At that time of year the incubating or brooding birds are extremely alert to any possible disturbance. They intensively mob any person or other possible threat to their nest or brood

Biological Profiles of Some Typical Sandhills Birds

Long-billed curlew, in flight

with diving calls and raucous screams from nearby dune tops.

Curlew clutches are almost invariably of four eggs, and incubation takes four weeks. In the Sandhills, hatching often occurs during the last week of May and the first week of June. All the chicks emerge from their eggs within a period of five hours or so. If they hatch late in the day, they are likely to spend the night in the nest, leaving it early the following morning. The highly mobile chicks are guarded by both adults. After the young are two to three weeks old, the female often abandons her brood, but the male continues to look after them until they fledge at about six weeks of age.

Fledging usually occurs before the end of July in the Sandhills, and after they congregate into local flocks the birds then undertake an early migration out of the region. During a study of the long-billed curlew in the Sandhills, Gregory (2010) banded two breeding curlews and attached radio collars that allowed continuous satellite tracking. One of the two flew from Nebraska to northern Texas in less than 24 hours. The other later took a week to get from Nebraska to southern Texas. Both of them spent the winter on the Gulf coast of northeastern Mexico. At least during the spring migration, these curlews travel in loose flocks of about 20 to 30 birds. I have watched dozens of such flocks flying determinedly north while silhouetted against a blood-red sunset and above featureless and still winter-brown prairie in western Kansas.

> Someone once wrote, and it could only have been Aldo Leopold, that in its biomass a ruffed grouse makes up only a minuscule part of the forest but to remove it is to remove much of the life from the forest. Similarly, a horned lark or Sprague's pipit represents an almost immeasurably tiny part of the prairie ecosystem, but a prairie without the song of a horned lark or a Sprague's pipit overhead is no prairie at all. And a place with no prairies at all is not a place that will stir the heart.
>
> —*Prairie Birds*

Introduction

Josef Kren

Natural History of the Nebraska Sandhills

One of the most impressive ecosystems in the lower 48 states of the United States lies at the heart of the North American grasslands. The Nebraska Sandhills are the largest sand dune system in the western hemisphere, covering much of the central and western parts of the state. For most people who have visited the Sandhills, the region is a mesmerizing, peaceful, and scenic landscape with numerous wetlands and lakes and very few hardtop roads, except for the scenic US Highway 2, which slices 200 miles through the heart of the Sandhills from Broken Bow to Alliance while passing through seven counties and only a single town of at least 2,000 people. Otherwise, there are uncountable miles of sandy roads or trails, where inexperienced drivers can easily get mired or lost.

Geography

The Nebraska Sandhills extend from about the 99th meridian on the east to the 103rd meridian on the west. The region covers an area of about 19,300 square miles (57,000 sq. km.) and extends about 265 miles from east to west. The Niobrara and Platte Rivers provide boundaries on the north and south, the Niobrara River on the north from whence sand dunes extend southward in almost unbroken continuity to the Platte River valley. Twenty-three counties of varying sizes encompass the Nebraska Sandhills. The five central counties comprise almost 4,000 square miles but have an average human population density of only 0.8 person per square mile (Map 1, Table 1). The Sandhills represent half of the state's overall 37,000 square miles of ranchland and pastures, which support 1.9 million cattle, as compared with a state population of 1.8 million people.

Until recently, the Sandhills have been viewed as a remnant from the Pleistocene epoch, but radiocarbon dating of organic-rich soils within the sand dunes and optically stimulated luminescence (OSL)

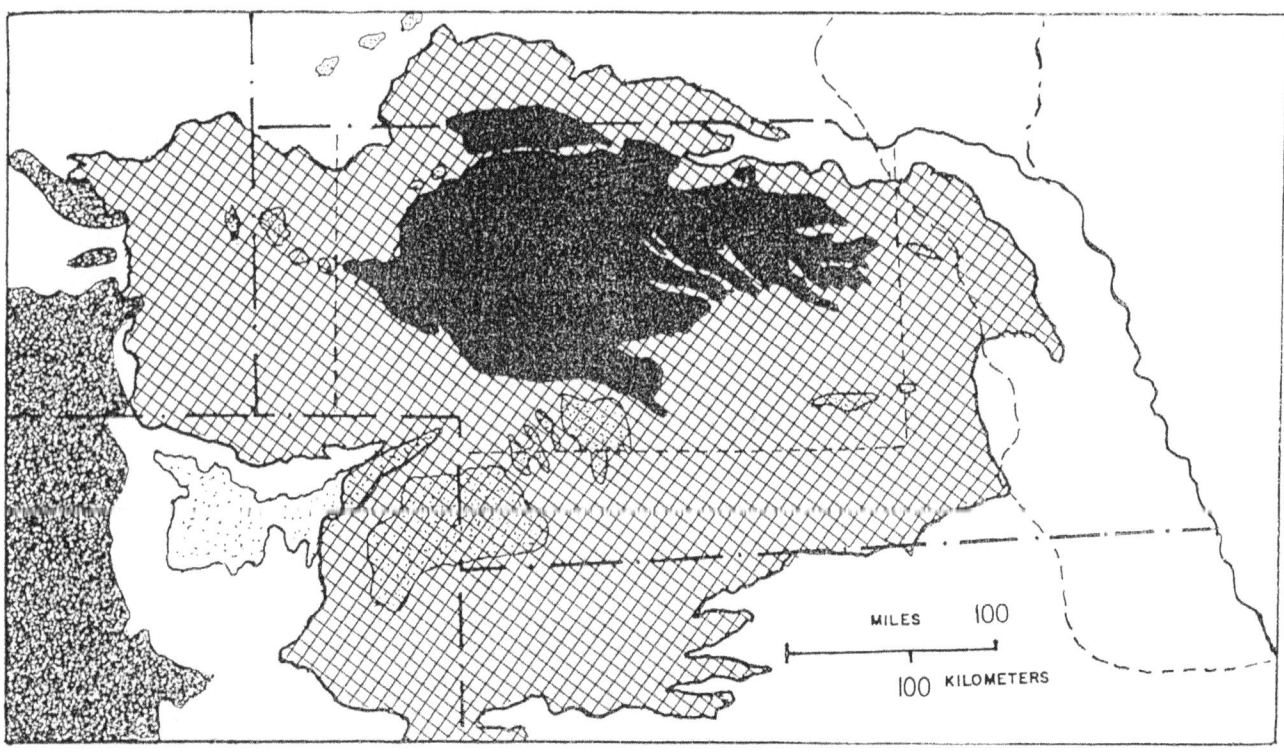

Map 1. Location of the Nebraska Sandhills (shaded), Ogallala aquifer (cross-hatched), Rocky Mountain piedmont (dark stippling), and peripheral regions. Dotted lines indicate approximate coverage of Sandhills regional maps in this book. From Johnsgard, 1995.

Table 1. Sandhills County Codes, Areas, and Human Populations

	Code	Area (sq. mi.)	Human population[a]	
Counties 90–100% within the Sandhills				**Total area 3,775 sq. mi.**
Arthur	Ar	715	465 (0.6)	
Grant	Gr	781	660 (0.8)	
Hooker	Ho	721	682 (0.94)	
McPherson	Mc	859	492 (0.6)	
Thomas	Th	720	699 (1.0)	
Total population (Density/sq. mi.)			2,998 (0.8)	
Counties 75–90% within the Sandhills				**Total area 9,640 sq. mi.**
Blaine	Bl	746	476 (0.6)	
Brown	Br	1,221	2,973 (2.4)	
Cherry	Ch	5,961	5,761 (0.96)	
Garfield	Grf	570	1,987 (3.5)	
Loup	Lo	570	618 (1.1)	
Wheeler	Wh	575	805 (1.4)	
Total population (Density/sq. mi.)			12,625 (1.3)	
Counties 50–75% within the Sandhills				**Total area 5,725 sq. mi.**
Garden	Gar	1,705	1,897 (1.1)	
Logan	Log	571	740 (1.3)	
Rock	Ro	1,008	1,360 (1.3)	
Sheridan	Sh	2,441	5,190 (2.1)	
Total population (Density/sq. mi.)			9,190 (1.6)	
Counties 25–50% within the Sandhills				**Total area 7,462 sq. mi.**
Holt	Hol	2,413	1,178 (4.2)	
Keith	Ke	1,061	8,021 (7.5)	
Lincoln	Li	2,564	35,185 (13.7)	
Morrill	Mo	1,424	4,686 (3.3)	
Total population (Density sq. mi.)			48,967 (6.56)	
Counties 5–25% within the Sandhills				**Total area 4,396 sq. mi.**
Antelope	An	563	6,336 (11.2)	
Boone	Bo	687	5,239 (7.6)	
Custer	Cu	2,576	10,840 (4.2)	
Greeley	Gre	570	2,356 (4.1)	
Total population (Density/sq. mi.)			24,771 (5.63)	

[a] Human population as of 2010; average densities per square mile are in parentheses.

dating of quartz grains indicate the sand dunes are much younger. Dune-forming activity in the region occurred several times during both the Pleistocene and Holocene epochs (Hartman, 2015).

Dune formation started about 10,000 years ago, and the largest dunes were formed between 8,000 and 5,000 years ago. The dunes occur at elevations of 2,201 to 4,298 feet (670–1,310 m) (Keech and Bentall, 1971). The sand was shaped by the prevailing northwest winds into relatively linear dunes, their long axes generally oriented from northeast to southwest. In the central Sandhills, where the sand is often more than 500 feet deep, some dune crests may reach heights of nearly 400 feet, and the interdune valleys are often so close to the underlying aquifer as to produce lush subirrigated meadows or shallow, vegetation-rich wetlands (Bleed and Flowerday, 1989; Johnsgard, 1995).

Although the dunes are now mostly stabilized with vegetation, during recurring periods of long-term drought over geologic time, they have been set into motion. They again become stabilized by a more mesic climate cycle, which permits vegetation to recolonize the region (Loope and Swinehart, 2000).

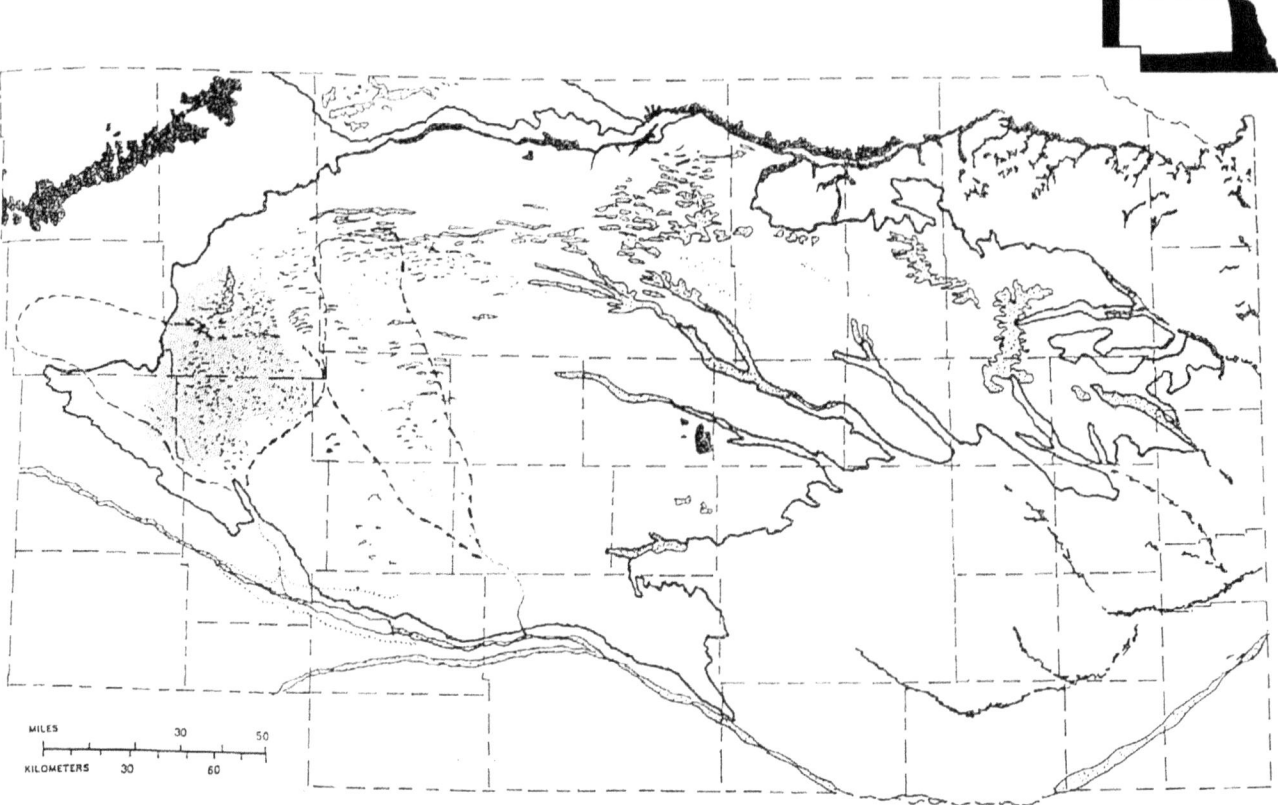

Map 2. Distribution of wetlands in the Nebraska Sandhills, showing region of poor drainage and highly alkaline wetlands in the western Sandhills (dark stippling), riparian woodlands (light stippling), and other regional forested areas (inked). An area of dune-blocked drainage of two Sandhills creeks is shown by a dashed line, and the extent of a now-extinct late Pleistocene lake is shown by a dotted line. From Johnsgard, 1995.

The topography of the Sandhills alternate between dunes and interdune valleys containing about 1,500 to 2,000 wetlands large enough to generously be called lakes, and approximately 80,000 acres (125 sq. mi.) of water, marshes, meadows, and dry basins. The total area of such at least periodically wetland habitats has been estimated at about 988,000 acres (1,540 sq. mi.) (McCarraher, 1977; Hayford and Baker, 2012) (Map 2).

Lakes and Rivers

The majority of the Sandhills lakes are shallow, their depth usually not exceeding 6.5 feet (2 m); the deepest (Cottonwood Lake in Cherry County) is 20 feet. An important source of water contributing to the lakes is related to groundwater discharge. If the groundwater discharge increases, the portion of lakes covered by wetland vegetation decreases, and vice versa. Thus, the ratio of free open water to wetland emergent vegetation varies and might fluctuate between as well as within seasons.

The extreme variation in lakes of the Sandhills is the basis for variations in their biological communities (Hayford and Baker, 2012). Sandhills lakes vary greatly in water chemistry. They range from nearly neutral in pH in the central and eastern regions to highly alkaline in the western Sandhills. An estimated total of 394,000 acres (615 sq. mi.) of wetlands having low alkalinity are associated with the main Sandhills region, while the hyperalkaline wetlands in the western Sandhills compose another 10,700 acres (17 sq. mi.). A small region of sandhill wetlands in the Loup River–Platte River valley adds another 8,000 acres (12.5 sq. mi.) (LaGrange, 2005; Johnsgard, 2012). The hydrology of the Sandhills was thoroughly described in Bleed and Flowerday's comprehensive monograph (1989), and the ecology of the Sandhills wetlands and their biotas have been outlined by Johnsgard (2012).

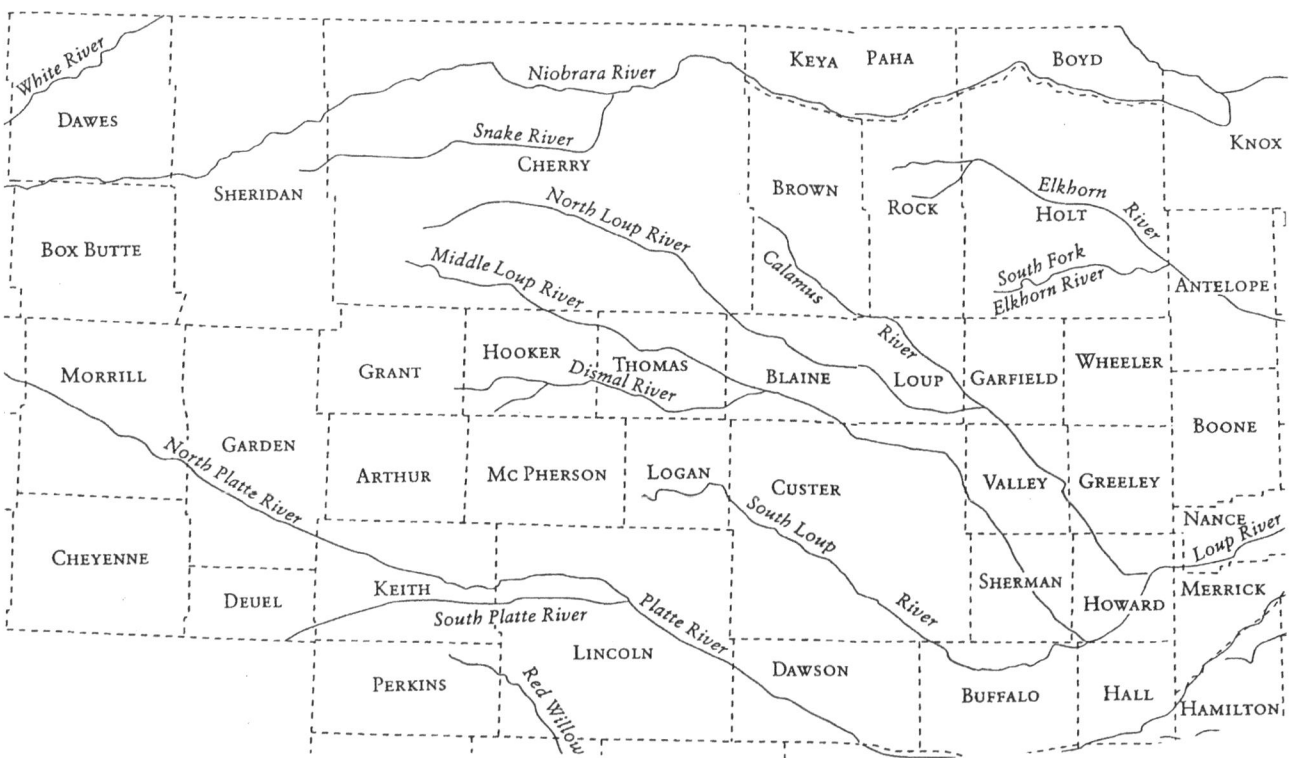

Map 3. Rivers and counties in the Nebraska Sandhills. Map courtesy of University of Nebraska Geography Department.

Most of the Sandhills lakes have large photic zones, with light penetrating the entire water column. The lakes are also characterized by variably elevated concentrations of total phosphorus and total nitrogen relative to lakes in nearby areas. The combination of high but not excessive concentrations of nutrients and large photic zones result in productive lake ecosystems. Such lakes are thus naturally eutrophic (Hayford and Baker, 2012).

Lakes of the Sandhills are seasonally and annually dynamic, varying in water level, lake area, and water chemistry, and most of them are too shallow to qualify as true lakes rather than as marshes. Two regions of the Nebraska Sandhills are notable in having many lakes of varied sizes, and portions of them have been designated national wildlife refuges (NWR): Crescent Lake NWR and Valentine NWR (Ginsberg, 1984; Ginsberg, 1985; Hayford and Baker, 2012; LaBaugh, 1986).

Besides numerous lakes, there are two major human-made reservoirs: Calamus Reservoir, 5,124 acres (8 sq. mi.) in Garfield and Loup Counties, and Merritt Reservoir, 2,906 acres (4.5 sq. mi.) in Cherry County. As mentioned, two major rivers form natural borders to the Sandhills. The Niobrara River rises in eastern Wyoming and, from both underground and surface water sources, flows eastward along the northern edge of the Sandhills before conferencing with the Missouri River. Unlike other Nebraska rivers, much of it flows over shale bedrock, so the water is notably clear. The North Platte River originates in central Colorado and skirts the southern edge of the western Sandhills, merging first with the South Platte to form the Platte River and finally also draining into the Missouri River. The major rivers that feed the Platte and originate within the Sandhills are the South Loup, North Loup, Middle Loup, Calamus, Dismal, Snake, and Elkhorn (Map 3). These rivers are all spring-fed, sand-bottomed, and year-round. All of these Sandhills rivers are dependent upon the vast capacity of the underground Ogallala aquifer to store and release water.

The Ogallala aquifer, underlying an area of about 174,000 square miles (450,000 sq. km.) below eight states (South Dakota, Nebraska, Wyoming, Colorado, Kansas, Oklahoma, New Mexico, and Texas), is a massive storage site of ancient groundwater. The aquifer's formation began 50 million to 70 million years ago, when permeable surface sediments of the

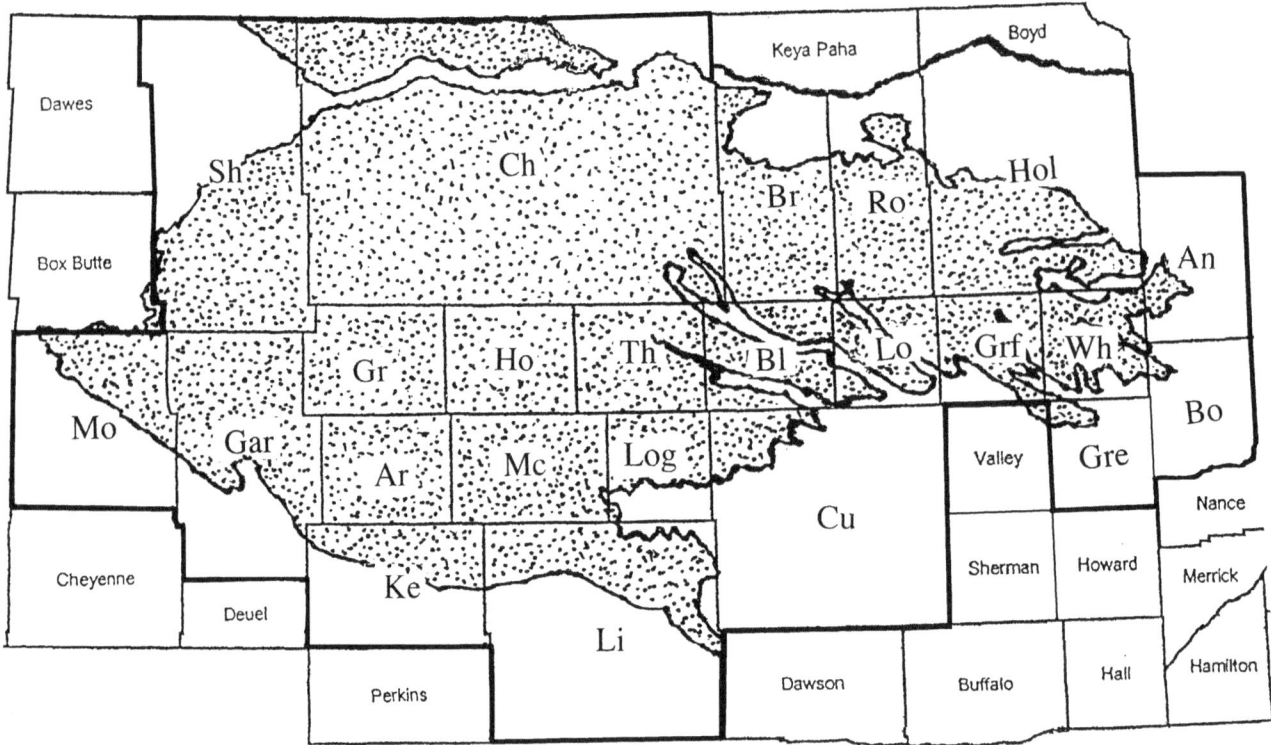

Map 4. The extent of surface sand (stippled) and associated counties in the Nebraska Sandhills. The counties are here identified by the codes used in this book.

Great Plains allowed water to collect in an underground reservoir overlaying impermeable bedrock (Bittinger and Green, 1980), a process that was probably greatly aided by melting glaciers during the past 20,000 years. About 10,000 years ago, the last of the Great Plains glaciers withdrew, and their associated rivers dried or were diverted southward, leaving the aquifer with little or no recharge (Opie, 2000).

The first uses of the Ogallala's ancient waters for irrigation in western Nebraska occurred in the early 1900s. The amount drawn from the aquifer was minimal until the 1930s, when a series of droughts changed this situation. Vast areas of cultivated land received very little rain, and the soil uncovered by cultivation became dry and easily erodible. As winds increased the clay and silt particles became airborne, creating the infamous storms of the Dust Bowl.

To keep farmers on these fragile lands, the federal government began subsidizing irrigation projects. Improved drilling technologies plus subsidization prompted the development of vast tracts of farmland, all dependent on water from the Ogallala aquifer. By 1980, the aquifer fed about 20 percent of the irrigated land in the United States. It provided 30 percent of the irrigation groundwater used in the US. It then also watered the crops that fed over 40 percent of the cattle slaughtered in the US. Unfortunately, all the pumping from the aquifer has had a disastrous impact. Since about 1950, the amount of water in the Ogallala aquifer has dropped by 9 percent, with the southernmost parts of it almost entirely depleted. Depletion of aquifer levels is still rapidly occurring as a result of an ever increasing number of irrigation wells and lands previously unsuited to irrigation being watered by new technology, with an estimated 2 percent loss of the aquifer between 2001 and 2009 (Fleming et al., 2012).

Wetlands

Wetlands are considered to be among the most productive ecosystems in the world. Numerous species of vertebrates are associated with wetlands, either year-round, during migration, or during reproduction. In spite of the importance of wetlands, they are

WETLANDS

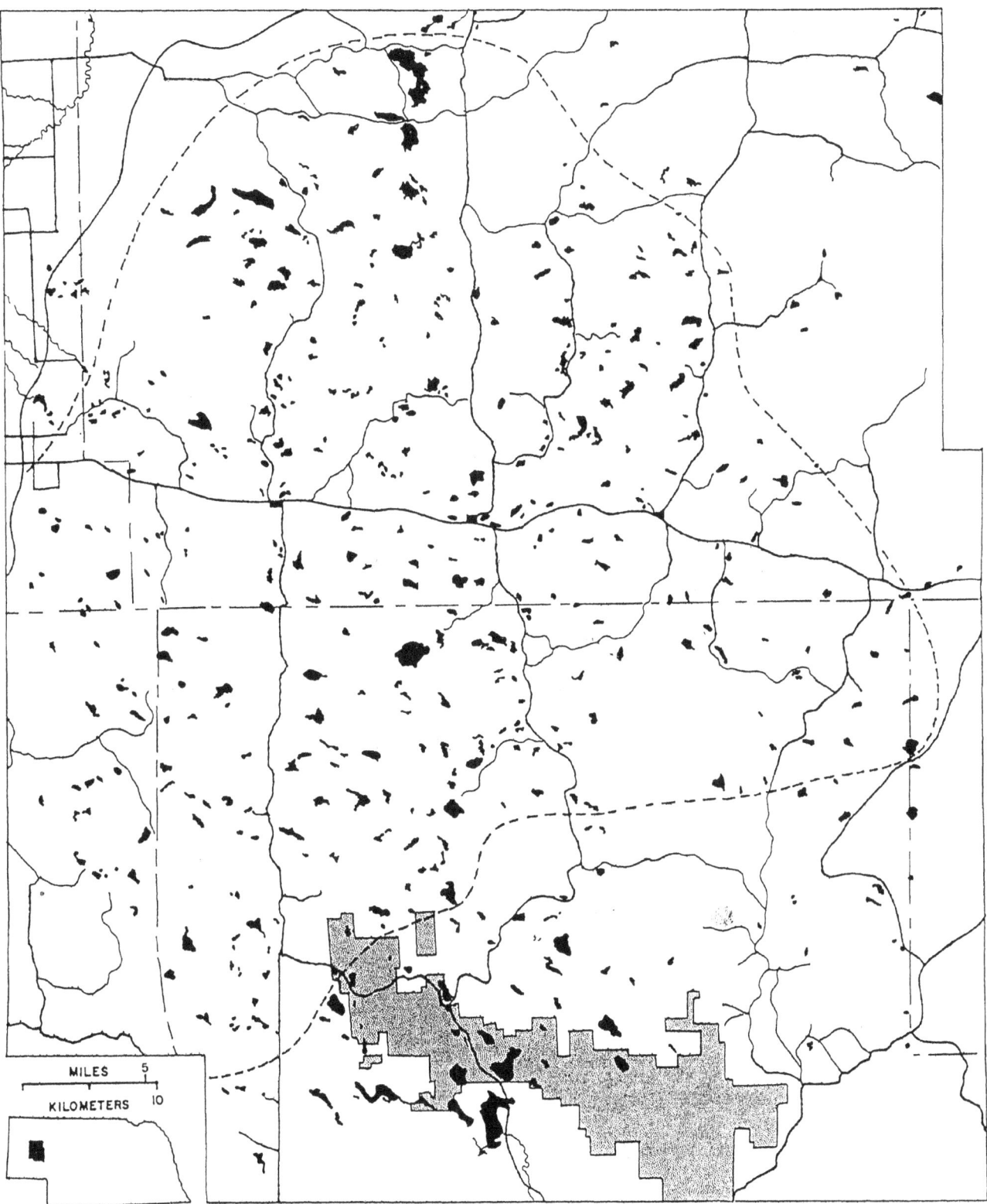

Map 5. Wetlands (inked) and roads in the western Sandhills of Garden County and southern Sheridan County. Crescent Lake National Wildlife Refuge (shaded) and the approximate limits of a region of highly alkaline wetlands (dashed line) are also indicated. From Johnsgard, 1995.

being lost worldwide because of numerous factors as human activities and climate change. However, the Nebraska Sandhills wetlands have been little or not at all affected by human-caused disturbances, are relatively abundant in many counties (Map 4), and provide habitat for numerous migrating and nesting species of birds. In low interdune depressions of the Sandhills, wet meadows and marshes are formed where the top of the Ogallala aquifer reaches the sand surface, producing thousands of relatively small and shallow wetlands of great value to wetland birds (Novacek, 1989; Johnsgard, 1995, 2001, 2012). The importance of wetlands to many taxa of Nebraska vertebrates, including some endangered species of fish, amphibians, and birds, has been discussed by Dinan, Jorgensen, and Bomberger (2018); Johnsgard and Dinan (2005); and Johnsgard (2012).

Nebraska wetlands are classified into two major categories (Johnsgard, 2012), including riverine wetlands, such as the Niobrara, Calamus, and Loup Rivers, and standing-water wetlands, including lakelike (lacustrine) and marshlike (palustrine) wetlands. Some lakelike wetlands occur in the Sandhills, although most Sandhills lakes are best described as "lacustrine lagoon marshes" (1). Other wetland types include (2) emergent vegetation marshes, typically surrounded by shoreline and emergent aquatic vegetation; (3) alkaline and saline wetlands, found mainly in the western part of the Sandhills and the North Platte River valley (Map 5); (4) wet meadows and fens, the fens (boglike wetlands having relatively good nutrient sources) being mainly found in Cherry County; (5) seeps from underground water sources; and (6) river backwaters and reservoir inflows, such as Clear Creek Wildlife Management Area at the western end of Lake McConaughy and the western end of Lewis and Clark Lake in Knox County (Johnsgard, 2012).

Wetlands loss in the Sandhills has occurred primarily through draining by surface ditches, which began as early as 1900 (McMurtrey, Craig, and Schildmann, 1972). With the introduction of center-pivot irrigation systems to the Sandhills in the early 1970s along with land leveling and shaping and local water table declines have increasingly resulted in extensive wetland losses in some peripheral areas of the Sandhills (LaGrange, 2005).

Landscape Ecology

The Nebraska Sandhills remain a semiwilderness that is almost entirely covered with native grassland vegetation (Kaul, 1998; Kaul, Sutherland, and Rolfsmeier, 2012). This unique prairie community, the Sandhills mixed-grass prairie, is adapted to its fragile sandy substrate, and flourished after it was formed by the deposition of sand and fine gravels produced by glacial melting during late Pleistocene times (Bleed and Flowerday, 1989; Johnsgard, 1995).

Based on Omernik's (1995) concepts of the ecogeography of the United States, the Sandhills is a major ecoregion (Chapman et al., 2001). Ecological regions can be identified and defined by analyzing the patterns and composition of biotic and abiotic phenomena that affect or reflect differences in ecosystem quality and integrity. These variables include geology, physiography, vegetation, climate, soils, land use, wildlife, and hydrology (Chapman et al., 2001).

The Nebraska Sandhills are subdivided into four lower-level ecoregions. The largest, the Sandhills Ecoregion, covers approximately 75 percent of the entire Sandhills region. Much smaller in size, the Alkaline Lakes and Lakes Ecoregion is characterized by numerous small lakes that arise from the intersection of the water table with dune topography. These valuable wetland areas are used predominantly by ranchers as rangeland. The Wet Meadow and Marsh Plain Ecoregion, also smaller in extent, is mostly located at the northeastern edge of the Sandhills and is characterized by extensive wet meadows and some small areas in crops. The central Sandhills are generally devoid of croplands except for occasional irrigated or subirrigated areas used to grow winter forage (Doubková and Henebry, 2005).

The vegetation in the Sandhills suggests that its flora has been recruited largely from the surrounding prairie flora. Hayden's penstemon (*Penstemon haydenii*) is an exception and is the only endemic vascular plant in the region. It is likely that long-term changes in the Sandhills biota have been extensive and dynamic. The present sand-related flora, and its associated fauna, may have been widely distributed at the end of the Pleistocene epoch. Most of the introduced plant species occur in disturbed areas such as roadsides, cultivated fields, and heavily grazed rangeland, which constitute a small fraction of the total Sandhills area (Whitcomb, 1989) but compose more than 40 percent of the vascular plant diversity of Keith County (Johnsgard, 1995).

About 720 species of vascular plants are native to the Sandhills, or less than a third of those reported for the entire state, as a reflection of environmental constraints such as those caused by the low water-holding capacities of sand and the highly unstable dune substrate. Of the 720 species, approximately 670 of them are native and 50 are introduced "exotics" (Whitcomb, 1989). The Sandhills prairie, especially on xeric and mesic sites, is dominated by arid-adapted perennial grasses, especially little bluestem (*Schizachyrium scoparium*). Kaul (1989) recognized eight native Sandhills plant communities: (1) bunchgrass, consisting of a mixture of little bluestem, junegrass (*Koeleria*), needle-and-thread (*Stipa*), and switchgrass (*Panicum*); (2) sand muhly (*Muhlenbergia*); (3) blowout grass (*Redfieldia*); (4) needle-and-thread (*Stipa*); (5) three-awn grass (*Aristida*); (6) short-grass meadow; (7) wet meadow; and (8) marsh and aquatic communities.

Common forbs and shrubs in upland communities include Arkansas rose (*Rosa arkansana*), bush morning glory (*Ipomoea leptophylla*), leadplant (*Amorpha canescens*), lemon scurfpea (*Psoralea lanceolata*), New Jersey tea (*Ceanothus herbaceus*), pincushion cactus (*Coryphantha vivipara*), poison ivy (*Toxicodendron rydbergii*), and sand cherry (*Prunus pumila*). A variety of composites, such as asters (*Aster* spp.) and sunflowers (*Helianthus* spp.), also commonly occurs in these communities and represents the most species-rich family of the Sandhills' vascular plants, exclusive of grasses (Johnsgard, 1995). Some of these are important food and nesting or escape cover plants for birds.

In marshes, wet meadows, and aquatic habitats, a wide variety of sedges, rushes, and reed species are found, as are such aquatic or semiaquatic forbs as arrowheads (*Sagittaria* spp.), cow lily (*Nuphar luteum*), duckweeds (*Lemna* spp.), floating azolla (*Azolla mexicana*), giant duckweed (*Spirodela polyrhiza*), horned pondweed (*Zannichellia palustris*), water milfoil (*Myriophyllum* spp.), naiad (*Najas* spp.), pondweeds (*Potamogeton* spp.), smartweeds (*Polygonum* spp.), swamp milkweed (*Asclepias incarnata*), watercress (*Nasturtium officinale*), water lilies (*Nymphaea* spp.), watermeal (*Wolffia* spp.), waterweed (*Elodea* spp.), water hemlock (*Cicuta* spp.), water plantain (*Alisma* spp.), and widgeon grass (*Ruppia maritima*). At least in Keith County, riparian and lowland–prairie meadow species compose almost half of the taxonomic diversity of the county's vascular plants (Johnsgard, 1995). These too are important food plants, especially for aquatic birds (Oberholser and McAtee, 1920).

About 224,000 acres (350 sq. mi.) of wooded vegetation also occur in the Sandhills, mainly along river valleys, although the partially planted Nebraska National Forest provides additional upland acreage. The Bessey Ranger District includes the 20,000-acre human-planted Halsey portion of the Nebraska National Forest, and the similarly planted 116,000-acre Samuel R. McKelvie National Forest in Cherry County. Most of the Sandhills' passerine birds, and some non-passerine such as hawks, owls, cuckoos, and woodpeckers are dependent on forest habitats.

Climate

The Sandhills region is large enough to exhibit considerable climatic variation. Annual precipitation in the Sandhills ranges from about 23 inches (580 mm) in the east to less than 17 inches (430 mm) in the west (Wilhite and Hubbard, 1989). As much as half of the precipitation is received during the primary growing season from May through July. Mean precipitation values for the Sandhills can be deceiving, since precipitation varies greatly from year to year. Snowfall, which ranges from about 22 inches (560 mm) in the south to about 56 inches (1,440 mm) in the north, is also an important factor in groundwater recharge. The Sandhills area was affected by the "great drought" of the 1930s but suffered less than many other Great Plains regions, largely because the region's flora is well adapted to withstand such variations in precipitation.

Mean annual temperatures in the Sandhills range from 68° to 77° F (20°–25° C). The freeze-free season varies from 150 days in the east to 120 days in the west, which is primarily a reflection of elevational differences. Prevailing winds usually have a westerly component but frequently also are northerly or southerly; east winds are uncommon (Wilhite and Hubbard, 1989). Long prevailing northwesterly winds have shaped the dune topography and directional orientation.

For much of the twentieth century, and especially during the past few decades, the Great Plains has experienced a warming trend that is part of a global phenomenon. In the Great Plains this warming trend has been most apparent in recent milder winter temperatures. Such changes and availability of open water, mainly on rivers in the Sandhills, have greatly increased the diversity and abundance of overwintering waterfowl and shifted the usual wintering distributions of many bird species (Johnsgard, 2012).

Birds and Humans in the Nebraska Sandhills

Evidence of permanent settlements of plains tribes along the streams of the Sandhills has been dated to 1,000 to 2,000 years ago. At least eight Native American tribes have lived in the region, hunting and growing crops such as beans, corn, and squash. Bison seasonally migrated through the region in herds of uncountable numbers and were hunted by the Pawnees, Lakotas, Cheyenne, and other horse-centered cultures until the bison were extirpated in the late 1880s. As they disappeared, so did predators and scavengers such as wolves and ravens. Archaic buffalo wallows can still be found in many parts of the Sandhills (Hayford and Baker, 2012). Native Americans, such as the Pawnees, were familiar with the bird life of the Sandhills. They were an important food source and were also considered spiritual creatures, appearing in tribal myths and ceremonies. Tribal seasonal and daily activities were also closely linked to avian breeding and migratory seasons (Ducey, 2000).

The Nebraska Sandhills were not studied ornithologically during the early exploratory expeditions across the central Great Plains, although a few survey groups passed through the region. The Gouverneur Warren exploratory expeditions into Nebraska Territory (1855–1857) provided documentation of almost thirty bird species, but few if any other Sandhills species were documented during this period (Ducey, 2000).

In 1862 President Abraham Lincoln signed the Homestead Act, under which settlers were given title to tracts of 160 acres of surveyed public domain if they cultivated the land and lived on it for at least five years. Encouraged by the construction of railroads, floods of settlers arrived in the plains in the 1880s to take up either farming or cattle ranching. They were supplemented by others with the later passage of the more land-generous Kinkaid Act, which provided 640 acres in many of the Sandhills and other drier portions of western Nebraska where it is impossible for a person to scratch out a living on only 160 acres. By the turn of the twentieth century, Sandhills ranching had become a large-scale operation (Whitcomb, 1989).

Human Impacts on Birds

The Nebraska Sandhills region is one of the most intact mixed-grass prairie regions in North America. One current threat is the combination of warming climate and an increase in center-pivot agriculture along the river valleys and southern and eastern margins of the region. Climate projections forecast increased drought and significant warming in the Great Plains. As the climate becomes warmer, the shallow lakes will receive less precipitation and will need to receive more groundwater inflow to maintain water levels.

Less precipitation will mean that row crops will require more irrigation. Increased center-pivot irrigation will further reduce water levels in the Ogallala aquifer, resulting in less groundwater being available to maintain wetlands and irrigate crops, as has already occurred in all of the Great Plains states south of Nebraska. It is possible that future droughts and warming will reduce the number of lakes and wetlands in the Sandhills (Hayford and Baker, 2012).

Another current threat to the Sandhills is overgrazing. Sandhills ranchers have a tradition of good management practices for their rangeland, as the thin Sandhills soil is easily disrupted, leading to erosion and openly eroding exposures of sand ("blowouts"). Consequently, ranchers can quickly see when grazing is destroying the soil and vegetation, and can take corrective actions. The water-land interface can also easily degrade under grazing pressures. Cattle that are allowed to graze along the shorelines of lakes and streams destabilize banks and shorelines, and introduce ammonia and organic waste into these waters (Hayford and Baker, 2012).

Ornithological Research and Regional Birding

The first scientific ornithological research in the Nebraska Sandhills was probably conducted by the

University of Nebraska's Professor Lawrence Bruner (1902), who compared the bird life in Holt County in 1883–84 and 1891. At the end of the nineteenth and early twentieth century, the Sandhills had still not attracted much attention from biologists, whereas birds in the eastern part of the state and some areas along the lower Platte River were being studied more extensively. The activities of the Nebraska Ornithologists' Union gradually improved this situation after its formation in 1899, and especially with the initiation of its quarterly research journal, the *Nebraska Bird Review*, in 1931 (Johnsgard, 1999, 2001).

It was not until mid-1900s that some parts of the Nebraska Sandhills attracted the attention of professional ornithologists. The mid-1950s was a time of great interest in Nebraska's Platte River valley birds by some nationally known ornithologists. Professor Charles Sibley of Cornell University led several students on a series of summer expeditions to the Platte valley of central Nebraska, studying the breeding biology and collecting specimens of several east-west species pairs of birds that hybridize extensively there as a result of post-Pleistocene secondary contact. These studies (Sibley and Short, 1959, 1964; Sibley and West, 1959; West, 1962; Short, 1965) proved the biological and zoogeographic importance of the central Platte valley, and to a lesser extent the Niobrara River valley, as dispersal corridors and major evolutionary "suture zones" between eastern and western avifaunas, primarily among woodland nesting species that have undergone range expansion as mature riparian forests have developed following the suppression of prairie fires (Johnsgard, 2001) (Table 2).

Table 2. Geographic and Ornithological Aspects of the Nebraska Sandhills Counties

County name[a]	Grassland (sq. mi.)[b]	Woodlands (sq. mi.)[b]	Water (acres)[c]	Bird Species[d]
Antelope	300	33	900	257
Arthur	670	0.3	3,000	162
Blaine	700	2.5	1,000	187
Boone	250	4.1	1,100	208
Brown	1,100	26	8,000	212
Cherry	5,800	26	40,000	283
Custer	1,700	16	2,100	205
Garden	1,400	0.8	22,000	273
Garfield	500	8.6	6,000	170
Grant	500	0.6	3,500	193
Greeley	450	4.7	2,500	164
Holt	1,700	11	12,000	211
Hooker	700	3.8	400	182
Keith	500	9.4	41,000	386
Lincoln	1,900	56	10,000	259
Logan	500	0.5	250	174
Loup	550	7.8	7,000	209
McPherson	800	1.5	600	164
Morrill	1,000	47	5,000	189
Rock	950	17.2	11,000	179
Sheridan	1,900	78	20,000	209
Thomas	600	2.5	1,500	161
Wheeler	500	37	1,300	269

[a] Interior counties are shown in **bold**; remaining peripheral Sandhills counties were identified from maps in Bleed and Flowerday (1989).
[b] "Grassland" includes Sandhills prairie, other native grasslands, and pastures. "Woodlands" include natural and planted woody stands. Estimates were based on various sources. After Johnsgard (2001).
[c] Surface water, including wetlands, reservoirs, and rivers. After Johnsgard (2001).
[d] Totals are based on those reported in this book. They are mostly smaller than those reported on the Nebraska Ornithologists' Union website (2020) (https://noubirds.org/Birds/CountyTotals.aspx), which are based on personal field records provided by its members.

An important event in exploring the avifauna of the Nebraska Sandhills, particularly the western part, was the 1975 establishment of the University of Nebraska's Cedar Point Biological Station. Ornithology classes have been offered there annually since 1976. Several associated major ornithological and ecological studies have been conducted in the general vicinity of Lake McConaughy and at the university's upland prairie research site at Arapahoe Prairie in southern Arthur County.

Additional investigations of birds at Cedar Point Biological Station occurred between 1992 and 1996, when Professor William Scharf and his associates began a mist-netting and bird-banding program. More than 11,000 birds of 84 species were banded, weighed, and later sometimes recaptured from locations as far away as central Alaska (Brown et al., 1996).

More than 20 theses, dissertations, and other ornithological research studies at Cedar Point were published during a three-decade period in the late 1900s, including groundbreaking research on the biological costs and ecological benefits of cliff swallow sociality by Professors Charles and Mary B. Brown (Brown and Brown, 1996). Several theses and dissertations were also completed during the later 1900s under the direction of Professor Paul Johnsgard at Cedar Point and the central Sandhills, including those by Curtis Twedt (1974), Sharon Clawson (1980), Mary Bomberger (1982), Timothy Bergin (1987), and Josef Kren (1996).

Richard Rosche (1982, 1994), then a resident of Chadron, also significantly contributed to the knowledge of the birds of western Nebraska and the Sandhills, particularly the northwestern Sandhills. C. Fred Zeillemaker, the refuge manager at Crescent Lake NWR from 1977 to 1982, also contributed to a better understanding of the avifauna at the refuge and surrounding areas through his local bird-netting and observations. Stephen Jones later described the biology and botany of the western Sandhills in his book *The Last Prairie* (2000). *The Birds of Nebraska*, published in 2001 by Roger Sharpe, Ross Silcock, and Joel Jorgensen, provides an excellent summary of the status of Nebraska ornithology at the start of the twenty-first century.

Students of the University of Nebraska's School of Natural Resources have also been conducting ornithological research in the Nebraska Sandhills. Since 1981 some of it has centered at the University of Nebraska's Gudmundsen Sandhills Laboratory in Grant, Hooker, and Cherry Counties. Several PhD dissertations and papers centered on the biology of this area of the Sandhills have been produced.

Another important milestone in the distribution of Nebraska's avifauna was a statewide survey of breeding birds that began in 1984 and resulted in *The Nebraska Breeding Birds Atlas, 1984–1989* (Mollhoff, 2001). Field work for a second breeding atlas edition was conducted between 2006 and 2011, and the results were published in 2016 (Mollhoff, 2016). One of Mollhoff's interesting findings (2016) was that six Sandhill counties were among the ten most species-rich counties in the state during the first atlas surveys, and seven were among the ten most species-rich counties during the second atlas surveys. Five of the counties (Cherry, Sheridan, Garden, Morrill, and Lincoln) were in the top ten lists during both survey periods.

The North American Breeding Bird Survey, organized by the US Geological Survey's Patuxent Wildlife Research Center, was initiated in 1966. Its purpose is to monitor the status and trends of North American bird populations by collecting long-term data on the populations of breeding birds. Several designated routes in the Nebraska Sandhills are surveyed annually. The annual National Audubon Society's Christmas Bird Counts are another important national survey of birds. Although regularly conducted in only two Sandhills counties, Keith and Lincoln, they significantly contribute to our understanding of the winter bird populations of the Sandhills.

Many birders now travel through the Nebraska Sandhills. Some report their sightings on two internet-based databases, eBird and NEBirds. The internet site eBird is an online database of bird observations with a relatively large volume of data from Nebraska. It is always useful to review when planning a Sandhills trip. NEBirds is another form of reporting system and is commonly used by observers who do not use eBird. Although interest in birding in Nebraska's Sandhills has increased significantly over the past few decades, countless lakes, marshes, and other habitats are still unvisited by birdwatchers and ornithologists, and many are still so isolated they are probably accessible only on horseback, the transportation form McCarraher (1960) used when he inventoried the lakes of the region.

As a general overview of the Sandhills' breeding bird community, Table 3 shows an approximate estimate of the relative spring and summer abundance of 44 mostly breeding species in three Nebraska Sandhills refuges.

Table 3. Relative Spring and Summer Abundance Indices of Mostly Wetland Bird Species in Three Nebraska Sandhills National Wildlife Refuges[a]

Blue-winged teal (28)	Black tern (18)	Greater prairie-chicken (12)
Red-winged blackbird (28)	Forster's tern (16)	Trumpeter swan (9)
Barn swallow (28)	Long-billed curlew (16)	Belted kingfisher (9)
Mallard (27)	Ruddy duck (16)	Black-crowned night-heron (8)
Northern shoveler (26)	Sora (16)	Lesser scaup (7)
Gadwall (25)	Double-crested cormorant (16)	Great blue heron (7)
Killdeer (25)	Pied-billed grebe (15)	Green-winged teal (7)
Wilson's snipe (25)	Eared grebe (15)	Spotted sandpiper (6)
Upland sandpiper (24)	Western grebe (15)	Franklin's gull (6)
Common yellowthroat (23)	American bittern (15)	Northern rough-winged swallow (6)
Redhead (20)	Northern harrier (14)	Swamp sparrow (6)
Marsh wren (20)	Bobolink (13)	Wood duck (4)
Northern pintail (19)	American wigeon (13)	Cinnamon teal (4)
Canada goose (15)	Willet (12)	Black-necked stilt (4)
Yellow-headed blackbird (18)	Virginia rail (12)	Song sparrow (2)
American coot (18)	American avocet (12)	
Wilson's phalarope (18)	Canvasback (12)	

[a] Based on summed spring and summer relative abundance estimates for wetland-associated birds at Crescent Lake, Valentine, and Fort Niobrara National Wildlife Refuges, as identified and summarized by Novacek (1989). Abundance numerical key: Abundant = 5, Common = 4, Uncommon = 3, Occasional = 2, Rare = 1.

Upland sandpiper

Species Acccounts

Terms and Inclusion Criteria for Species Accounts

Terms and Criteria of Temporal Occurrence

Permanent resident. Present throughout the year and presumably breeding.

Summer resident. Present during the summer, presumably breeding, but migrating out of the state for part of the year. The English name of species judged to be breeding in the Sandhills are identified in these species accounts by being shown in **bold** font.

Migrant. Passes through the state in spring or fall or both, but normally not remaining in Sandhills counties through summer or winter. The term "straggler" is used for rare migrants or individuals of regular migrant species that sometimes remain in the area beyond their normal period. The arrival and departure times shown are based on statewide averages from records in the *Nebraska Bird Review* and are several decades old (terminating in the mid-1980s). Because of more recent climate change, mean spring arrival dates should usually be moved about two weeks earlier, and mean fall departure dates to about two weeks later (Johnsgard, 2018).

Vagrant. Refers to species normally migratory in other areas, individuals of which sometimes stray well outside their usual range and are of "accidental" occurrence in the region.

Winter visitor. Species normally present in the area only between November 1 and May 1. The term "late winter visitor or spring migrant" refers to those species usually not appearing until mid-January and sometimes remaining in Sandhills counties until late May.

Relative Abundance Terms

Abundant. Present in such quantity that large numbers are likely to be encountered daily during the proper season and in appropriate habitats.

Common. Present in such quantity that several are likely to be encountered daily during the proper season and in appropriate habitats.

Uncommon. A few are likely to be seen each year in the appropriate habitats.

Occasional. Not observed every year but reported periodically in the Sandhills region.

Rare. Reported from five to ten Sandhills counties, according to sources in "Distribution Criteria."

Very rare. Highly local (if resident) or rare vagrant (if migratory); reported from three to four Sandhills counties, according to sources in "Distribution Criteria."

Accidental. Reported (one or more times) from one or two Sandhills counties.

Distribution Criteria

Distributional categories assigned in the species accounts were chosen largely based on county occurrence data on the 2019 Nebraska Ornithologists' Union (NOU) website, plus information in the *Nebraska Bird Review*, national wildlife refuge checklists, and other regional literature to 2020.

The descriptive species accounts of these species are mostly confined to county occurrence information and lack full documentation for the rarer species. Details on rare and accidental occurrences can be found in Johnsgard (2012b); Sharpe, Silcock, and Jorgensen (2001); and in Birds of Nebraska–Online (https://birds.outdoornebraska.gov/browse-species/). Sightings of rare birds in Nebraska are also periodically evaluated and summarized in annual reports of the NOU Records Committee and published in the *Nebraska Bird Review* (https://digitalcommons.unl.edu/nebbirdrev/).

Distribution Terms

Local. Reported from 5 to 10 Sandhills counties, according to sources in "Distribution Criteria."

Regional. Reported in 11 to 15 Sandhills counties, according to sources in "Distribution Criteria."

Widespread. Reported in 16 to 20 Sandhills counties, according to sources in "Distribution Criteria."

Ubiquitous. Reported in 21 to 22 Sandhills counties, according to sources in "Distribution Criteria."

Pandemic. The species has a very wide distribution,

sometimes extending throughout the North American continent.

Endemic. The species is essentially limited to a particular region (such as the Sandhills region) or unique habitat (such as Sandhills prairie).

Extirpated. The species is now absent from the Sandhills region but once was more numerous.

Extinct. The species is no longer alive anywhere. (Extinct species are not discussed in this book.)

Breeding and County Records Criteria

County occurrence records are largely based on NOU website records, plus the *Nebraska Bird Review* and other sources, including personal observations. Older county records that occurred from 1961 to 1984 are considered "quasihistoric." As summarized by Ducey (1988), records from 1921 to 1960 are considered "historic" and are followed by "(H)." County records that Ducey summarized from the 1800s to 1920 are identified by the county name abbreviations followed by asterisks, with those counties having breeding records indicated in **bold**. Species name is in **bold** if confirmed breeding records for the species exist for the overall Sandhills region, as judged by Ducey (1988); Labedz (1989); Sharpe, Silcock, and Jorgensen (2001); and/or Johnsgard (2018).

Individual county breeding records from 1920 to 1987 are based primarily on Ducey (1988). Those from 1984 to 1989 and from 2005 to 2015 are based on two *Nebraska Breeding Bird Atlas*es (Mollhoff, 2001, 2016). Interim breeding records between atlasing years (1989–2005) and records occurring from 2015 to 2019 are based on information in the *Nebraska Bird Review*, Birds of Nebraska–Online, and (in some cases) eBird records.

Technical Nomenclature

The English names, family and species sequence and Latin nomenclature used here follow the American Ornithologists' Society's (AOS) *Check-list of North American Birds*, with supplements through 2019 (Chesser et al., 2019). Hypothetical species lacking adequate occurrence documentation are parenthetically indicated.

Additional recent information on Nebraska's birds can be found at Birds of Nebraska–Online. Likewise, the website of the Nebraska Ornithologists' Union (hereafter referred to as the NOU website; https://www.noubirds.org/) provides a wealth of information on Nebraska birds.

Family Anatidae (Swans, Geese, and Ducks)

Black-bellied Whistling-Duck,
Dendrocygna autumnalis
Ch, Gar, Hol, Li

Very rare. The vagrant black-bellied whistling-duck has been reported several times in the Sandhills during recent years, which might reflect the early stages of a slow northern expansion of the species' once-tropical range (Johnsgard, 2018).

Snow Goose, *Anser caerulescens*
An, Ar, Bo, Br, Ch, Cu, Gar, Gre, Grf, Hol, Ke, Li, Lo, Log, Mc, Mo, Ro, Sh, Wh

Status. The snow goose is an abundant spring and fall migrant throughout the Sandhills. The bluish morph ("blue goose") and less common intermediate (heterozygotic) types compose about a third of the total snow goose population in eastern Nebraska but are much less frequent westward. Migrants are abundant during spring and fall throughout the Great Plains states, which supported a midcontinental population of white geese (including Ross's geese) of about 12 million birds by 2017 (US Fish and Wildlife Service, 2019), and which is still increasing at a substantial rate.

Migration. Thirty-six initial spring sightings range from January 8 to March 28, with a median of March 9. Twenty-six final spring sightings are from March 6 to May 20, with a median of April 20. Forty initial fall sightings are from August 19 to December 16, with a median of October 4. Thirty-eight final fall sightings are from October 26 to December 31, with a median of December 2.

Habitats. Marshes, sloughs, riverbottom meadows, and croplands such as cornfields are used on migration. Lakes or reservoirs near croplands are utilized for roosting.

Adult snow geese in flight, two blue morph, one white morph

Ross's Goose, *Anser rossii*
An, Bo, Br, Gre, Ke, Li, Lo, Log, Mc, Sh, Wh

Status. The Ross's goose is an increasingly common and regular spring and fall migrant in the Sandhills. It is present each spring in the Sandhills wetlands and many other eastern and Platte River valley counties, typically in the company of large flocks of snow geese. Ross's geese now make up at least 2 to 3 percent of Nebraska's snow goose flocks (Johnsgard, 2012a). This tiny goose is now a regular and uncommon migrant throughout the Great Plains states, and it occasionally hybridizes with snow geese. When hybridization involves the blue-morph snow goose, "blue Ross's geese" phenotypes might result (Johnsgard, 2014).

Migration. Six spring records are from March 10 to April 13, with a mean of March 29. Five fall records are from November 10 to December 22, with a mean of November 26.

Habitats. Found in the same habitats as snow geese.

Greater White-fronted Goose, *Anser albifrons*
An, Ar, Bl, Bo, Ch, Cu, Gar, Gre, Grf, Hol, Ke, Li, Log, Ro, Sh, Th, Wh

Status. The greater white-fronted goose is a common spring and fall migrant throughout Nebraska. Migrants occur throughout the Great Plains states but are more common in western and central areas than toward the east. The species had a midcontinental population of about 775,000 birds by 2018–19 (US Fish and Wildlife Service, 2019).

Migration. Twenty-nine initial spring sightings are from February 12 to May 12, with a median of March 12. Seventeen final spring sightings are from March 23 to May 18, with a median of April 14. Nineteen initial fall sightings are from September 14 to November 21, with a median of October 23. Fifteen final fall sightings are from October 12 to December 29, with a median of November 6.

Habitats. Migrants are associated with large marshes, shallow lakes, wide rivers with bars and islands, and adjacent agricultural grainfields. This goose usually does not associate closely with either Canada geese or snow geese and is more wary than both.

Brant, *Branta bernicla*
Gar, Ke

Accidental. Besides being reported from Crescent Lake NWR, brant have also been observed in Keith County at various times, mostly during November and December (Brown, Dinsmore, and Brown, 2012).

Cackling Goose, *Branta hutchinsii*
An, Ar, Bl, Bo, Br, Ch, Cu, Gar, Gr, Gre, Grf, Ho, Ke, Li, Lo, Log, Mo, Ro, Th, Wh

Status. The cackling goose is a common migrant, especially in central Nebraska (*Nebraska Bird Review* 74: 99–105), including the Sandhills. In 1934 Swenk (*Nebraska Bird Review* 2: 103–16) classified 17 of 404 Nebraska-shot Canada goose specimens as *hutchinsii*. He identified the majority of the birds as intermediate *leucopareia*, which would probably include the forms currently represented by the taxa *parvipes* and *taverneri* (the latter is now considered part of *hutchinsii*). Typical *hutchinsii* types are seemingly most common in the central Platte River valley, and some wintering may occur in southwestern Nebraska and adjacent western Kansas. The species had an estimated national population of about 200,000 birds by 2018–19 (US Fish and Wildlife Service, 2019).

Migration. Some wintering may occur in southwestern Nebraska and adjacent western Kansas.

Habitats. Cackling geese use the same habitats as, and often associate with, Canada geese while they are in Nebraska, but also at times consist of single-species flocks. Less often they might mix with snow geese or greater white-fronted geese while resting or foraging.

Canada Goose, *Branta canadensis*
An, Ar, Bl, Bo, Br, Ch, Cu, Gar, Gr, Gre, Grf, Ho, Hol, Ke, Li, Lo, Log, Mc, Mo, Ro, Sh, Th, Wh

Status. A common to abundant migrant throughout the Sandhills with widespread breeding and local overwintering. Canada geese have been released widely, and breeding now occurs throughout the state. Overwintering is now normal in the Platte valley and even some cities, especially by the larger races. Breeding Bird Surveys between 1966 and 2015 indicate the species collectively

underwent a survey-wide population increase (9.17% annually) during that period, and Nebraska underwent an estimated and hardly believable 13.58 percent rate of annual increase. The western prairies and Great Plains region supported a midcontinental population of about 1.4 million birds by 2018–19 (US Fish and Wildlife Service, 2019), which is still increasing at a substantial rate.

Migration. Forty-five initial spring sightings are from January 4 to April 3, with a median of March 27. Forty-one final spring sightings are from March 19 to May 30, with a median of April 28. Fifty-three initial fall sightings are from July 28 to December 20, with a median of October 13. Fifty-four final fall sightings are from October 18 to December 31, with a median of December 10.

Habitats. Migrant birds are found on large marshes, lakes or reservoirs, and nearby grainfields. Breeding is typical on prairie marshes, or sometimes on larger lakes with islands or muskrat houses. Canada geese and cackling geese are often seen in mixed flocks when foraging or roosting but tend to separate in flight owing to differences in flight speeds.

Trumpeter Swan, *Cygnus buccinator*
An, **Ar**, Bo, **Br**, **Ch**, Cu, **Gar**, **Gr**, Grf, Ho, **Hol**, Ke, Lo, **Log, Mc, Ro, Sh, Wh**

Status. The trumpeter swan is an occasional spring and fall migrant and local permanent resident in the Sandhills. This species originally nested in the state but was extirpated and apparently absent until the late 1960s, when recolonization occurred as a result of releases made in South Dakota. Nesting has since occurred in many Sandhills lakes, mainly in Cherry and Grant Counties but with breeding-season usage also reported from marshes in Sheridan, Garden, and Brown Counties. By 1995 the Nebraska population totaled about 150 birds. Recent studies indicate a gradual increase in fall and winter numbers to about 600 birds in the Nebraska–South Dakota region (Johnsgard, 2018), and the national population had totaled more than 60,000 birds by 2015 (Johnsgard, 2020a).

Migration. Eight spring sightings are from January 24 to May 23, with a mean of March 28. Six fall sightings are from August 10 to November 7, with a mean of October 6. However, many birds overwinter in ice-free rivers of the Sandhills. Traditional wintering sites include Blue Creek in Garden County, the Snake River in Cherry County, portions of the Loup River system, and the North Platte River at Lake Ogallala in Keith County (Silcock and Jorgensen, various dates).

Habitats. Migrants are found on lakes, large marshes, and impoundments. Breeding occurs on large shallow marshes or lakes having abundant submerged vegetation, emergent plants, and stable water levels. Wetlands used during the breeding season in Nebraska average about 180 acres with about 75 percent open water and having slight to (infrequently) medium salinity levels (Ducey, 1984).

Tundra Swan, *Cygnus columbianus*
An, Gar, Hol, Ke, Li, Log

Status. The tundra swan is an occasional spring and fall migrant in Nebraska, primarily in eastern and northeastern areas, but it has been observed as far west in the Sandhills as Garden County, usually in company with trumpeter swans. It is a regular and common migrant in the northern portions of the Great Plains, but the Atlantic and Pacific wintering breeding populations' migration routes diverge in North Dakota, and only a few stray birds reach Nebraska (Johnsgard, 2020a).

Migration. Twenty spring sightings range from January 1 to May 15, with a median of March 27. Eleven fall sightings are from October 21 to December 14, with a median of November 22.

Habitats. Tundra swans are usually found as individuals or pairs among flocks of migrating trumpeter swans, where they generally make up far less than 1 percent of the flocks. Nebraska is south of the species' usual migratory routes to the Atlantic and Pacific coasts.

Wood Duck, *Aix sponsa*
An, Ar, Bl, Bo, Br, Ch, Cu, Gar, Gr, Gre, Grf, Ho, Hol, Ke, Li, Lo, Log, Mc, Mo, Ro, Sh, Th, Wh

Status. The wood duck is a common spring and fall migrant and summer resident in eastern Nebraska but less common westwardly. It is only locally common in the Sandhills, although it has been reported from all the Sandhills counties. The

Trumpeter swan family. *Photo by P. Johnsgard.*

birds are most common along wooded rivers and creeks. Breeding Bird Surveys between 1966 and 2015 indicate the species collectively underwent a survey-wide population increase (1.63% annually) during that period, and Nebraska underwent an estimated 6.26 percent rate of annual increase.

Migration. Sixty-nine initial spring sightings are from January 17 to June 7, with a median of March 28. Half of the sightings fall within the period March 13–April 8. Thirty-five final fall sightings are from September 10 to December 31, with a median of October 21. Half of the records fall within the period October 3–30.

Habitats. Throughout the year this species is associated with tree-lined rivers, creeks, oxbows, and lakes and usually breeds near slow-moving rivers, sloughs, or ponds where large trees are found. Nest-box erection has helped facilitate the species' western expansion across Nebraska.

Blue-winged Teal, *Spatula discors*
An, Ar, Bl, Bo, Br, Ch, Cu, Gar, Gr, Gre, Grf, Ho, Hol, Ke, Li, Lo, Log, Mc, Mo, Ro, Sh, Th, Wh

Status. The blue-winged teal is an abundant spring and fall migrant and common summer resident throughout the Sandhills, especially common in smaller Sandhills marshes. Breeding Bird Surveys between 1966 and 2015 indicate the species collectively underwent a survey-wide population increase (0.29% annually) during that period, and Nebraska showed an estimated 1.43 percent rate of annual increase. Blue-winged teal are probably the most common nesting duck in the Sandhills, followed closely by the mallard, gadwall, and northern shoveler. The species had an estimated breeding population of about 5.4 million birds in the US Fish and Wildlife Service (USFWS) traditional survey area in 2018–19 (US Fish and Wildlife Service, 2019).

Migration. Sixty-eight initial spring sightings range from February 10 to June 1, with a median of April 2. Half of the sightings fall within the period March 28–April 10. Eighty-eight final fall sightings are from August 19 to December 31, with a median of October 10. Half of the records fall within the period September 24–October 23. The only documented records of presumed overwintering birds are of an immature male seen at Lake Ogallala, Keith County, on December 16, 1999, and January 29, 2000, and an adult in an open spring-fed pond in Lincoln County on January 12, 1991 (Silcock and Jorgensen, various dates).

Habitats. Migrants are found on generally shallow ponds, ditches, marshes, and the like, and rarely occur in deep open water. Breeding is typically in marshes surrounded by native prairies and grassy sedge meadows (Johnsgard, 2017a).

Cinnamon Teal, *Spatula cyanoptera*
An, Ar, Ch, **Gar**, Ho, Ke, Li, **Log**, Mc, **Mo**, Ro, **Sh**

Status. The cinnamon teal is an uncommon spring and fall migrant in the western half of Nebraska, becoming rarer eastwardly. It is probably a local summer resident in the Sandhills, but confusion with the blue-winged teal during summer makes the species' breeding status unclear. The birds are regularly present at Crescent Lake NWR during summer, and there is a nesting record for that refuge (Mollhoff, 2001). Breeding Bird Surveys between 1966 and 2015 indicate the species collectively underwent a survey-wide population decline (2.97% annually) during that period.

Migration. Sixty-two initial spring sightings are from January 9 to June 6, with a median of April 26. Half of the sightings fall within the period April 8–May 10. Six fall records are from July 13 to November 14, with a mean of September 19.

Habitats. This species occupies the same habitats as the blue-winged teal in Nebraska and usually is found in flocks of that species. To see this beautiful little duck, consider visiting Crescent Lake NWR in June, when as many as six to eight males might be seen on a good day, especially in western parts of the refuge.

Northern Shoveler, *Spatula clypeata*
An, **Ar**, Bl, **Bo, Br, Ch**, Cu, **Gar**, Gr, **Gre, Grf, Ho, Hol, Ke, Li**, Lo, **Log, Mc, Mo, Ro, Sh, Th, Wh**

Status. A common to abundant spring and fall migrant, and a common to uncommon summer resident in Nebraska, with breeding most frequent in the Sandhills and decreasing southeastwardly. Breeding Bird Surveys between 1966 and

Wood duck, male. *Photo by J. Kren.*

2015 indicate the species collectively underwent a survey-wide population increase (2.00% annually) during that period, and Nebraska underwent an estimated 2.07 percent rate of annual decline. The species had an estimated breeding population of about 3.6 million birds in the USFWS traditional survey area in 2018–19 (US Fish and Wildlife Service, 2019).

Migration. Seventy initial spring sightings are from January 27 to June 6, with a median of March 23. Half of the sightings fall within the period March 11–30. Sixty-two final fall sightings range from September 5 to December 31, with a median of November 4. Half of the records fall within the period October 20–November 20.

Habitats. Migrants use aquatic habitats rich in zooplankton and phytoplankton, and during the nesting season the birds favor shallow prairie marshes rich in those food sources. Wetlands with non-wooded shorelines are preferred over those with wooded shores, and mud-bottom ponds are also apparently preferentially used over those with sand bottoms (Johnsgard, 2017a).

Gadwall, *Mareca strepera*
An, Ar, Bl, Bo, Br, Ch, Cu, Gar, Gr, Gre, Grf, Ho, Hol, Ke, Li, Lo, Log, Mc, Mo, Ro, Sh, Th, Wh

Status. The gadwall is a common to abundant spring and fall migrant and a common summer resident in Nebraska, especially in the Sandhills. Breeding Bird Surveys between 1966 and 2015 indicate the species collectively underwent a survey-wide population increase (2.66% annually) during that period, and Nebraska underwent an estimated 4.34 percent rate of annual decline. The species had an estimated breeding population of about 3.2 million birds in the USFWS traditional survey area in 2018–19 (US Fish and Wildlife Service, 2019).

Migration. The range of 48 initial spring sightings is from January 3 to June 8, with a median of March 28. Half of the records fall within the period March 6–April 8. Fifty final fall sightings range from October 4 to December 31, with a median of November 21. Half of the records fall within the period November 2–December 2.

Habitats. Migrants are normally found in shallow marshes and sloughs, and sometimes on deeper waters such as lakes and reservoirs. Nesting occurs preferentially on shallow prairie marshes, especially those having grassy or weedy islands or surrounding weedy cover (Johnsgard, 2017a).

Eurasian Wigeon, *Mareca penelope*
Ch, Ke, Li, Mo

Status. This wigeon is a rare spring Eurasian vagrant. The species was reported within the Sandhills region in Lincoln County during November 1966, and it has been observed at Valentine NWR, Cherry County, and on the Clear Creek marshes in May 1998 (Brown, Dinsmore, and Brown, 2012).

Habitats. Shallow lakes, marshes, and adjacent flooded fields are used by migrants. Fall plumages are very difficult to distinguish from those of the American wigeon. In recent years reports suggest the species is a regular spring migrant. One probable Eurasian × American wigeon hybrid has been reported in Nebraska (*Nebraska Bird Review* 66: 35), but no Eurasian wigeon breeding records in North America are yet known to our knowledge.

American Wigeon, *Mareca americana*
An, **Ar**, Bl, Bo, **Ch**, Cu, **Gar**, **Gr**, Gre, Grf, **Ho**, Hol, Ke, **Li**, Lo, Log, **Mc**, **Mo**, Ro, **Sh**, Th, Wh

Status. The American wigeon is a common to locally abundant spring and fall migrant throughout Nebraska and a local and generally uncommon breeder. It apparently is mostly confined to the northwestern parts of the Sandhills (south and east to Garden and Holt Counties, and possible breeding east to Holt County). Breeding Bird Surveys between 1966 and 2015 indicate the species collectively underwent a survey-wide population decline (2.13% annually) during that period. The species had an estimated breeding population of about 2.8 million birds in the USFWS traditional survey area in 2018–19 (US Fish and Wildlife Service, 2019).

Migration. Sixty-seven initial spring sightings range from January 9 to May 28, with a median of March 22. Half of the sightings fall within the period March 6–30. Thirty-four final spring sightings are from March 27 to June 6, with a median of May 3. Fifty initial fall sightings are from August 28 to December 17, with a median of September 30. Fifty final fall sightings are from

October 9 to December 31, with a median of November 18.

Habitats. During migration these birds are sometimes found on large lakes or reservoirs, but they forage where submerged plants can easily be reached from the surface or around shorelines in grassy meadows. Breeding is usually done on marshes or lakes with abundant aquatic food at or near the surface and especially on those with adjacent sedge meadows for nesting or brushy, partially wooded habitats nearby (Johnsgard, 2017a).

Mallard, *Anas platyrhynchos*
An, Ar, Bl, Bo, Br, Ch, Cu, Gar, Gr, Gre, Grf, Ho, Hol, Ke, Li, Lo, Log, Mc, Mo, Ro, Sh, Th, Wh

Status. The mallard is an abundant migrant and a locally common summer resident throughout Nebraska, including the Sandhills, where it is the most common breeding duck, followed by the blue-winged teal, gadwall, northern shoveler, and northern pintail (Vrtiska and Powell, 2011). Wintering birds are common wherever open water occurs and very common throughout the Sandhills region. Breeding Bird Surveys between 1966 and 2015 indicate the species collectively underwent a survey-wide population increase (0.30% annually) during that period, and Nebraska underwent an estimated 1.67 percent rate of annual increase. The species had an estimated breeding population of about 9.4 million birds in the USFWS traditional survey area in 2018–19 (US Fish and Wildlife Service, 2019).

Migration. Forty-three initial spring sightings are from January 1 to May 29, with a median of March 12. Half of the records fall within the period March 2–April 3. Sixty-four final fall sightings are from August 25 to December 31, with a median of November 27. Half of the sightings fall within the period November 21–December 28.

Habitats. Breeding birds favor fairly shallow waters, either still or slowly flowing, and surrounding dry areas of nonforested vegetation. Migrants are often found on large marshes, lakes, and reservoirs, especially where nearby grainfields provide food (Johnsgard, 2017a).

American Black Duck, *Anas rubripes*
An, Bo, Br, Ch, Gar

Status. The black duck is an occasional migrant in eastern Nebraska, becoming rarer westwardly but reported in at least five Sandhills counties.

Migration. Migration patterns closely follow those of the mallard.

Habitats. In Nebraska, black ducks are often seen in company with mallards, and hybrids between the two are quite common. Hybrids might range from being of intermediate plumage to closely approaching either of the parental species because of the complete interfertility of the two populations (Johnsgard, 2017a).

Northern Pintail, *Anas acuta*
An, **Ar**, **Bl**, Bo, **Br**, **Ch**, Cu, **Gar**, **Gr**, **Gre**, **Grf**, **Ho**, **Hol**, **Ke**, **Li**, **Lo**, **Log**, **Mc**, **Mo**, **Ro**, **Sh**, **Th**, **Wh**

Status. The northern pintail is an abundant spring and fall migrant and a common summer resident throughout the Sandhills that breeds locally in suitable habitats. It frequently overwinters in considerable numbers where open water occurs. Breeding Bird Surveys between 1966 and 2015 indicate the species collectively underwent a survey-wide population decline (2.40% annually) during that period, and Nebraska underwent an estimated 6.17 percent rate of annual decline. The species had an estimated breeding population of about 2.5 million birds in the USFWS traditional survey area in 2018–19 (US Fish and Wildlife Service, 2019).

Migration. Sixty initial spring sightings range from January 18 to May 29, with a median of March 12. Half of the records fall within the period February 27–March 20. Fifty-seven final fall sightings range from September 16 to December 31, with a median of November 19. Half of the records fall within the period November 6–December 18.

Habitats. While on migration nearly all aquatic habitats are used, ranging from flooded fields to large lakes and reservoirs. Breeding is also near water areas ranging from small ponds, including tundra ponds, to permanent marshes, but it usually occurs where the surrounding land is quite open and well drained (Johnsgard, 2017a).

Green-winged Teal, *Anas crecca*
An, **Ar**, Bl, Bo, Br, **Ch**, Cu, **Gar**, **Gr**, Gre, **Grf**, **Ho**, **Hol**, Ke, Li, **Lo**, Log, **Mc**, Mo, Ro, Sh, **Th**, Wh

Status. The green-winged teal is an abundant spring and fall migrant and an occasional summer resident in the Sandhills region. Breeding is essentially limited to the northern half of the state and is concentrated in the western Sandhills. Breeding Bird Surveys between 1966 and 2015 indicate the species collectively underwent a survey-wide population decline (0.14% annually) during that period, and Nebraska underwent an estimated 1.88 percent rate of annual decline. The species had an estimated breeding population of about 3.1 million birds in the USFWS traditional survey area in 2018–19 (US Fish and Wildlife Service, 2019).

Migration. Fifty-eight initial spring sightings range from January 1 to June 4, with a median of March 20. Half of the records fall within the period March 12–30. Fifty-five final spring sightings are from April 4 to June 10, with a median of May 10. Forty-six initial fall sightings are from August 3 to October 18, with a median of September 12. Forty-nine final fall sightings are from September 20 to December 31, with a median of November 2.

Habitats. Migrants are associated with almost all standing or slowly flowing aquatic habitats in Nebraska, and breeding normally occurs where ponds or sloughs are surrounded by a mixture of grassland, sedge meadows, and well-drained areas that support shrubby or tall woody vegetation (Johnsgard, 2017a).

Canvasback, *Aythya valisineria*
An, **Ar**, Bl, Bo, **Br**, **Ch**, Cu, **Gar**, **Gr**, Gre, Grf, **Ho**, Hol, Ke, Li, Lo, Log, **Mc**, **Mo**, Ro, **Sh**, Th, Wh

Status. The canvasback is an uncommon to locally common spring and fall migrant statewide, and a local summer resident in the western Sandhills (especially Valentine and Crescent Lake NWRs). Breeding Bird Surveys between 1966 and 2015 indicate the species collectively underwent a survey-wide population increase (0.20% annually) during that period, and Nebraska underwent an estimated 4.47 percent rate of annual increase. The species had an estimated breeding population of about 650,000 birds in the USFWS traditional survey area by 2018–19 (US Fish and Wildlife Service, 2019).

Migration. Sixty-eight initial spring sightings are from February 12 to May 21, with a median of March 18. Half of the records fall within the period March 7–30. Thirty-nine final fall sightings are from October 12–December 31, with a median of November 14. Half of the records fall within the period October 29–November 23.

Habitats. On migration this species uses marshes, rivers, and shallow lakes rich in submerged pondweeds and similar vegetation. Prairie marshes with abundant emergent vegetation and some areas of open water large enough for takeoffs and landings are favored for nesting (Johnsgard, 2017a).

Redhead, *Aythya americana*
An, **Ar**, Bl, Bo, **Br**, **Ch**, **Cu**, **Gar**, **Gr**, Gre, **Grf**, **Ho**, **Hol**, **Ke**, **Li**, **Lo**, Log, **Mc**, **Mo**, **Ro**, **Sh**, Th, **Wh**

Status. The redhead is a common spring and fall migrant statewide and a locally common summer resident in the Sandhills west to Garden County. Breeding Bird Surveys between 1966 and 2015 indicate the species collectively underwent a survey-wide population increase (0.74% annually) during that period, and Nebraska underwent an estimated 1.63 percent rate of annual increase. The species had an estimated breeding population of about 730,000 birds in the USFWS traditional survey area by 2018–19 (US Fish and Wildlife Service, 2019).

Migration. Sixty initial spring sightings range from February 9 to May 25, with a median of March 13. Half of the sightings fall within the period March 1 through March 20. Fifty-six final fall sightings are from October 9 to December 1, with a median of November 9. Half of the records fall within the period October 28 to November 19.

Habitats. Migrants are found on large prairie marshes, lakes, and reservoirs, especially where submerged vegetation is abundant. Nesting typically occurs on marshes at least an acre in size that have both open areas and stands of emergent vegetation (Johnsgard, 2017a).

Northern pintail, males. *Photo by J. Kren.*

Ring-necked Duck, *Aythya collaris*
An, Ar, Bo, **Br** (H), Ch, Cu, Gar (H), Gr, Gre, Grf, Ho, Hol, Ke, Li, Lo, Log, Mc, **Mo** (H), Ro, Sh, Th, Wh

Status. The ring-necked duck is an uncommon to common spring and fall migrant almost statewide, becoming less common in the panhandle. It possibly bred historically in the Sandhills and was reported by Oberholser and McAtee (1920) to possibly breed in Cherry and Brown Counties but without firm evidence. Ducey (1988) accepted a historic breeding record for Brown County. Nebraska is outside the regular breeding range of this species, which favors conifer-edged and often somewhat acidic wetlands for breeding. There are no actual breeding records for Crescent Lake or Valentine NWRs.

Migration. Forty-two initial spring sightings are from February 12 to May 25, with a median of March 21. Half of the records fall within the period March 7–30. Twenty-six final spring sightings are from March 24 to May 30, with a median of April 21. Twenty-seven initial fall sightings are from September 17 to December 7, with a median of October 12. Twenty-three final fall sightings are from October 27 to December 31, with a median of November 17.

Habitats. Migrants are found on large prairie marshes, lakes, and reservoirs, but prairie marshes are only secondary breeding habitats. Rather acidic swamps and bogs surrounded by shrubby cover in a coniferous forest matrix are the primary breeding habitat (Johnsgard, 2017a).

Tufted Duck, *Aythya fuligula*
Ke

Accidental. A male tufted duck was seen for five consecutive years at Lake Ogallala, Keith County, between November and May (Brown, Dinsmore, Brown, 2012).

Greater Scaup, *Aythya marila*
An, Bo, Br, Ch, Cu, Gar, Gre, Grf, Ho, Ke, Li, Ro, Sh, Th, Wh

Status. The greater scaup is an occasional migrant and winter visitor in the Sandhills, probably more common than the published records would suggest. It is probably regular during late fall, winter, and early spring on larger reservoirs and lakes.

Migration. Twenty-seven total spring records are from January 11 to May 18, with the largest number (12) for March, followed by April (8), and then February and May (3 each). Fall records span October 27 to December 30.

Habitats. Migrants and wintering birds use lakes and reservoirs in the interior, but most birds winter coastally.

Lesser Scaup, *Aythya affinis*
An, **Ar**, Bo, Br, **Ch** (H), Cu, Gar, Gr, Gre, Grf, Ho, Hol, Ke, Li, Lo, Log, Mc, Mo, Ro, Sh, Th, Wh

Status. The lesser scaup is a common to abundant spring and fall migrant statewide and an occasional summer resident in the Sandhills (probably in Garden, Morrill, Cherry, and Brown Counties). It is reported to have nested at Crescent Lake NWR but not at Valentine NWR, and current breeding is very doubtful. Some birds overwinter locally where open water is present. Breeding Bird Surveys between 1966 and 2015 indicate the species collectively underwent a survey-wide population decline (1.84% annually) during that period. Mollhoff (2016) indicated possible or probable breeding in the following counties: Arthur, Brown, Cherry, Garden, Holt, Lincoln, Loup, and Sheridan. The two scaup species had a combined estimated breeding population of about 3.5 million birds in the USFWS traditional survey area in 2018–19 (US Fish and Wildlife Service, 2019).

Migration. Sixty-nine initial spring sightings are from February 12 to May 20, with a median of March 19. Half of the records fall within the period March 5 through March 25. Forty-three final spring records are from March 10 to June 6, with a median of May 11. Forty-five initial fall sightings are from July 20 to December 15, with a median of October 18. Thirty-one final fall sightings are from November 22 to December 31, with a median of December 14.

Habitats. Deeper marshes, reservoirs, borrow pits, and lakes are commonly used by migrating birds. Prairie marshes surrounded by partially wooded uplands are favored for breeding, especially those supporting large populations of amphipods ("scuds") (Johnsgard, 2017a).

Harlequin Duck, *Histrionicus histrionicus*
Ch, Gar, Grf (NOU website checklist)

Very rare. Harlequin ducks are normally found on swiftly flowing mountain streams no closer than western Wyoming, where they locally breed on a few mountain streams in the northwestern corner of that state (Johnsgard, 2019). There are two records from the Sandhills: a subadult male from Calamus Reservoir, Garfield County, November 6, 1992, and four individuals at Goose Lake, Holt County, November 12, 2006 (Silcock and Jorgensen, various dates).

Common Eider, *Somateria mollissima*
Li

Accidental. One specimen record exists of a female common eider shot during the late fall of 1967 in Lincoln County (Brown, Dinsmore, and Brown, 2012; Johnsgard, 2018).

Surf Scoter, *Melanitta perspicillata*
Ch, Gar, Ke, Sh

Status. The surf scoter is a rare migrant in Nebraska, occurring primarily in the fall. As of the early 2000s, it had been seen repeatedly in Keith County. It is a rare spring, fall, and early winter migrant at Lake McConaughy (Brown, Dinsmore, and Brown, 2012). Like the other scoters, most reports are of females or immature males that are often overlooked or confused with other species.

White-winged Scoter, *Melanitta deglandi*
An, Gar, Gre, Ke, Li, Lo, Sh

Status. The white-winged scoter is an occasional spring and fall migrant in the Sandhills, more common in the fall than spring. Most of the Nebraska records are from counties bordering the Platte or Missouri Rivers. As of the early 2000s, it had been recorded at least twice in Lincoln County, and it is an uncommon spring, fall, and early winter migrant at Lake McConaughy (Brown, Dinsmore, and Brown, 2012). This scoter is probably an annual visitor to the state, especially along the Missouri River and on the larger reservoirs.

Black Scoter, *Melanitta americana*
Ke, Li

Accidental. The black scoter has been observed from mid-October to mid-January in the Lake McConaughy–Ogallala area, Keith County (Brown, Dinsmore, and Brown, 2012), and in Lincoln County. An immature/female was observed at Sutherland Reservoir, March 9, 2020 (Silcock and Jorgensen, various dates). This coastal species is the scoter that is most often interior in its wintering range, and, as for the other rare sea ducks, most of the birds seen are in immature female-like plumage.

Long-tailed Duck, *Clangula hyemalis*
Bo, Br, Gar, Ke, Li, Sh

Status. The long-tailed duck is a rare fall and spring migrant statewide but is perhaps slightly more common eastwardly, where overwintering commonly occurs on large deep lakes and coastally. As of the early 2000s, two or more records existed for at least Keith, Lancaster, Douglas, and Washington Counties, with at least eight for Douglas County. This duck is more common now than before the formation of large reservoirs. As of 1933, less than a dozen definite records for the state existed (*Nebraska Bird Review* 1: 11), but the species is now regular during early winter at Lakes McConaughy and Ogallala, with up to nine reported at one time in early December.

Bufflehead, *Bucephala albeola*
An, Ar, Bl, Bo, Br, Ch, Cu, Gar, Gr, Gre, Grf, Ho, Hol, Ke, Li, Lo, Log, Mc, Mo, Ro, Sh, Th, Wh

Status. The bufflehead is a common to uncommon migrant statewide, including the Sandhills, where larger and deeper marshes are commonly used. Occasionally stragglers remain through the summer. Breeding Bird Surveys between 1966 and 2015 indicate the species collectively underwent a survey-wide population increase (2.80% annually) during that period. Possible breeding has occurred in Garden and Grant Counties (Mollhoff, 2016).

Migration. Fifty-three initial spring sightings are from February 21 to May 1, with a median of March 18. Half of the records fall within the period March 6 through March 24. Thirty-eight final spring sightings are from March 15 to May 29, with a median of April 21. Thirty-four initial fall sightings are from August 14 to December 16, with a median of October 19. Thirty-one final fall sightings are from October 29 to December 31, with a median of November 24.

Habitats. Lakes, reservoirs, and relatively vegetation-free marshes are used by migrating birds. Nesting often occurs in abandoned tree cavities made by larger woodpecker species (Johnsgard, 2016e).

Common Goldeneye, *Bucephala clangula*
An, Ar, Bl, Bo, Br, Ch, Cu, Gar, Grf, Gr, Gre, Hol, Ho, Ke, Li, Log, Lo, Mc, Mo, Ro, Sh, Th, Wh

Status. The common goldeneye is a common to uncommon spring and fall migrant statewide, including the Sandhills. It occasionally overwinters where open water is available. Breeding Bird Surveys between 1966 and 2015 indicate the species collectively underwent a survey-wide population increase (0.21% annually) during that period. A few summer reports indicate sightings from Garden, Keith, and Sheridan Counties (Silcock and Jorgensen, various dates).

Migration. Thirty-five initial spring sightings range from January 1 to April 12, with a median of March 5. Twenty-four final spring sightings are from March 9 to May 8, with a median of March 30. Thirty-four initial fall sightings are from October 10 to December 31, with a median of November 21. Thirty-one final fall sightings are from November 22 to December 31, with a median of December 14. This species has been reported at Lake McConaughy from September 9 to June 13 (Brown, Dinsmore, and Brown, 2012).

Habitats. Deeper marshes, rivers, lakes, and reservoirs are used during migration.

Barrow's Goldeneye, *Bucephala islandica*
Gar, Ke, Li

Status. Barrow's goldeneye is a rare winter and spring vagrant in Nebraska, probably mainly occurring westwardly on larger and deeper waters. It is a rare to uncommon spring, fall, and early winter (mid-November to mid-April) migrant at Lake McConaughy (Brown, Dinsmore, and Brown, 2012). This goldeneye is also reported from Garfield (Crescent Lake NWR bird checklist) and Lincoln Counties.

Migration. Eight spring records range from February 15 to April 2, with a mean of March 19. Three fall records are from November 26 to December 21. Barrow's goldeneye has been reported at Lake McConaughy from November 14 to April 19 (Brown, Dinsmore, and Brown, 2012).

Habitats. While on migration this species uses the same habitats as the common goldeneye, but it is more likely to winter in coastal or brackish waters.

Hooded Merganser, *Lophodytes cucullatus*
An, Ar, Bl, Bo, Br, **Ch** (H), Cu, Gar, Gr, Gre, Grf, Ho, Hol, Ke, Li, Lo, **Log, Mo**, Ro, Sh, Th, Wh

Status. The hooded merganser is an uncommon to occasional spring and fall migrant in eastern Nebraska, with scattered sightings throughout the Sandhills region, usually on clearwater streams with wooded edges. Possible recent breeding has been reported from Cherry, Garden, Holt, Lincoln, and Loup Counties (Mollhoff, 2016). Breeding Bird Surveys between 1966 and 2015 indicate the species collectively underwent a survey-wide population increase (3.89% annually) during that period.

Migration. Seventy-four initial spring sightings range from January 16 to May 30, with a median of March 26. Half of the records fall within the period March 13 to March 28. Fourteen final spring records are from March 19 to May 30, with a median of April 25. Sixteen initial fall sightings are from September 14 to November 27, with a median of November 5. Nineteen final fall sightings are from November 6 to December 17, with a median of November 22.

Habitats. Migrants are found on clearwater rivers, lakes, reservoirs, and deeper marshes. Breeding is usually done along rivers, creeks, and oxbows that are bordered by woods and support good populations of fish (Johnsgard, 2016e).

Common Merganser, *Mergus merganser*
An, Ar, Bl, Bo, **Br**, Ch (H), **Cu**, Gar, Gr, Gre, Grf, Ho, Hol, Ke, Li, Lo, Mc, Mo, Ro, Sh, Th, Wh

Status. The common merganser is a regular spring and fall migrant statewide, varying in abundance from very common to occasional. It overwinters commonly where open water persists. Stragglers sometimes remain through the summer, such as on Lake McConaughy and Lake Ogallala. Possible recent breeding has been reported from Garden County and probable breeding from Keith County (Mollhoff, 2016). Breeding Bird Surveys between 1966 and 2015 indicate the species collectively underwent a survey-wide population decline (1.98% annually) during that period.

Migration. Fifty initial spring sightings are from January 14 to April 25, with a median of March 9. Half of the records fall within the period March 3 through March 27. Thirty-nine final spring sightings are from March 4 to May 30, with a median of April 6. Thirty-eight initial fall sightings are from September 18 to December 31, with a median of November 13. Thirty-six final fall sightings are from November 20 to December 31, with a median of December 17.

Habitats. Migrants and wintering birds are found on rivers, lakes, reservoirs, and any other large water areas that support fish populations. Most nesting occurs on forest-lined lakes and ponds near rivers, but it also rarely occurs in treeless areas in rock crevices or other natural cavities (Johnsgard, 2016e).

Red-breasted Merganser, *Mergus serrator*
An, Ar, Ch, Gar, Gre, Grf, Ho, Ke, Li, Lo, Sh

Status. The red-breasted merganser is an occasional to rare spring and fall migrant in the Sandhills region. It has been reported at Lake McConaughy from August 7 to June 7 (Brown, Dinsmore, and Brown, 2012).

Migration. Sixty-one initial spring sightings are from January 15 to May 12, with a median of March 29. Half of the records fall within the period March 19 to April 7. Twenty-four final spring sightings are from February 14 to May 18, with a median of April 20. Sixteen total fall sightings are from September 21 to December 31, with a median of November 18. Half of the records fall within the period November 4–27.

Habitats. Lakes, reservoirs, and large rivers are used by migrants. Wintering more often occurs coastally.

Ruddy Duck, *Oxyura jamaicensis*
An, **Ar**, Bo, **Br**, **Ch**, Cu, **Gar**, **Gr**, Gre, **Grf**, **Ho**, **Hol**, Ke, Li, **Lo**, Log, **Mc**, Mo, **Ro**, **Sh**, **Wh**

Status. The ruddy duck is a common spring and fall migrant statewide and an uncommon and very local summer resident in some of the aquatic-vegetated and more permanent marshes of the Sandhills. It is considered a common breeder at both Valentine and Crescent Lake NWRs. Breeding Bird Surveys between 1966 and 2015 indicate the species collectively underwent a survey-wide population increase (0.94% annually) during that period, and Nebraska underwent an estimated 0.81 percent rate of annual decline.

Migration. Sixty-seven initial spring sightings are from February 12 to June 9, with a median of April 3. Half of the records fall within the period March 14 to April 19. Fifty-nine final fall records are from August 30 to December 31, with a median of November 27. Half of the records fall within the period October 10–November 27.

Habitats. Migrants may be found on lakes, reservoirs, larger marshes, and similar habitats offering considerable open water and mud-bottom foraging areas, where the birds can extract microrganisms with their specialized bill structure. Breeding occurs on permanent prairie marshes having stable water levels and an abundance of emergent vegetation, along with some areas of open water for display, landings, and takeoffs (Johnsgard 2017a).

Family Odontophoridae (New World Quails)

Northern Bobwhite, *Colinus virginianus*
Bo, Br, Ch, Cu, Gar, Gre, Grf, Hol, **Ke**, **Li**, Lo, Log, Mc, Mo, Sh, Th, Wh

Status. The northern bobwhite is a fairly common permanent resident almost statewide, becoming rarer westwardly. It extends into the Sandhills along river drainages. Although there is no record of confirmed breeding, possible or probable breeding has recently been reported from the following counties: Antelope, Blaine, Boone, Brown, Cherry, Custer, Garden, Garfield, Holt, Keith, Lincoln, Logan, Loup, Rock, Sheridan, Thomas, and Wheeler (Mollhoff, 2016). The species' western and northern range limits are highly variable, largely depending on yearly weather conditions during the breeding season. A continent-wide population decline in this species has also occurred in recent decades. Breeding Bird Surveys between 1966 and 2015 indicate the species collectively underwent a survey-wide population decline (3.48% annually) during that period, with many states losing up to about 80 to 90 percent of their bobwhite populations (Johnsgard 2017b).

Habitats. Throughout the year this species is normally found where there is a combination of grassy nesting cover, cultivated crops, and brushy cover or woodlands with a brushy understory. A sandy area for dusting is also favored. Nesting is typically done in open herbaceous cover consisting of rather short vegetation that does not obstruct easy entry and exit but is sufficient to provide concealment from above.

Family Phasianidae (Pheasants, Grouse, and Turkeys)

Gray Partridge, *Perdix perdix*
An, **Ch**, Gar, Gre, Hol, Wh

Status. The gray partridge is an uncommon and local permanent resident in northeastern Nebraska; it occasionally wanders into the northern Sandhills from South Dakota.

Habitats. A combination of small-grain agriculture during fall and winter and nesting cover in the form of native grassland vegetation or hayfield pasturelands provide for the basic needs of this species.

(Chukar, *Alectoris chukar*)
Lo, **Sh**

The chukar was introduced to the Sandhills unsuccessfully; early breeding records exist for Logan and Sheridan Counties (Ducey, 1988). Game farm releases occasionally result in recent sightings.

Ring-necked Pheasant, *Phasianus colchicus*
An, Ar, Bl, Bo, **Br**, **Ch**, Cu, Gar, Gr, Gre, **Grf**, Ho, **Hol**, Ke, **Li**, **Lo**, Log, **Mc**, Mo, Ro, **Sh**, Th, Wh

Status. The ring-necked pheasant is an introduced permanent resident, now fairly common almost statewide, and fairly common throughout the Sandhills, especially near water sources. Possible or probable breeding has been reported from all of the Sandhills counties (Mollhoff, 2016). Breeding Bird Surveys between 1966 and 2015 indicate the species collectively underwent a survey-wide population decline (0.64% annually) during that period, and Nebraska underwent an estimated 1.78 percent rate of annual decline.

Habitats. Throughout the year a combination of small-grain croplands and adjacent heavier covers such as weedy ditches, sloughs, wooded areas, or shelterbelts provide optimum habitat. Nesting is often done in roadside ditches, in alfalfa or sweet clover fields, or in heavy grass cover.

Sharp-tailed Grouse, *Tympanuchus phasianellus*
An, Ar, Bl, **Ch**, Cu, Gar, Gr, Gre, Grf, Ho, **Hol**, Ke, Li, Lo, Log, Mc, Mo, **Ro**, **Sh**, Th, Wh

Status. The sharp-tailed grouse is a locally common permanent resident over much of Nebraska. It is most common in the Sandhills, with its eastern and southern limits approximating those of the Sandhills. Possible or probable breeding has been reported from all of the Sandhills counties where sharp-tailed grouse commonly occur, except

Sharp-tailed grouse, male. *Photo by P. Johnsgard.*

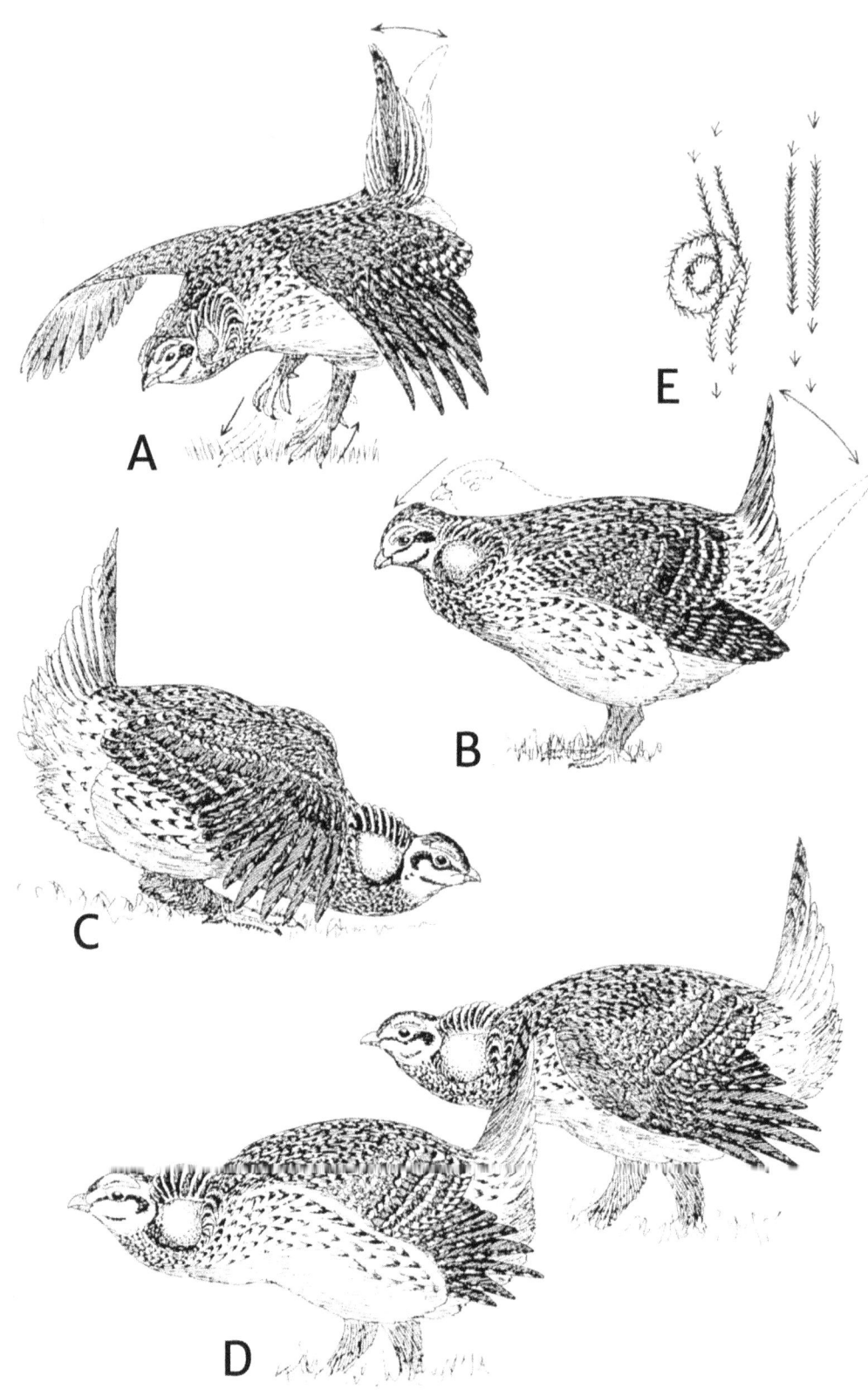

Display postures of male sharp-tailed grouse, including (A) dancing, (B) cooing, (C) defensive-threat, (D) parallel running, and (E) footprints of dancing

Antelope County (Mollhoff, 2016). Breeding Bird Surveys between 1966 and 2015 indicate the species collectively underwent a survey-wide population decline (0.37% annually) during that period, and Nebraska underwent an estimated 0.56 percent rate of annual decline.

Habitats. Open grassland habitats, where trees are absent or nearly so, is the typical Nebraska habitat. Brushy cover with a 5–30 percent extent over the land is used by this grouse in more northerly areas, especially where winter snow accumulation is considerable. Like prairie-chickens, sharp-tailed grouse offer early risers a chance to witness the visual poetry of several males dancing in nearly perfect synchrony on their traditional leks (display grounds). In some areas of the Sandhills, both species display on the same grounds, and hybrids occasionally result (Johnsgard and Wood, 1968). The displays and vocalizations of the two species are quite different, but females sometimes are attracted to the wrong species for mating (Johnsgard, 1973, 2017b).

Greater Prairie-Chicken, *Tympanuchus cupido*
An (H), Bl, Bo, Br, **Ch**, Cu, Gar, Gr, Gre, **Grf**, Ho, **Hol**, **Ke**, **Li**, Lo, **Log**, Mc, Mo, **Ro**, Sh, Th, Wh

Status. The greater prairie-chicken is a locally common to uncommon permanent resident, especially in the eastern half of the Sandhills. Possible or probable breeding has been reported from all of the other Sandhills counties except Keith County (Mollhoff, 2016). The species' range is discontinuous and probably declining as native grasslands disappear, but Nebraska's populations are perhaps the best of all the few remaining in the Sandhills counties. Breeding Bird Surveys between 1966 and 2015 indicate the species collectively underwent a survey-wide population increase (2.80% annually) during that period, and Nebraska underwent an estimated 6.79 percent rate of annual increase.

Habitats. Greater prairie-chickens are primarily associated with native grasslands and where native grasslands and grain croplands interdigitate. Nesting usually occurs in grassy open habitats such as ungrazed meadows or hayfields, usually in rather dry sites, but sometimes nests are placed in brushy vegetation or in open woods or at the edge of woods. Nebraska is one of the few states in which prairie-chickens are still sufficiently common to be major game birds. The eastern edge of the Sandhills probably represents prime prairie-chicken habitat; here a mixture of native grasses and grain crops such as corn provide both nesting cover and winter foods for these birds (Johnsgard, 1973, 1979, 2002a, 2017b).

Wild Turkey, *Meleagris gallopavo*
An, **Ar**, Bl, Bo, **Br**, **Ch**, Cu, **Gar**, Gr, Gre, **Grf**, Ho, **Hol**, **Ke**, **Li**, **Lo**, Log, Mc, Mo, **Ro**, **Sh**, **Th**, **Wh**

Status. The wild turkey was originally native to Nebraska but extirpated and now is reestablished as a permanent resident in many areas, especially along all the state's major wooded river systems. Possible or probable breeding has been reported from all the Sandhills counties (Mollhoff, 2016). In the Sandhills, wild turkeys are attracted to grainfields and to the vicinity of small towns where it can raid bird feeders and obtain other sources of waste grain. Breeding Bird Surveys between 1966 and 2015 indicate the species collectively underwent a survey-wide population increase (7.51% annually) during that period, and Nebraska underwent a mind-boggling estimated 12.7 percent rate of annual increase.

Habitats. Although various races differ greatly in habitats utilized, in Nebraska the birds in most parts of the state are found in floodplain forests that have a variety of hardwood trees, especially those bearing acorns or other large and edible seeds. Nesting occurs in forested areas, with the nests being well concealed, often under a log or at the base of a tree.

Pheasants, Grouse, and Turkeys

Display postures of male greater prairie-chicken, including (A) booming, (B) territorial cackling, (C) flutter-jumping, (D) bowing, and (E) fighting

Greater prairie-chicken, male booming. *Photo by P. Johnsgard.*

Family Podicipedidae (Grebes)

Pied-billed Grebe, *Podilymbus podiceps*
An, **Ar**, Bl, Bo, **Br, Cu**, Gar, **Gr, Gre, Grf, Ho, Hol**, Ke,
Li, Lo, Log, Mc, Mo, Ro, **Sh**, Th, **Wh**

Status. The pied-billed grebe is a common spring and fall migrant and local summer resident throughout the Sandhills wetlands. Breeding Bird Surveys between 1966 and 2015 indicate the species collectively underwent a survey-wide population increase (0.68% annually) during that period, and Nebraska underwent an estimated 2.76 percent rate of annual decline.

Migration. A total of 116 initial spring sightings range from February 27 to June 10, with a median of April 5. Half of the sightings fall within the period March 24–April 22. Eighty-four final fall sightings are from August 21 to December 6, with a median of November 6. Half of the sightings fall within the period October 10–November 16.

Habitats. Breeding occurs on small ponds, river impoundments, and lakes that range from quite small to large but always having extensive stands of heavy emergent vegetation and adjacent areas of open water.

Horned Grebe, *Podiceps auritus*
An, Ar, Ch, Cu, Gar, Gre, Grf, Ho, Hol, Ke, Li, Lo,
Log, Sh, Wh

Status. The horned grebe is an uncommon spring and fall wetland migrant throughout Nebraska and a reported accidental overwintering migrant. It reportedly bred in Cherry County more than 100 years ago (Silcock and Jorgensen, various dates). Breeding Bird Surveys between 1966 and 2015 indicate the species collectively underwent a survey-wide population decline (0.47% annually) during that period.

Migration. Sixty-two initial spring sightings range from February 20 to June 4, with a median of April 16. Twenty-four final spring sightings are from April 14 to May 22, with a median of May 6. Seventeen initial fall sightings are from September 5 to November 11, with a median of October 8. Seventeen final fall sightings are from October 9 to November 27, with a median of November 11.

Habitats. Rivers, lakes, and reservoirs are used while on migration. Breeding occurs on ponds and marshes ranging in size from less than an acre to several hundred acres, which may be seasonal or permanent. Submerged aquatic vegetation is typically abundant, but emergent growth may be rather sparse.

Red-necked Grebe, *Podiceps grisegena*
An, Ke, Li

Status. The red-necked grebe is a very rare wetland migrant in the Sandhills region; most of the state records come from the easternmost counties.

Migration. A small sample of spring records for Nebraska center around April 9, and a similar number of fall records center around October 30. In the Lake McConaughy area, this species has been seen primarily from early September to early January, with rare overwintering (Brown, Dinsmore, and Brown, 2012).

Habitats. In their breeding areas, red-necked grebes favor large marshes and the variably vegetated edges of lakes for nesting territories. As with other grebes, their nests are untidy piles of waterlogged vegetation and often are quite conspicuous.

Eared Grebe, *Podiceps nigricollis*
An, Ar, **Ch**, Cu, **Gar**, Gr, Gre, Grf, Ho, Hol, Ke, **Li**, Lo,
Log, **Mc**, Mo, Ro, **Sh**, Th, Wh

Status. The eared grebe is an uncommon spring and fall wetland migrant throughout Nebraska and a fairly common summer resident, especially in the Sandhills. Possible or probable recent breeding has been reported from the following counties: Arthur, Cherry, Grant, Holt, Hooker, McPherson, Morrill, and Rock (Mollhoff, 2016). Breeding Bird Surveys between 1966 and 2015 indicate the species collectively underwent a survey-wide population increase (1.11% annually) during that period, and Nebraska underwent an estimated 0.22 percent rate of annual increase.

Migration. A total of 105 initial spring sightings range from February 19 to June 5, with a median of April 22. Half of the sightings fall within the period of

Pied-billed grebe, adult in breeding plumage. *Photo by J. Kren.*

April 11 to May 5. Twenty-three final fall sightings are from August 23 to November 15, with a median of October 16. Half of the sightings fall within the period October 8–30.

Habitats. Rivers, lakes, and reservoirs are used during migration. Breeding occurs on ponds, marshes, and shallow river impoundments that are usually rich in submerged aquatic plants. Large open ponds that provide abundant feeding areas and also some sheltered locations with emergent aquatic plants for nesting sites seem to be favored. Colonial breeding is typical.

Western Grebe, *Aechmophorus occidentalis*
An, Ar, Bl, **Ch**, Cu, **Gar**, Grf, Gr, Hol, Ho, Ke, Li, Log, Lo, **Mc**, Mo, Ro, **Sh**, Th, Wh

Status. The western grebe is a common spring and fall wetland migrant in the western part of Nebraska, rarer eastwardly, and a summer resident in western areas. Breeding occurs primarily on the larger Sandhills marshes, including Crescent Lake and Valentine NWRs, which represent the southeastern limit of breeding of this species in the Great Plains states. Possible or probable breeding has been recently reported from the following counties: Brown, Grant, Holt, Hooker, Keith, Lincoln, and Rock (Mollhoff, 2016). Many apparent nonbreeders and a few breeders occur during summer on Lake McConaughy and Lake Ogallala. Adults with young were seen at the western end of Keystone Lake in late July 1993 (Rosche, 1994). Large numbers bred at the western end of Lake McConaughy in 1995 (Brown, Dinsmore, and Brown, 2012). Breeding Bird Surveys between 1966 and 2015 indicate the western and Clark's grebes collectively underwent a survey-wide population decline (2.02% annually) during that period, and Nebraska underwent an estimated 4.61 percent rate of annual decline.

Migration. Seventy-seven initial spring sightings range from March 10 to June 10, with a median of May 6. Half of the sightings fall within the period April 19–May 18. Forty-three final fall sightings are from September 10 to December 7, with a median of October 3. Half of the sightings fall within the period October 1–24.

Habitats. Rivers, lakes, and reservoirs are used while on migration. Breeding is on ponds and lakes that usually have large expanses of open water and on some marshes that are at least 50 acres in area.

Clark's Grebe, *Aechmophorus clarkii*
Ch, Gar, Gr, Ke, Li, Mo, **Sh**

Status. The Clark's grebe is probably a regular but very local breeder on permanent Sandhills wetlands. The state's first record was of an adult in breeding plumage found dead at Keystone Lake, Keith County, on June 1, 1986. Since then a considerable number of sightings have been reported in western Nebraska, including adults with young at the western end of Keystone Lake in late July 1993 (Rosche, 1994). Clark's grebes have also been reported at Crescent Lake NWR, and apparent western × Clark's grebe hybrids have been seen at Lake McConaughy (Brown, Dinsmore, and Brown, 2012). A 2002 breeding was observed at Willy Lake, Sheridan County (Mollhoff, 2016), and possible recent breeding has been reported from Cherry, Garden, and Hooker Counties (Mollhoff, 2016).

Family Columbidae (Pigeons and Doves)

Rock Pigeon, *Columba livia*
An, Ar, Bl, Bo, Br, Ch, Cu, Gar, Gr, Gre, Grf, Ho, Hol, **Ke**, Li, Lo, Log, Mc, Mo, Sh, Th, Wh

Status. The rock pigeon is an introduced and common permanent resident statewide, especially in towns and around farms, but feral in a few western locations. It is also a resident throughout the entire Great Plains. Confirmed breeding was not documented in any Sandhills county (Mollhoff, 2016). However, possible or probable breeding has been reported from Antelope, Blaine, Brown, Cherry, Custer, Garden, Holt, Hooker, Keith, Lincoln, Logan, Loup, Thomas and Wheeler Counties (Mollhoff, 2016).

Habitats. This species is mostly associated with human habitations in cities and villages and on farms, but it also occurs to a limited extent as feral populations around bluffs and cliffs in western Nebraska.

Eared grebe, adults in breeding plumage. *Photo by J. Kren.*

Eurasian Collared-Dove, *Streptopelia decaocto*
An, Ar, Bl, Bo, Br, Ch, Cu, Gar, Gr, Gre, Grf, Ho, Hol, **Ke**, Li, Lo, Log, Mc, Mo, Ro, Sh, Th, Wh

Status. This introduced and increasing species has become common and widespread since first being reported in 1997 (*Nebraska Bird Review* 65: 168; 66: 42). By 2007 the Eurasian collared-dove had been reported from all of Nebraska's counties (*Nebraska Bird Review* 75: 9). No breeding was confirmed in any Sandhills counties as of 2016, but possible or probable breeding has been reported from all Sandhills counties except McPherson and Rock Counties (Mollhoff, 2016). Breeding Bird Surveys between 1966 and 2015 indicate the species underwent an amazing rate of population increase (18.3% annually) during that period.

Migration. The collared-dove is nonmigratory, although dispersal tendencies have resulted in a rapid range expansion.

Habitats. To a greater degree than mourning doves, collared-doves are likely to be found in small towns and villages, especially where grain elevators are present. In both species wooded habitats are most favored, with human-based habitats having a lower incidence of usage. Collared-doves are much less likely to occur in open, grass-dominated habitats, except around farmsteads. They are also less likely to be found in croplands, shrubs, and around water (Mollhoff, 2016).

White-winged Dove, *Zenaida asiatica*
Bo, Br, Gar, Li

Status. The white-winged dove is a rare to occasional local summer resident. In recent years this southern dove has been reported several times per year, but breeding records are few, the first reports occurring in 2005 and 2007 (*Nebraska Bird Review* 75: 78; 78: 95).

Migration. Too little data are available to judge migration patterns, but they are probably similar to those of mourning doves.

Habitats. Little information on the Nebraska habitats of these birds is available. In general they are better adapted to drier and hotter habits and less tolerant of cold weather than are mourning doves. White-winged doves appear to be more cold sensitive than mourning doves; individuals with frost-bitten toes have been seen as far north as Kansas.

Mourning Dove, *Zenaida macroura*
An, Ar, Bl, Bo, Br, Ch, Cu, Gar, Gr, Gre, Grf, Ho, Hol, Ke, Li, Lo, Log, Mc, Mo, Ro, Sh, Th, Wh

Status. The mourning dove is an abundant spring and fall migrant and summer resident statewide and perhaps the most common of all terrestrial Sandhills birds. Overwintering often occurs during mild winters and in sheltered locations. Breeding Bird Surveys between 1966 and 2015 indicate the species collectively underwent a survey-wide population decline (0.29% annually) during that period, and Nebraska underwent an estimated 0.22 percent rate of annual decline.

Migration. Sixty-two initial spring sightings range from January 1 to May 29, with a median of March 26. Half of the records fall within the period March 9–April 8. Ninety final fall sightings range from August 30 to December 31, with a median of November 1. The wide spread of fall departure dates suggests that the species frequently overwinters in the state.

Habitats. This dove is one of the most abundant North American land birds and ranked first in number of occurrences within survey blocks during the first and second *Nebraska Breeding Bird Atlas*es (Mollhoff, 2001, 2016). It is a widely adaptable species, occurring in open woods and edge areas, in parks and cities, on grasslands far from trees, and in cultivated fields. Although nests are most often placed in trees or shrubs, in treeless areas the birds regularly nest on the ground.

Inca Dove, *Columbina inca*
Ke

Accidental. Observed at Keystone, Keith County, December 28, 2006.

Clark's (front) and western grebe, adults in breeding plumage. *Photo by P. Johnsgard.*

Family Cuculidae (Cuckoos)

Yellow-billed Cuckoo, *Coccyzus americanus*
An, **Bl**, Bo, Br, Ch, Cu, **Gar**, Gre, Grf, Hol, Ke, Li, Lo, **Log**, Mc, Mo, Ro, Sh, Th, Wh

Status. The yellow-billed cuckoo is a spring and fall migrant and summer resident statewide, common in the east but less common westwardly and becoming rare in the panhandle. The Sandhills breeding records are concentrated in the east and along wooded rivers. Breeding Bird Surveys between 1966 and 2015 indicate a national population decline (1.48% annually) during that period, and Nebraska underwent an estimated 1.83 percent rate of annual decline.

Migration. The range of 170 initial spring sightings is from April 12 to June 10, with a median of May 23. Half of the records fall within the period May 15 to 29. The range of 101 final fall sightings is from July 23 to October 14, with a median of September 15. Half of the records fall within the period September 1–27.

Habitats. Migrating and breeding birds favor moderately dense thickets near watercourses, second-growth woodlands, deserted farmlands overgrown with shrubs and brush, and brushy orchards. Yellow-billed cuckoos additionally use lowland mixed woodlands and wooded shelterbelts (Mollhoff, 2016). Extremely dense woods are avoided. Habitats with large populations of tent caterpillars, a favorite food, are preferred.

Black-billed Cuckoo, *Coccyzus erythropthalmus*
An, Bl, **Br**, Ch, Cu, Gar, Grf, Hol, Ke, Li, Lo, Mo, Sh, Th (H)

Status. The black-billed cuckoo is a spring and fall migrant and summer resident almost statewide, most common in the northeast, rarer in the south and west, and nearly absent from parts of the panhandle. In the Sandhills the number of survey blocks in which this species was reported was only about one-fourth the number reported for the yellow-billed cuckoo (Mollhoff, 2016). Breeding Bird Surveys between 1966 and 2015 indicate the species collectively underwent a survey-wide population decline (1.62% annually) during that period, and Nebraska underwent an estimated 5.29 percent rate of annual decline.

Migration. The range of 163 initial spring sightings is from April 1 to June 10, with a median of May 24. Half of the records fall within the period May 16–30. The range of 60 final fall sightings is from July 28 to October 9, with a median of August 30. Half of the records fall within the period August 25–September 9.

Habitats. Relatively dense wooded habitats are favored by this species, especially those that provide a variety of trees, bushes, and vines for possible nesting sites. Favored breeding habitats include upland and lowland deciduous woodlands, mixed deciduous–coniferous woodlands, and woodlands with scattered trees. This species is considerably less common than the yellow-billed cuckoo in Nebraska. Both species feed largely on hairy caterpillars such as tent caterpillars, and the birds' yearly abundance varies greatly, probably in relation to food supplies.

Family Caprimulgidae (Goatsuckers)

Common Nighthawk, *Chordeiles minor*
An, Ar, Bl, Bo, **Br**, Ch, Cu, Gar, Grf, Gr, Gre, **Hol** (H), Ho, **Ke**, **Li**, **Log**, Lo, Mc, **Me**, Mo, Ro, **Sh**, **Th**, Wh

Status. The common nighthawk is a progressively less common spring and fall migrant and summer resident statewide, particularly around cities. Possible or probable breeding has been reported from all Sandhills counties (Mollhoff, 2016). It is a regular migrant and breeder throughout the Sandhills region, where it once could be regularly seen perched on wooden fenceposts or horizontal tree branches—but it has largely disappeared in recent years. Breeding Bird Surveys between 1966 and 2015 indicate the species collectively underwent a survey-wide population decline (1.62% annually) during that period, and Nebraska underwent an estimated 5.29 percent rate of annual decline.

Migration. The range of 170 initial spring records is from April 16 to June 7, with a median of May 21. Half of the records fall within the period May 16–28. The range of 137 final fall records is from July 21 to October 24, with a median of September 18. Half of the records fall within the period September 8–October 2.

Habitats. During its stay in Nebraska, this species occurs widely in open habitats such as grasslands, sparse woods, and cities. Perhaps it is more common near humans and their structures than anywhere else because the stone-surfaced tops of flat-roofed buildings provide perfect camouflage for nests. This is easily the most common of Nebraska's "nightjars," a group of aerial-foraging, insect-eating, and seminocturnal birds mostly recognized (and usually named for) their distinctive vocalizations. Like many nocturnal birds, the nightjars have acquired a rich diversity of myths and medieval beliefs, such as "goatsucking."

Common Poorwill, *Phalaenoptilus nuttallii*
Br, Ch, Gar, Hol, Ke, Li, **Mo**, **Th**

Status. The common poorwill is a common spring and fall migrant and summer resident in western Nebraska. The species seemingly mostly avoids the Sandhills and occurs more often in rocky terrain west of a line from Cherry to Harlan Counties. Breeding Bird Surveys between 1966 and 2015 indicate the species collectively underwent a survey-wide population decline (1.86% annually) during that period.

Migration. Thirty-three initial spring records range from April 25 to June 9, with a median of May 6. Half of the records fall within the period May 1–16. Eighteen final fall records are from July 20 to November 1, with a median of September 4. Half of the records fall within the period August 18–September 16.

Habitats. Although this species is most common in eroded and rocky habitats with scrubby brush cover or dry woodlands, it also extends locally into rocky grasslands—but evidently not into sandy grasslands.

Chuck-will's-widow, *Antrostomus carolinensis*
Hol, Th

Accidental. The chuck-will's-widow is associated with the mature riverine forests of the Missouri River valley but apparently is slowly extending its breeding range west into the Niobrara valley. It is not a proven part of the Sandhills breeding biota but has been reported from Holt and Thomas Counties, where riverbottom woodlands exist.

Eastern Whip-poor-will, *Antrostomus vociferous*
An, Ch, Hol

Status. The eastern whip-poor-will is a rare migrant and probable summer breeder, although nesting is undocumented in a few northern Sandhills counties that are mostly peripheral to the Sandhills proper, and where good-sized stands of mature upland deciduous trees are present. Breeding Bird Surveys between 1966 and 2015 indicate the species collectively underwent a survey-wide population decline (2.76% annually) during that period.

Migration. Thirty-four initial spring records range from April 14 to May 21, with a median of May 2. Half of the records fall within the period April 25–May 7. Fifteen final fall records range from July 31 to October 1, with a median of September 2. Half of the records fall within the period August 26–September 7.

Habitats. During the breeding season this species occupies open hardwood or mixed woodlands, especially younger stands in fairly dry habitats. Woodlands with scattered clearings also seem to be preferentially used.

Family Apodidae (Swifts)

Chimney Swift, *Chaetura pelagica*
An, Ar, Bl, **Bo**, Br, Ch, Cu, **Gar**, Gr, Gre, Grf, Ho, **Hol** (H), Ke, **Li**, Lo, Log, Mc, Mo, **Ro**, **Sh**, Th, Wh

Status. The chimney swift is an abundant spring and fall migrant and summer resident throughout the Sandhills but becomes less common westwardly. It breeds almost throughout the entire region of the Great Plains states but is rare or absent in extreme western areas. Breeding Bird Surveys between 1966 and 2015 indicate the species collectively underwent a survey-wide population decline (2.5% annually) during that period, and Nebraska underwent an estimated 2.03 percent rate of annual decline.

Migration. The range of 129 initial spring records is from March 7 to June 6, with a median of April 27. Half of the records fall within the period April 20–May 4. The range of 111 final fall records is from July 22 to October 14, with a median of October

7. Half of the records fall within the period October 2–14.

Habitats. Like the common nighthawk, this species occurs in a wide variety of open habitats but is probably most common in cities, where chimneys and other similarly hollow human-made structures provide roosting and nesting sites, replacing the historic use of large hollow trees.

White-throated Swift, *Aeronautes saxatalis*
Ke, Li

Accidental. This western species of swift is adapted to the steep cliffs and deep canyons of the Nebraska's panhandle and is likely to be seen in the Sandhills region as only an accidental vagrant. One was seen in July 2000 at Lake McConaughy, Keith County (Brown, Dinsmore, and Brown, 2012), and there are also sight records from Sheridan County. The records are from May 25, 2019; May 6, 2018; May 6, 2017; May 21, 2012; May 16, 2010; and May 14, 1993. A bird was picked up at a North Platte, Lincoln County, grain elevator October 11 and died October 13, 2005 (Silcock and Jorgensen, various dates). White-throated swifts are regularly seen in Scotts Bluff County.

Family Trochilidae (Hummingbirds)

Ruby-throated Hummingbird, *Archilochus colubris*
An, Bo, Br, Ch, Gar, Grf, Hol, **Ke**, Li, Ro, Sh, Th, Wh

Status. The ruby-throated hummingbird is an uncommon to common spring and fall migrant and summer resident in eastern Nebraska, with nesting occurring at least in the Missouri River's forested valley and west along the Platte valley locally at least to Keith County (*Nebraska Bird Review* 76: 60, 105; Brown, Dinsmore, and Brown, 2012). Vagrants appear farther west during migration, sometimes as far into the Sandhills as Garden County. Breeding Bird Surveys between 1966 and 2015 indicate the species collectively underwent a survey-wide population increase (1.44% annually) during that period.

Migration. The range of 160 initial spring sightings is from April 7 to June 10, with a median of May 12. Half of the records fall within the period May 5–17. Sixty-four final fall sightings are from July 30 to October 8, with a median of September 13. Half of the records fall within the period September 2–18.

Habitats. Migrants often appear in city gardens or other areas where nectar-bearing flowers occur, but breeding is done in woodlands, orchards, and parks where large trees as well as flowering herbs and shrubs are available. During spring males are usually the first to arrive in Nebraska, and in fall they also precede the arrival of females and immature birds.

Costa's Hummingbird, *Calypte costa*
Ke

Accidental. This western hummingbird, the Costa's hummingbird, has a single Sandhills county record for Keith County, where an immature male was photographed at Lake McConaughy between September 5 and October 23, 2013 (Silcock and Jorgensen, various dates).

Broad-tailed Hummingbird, *Selasphorus platycercus*
Gar, Ke, Li, Mc, Sh

Status. The broad-tailed hummingbird is an occasional migrant in western Nebraska, mostly in fall but also in summer. Most of the Nebraska records are for the westernmost counties, but it has also been seen in at least five Sandhills counties.

Migration. Fifteen initial fall records of this autumn migrant range from July 20 to September 13, with a median of August 4. Sixteen final fall records are from August 3 to September 14, with a median of August 14. Half of the total fall records are within the period July 29–August 16. There is a single spring sighting record in May. A few records from Keith County extend from early August to early September (Brown, Dinsmore, and Brown, 2012).

Habitats. Migrants are normally associated with open plains, forest clearings, and mountain parklands but sometimes appear in gardens or at hummingbird feeders as well. Broad-tailed hummingbirds are very common nesters in the mountains of Colorado and Wyoming, and probably the birds seen in western Nebraska are vagrants from there, or perhaps are migrants from the Black Hills.

Rufous Hummingbird, *Selasphorus rufus*
Bo, Br, Gr, Ke

Status. The rufous hummingbird is an occasional fall migrant in western Nebraska and the Sandhills but rare in eastern Nebraska. Most of the state records are for Scotts Bluff County. The nearest breeding area is in northwestern Wyoming (Johnsgard, 2019), but rufous hummingbirds often stray well to the east of their breeding and wintering ranges during fall migration.

Migration. Sixteen fall sightings of this species range from July 30 to September 14, with a median of August 12. Half of the records fall within a period August 9–17.

Habitats. Migrants are associated with plains, foothills, and urban gardens and have become increasingly frequent fall migrants as hummingbird feeders become commonplace in the Great Plains and on the Gulf Coast.

Calliope Hummingbird, *Selasphorus calliope*
Ke, Ro

Accidental. A calliope hummingbird was reported once at Ogallala, Keith County, August 4, 2003 (Brown, Dinsmore, and Brown, 2012). The other records from Keith County are from Lake McConaughy on August 31, 2012, and July 25–26, 2014. A record from Bassett, Rock County, is from August 21, 2002, and a record from Lincoln County is from September 26–30, 2017. The earliest record from the Sandhills seems to be a female found dead about 25 miles northwest of North Platte, Lincoln County, and identified by Emmet R. Blake at the Field Museum of Natural History (Silcock and Jorgensen, various dates). It has also been reported from Garfield County. This western hummingbird breeds as close to Nebraska as Wyoming's Bighorn Mountains (Canterbury, Johnsgard, and Downing, 2013), so it is surprising that so few Sandhills records have accumulated. Like the rufous hummingbird, migrants are associated with plains, foothills, and urban gardens.

Family Rallidae (Rails, Gallinules, and Coots)

Yellow Rail, *Coturnicops noveboracensis*
Bo, Br, Ch

Status. The yellow rail is a very rare spring and probably fall migrant in Nebraska. At least two June Sandhills records exist, suggesting possible Nebraska breeding (*Nebraska Bird Review* 41: 24), but the nearest area of known breeding is southern Minnesota.

Migration. Eight total spring records are from April 26 to June 10, with a mean of May 6. Apparently, there are no fall records for the species in Nebraska, but it has been seen as late as August 26 in South Dakota and to September 30 in North Dakota.

Habitats. During migration, this species is likely to be found in marshes with extensive grassy or sedge vegetation. When these birds occur in the same marshes with Virginia and sora rails they tend to occupy the densest areas of sedges, while the other species are more often found in areas of cattails and bulrushes.

Black Rail, *Laterallus jamaicensis*
Gar, Ch

Status. Accidental. The black rail is possibly an extremely rare spring and fall migrant or very rare summer wetland resident in the Sandhills. Nebraska is slightly outside this rail's known breeding range in Kansas. Records include Crescent Lake NWR between May 31 and September 6 (*Nebraska Bird Review* 63: 73). Playback of recordings of black rail calls at Crescent Lake have suggested that a breeding population may occur there, but this remains to be proven.

Migration. The few Nebraska records for black rails extend from May 13 to September 20. In Kansas, where this species breeds, it has been reported from as early as March 18 to as late as September 26.

Habitats. In the Great Plains, this species occupies marshy meadows that are heavily overgrown with sedges and grasses. Like the yellow rail, it is much more likely to be heard than seen.

King Rail, *Rallus elegans*
Ch (Valentine NWR checklist), Gar (Crescent Lake NWR checklist), Li, Mo, Sh

Status. The king rail is a rare summer resident in eastern Nebraska. Few have been sighted in the Sandhills, but it probably breeds locally and rarely east of a line from Jefferson to Knox Counties. It possibly also nests in the Clear Creek–Lewellen marshes at the west end of Lake McConaughy.

Migration. Nine total spring records are from April 2 to June 9, with a mean of May 6. Five fall records are from July 10 to September 11, with a mean of August 7.

Habitats. During the breeding season, this species is associated with freshwater marshes up to four feet deep with abundant shoreline and emergent vegetation.

Virginia Rail, *Rallus limicola*
An (H), **Ar**, **Ch**, Cu, **Gar**, Gr, Grf, Ho, **Hol**, Ke, Li, Lo, **Log**, Mo, Ro, **Sh**, Wh

Status. The Virginia rail is an uncommon spring and fall migrant and local wetland summer resident throughout the Sandhills region. There are a few widely scattered breeding records. Breeding Bird Surveys between 1966 and 2015 indicate the species collectively underwent a survey-wide population increase (1.10% annually) during that period. Density studies of this rail have been performed by Dinan, Jorgensen, and Bomberger (2018).

Migration. Thirty-six initial spring sightings are from February 14 to June 1, with a median of May 8. Half of the records fall within the period April 29–May 16. Thirteen final fall sightings are from July 21 to October 13, with a median of September 16.

Habitats. The primary breeding habitats are marshes with extensive stands of emergent vegetation, such as taller grasses, bulrushes, and sedges. Nests are built over wet ground or in shallow water among emergent vegetation.

Clapper Rail, *Rallus longirostris*
Log

Accidental. The clapper rail is not known to breed in Nebraska. The only Sandhills record was of one caught in a mink trap about 12 miles east of Stapleton in Logan County on January 30, 1951. The identification was confirmed by J. Van Tyne, who determined it to be a "typical" northern clapper rail of the Atlantic coast subspecies *crepitans* (Silcock and Jorgensen, various dates).

Sora, *Porzana carolina*
An (H), Ar, Bo, Br, **Ch**, Cu, **Gar**, Gr, Grf, Hol, **Ke**, Lo, Log, **Mc**, Mo, Ro, Sh, Th

Status. The sora is a common spring and fall migrant and locally common wetland summer resident nearly statewide. It is more local in the Sandhills but is probably common on every vegetation-covered marsh. Breeding Bird Surveys between 1966 and 2015 indicate the species collectively underwent a survey-wide population increase (0.43% annually) during that period. Undocumented nesting has been reported in Sandhills counties (Mollhoff, 2016), although as a possible or probable breeder it occurs in the majority of the counties (Mollhoff, 2016; Silcock and Jorgensen, various dates). Population density studies of this rail in Nebraska have been performed by Dinan, Jorgensen, and Bomberger (2018).

Migration. Of 108 initial spring records, the range is from March 10 to June 3, and the median is May 6. Half of the records fall within the period April 30–May 12. Twenty-five final fall sightings are from July 27 to November 27, with a median of September 30.

Habitats. Habitats are apparently almost identical to those of the Virginia rail, namely marshlands with extensive stands of dense emergent vegetation, especially grasses and grassland plants. Nesting tends to occur in deeper water than is used by the Virginia rail, often in water 9–12 inches deep and well concealed in cattails, bulrushes, or sedges.

Common Gallinule, *Gallinula galeata*
Ch, **Li** (H)

Accidental. The common gallinule has a historic breeding record from Lincoln County (Ducey, 1988). The only fall report not known to be associated with breeding is one without details in Cherry County, August 29–September 3, 1933 (Silcock and Jorgensen, various dates).

Sora, adult in breeding plumage. *Photo by J. Kren.*

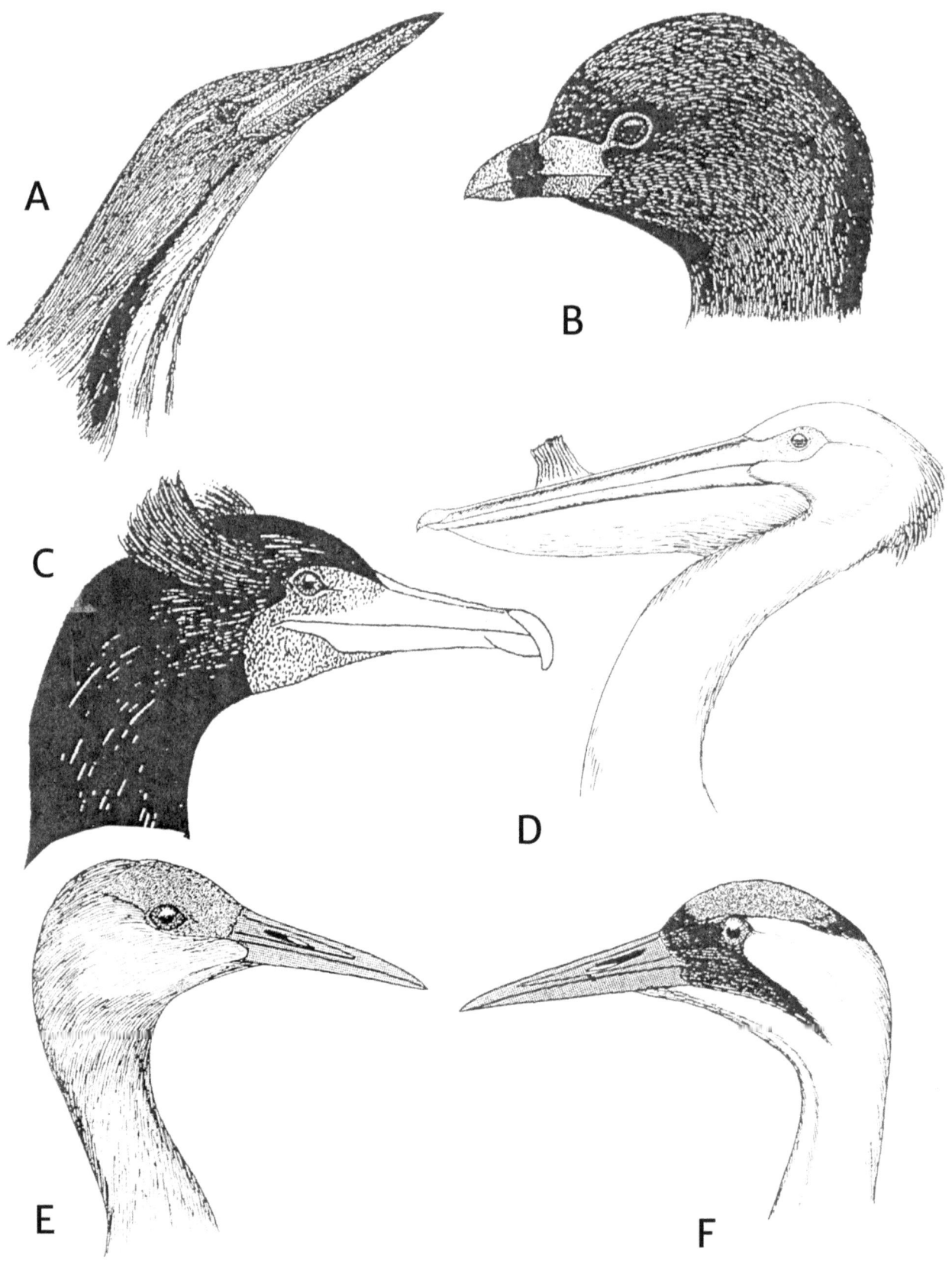

Aquatic and marsh birds, including (A) American bittern, (B) pied-billed grebe, (C) double-crested cormorant, (D) American white pelican, (E) sandhill crane, and (F) whooping crane

American Coot, *Fulica americana*
An, **Ar**, Bl, Bo, **Br**, **Ch**, Cu, **Gar**, Gr, Gre, **Grf**, **Ho**, **Hol** (H), Ke, **Li**, Lo, Log, Mc, Mo, Ro, Sh, Th, **Wh**

Status. The American coot is a common to abundant spring and fall migrant and summer resident throughout the state, most abundant in the Sandhills marshes. Sometimes it overwinters where open water exists. Breeding Bird Surveys between 1966 and 2015 indicate the species collectively underwent a survey-wide population increase (0.61% annually) during that period, and Nebraska underwent an estimated 2.03 percent rate of annual increase.

Migration. Seventy-four initial spring sightings are from February 4 to June 7, with a median of March 29. Half of the records fall within the period March 19–April 24. Eighty-two final fall records are from July 25 to December 31, with a median of November 2. Half of the records fall within the period October 14–November 21.

Habitats. A wide variety of wetlands, ranging from small ponds or large lakes and reservoirs are used throughout the year, but those that are fairly shallow and rich in submerged aquatic plants are favored. Nesting usually occurs on vegetation mounds among emergent vegetation.

Family Gruidae (Cranes)

Sandhill Crane, *Antigone canadensis*
An, Ar, Bl, Bo, Br, Ch, Cu, Gar, Gr, Gre, Grf, Hol, Ke, Li, Lo, Log, Mc, **Mo**, **Ro**, Sh, Th, Wh

Status. The sandhill crane is an abundant spring and fall migrant in the Platte River valley from Grand Island west to Lewellen and farther west locally along the Platte–North Platte valley to Scottsbluff. It is also a local or irregular breeder in the Sandhills and Rainwater Basin. Since 1996, breeding by the greater sandhill crane has occurred in central Nebraska's Rainwater Basin on several occasions as well as within the Sandhills region in Morrill County (*Nebraska Bird Review* 77: 100) and Rock County (Mollhoff, 2016). Breeding Bird Surveys between 1966 and 2015 indicate the species collectively underwent a survey-wide population increase (4.74% annually) during that period, but this rate of increase is probably typical only of the eastern migratory flock of greater sandhill cranes. The lesser sandhill cranes' much larger midcontinent flock has been increasing at a much slower rate, very probably because of heavy hunting pressures along major migration routes, such as in North Dakota and Saskatchewan.

Migration. Fifty-seven initial spring sightings are from January 8 to May 1, with a median of March 1. Half of the records fall within the period February 10–March 20. Thirty final spring sightings are from March 9 to June 1, with a median of April 7. Fifty-five initial fall sightings are from September 2 to November 24, with a median of October 8. Half of the records fall within the period September 28 to October 22. Fifty-three final fall sightings are from October 1 to December 31, with a median of November 5.

Habitats. Slowly flowing rivers with relatively bare bars and islands for roosting and adjacent wet meadows and croplands for foraging are used by this species during migration. The Platte River valley is evidently the optimum spring habitat for this species in the entire Great Plains region. Spring concentrations of (predominantly) lesser sandhill cranes there are unequaled anywhere in North America, usually peaking at about 500,000 to 700,000 in late March.

Common (Eurasian) Crane, *Grus grus*
Ga, Ke, Li

Very rare. The common crane is a very rare spring vagrant. The first Nebraska record was a bird seen several times March 25–31, 1972, between Hershey and North Platte in Lincoln County (Silcock and Jorgensen, 2020). It was also reported from Keith and Lincoln Counties between March 12 and April 6, 2008, 2009, and 2010 (Brown, Dinsmore, and Brown, 2012). The other records are from Lewellen, Garden County. Single birds were also seen on March 10, 2007; March 18–21, 2009; April 10, 2019; and March 12, 2020. No North American breeding is known, but possible wild hybrids with sandhill cranes have been described.

CRANES · STILTS AND AVOCETS

Whooping Crane, *Grus americana*
An, Grf, Li, Lo

Status. The whooping crane is an occasional spring and fall migrant in Nebraska, more often seen in spring than in fall. It has been observed in at least 26 counties but most commonly in Buffalo and Kearney Counties. Within the Sandhills region it has been observed at least ten times in Lincoln County.

Migration. More than 90 percent of the sightings have occurred within 30 miles of the Platte River, and about 80 percent have occurred between Lexington and Grand Island (*Nebraska Bird Review* 45: 54–56). Migration records for whooping cranes indicate the spring migration usually extends from early March to late May, with a peak during the period April 1–15. The earliest spring record is February 10. The fall migration extends from mid-September to early November, with a peak during the period October 11–25. Recent studies indicate that both spring and fall migration phenologies have been influenced by climate change.

Habitats. While in Nebraska, the Platte River valley is the whooping crane's primary habitat. A wide and slowly flowing river, with numerous sandbars and islands, and adjacent wet meadows, grainfields, and marshlands, is evidently an important combination of habitat characteristics. The species migrates later in spring than does the sandhill crane, and thus does not normally associate with it. It also uses marshy areas, seasonal "lagoons," and similar shallow wetlands for foraging to a larger degree than does the sandhill crane.

Family Recurvirostridae (Stilts and Avocets)

Black-necked Stilt, *Himantopus mexicanus*
An, Ch, **Gar**, Ke, Li, **Sh**

Status. The black-necked stilt is an occasional spring migrant that had no evidence of nesting within the state until it began at Crescent Lake NWR in 1985. Breeding has also occurred near Lakeside, Sheridan County, since at least 1985. There are also scattered nonbreeding records from other Sandhills counties as far east as Antelope County but, as for the American avocet, the somewhat alkaline and shallow waters of the western Sandhills are preferred habitats. Breeding Bird Surveys between 1966 and 2015 indicate the species collectively underwent a survey-wide population increase (1.75% annually) during that period.

Migration. Eight records extend from April 30 to August 8. Five of the records are for the month of May.

Habitats. This stilt is generally associated with alkali ponds and marshes, often the same as those used by avocets.

American Avocet, *Recurvirostra americana*
An, Ar, Bl, **Ch**, Cu, **Gar**, **Gr**, Gre, Hol, **Ke**, Li, Lo, Log, Mc, **Mo**, **Ro**, **Sh**, Th, Wh

Status. The American avocet is an uncommon spring and fall migrant in the Sandhills region. It is common in central parts of the state and a common summer resident in the western, variably alkaline Sandhills. Breeding Bird Surveys between 1966 and 2015 indicate the species collectively underwent a survey-wide population decline (0.31% annually) during that period, and Nebraska underwent an estimated 3.90 percent rate of annual decline.

Migration. Eighty-two initial spring sightings range from April 2 to June 7, with a median of April 28. Half of the records fall within the period April 20–May 6. Thirty-eight final fall sightings are from July 25 to November 17, with a median of September 4. Half of the records fall within the period August 25–September 2.

Habitats. In Nebraska, avocets are associated with shallow ponds or marshes with exposed and sparsely vegetated shorelines, often in association with strongly alkaline waters. Nests are placed in exposed locations on mudflats, sandbars, and islands with little or no surrounding cover.

Black-necked stilt, adult in breeding plumage. *Photo by J. Kren.*

Family Charadriidae (Plovers)

Black-bellied Plover, *Pluvialis squatarola*
An, Bl, Ch, Gar, Gr, Ke, Li, Lo, Log, Sh

Status. The black-bellied plover is an uncommon spring and fall migrant in eastern Nebraska, becoming rarer westwardly. It is less common in fall than during spring but more common in both seasons than the American golden-plover. Both species are uncommon to occasional in the Sandhills region.

Migration. Sixty-six total spring sightings range from April 4 to June 9, with a median of May 16. Half of the records fall within the period May 12–23. Thirteen initial fall sightings are from July 27 to October 2, with a median of August 20. Thirteen final fall sightings are from August 27 to November 12, with a median of October 6.

Habitats. Mudflats, shallow ponds, and plowed fields are used by migrating birds.

American Golden-plover, *Pluvialis dominica*
An, Bl, Ch, Gar, Ke, Lo, Sh

Status. The American golden-plover is an uncommon to occasional migrant in eastern Nebraska, rarer westwardly. It migrates throughout the entire region, including the Sandhills. It is more common in spring than fall but present during both seasons.

Migration. Forty-nine total spring sightings are from April 6 to May 29, with a median of May 7. Half of the records fall within the period April 25–May 14. Ten initial fall sightings are from September 2 to October 9, with a median of September 28. Ten final fall sightings are from September 8 to November 20, with a median of October 12.

Habitats. Migrants favor grass stubble, short pasturelands, and newly plowed fields.

Killdeer, *Charadrius vociferous*
An, Ar, Bl, Bo, Br, Ch, Cu, Gar, Gr, Grf, Ho, Hol, Ke, Li, Lo, Log, Mc, Mo, Ro, Sh, Th, Wh

Status. The killdeer is a common to abundant spring and fall migrant and summer resident statewide, and an abundant breeder in the Sandhills. It overwinters infrequently in the state. Breeding Bird Surveys between 1966 and 2015 indicate the species collectively underwent a survey-wide population decline (1.09% annually) during that period, and Nebraska underwent an estimated 0.80 percent rate of annual increase.

Migration. The range of 86 initial spring sightings is from February 11 to May 27, with a median of March 13. Half of the records fall within the period March 8–19. The range of 110 final fall records is from August 18 to December 31, with a median of October 19. Half of the records fall within the period September 27–November 10.

Habitats. This highly adaptable species often occurs on open fields during migration, but it typically breeds near wetlands where there is exposed ground nearby. The birds prefer gravelly, stony, or sandy areas for nesting, but they will also nest in a wide variety of locations, sometimes even in garden plots and on building rooftops. The killdeer is one of the ten most common breeding birds of Nebraska (Mollhoff, 2016).

Semipalmated Plover, *Charadrius semipalmatus*
An, Bl, Ch, Gar, Gr, Hol, Ke, Li, Lo, Mo, Ro, Sh

Status. The semipalmated plover is an uncommon to occasional spring and fall migrant statewide, probably more common eastwardly. It is widespread but uncommon in the Sandhills region, favoring open sandy shorelines rather than those that are vegetated for foraging.

Migration. Eighty-two initial spring sightings are from March 24 to June 6, with a median of May 12. Sixteen initial fall sightings are from July 25 to September 24, with a median of August 11. Sixteen final fall sightings are from July 30 to October 14, with a median of September 18.

Habitats. Migrants favor mudflats, shallow ponds, and the muddy banks of slowly flowing rivers.

Piping Plover, *Charadrius melodus*
An, **Bl**, **Br**, Ch, Cu, **Gar**, **Hol**, **Ke**, Li, **Ro**, Sh

Status. The piping plover is an occasional to rare spring and fall migrant and a local rare summer resident along various river valleys, including the major Sandhills rivers. Most of the recent regional

American avocet, adult in breeding plumage. *Photo by P. Johnsgard.*

Long-billed curlew adult (above) and piping plover adult and chick

breeding records are for the Loup and Middle Loup Rivers and at Lake McConaughy, Keith County. Recent Breeding Bird Surveys indicate that 250 to 280 pairs breed in the state, mostly at Lake McConaughy and also on spoil piles associated with gravel operations. The Nebraska subspecies is currently federally listed as threatened.

Migration. Sixty-one initial spring sightings are from March 27 to June 1, with a median of May 3. Half of the records fall within the period April 21–May 12. Five final fall sightings are from July 27 to September 5, with a mean of August 19.

Habitats. Breeding birds are usually associated with sparsely vegetated shorelines of shallow lakes and impoundments, especially those having bare sand or salt-encrusted areas of gravel, sand, or pebbly mud.

Snowy Plover, *Charadrius nivosus*
An, **Ke**, Li

Status. The snowy plover is a rare summer resident. It has been a Sandhills nester at Lake McConaughy since 2000 and has been reported from May 13 to September 17 (*Nebraska Bird Review* 73: 154–156; Brown, Dinsmore, and Brown, 2012).

Migration. Six spring records for this species range from April 6 to May 17, with a mean of April 28. Five fall records are from August 7 to September 7, with a mean of August 21.

Habitats. Migrants are found on mudflats, alkaline flats, sandy shorelines, and in shallow ponds. Breeding occurs on open sandy flats and shorelines.

Mountain Plover, *Charadrius montanus*
Ke

Accidental. An individual mountain plover was observed at Clear Creek, Keith County, April 21, 1989 (Brown, Dinsmore, and Brown, 2012).

Family Scolopacidae (Sandpipers and Snipes)

Upland Sandpiper, *Bartramia longicauda*
An, **Ar**, **Bl**, **Bo**, **Br**, **Ch**, **Cu**, **Gar**, **Gr**, **Gre**, **Grf**, **Ho**, **Hol**, **Ke**, **Li**, **Lo**, **Log**, **Mc**, **Mo**, **Ro**, **Sh**, **Th**, **Wh**

Status. The upland sandpiper is an uncommon spring and fall migrant and local summer resident in natural grasslands nearly statewide, but it's most common in the Sandhills.

Migration. The range of 108 initial spring sightings is from March 9 to May 9, with a median of May 2. Half of the records fall within the period April 24–May 10. Seventy-five final fall sightings are from July 21 to October 28, with a median of August 20. Half of the records fall within the period August 10–26.

Habitats. During summer, this species occurs on native prairies (especially mixed-grass and tall grass), wet meadows, hayfields, retired croplands, and, to a limited extent, on fields planted to small grains.

Whimbrel, *Numenius phaeopus*
An, Ch, Gar, Ke

Status. The whimbrel is a very rare spring migrant in the Sandhills. There have been periodic sightings since 1949, with the largest number from Lincoln County. Large numbers were recorded at Lake McConaughy, Keith County, on May 16, 2004 (63 individuals), and May 16, 2005 (70 individuals) (Silcock and Jorgensen, various dates).

Migration. Eleven spring records are from April 12 to May 27, with a median of May 10.

Habitats. Migrating birds favor flooded grasslands, sandbars, and the shorelines of large impoundments.

Long-billed Curlew, *Numenius americanus*
Ar, Bl, **Br**, **Ch**, Cu, **Gar**, **Gr**, Gre, **Ho**, **Hol** (H), Ke, Li, Log, **Mc**, **Mo**, **Ro**, **Sh**

Status. The long-billed curlew is a common migrant and summer resident in central and western Nebraska, particularly in the Sandhills region. The eastern breeding limits reach at least Garfield and Holt Counties, near the eastern edge of the

Sandhills. Breeding Bird Surveys between 1966 and 2015 indicate the species collectively underwent a survey-wide population increase (0.17% annually) during that period, and Nebraska underwent an estimated 3.04 percent rate of annual decline. The Nebraska population has been estimated at about 24,000 birds (*Nebraska Bird Review* 79: 89), and it winters on the Gulf coast (Gregory, 2010).

Migration. Eighty-three initial spring sightings range from March 7 to June 7, with a median of April 11. Half of the records fall within the period April 5–21. Twenty-eight final fall sightings are from July 22 to September 21, with a median of August 18. Half of the records fall within the period August 5–September 1. Sometimes large flocks (of 50 or more) of curlews gather in Sandhills wet meadows in July just prior to fall migration, and similar-sized flocks can be seen migrating north through western Kansas during late April.

Habitats. In Nebraska, this species is associated with Sandhills grasslands, shortgrass plains, and other grassy environments that offer extensive foraging and nesting opportunities. Nests often are placed in prairie vegetation on upland slopes that are close to moist meadows for foraging. Although the nests are well scattered, alarm calls from a nesting pair of curlews will often attract other birds from distant territories to help in nest defense.

Hudsonian Godwit, *Limosa haemastica*
An, Ch, Cu, Gar, Grf, Hol, Ke, Li, Ro, Sh, Wh

Status. The Hudsonian godwit is an uncommon spring migrant in eastern Nebraska, becoming uncommon in the Sandhills and rare or absent in the west.

Migration. Sixty-nine initial spring records are from April 12 to May 27, with a median of May 2. Half of the records fall within the period April 22–May 12. Ten final spring sightings are from May 6 to May 25, with a median of May 15.

Habitats. This godwit is associated with marshy ponds, wet grasslands, and flooded fields while on migration.

Marbled Godwit, *Limosa fedoa*
An, Bo, Br, Ch, Gar, Grf, Ke, Li, Mc, Mo, **Sh**, Wh

Status. The marbled godwit is an uncommon to locally common migrant throughout Nebraska. A few recent state breeding records exist for the western and northern Sandhills (*Nebraska Bird Review* 76: 102), including Sheridan County (*Nebraska Bird Review* 73: 102, 76: 102; Mollhoff, 2016). Breeding Bird Surveys between 1966 and 2015 indicate the species collectively underwent a survey-wide population decline (0.41% annually) during that period.

Migration. The range of 117 initial spring sightings is from April 5 to May 26, with a median of April 29. Half of the records fall within the period April 22–May 10. Eleven final spring sightings are from April 19 to May 23, with a median of May 7. Eleven total fall records are from July 20 to October 24, with a median of September 9.

Habitats. Extensive mudflats, wet fields, sandbars, and the shorelines of impoundments are commonly used by migrating birds.

Ruddy Turnstone, *Arenaria interpres*
An, Bl, Ch, Gar, Ke, Li

Status. The ruddy turnstone is an occasional to rare spring migrant in eastern Nebraska, very rarely seen as far west in the Sandhills as Cherry and Garden Counties. It is rarely reported during fall; migrants are most common in the eastern portions of the Great Plains states.

Migration. Twenty-three total spring records are from April 19 to May 27, with a mean of May 18. Half of the records fall within the period May 14–25, with a median of May 18. Half the records fall between the period May 14–25. There are two fall records: September 10 and 17 (Rosche, 1982).

Habitats. Mudflats, shallow ponds, and plowed fields are used by migrating birds.

Sharp-tailed Sandpiper, *Calidris acuminata*
Sh

Accidental. A single Sandhills record for the sharp-tailed sandpiper is from Sheridan County on September 8, 1994 (Silcock and Jorgensen, various dates).

Upland sandpiper, adult in breeding plumage. *Photo by P. Johnsgard.*

Red Knot, *Calidris canutus*
Ch, Ke, Li, Sh

Status. The red knot is a rare spring and fall migrant in eastern Nebraska and west in the Sandhills to Sheridan County.

Migration. A total of six spring records range from May 7 to May 19, with a mean of May 14. Six fall records are from August 27 to October (no date), with a mean of September 12.

Habitats. Mudflats and sandbars are used by migrating birds.

Ruff, *Calidris pugnax*
An

Accidental. A female ruff was seen in northeast Antelope County on April 10, 1998 (Silcock and Jorgensen, various dates).

Stilt Sandpiper, *Calidris himantopus*
An, Ar, Bo, Br, Ch, Cu, Gar, Grf, Gr, Hol, Ho, Ke, Li, Log, Lo, Mo, Sh, Wh

Status. The stilt sandpiper is a common or uncommon spring and fall migrant almost statewide, and it is especially common in the Sandhills.

Migration. Ninety-nine initial spring sightings are from April 3 to May 29, with a median of May 11. Half of the records fall within the period May 9–19. Sixteen final spring sightings are from May 7 to May 30, with a median of May 17. Eleven initial fall sightings are from July 21 to September 19, with a median of August 11. Nine final fall sightings are from September 3 to October 21, with a median of September 20.

Habitats. Muddy flats, shallow mud-bottom ponds, and flooded fields are used by migrants; the birds feed in belly-deep water and are more likely to be in sheltered areas than on exposed shorelines than are many other shorebirds.

Sanderling, *Calidris alba*
An, Bl, Bo, Br, Ch, Gar, Grf, Hol, Ke, Li, Log, Lo, Mo, Sh, Wh

Status. The sanderling is a rare to occasional spring and fall migrant in Nebraska, mostly in the eastern and central parts of the state, becoming rare in the west. This species is widely but infrequently reported from the Sandhills.

Migration. Fifty-six initial spring sightings are from March 26 to June 2, with a median of May 6. Half of the records fall within the period April 25–May 15. Thirteen final spring sightings are from April 26 to June 10, with a median of May 13. Seventeen initial fall sightings are from July 27 to October 2, with a median of August 20. Twelve final fall sightings are from August 12 to October 19, with a median of October 4.

Habitats. Migrants are associated with sandy shorelines, sandflats, salt-encrusted flats, and, less frequently, muddy shorelines.

Dunlin, *Calidris alpina*
An, Bo, Br, Ch, Gar, Hol, Ke

Status. The dunlin is an occasional spring migrant in eastern Nebraska and rare in western parts of the state. It is apparently rare during fall migration in all areas. Dunlins have been observed at least as far west in the Sandhills as Cherry and Garden Counties.

Migration. Forty-eight spring sightings range from April 6 to June 2, with a median of May 13. Half of the records fall within the period May 19–21. Eleven fall records are from August 15 to November 20, with a median of September 11.

Habitats. Migrants use mudflats, shallow ponds, and open stretches of muddy shorelines, often mingling with other small sandpipers.

Baird's Sandpiper, *Calidris bairdii*
An, Ar, Bl, Bo, Br, Ch, Cu, Gar, Gr, Grf, Ho, Hol, Ke, Li, Lo, Log, Mc, Mo, Ro, Sh

Status. Baird's sandpiper is a common spring and fall migrant statewide—probably the most abundant of the smaller "peep" sandpipers in Nebraska, especially in the Sandhills.

Migration. The range of 125 initial spring sightings is from March 12 to May 24, with a median of April 21. Half of the records fall within the period April 6–May 4. Fifty-four final spring sightings are from April 7 to May 29, with a median of May 13. Thirty-two initial fall sightings are from July 20

Long-billed curlew, adult female incubating. *Photo by P. Johnsgard.*

to October 1, with median of August 12. Twenty-seven final fall sightings are from August 3 to December 5, with a median of October 6.

Habitats. Migrants use mudflats, shallow ponds, sandbars, and dried areas such as overgrazed pastures, salt plains, and similar open habitats while on migration.

Least Sandpiper, *Calidris minutilla*
An, Ar, Bl, Bo, Br, Ch, Cu, Gar, Grf, Gr, Gre, Hol, Ho, Ke, Li, Log, Lo, Mc, Mo, Ro, Sh, Th, Wh

Status. The least sandpiper is a common spring and fall migrant statewide, including the Sandhills region, but is less common westwardly.

Migration. The range of 102 initial spring sightings is from March 8 to May 29, with a median of May 2. Half of the records fall within the period April 20–May 10. Forty-one final spring sightings are from April 27 to June 2, with a median of May 12. Twenty-three final fall sightings are from July 20 to September 9, with a median of August 2. Twenty-three final fall sightings are from July 28 to November 11, with a median of September 18.

Habitats. Mudflats, shallow ponds, marsh edges, and flooded meadows are used by migrants, which frequently gather in small groups to forage in shallow puddles or wet grasslands well away from the larger "peep" sandpipers.

White-rumped Sandpiper, *Calidris fuscicollis*
An, Bl, Bo, Br, Ch, Cu, Grf, Hol, Ke, Li, Lo, Log, Ro, Sh, Th, Wh

Status. The white-rumped sandpiper is an abundant spring migrant statewide, including the Sandhill's region, but relatively few fall records exist.

Migration. The range of 100 initial spring sightings is from March 28 to June 1, with a median of April 29. Half of the records fall within the period May 1–16. Seventeen final spring sightings are from May 8 to May 25. Eleven total fall sightings are from July 20 to October 4, with a median of August 12.

Habitats. Migrants feed in shallow ponds, flooded pasturelands, flat shorelines, and muddy creeks. They are often seen with Baird's sandpipers, but they are less likely to forage in the dry areas that that species will use.

Buff-breasted Sandpiper, *Calidris subruficollis*
An, Gar, Ke, Log

Very rare. The buff-breasted sandpiper is a very rare spring and fall migrant. It was reported from July 30 to September 17 in Keith County (Brown, Dinsmore, and Brown, 2012). The only notable concentration observed outside of the Rainwater Basin was 321 individuals found in fields adjacent to a playa wetland in Antelope County (a location directly north of the basin) on May 15, 2006 (Silcock and Jorgensen, various dates). The other records from the Sandhills are from Clear Creek Wildlife Management Area, Garden and Keith Counties, on May 11, 1985, and from Logan County on May 22, 1939 (Silcock and Jorgensen, various dates).

Pectoral Sandpiper, *Calidris melanotos*
An, Bl, Bo, Br, Ch, Cu, Gar, Gr, Gre, Hol, Ke, Li, Lo, Log, Mc, Ro, Sh, Th, Wh

Status. The pectoral sandpiper is a common to abundant spring and fall migrant in the Sandhills, becoming less common to rare westwardly. It is a migrant throughout the entire Great Plains states region.

Migration. The range of 102 initial spring sightings is from March 4 to June 6, with a median of April 28 and half of the records falling within the period April 15–May 8. Thirty-nine final spring sightings are from April 5 to May 25, with a median of May 13. Twenty-eight fall sightings are from August 3 to November 20, with a median of October 4.

Habitats. Migrating birds use a variety of habitats, including muddy shorelines, creeks, flooded grasslands, and shallow marshy areas where the emergent vegetation is not too thick for easy wading.

Semipalmated Sandpiper, *Calidris pusilla*
An, Ch, Cu, Gar, Grf, Gr, Hol, Ke, Li, Log, Lo, Mo, Ro, Sh, Wh

Status. The semipalmated sandpiper is a common spring and fall migrant, locally abundant in the Sandhills region.

Migration. Eighty-nine initial spring sightings are from March 21 to June 10, with a median of April 28. Half of the records fall within the period April

20–May 10. Thirty-nine final spring sightings are from April 28 to June 1, with a median of May 15. Twenty-three initial fall sightings are from July 20 to September 8, with a median of August 5. Twenty-three final fall sightings are from July 28 to October 16, with a median of September 18.

Habitats. Migrating birds use mudflats, shallow ponds, and exposed sandbars as well as open shorelines, but they rarely move onto dry fields with Baird's sandpipers or wet grasslands with least sandpipers.

Western Sandpiper, *Calidris mauri*
An, Bo, Br, Ch, Cu, Gar, Hol, Ke, Li, Mo, Sh

Status. The western sandpiper is an occasional spring and uncommon fall migrant in Nebraska, becoming more common westwardly but considered rare at Crescent Lake NWR. The species' status in the state is still only poorly known. It is probably more common in western Nebraska during fall, since the spring migration closely follows the Pacific coastline.

Migration. Forty-one initial spring sightings are from April 7 to June 10, with a median of May 8. Half of the records fall within the period April 28–May 15. Ten final spring sightings are from May 3 to May 23, with a median of May 13. Fourteen initial fall records are from July 20 to September 19, with a median of August 12. Eleven final fall sightings are from August 26 to October 2, with a median of September 1.

Habitats. Mudflats, shallow ponds, and open shorelines are used by migrants, which avoid dry areas and prefer to forage while wading in shallow water. They usually forage at a slightly greater depth than do semipalmated sandpipers.

Short-billed Dowitcher, *Limnodromus griseus*
Bo, Br, Ch, Cu, Gar, Hol, Ke, Li, Sh, Wh

Status. The short-billed dowitcher is probably an occasional and local migrant in the Sandhills region, but identification problems and earlier consideration of the dowitchers as a single species make the species' distribution impossible to estimate.

Migration. Seven total spring sightings attributed to this species are from April 20 to May 18, with a median of May 14. Fourteen fall sightings are from early August to September 10, with most records between August 19 and September 10.

Habitats. Migrants use muddy flats and mud-bottom ponds, probably identical to the foraging habitats preferred by the long-billed dowitcher, at least in Nebraska. They are often seen with black-bellied plovers.

Long-billed Dowitcher, *Limnodromus scolopaceus*
An, Ar, Bl, Bo, Br, Ch, Cu, Gar, Grf, Gr, Gre, Hol, Ho, Ke, Li, Lo, Mc, Mo, Ro, Sh, W

Status. The long-billed dowitcher is a common spring and fall migrant statewide, including the Sandhills region. It is a regular migrant throughout the entire Great Plains states region.

Migration. Thirty-five initial spring sightings range from April 12 to May 23, with a median of May 1. Half of the records fall within the period April 20 to May 11. Thirteen final spring sightings are from May 4 to June 1, with a median of May 11. Eleven initial fall sightings are from July 20 to October 7, with a median of August 8. Thirteen final fall sightings are from August 1 to December 3, with a median of October 14.

Habitats. These birds are associated with muddy flats and mud-bottom ponds in Nebraska; foraging is done by probing in the shallow water of ponds or flooded grasslands.

Wilson's Snipe, *Gallinago delicata*
An, **Ar**, Bl, Bo, **Br**, **Ch**, Cu, **Gar**, **Gr**, Gre, **Ho**, **Hol**, Ke, **Li**, Lo, Log, **Mc**, Mo, **Ro**, **Sh**, **Th**, Wh

Status. Wilson's snipe is a common spring and fall migrant, and a rare or localized summer resident. Stragglers uncommonly overwinter in the state as well. It has recently bred in Garden, Rock, Cherry, Garfield, and Howard Counties (Mollhoff, 2016) and is regular during summer at the Clear Creek marshes, Garden County, and in the Pine Creek drainage north of Smith Lake in Sheridan County, so nesting there is quite likely. Regular nesting probably occurs from North Dakota and Minnesota southward to Nebraska, and migrants occur throughout the Great Plains states.

Migration. Eighty-one initial spring sightings range from January 1 to May 29, with a median of April 13. Half of the records fall within the period April

4–21. Twenty-three final spring records are from April 12 to May 28, with a median of April 29. Thirty-seven initial fall records are from July 21 to December 21, with a median of September 18. Forty-two final fall records are from July 27 to December 31, with a median of November 12. The data suggest that overwintering is rather rare in this species.

Habitats. Migrating birds are associated with marshes, sloughs, and other wetlands that support areas of mudflats or mucky organic soil, where foraging by probing is readily performed. Marshes rich in shoreline and emergent vegetation are preferred over more open areas.

Spotted Sandpiper, *Actitis macularius*
An, Ar, **Bl**, Bo, **Br**, **Ch**, Cu, **Gar**, Gr, Gre, Grf, Ho, **Hol**, **Ke**, **Li**, **Lo**, Log, Mc, Mo, **Ro**, Sh, **Th**, Wh

Status. The spotted sandpiper is a common spring and fall migrant and summer resident statewide, including the Sandhills region. Breeding Bird Surveys between 1966 and 2015 indicate the species collectively underwent a survey-wide population decline (1.35% annually) during that period, and Nebraska underwent an estimated 0.05 percent rate of annual increase.

Migration. The range of 105 initial spring records is from March 3 to June 5, with a median of May 4. Half of the records fall within the period April 26–May 3. Sixty-two final fall records are from July 26 to October 26, with a median of September 9. Half of the records fall within the period August 27–September 22.

Habitats. Throughout its stay in Nebraska, this species is associated with wetlands that have exposed or sparsely vegetated shorelines or islands and water availability ranging from fairly rapidly flowing streams to stillwater ponds.

Solitary Sandpiper, *Tringa solitaria*
An, Ar, Bl, Bo, Br, Ch, Cu, Gar, Grf, Gr, Gre, Hol, Ho, Ke, Li, Log, Lo, Mc, Mo, Ro, Sh, Th, Wh

Status. The solitary sandpiper is a common to uncommon spring and fall migrant statewide, including the Sandhills region. Breeding Bird Surveys between 1966 and 2015 indicate the species collectively underwent a survey-wide population increase (0.34% annually) during that period.

Migration. Eighty-eight initial spring sightings are from March 17 to June 7, with a median of May 4. Half of the records fall within the period April 28–May 11. Twenty-nine final spring sightings are from May 6 to June 10, with a median of May 13. Thirty-six initial fall sightings are from July 20 to September 9, with a median of August 9. Thirty-five final fall sightings are from August 5 to November 26, with a median of September 1.

Habitats. Wooded ponds, streams, and flooded meadows are used by migrants.

Lesser Yellowlegs, *Tringa flavipes*
An, Ar, Bl, Bo, Br, Ch, Cu, Gar, Grf, Gr, Hol, Ho, Ke, Li, Log, Lo, Mc, Mo, Ro, Sh, Th, Wh

Status. The lesser yellowlegs is a common spring and fall migrant statewide, including the Sandhills region. It is usually somewhat more abundant than the greater yellowlegs. Breeding Bird Surveys between 1966 and 2015 indicate the species collectively underwent a survey-wide population decline (1.87% annually) during that period.

Migration. The range of 124 initial spring sightings is from March 13 to May 29, with a median of April 14. Half of the records fall within the period April 10 to June 1, with a median of May 13. Thirty-five initial fall sightings are from July 20 to September 22, with a median of August 15. Half of the records fall within the period August 8–September 5. Forty-two final fall sightings are from August 20 to November 23, with a median of October 5.

Habitats. Ponds, marshes, creeks, mudflats, and flooded meadows are used by migrants. There is no apparent ecological separation between migrating greater and lesser yellowlegs.

Willet, *Tringa semipalmata*
An, **Ar**, **Ch**, **Gar**, **Gr**, Grf, Ho, **Hol**, Ke, Li, Lo, **Mc**, **Mo**, Ro, **Sh**, Wh

Status. The willet is an uncommon to locally common spring and fall migrant statewide and a locally common summer resident in the Sandhills. The Sandhills region apparently represents the species' southern limits of breeding in the Great

Short-billed dowitcher, adults in breeding plumage. *Photo by J. Kren.*

Plains. Breeding Bird Surveys between 1966 and 2015 indicate the species collectively underwent a survey-wide population decline (0.48% annually) during that period, and Nebraska underwent an estimated 1.08 percent rate of annual increase.

Migration. The range of 104 initial spring sightings is from March 18 to June 10, with a median of April 27. Half of the records fall within the period April 19–May 5. Sixteen final fall sightings are from August 10 to November 9, with a median of August 24. Half of the records fall within the period August 19–September 1.

Habitats. Breeding birds use a rather wide variety of wetland habitats, including streams, ponds, and marshes or shallow lakes, provided that prairie vegetation is located nearby. Less often hayfields or croplands may be used for nesting.

Greater Yellowlegs, *Tringa melanoleuca*
An, Ar, Bl, Bo, Br, Ch, Cu, Gar, Gre, Grf, Ho, Hol, Ke, Li, Log, Mc, Mo, Ro, Sh, Th, Wh

Status. The greater yellowlegs is a common spring and fall migrant statewide, including the Sandhills region. Breeding Bird Surveys between 1966 and 2015 indicate the species collectively underwent a survey-wide population increase (3.17% annually) during that period.

Migration. The range of 115 initial spring sightings is from March 13 to June 10, with a median of April 13. Half of the records fall within the period April 2–14. The range of 55 final spring sightings is from April 11 to May 30, with a median of May 5. Thirty-eight initial fall sightings are from July 20 to October 16, with a median of August 18. Half of the records fall within the period August 4–September 3. Thirty-eight final fall sightings are from August 14 to November 16, with a median of October 7.

Habitats. Ponds, marshes, creeks, mudflats, and flooded meadows are all used by migrants.

Wilson's Phalarope, *Phalaropus tricolor*
An, **Ar**, **Bl**, Bo, **Br**, Ch, Cu, **Gar**, **Gr**, Grf, **Ho**, **Hol**, Ke, Mc, **Li**, **Lo**, **Log**, **Mc**, **Mo**, **Ro**, **Sh**, **Th**, Wh

Status. Wilson's phalarope is a common to abundant spring and fall migrant, and a common summer resident, breeding over much of Nebraska, especially in the Sandhills region. Breeding occurs from North Dakota to central Kansas, and migrants appear throughout the region. Breeding Bird Surveys between 1966 and 2015 indicate the species collectively underwent a survey-wide population decline (0.48% annually) during that period, and Nebraska underwent an estimated 0.61 percent rate of annual decline.

Migration. A range of 115 initial spring sightings is from April 6 to June 6, with a median of May 2. Half of the records fall within the period April 25–May 10. Thirty-eight final fall sightings are from July 26 to October 20, with a median of September 8. Half of the records fall within the period August 19–September 12.

Habitats. Breeding occurs in wet meadows near aquatic habitats ranging from flooded ditches to ponds and marshes or shallow lakes, especially somewhat alkaline waters. This species breeds commonly around Border Lake, a hyperalkaline lake at the western edge of Crescent Lake NWR. Migrants forage by swimming in open water, capturing surface invertebrates, often paddling together in a tight circle, which produces a vortex that draws invertebrates up from below. Phalaropes are notable in that they exhibit "sex reversal" traits in which females are larger and more colorful than males. Female phalaropes also transfer incubation and brood-rearing chores to males, and to varying degrees in different species are reportedly polyandrous, although their short breeding seasons at high latitudes would seemingly limit their potential for effective polyandry.

Red-necked Phalarope, *Phalaropus lobatus*
An, Ar, Ch, Gar, Ho, Hol, Ke, Li, Mc, Mo, Sh, Wh

Status. The red-necked phalarope is an uncommon to rare spring migrant in northern and western Nebraska, including the Sandhills region. It is less common during fall migration because of a coastally oriented route.

Migration. Forty-two initial spring sightings range from April 19 to May 27, with a median of May 14. Half of the records fall within the period May 8–19. Seven final spring sightings are from May 9 to May 25, with a mean of May 19. Ten initial fall

Wilson's snipe, territorial adult calling. *Photo by J. Kren.*

sightings are from July 20 to September 21, with a median of August 10. Eleven final fall sightings are from August 20 to October 14, with a median of September 27.

Habitats. Migrants use the same habitats as do Wilson's phalaropes, namely open water areas of marshes and shallow lakes, where the invertebrate life is abundant and can be captured by surface foraging.

Red Phalarope, *Phalaropus fulicarius*
Ch, Ke, Sh

Very rare. The red phalarope is a very rare migrant in the Sandhills. The first specimen was collected during the fall in the 1930s in Cherry County (*Nebraska Bird Review* 2: 38). Since then there have been additional fall records, mostly of young birds (*Nebraska Bird Review* 70: 14). Keith County records, mostly from Lake McConaughy, extend from August 26 to September 17 (Brown, Dinsmore, and Brown, 2012).

Family Laridae (Gulls and Terns)

Black-legged Kittiwake, *Rissa tridactyla*
Ke

Accidental. One specimen record of a black-legged kittiwake is from Keith County, an adult found dead in May 1990 on Keystone Lake (a once semi-isolated eastern section of Lake Ogallala) (*Nebraska Bird Review* 58: 75). This species is an accidental or rare migrant at Lake McConaughy and has been reported January 29 to March 27 (Brown, Dinsmore, and Brown, 2012).

Sabine's Gull, *Xema sabini*
Gar, Ke, Li, Sh

Very rare vagrant. Sandhills records for the Sabine's gull were obtained August 27 to October 17 in Lincoln and Keith Counties (*Nebraska Bird Review* 65: 42–43; Brown, Dinsmore, and Brown, 2012) along with three sightings from Lincoln County during September 1996 (Brogie, 1997). It was also seen in Garden County during October 1978.

Habitats. Large rivers, lakes, and reservoirs are sometimes used, but most migration occurs coastally.

Bonaparte's Gull, *Chroicocephalus philadelphia*
An, Bl, Bo, Br, Ch, Cu, Gar, Grf, Hol, Ke, Li, Lo, Mc, Sh

Status. Bonaparte's gull is an uncommon spring and fall migrant in eastern Nebraska, becoming rarer westwardly but reported at least as far west in the Sandhills as Cherry, Lincoln, and Garden Counties.

Migration. Thirty-six total spring sightings are from April 3 to May 27, with a median of April 23. Half of the records fall within the period April 12–May 9. Twenty fall sightings are from August 18 to November 21, with a median of October 26.

Habitats. Migrants are associated with rivers, marshes, and lakes, especially large lakes.

Black-headed Gull, *Chroicocephalus ridibundus*
Ke, Sh

Accidental. One adult black-headed gull was observed at Lake McConaughy, Keith County, on December 19–20, 2003 (Brown, Dinsmore, and Brown, 2012), and one was observed at Lake Walgren, Sheridan County, on August 12, 1979 (Silcock and Jorgensen, various dates).

Little Gull, *Hydrocoloeus minutus*
Gre, Ke, Li

Very rare. A vagrant little gull was recorded from April to December at Lake McConaughy, Keith County (Brown, Dinsmore, and Brown, 2012).

Ross's Gull, *Rhodostethia rosea*
Li

Accidental. A Ross's gull was observed at Sutherland Reservoir, Lincoln County, on December 17, 1992 (Brown, Dinsmore, and Brown, 2012).

Wilson's phalarope, adults copulating. *Photo by J. Kren.*

Laughing Gull, *Leucophaeus atricilla*
Ke, Li

Accidental. The laughing gull is a rare late spring and summer transient, May 27–June 30, Keith and Lincoln Counties (Brown, Dinsmore, and Brown, 2012).

Franklin's Gull, *Leucophaeus pipixcan*
An, Ar, Bl, Br, Ch, Cu, **Gar**, Gr, Gre, Grf, Hol, Ke, Li, Lo, Log, Mc, Mo, Ro, Sh, Th, Wh

Status. Franklin's gull is an abundant spring and fall migrant and a very rare or accidental summer resident in the Sandhills, with the only known breeding records from Garden County (*Nebraska Bird Review* 34: 63; 35: 32). Stragglers sometimes are present during the summer in the Sandhills. Breeding Bird Surveys between 1966 and 2015 indicate the species collectively underwent a survey-wide population decline (2.95% annually) during that period.

Migration. Eighty-nine initial spring sightings range from March 6 to June 8, with a median of April 10. Half of the records fall within the period March 27–April 21. Fifty-eight final spring sightings are from April 2 to June 2, with a median of May 14. Fifty-two initial fall sightings are from July 20 to October 24, with a median of September 7. Fifty-eight final fall sightings are from August 17 to December 20, with a median of October 17. Half of the records are for the period October 3–November 2.

Habitats. Migrants are often found on plowed fields, often closely following moving plows in large flocks. Breeding occurs on large prairie marshes that have extensive areas of semi-open emergent vegetation for nesting.

Mew Gull, *Larus canus*
Ke, Li

Accidental. The mew gull is a rare late winter and spring Sandhills transient, May 27 to June 30, Keith and Lincoln Counties (Brown, Dinsmore, and Brown, 2012).

Ring-billed Gull, *Larus delawarensis*
An, Ar, Bl, Bo, Br, Ch, Cu, Gar, Gr, Gre, Ho, Hol, Ke, Li, Lo, Log, Mc, Mo, Ro, Sh, Th, Wh

Status. The ring-billed gull is a common to abundant spring and fall migrant statewide, including the Sandhills region, with stragglers sometimes remaining in Sandhills counties through the summer months. Breeding Bird Surveys between 1966 and 2015 indicate the species collectively underwent a survey-wide population increase (1.61% annually) during that period.

Migration. Eighty initial spring sightings range from January 3 to May 15, with a median of March 16. Half of the records fall within the period March 5–26. Fifty final spring sightings are from March 12 to June 7, with a median of May 12. Forty-eight initial fall sightings are from July 20 to November 15, with a median of September 12. Fifty-seven final fall sightings are from August 25 to December 21, with a median of November 28.

Habitats. A wide variety of lakes, reservoirs, rivers, marshes, and other water areas are used by migrants.

California Gull, *Larus californicus*
Ar, Ch, Gar, Ke, Li, Lo

Status. The California gull is a rare migrant or winter vagrant in most of Nebraska, including the Sandhills region, but apparently most regular and uncommon in northwestern Nebraska (Rosche, 1982). In the Lake McConaughy area, it is a permanent nonbreeding visitor (Brown, Dinsmore, and Brown, 2012).

Migration. Seven spring records are from March 19 to April 26, with a mean of March 28. There is at least one June record. Ten late summer and fall records are from July 18 to November 10. Nine winter records extend from December 13 to February 15.

Habitats. Lakes, large marshes, and similar habitats are used by migrants.

Herring Gull, *Larus argentatus*
An, Bo, Br, Ch, Gr, Gre, Ke, Li, Lo, Mo, Sh

Status. The herring gull is an uncommon spring and fall migrant throughout Nebraska, including the Sandhills region. Breeding Bird Surveys between

1966 and 2015 indicate the species collectively underwent a survey-wide population decline (3.53% annually) during that period.

Migration. Forty-seven initial spring records range from January 13 to May 13, with a median of March 18. Half of the records fall within the period March 2–April 1. Twenty-seven final spring sightings are from March 5 to May 28, with a median of April 21. Twenty-four initial fall sightings are from July 21 to November 24, with a median of October 26. Eighteen final fall sightings are from August 29 to December 21, with a median of November 28.

Habitats. Migrating birds are widely distributed over rivers, lakes, reservoirs, and other larger water areas, but some scavenging might occur on land.

Iceland Gull (including Thayer's Gull,
L. g. thayeri), *Larus glaucoides*
Ke

Accidental. The Iceland gull is a spring and fall transient and uncommon winter visitor in the Lake McConaughy area, Keith County. Both typical Iceland gull and Thayer's gull plumage types have been observed (Brown, Dinsmore, and Brown, 2012). Recent reports at Lake McConaughy indicate this species winters regularly, sometimes in numbers; most reports are of the race formerly recognized as Thayer's gull. Overwintering is unknown away from Lake McConaughy, Keith County, and Sutherland Reservoir, Lincoln County. At the latter location, six were present January 14, 1998, five on December 31, 1998, and five on January 29, 2000 (Silcock and Jorgensen, 2020).

Lesser Black-backed Gull, *Larus fuscus*
Li, Lo

Accidental. The lesser black-backed gull is rare in Keith County. It was first reported at Kingsley Dam in February and March, 1994 (*Nebraska Bird Review* 64: 39). This gull is now considered a rare spring, fall, and winter migrant at Lake McConaughy (Brown, Dinsmore, and Brown, 2012).

Glaucous Gull, *Larus hyperboreus*
Ke, Li, Lo

Accidental. The glaucous gull is a spring and fall transient and winter visitor in the Lake McConaughy area, Keith County (Brown, Dinsmore, and Brown, 2012). It is also reported from Loup and Lincoln Counties (Silcock and Jorgensen, various dates).

Glaucous-winged Gull, *Larus glaucesens*
Ke, Li

Accidental. The glaucous-winged gull is a rare year-round nonbreeding resident in the Lake McConaughy region, Keith and Lincoln Counties (Brown, Dinsmore, and Brown, 2012).

Great Black-backed Gull, *Larus marinus*
Grf, Ke, Li

Very rare. The great black-backed gull is a rare year-round nonbreeding resident in the Lake McConaughy area, Keith County (Brown, Dinsmore, and Brown, 2012). It was also found at Calamus Reservoir, Garfield County, on March 25, 2017, and at Lake Maloney on December 18, 2010, and Sutherland Reservoir on February 21, 1988, and January 14, 1989, both in Lincoln County (Silcock and Jorgensen, various dates).

Least Tern, *Sternula antillarum*
Bo, **Br**, Ch, Cu, Gar, Grf, Hol, **Ke**, **Li**, Lo, **Ro**, Sh, Wh

Status. The least tern is an uncommon spring and fall migrant in eastern and central Nebraska, including the Sandhills region. It is also a local and rare summer resident in the state's major valleys and around the sandy shorelines of Lake McConaughy (*Nebraska Bird Review* 59: 133–150 (Brown, Dinsmore, and Brown, 2012). Breeding Bird Surveys between 1966 and 2015 indicate the species collectively underwent a survey-wide population decline (4.13% annually) during that period. The inland population of the least tern (the interior least tern) is federally listed as an endangered species.

Migration. Eighty-seven initial spring sightings range from March 8 to June 10, with a median of May 23. Half of the records fall within the period May

16–30. Twenty-six final fall sightings are from July 20 to October 6, with a median of August 14.

Habitats. The least tern is associated with rivers, lakes, and impoundments during migration; nesting is mostly on river sandbars or islands but sometimes also on barren shorelines of large impoundments, gravel beaches, or even newly cleared land. Nesting is typically done in colonies, on a sand or gravel substrate.

Caspian Tern, *Hydroprogne caspia*
Ch, Ke, Li, Mo, Sh

Status. The Caspian tern is an uncommon spring and fall migrant in eastern Nebraska but is also regularly reported in the Sandhills as far west as Sheridan, Garden, Keith, and Lincoln Counties. A few nonbreeding birds often summer in the Lake McConaughy area (Brown, Dinsmore, and Brown, 2012).

Migration. Twenty-seven total spring sightings are from March 23 to May 28, with a median of May 10. Half of the records fall within the period May 3–17. Twenty-four fall records are from July 20 to October 14, with a median of September 19. Half of the records fall within the period September 4–25.

Habitats. Larger rivers, deep marshes, lakes, and reservoirs are used by migrants.

Black Tern, *Chlidonias niger*
An, **Ar**, Bl, Bo, **Br**, **Ch**, Cu, **Gar**, **Gr**, Gre, Grf, Ho, **Hol**, Ke, Li, Log, Lo, **Mc**, **Mo**, **Ro**, **Sh**, Th, Wh

Status. The black tern is a previously abundant spring and fall migrant statewide, and a common summer resident primarily in the Sandhills, but locally common elsewhere as well. Breeding Bird Surveys between 1966 and 2015 indicate the species collectively underwent a survey-wide population decline (1.37% annually) during that period, whereas Nebraska underwent a much greater estimated 5.74 percent rate of annual decline, and little nesting still occurs in the state.

Migration. The range of 130 initial spring sightings is from April 9 to June 5, with a median of May 12. Half of the records fall within the period May 6–18. Sixty-six final fall sightings are from July 21 to October 5, with a median of September 2. Half of the records fall within the period August 19–September 11.

Habitats. Migrants are found over a variety of aquatic habitats; they sometimes also forage well away from water over adjoining grasslands. Breeding occurs on small to large marsh areas that have a combination of open water and stands of emergent vegetation.

Common Tern, *Sterna hirundo*
An, Ch, Gar, Ke, Li

Status. The common tern is an uncommon to rare spring and fall migrant in eastern Nebraska, becoming rarer westwardly and relatively rare in the Sandhills region. Frequent confusion with the Forster's tern makes the status of this species somewhat uncertain, but it is probably fairly common only in eastern Nebraska.

Migration. Sixty-five initial spring sightings are from March 18 to June 7, with a median of May 5. Half of the records fall within the period April 24–May 15. Fourteen final spring sightings are from April 25 to June 6, with a median of May 11. Eleven initial fall sightings are from August 9 to October 14, with a median of September 2.

Habitats. Migrants use lakes, reservoirs, and rivers and less often are found on smaller marshes and ponds.

Arctic Tern, *Sterna paradisaea*
Ke

Accidental. Adult Arctic terns have been seen on two occasions in May and June at Lake McConaughy, Keith County (Brown, Dinsmore, and Brown, 2012).

Forster's Tern, *Sterna forsteri*
An, **Ar**, **Ch**, Cu, **Gar**, **Gr**, Gre, Grf, Ho, Hol, Ke, Lo, Mc, Mo, **Sh**, Th, Wh

Status. Forster's tern is a common spring and fall migrant statewide and a rather localized summer resident in the Sandhills, especially in Garden, Cherry, and Grant Counties. It probably still breeds in some Sheridan County marshes. Breeding Bird Surveys between 1966 and 2015 indicate the species collectively underwent a survey-wide population decline (1.60% annually) during that period, whereas Nebraska underwent an estimated 0.94 percent rate of annual decline.

Gulls and Terns

Forster's tern, pair mating

Migration. Fifty-eight initial spring sightings are from April 11 to June 8, with a median of April 28. Half of the records fall within the period April 19–May 5. Twenty-one final spring sightings are from April 24 to June 6, with a median of May 17. Thirteen initial fall records are from July 21 to September 22, with a median of August 1. Twenty final fall sightings are from August 1 to October 8, with a median of September 11.

Habitats. This species is associated with lakes, rivers, and marshes while on migration. Breeding occurs in large marshes that have extensive areas of emergent vegetation or muskrat houses for nesting sites.

Family Stercorariidae (Jaegers)

Pomarine Jaeger, *Stercorarius pomarinus*
Ch, Ke

Accidental. The pomarine jaeger has been observed from July 23 to December 3 at Lake McConaughy, Keith County (Brown, Dinsmore, and Brown, 2012). It was also reported from Merritt Reservoir, Cherry County, August 28–29, 1999 (Silcock and Jorgensen, various dates).

Parasitic Jaeger, *Stercorarius parasiticus*
Ke, Sh

Accidental. The parasitic jaeger was observed in mid-September and early October at Lake McConaughy, Keith County (Brown, Dinsmore, and Brown, 2012). It was also reported from near Hay Springs, Sheridan County, August 23–24, 1968 (Silcock and Jorgensen, various dates).

Long-tailed Jaeger, *Stercorarius longicaudus*
Grf, Ke

Accidental. The long-tailed jaeger was observed in June, September, and October at Lake McConaughy, Keith County (Brown, Dinsmore, and Brown, 2012). An adult light-phase was documented at Calamus Fish Hatchery, Garfield County, September 16–20, 2019 (Silcock and Jorgensen, 2019).

Family Gaviidae (Loons)

Red-throated Loon, *Gavia stellata*
Ke, Li, Sh

Status. The red-throated loon is an extremely rare spring and fall migrant statewide.

Migration. Five spring records are from April 17 to May 7, with a mean of April 28, and eight fall records are from October 31 to December 2, with a mean of November 17. There is also one mid-June record.

Habitats. Larger rivers, lakes, and reservoirs are used while on migration.

Pacific Loon, *Gavia pacifica*
Ga, Ke

Accidental. The Pacific loon is a rare year-round visitor at Lake McConaughy and Lake Ogallala, Keith County, reported January 2 to December 15 (Brown, Dinsmore, and Brown, 2012). An adult was observed at Crescent Lake NWR, Garden County, on December 7, 2017 (Silcock and Jorgensen, various dates).

Common Loon, *Gavia immer*
An, Bl, Ch, Grf, Hol, Ke, Li, Lo, Sh, Th

Status. The common loon is an uncommon spring and fall migrant throughout Nebraska, including the Sandhills region. This species has been observed numerous times in Keith County.

Migration. Excepting two January records, 55 initial spring sightings range from March 18 to May 27, with a median of May 7. Fourteen final spring sightings are from April 12 to May 28, with a median of May 16. Twenty-five initial fall sightings are from July 20 to November 2, with a median of October 24. Seventeen final fall sightings are from October 25 to December 7 with a median of November 2. Of a total of 135 records, the largest number (37) are for April, followed by May (35), November (26), and October (15). Records exist for all months except February.

Habitats. Larger rivers, lakes, and reservoirs are used while on migration.

Yellow-billed Loon, *Gavia adamsii*
Ke

Accidental. The yellow-billed loon has been seen twice, in September and October at Lake McConaughy, Keith County (Brown, Dinsmore, and Brown, 2012).

Family Phalacrocoracidae (Cormorants)

Neotropic Cormorant, *Phalacrocorax brasilianus*
Ch, Hol, Li

Very rare. The neotropic cormorant is very rare; the first Sandhills specimen was obtained October 2, 1982, at Sutherland Reservoir, Lincoln County (*Nebraska Bird Review* 51: 18). It has since been photographed at Hackberry Lake, Cherry County, on September 4, 1993 (*Nebraska Bird Review* 64: 31), and seen at Valentine NWR, July 19, 1995 (*Nebraska Bird Review* 63: 71), and at Chambers, Holt County, May 20–30, 1996 (*Nebraska Bird Review* 64: 44). This tropical species is apparently slowly expanding north into the central Great Plains.

Double-crested Cormorant, *Phalacrocorax auritus*
Ar, Bl, Bo, Br, **Ch**, Cu, **Gar**, Gr, Gre, Grf, Ho, Hol, **Ke**, **Li**, Lo, Mc, Mo, Ro, **Sh**, Th, Wh

Status. The double-crested cormorant is an uncommon spring and fall migrant throughout Nebraska, including the Sandhills region. It is a summer resident in several locations in the western half of the state, east to at least Cherry County. Probable or possible breeding was also reported from most of the Sandhills counties except Antelope, Blaine, Boone, Custer, Garfield, Logan, and Thomas (Mollhoff, 2016). Breeding Bird Surveys between 1966 and 2015 indicate the species collectively underwent a survey-wide population increase (3.76% annually) during that period, and Nebraska underwent an estimated 0.76 percent rate of annual increase.

Migration. Of 102 initial spring sightings, the range is March 14 to May 29, and the median is April 12. Half of the records fall during the period April 14–25. Thirty-nine final spring records range from April 17 to June 2, with a median of May 1. Thirty-one initial fall sightings are from August 7 to October 20, with a median of September 21. Thirty-one final fall sightings are from September 17 to December 14, with a median of October 23.

Habitats. Migrating birds use deeper marshes, lakes, rivers, and reservoirs. Breeding occurs on islands, trees, or cliffs near water, usually within about ten miles of an adequate fish supply. The increase in fish-raising farms in the southern states has benefited this species but provoked ire among the farms' owners.

Family Pelecanidae (Pelicans)

American White Pelican, *Pelecanus erythroryhnchos*
An, Ar, Bl, Cu, Gar, Gr, Gre, Grf, Ho, Hol, Ke, Li, Lo, Log, Mc, Mo, Ro, Sh, Th, Wh

Status. The American white pelican is a common migrant throughout Nebraska, including the Sandhills region. Nonbreeders commonly occur on Lake McConaughy, but there are no breeding records for the state. Breeding Bird Surveys between 1966 and 2015 indicate the species collectively underwent a survey-wide population increase (4.02% annually) during that period.

Migration. Eighty-four initial spring sightings range from February 21 to May 22, with a median of April 28. Half of the records fall within the period May 10–24. Thirty final spring sightings are from April 12 to June 1, with a median of April 28. Twenty-eight initial fall sightings range from August 5 to November 21, with a median of September 24. Twenty-eight final fall sightings are from September 16 to November 10, with a median of October 16.

Habitats. Deeper marshes, lakes, and reservoirs are used by migrating and nonbreeding birds. The nearest breeding site for this species is at LaCreek NWR near Martin, South Dakota. Probably many of the birds seen in Nebraska are migrants going to and from this refuge or probably immature nonbreeders spending their summers away from the crowded breeding colonies.

Brown Pelican, *Pelecanus occidentalis*
Ch, Cu, Li

Very rare. An adult of the brown pelican Pacific Coast subspecies *californicus* (based on its seasonal reddish proximal gular pouch coloration) was seen at Sutherland Reservoir, Lincoln County, between December 26, 2014, and March 15, 2015 (Silcock and Jorgensen, various dates). Older records from the Sandhills are from North Platte, Lincoln County, on May 18, 1930, and May 9, 1937; Cherry County on April 18, 1955; and near Milburn, Custer County, on May 28, 1977 (Silcock and Jorgensen, various dates).

Family Ardeidae (Herons and Egrets)

American Bittern, *Botaurus lentiginosus*
An, Ar, **Ch**, **Cu**, **Gar**, Gr, Grf, Hol, Ke, Li, Lo, Log, Mc, Mo, Ro, **Sh**, Wh

Status. The American bittern is a common spring and fall migrant throughout Nebraska and a locally common summer resident. Possible or probable breeding was reported from Arthur, Blaine, Brown, Grant, Holt, Hooker, Lincoln, Loup, McPherson, and Rock Counties (Mollhoff, 2016). This bittern breeds throughout the state in suitable habitats, with the Sandhills marshes providing optimum habitat. Breeding Bird Surveys between 1966 and 2015 indicate the species collectively underwent a survey-wide population decline (0.52% annually) during that period, and Nebraska underwent an estimated 0.38 percent rate of annual decline.

Migration. The range of 109 initial spring sightings is from March 26 to June 10, with a median of May 3. Half of the records fall within the period April 23–May 11. Forty-four final fall sightings are from July 14 to December 17, with a median of October 6. Half of the sightings fall within the period October 1–27.

Habitats. Normally this species is found in marshes, swamps, and bogs that have heavy emergent vegetation or adjacent wet swales or tall grassy meadows. Its unique courtship involving the exposure of normally hidden aigrette-like shoulder plumes for display has been described and illustrated by Johnsgard (1980b, 2016a).

Least Bittern, *Ixobrychus exilis*
An, Ar, **Bl**, Bo, Br, **Ch**, **Gar**, Ke, Li, **Lo**

Status. The least bittern is an uncommon spring and fall migrant and seemingly rare summer Sandhills resident. It breeds locally in the eastern half of the state and perhaps has its western nesting limits in Garden County, where it has been observed during summer at the Ash Hollow State Historical Park marshes, Garden County, and Crescent Lake NWR. Breeding Bird Surveys between 1966 and 2015 indicate the species collectively underwent a survey-wide population increase (0.17% annually) during that period.

Migration. Thirty-nine initial spring sightings range from March 30 to June 4, with a median of May 15. Half of the records fall within the period May 4–24. Ten final fall sightings are from July 28 to September 19, with a median of August 17.

Habitats. In Nebraska this species is usually found in freshwater or slightly brackish marshes or lake edges that have extensive stands of emergent vegetation and scattered bushes or similar woody growth.

Great Blue Heron, *Ardea herodias*
An, Ar, Bl, **Bo**, Br, **Ch**, Cu, **Gar**, Gr, Gre, **Grf**, Ho, **Hol**, **Ke**, **Li**, **Lo**, **Log**, Mc, Mo, Ro, **Sh**, **Th**, Wh

Status. The great blue heron is a common migrant and a local summer resident that breeds in colonies in various locations throughout Nebraska but especially along major rivers and locally in the Sandhills. Possible or probable recent nesting occurs in all of the Sandhills counties (Mollhoff, 2016).

Migration. The range of 87 initial spring sightings is from January 6 to June 6, with a median of April 2. Half of the records fall within the period March 26–April 30. Of 103 final fall sightings, the range is August 8 to December 30, and the median is October 13. Half of the records fall within the period September 23–November 7.

Habitats. Migrants are found around all water areas that support a fish population and have shallows for foraging. Nesting usually occurs among groves

American bittern, adult male displaying shoulder plumes. *Photo by P. Johnsgard.*

of tall trees but sometimes also has been reported on the ground, on rock ledges, among bulrushes, or on other elevated situations. Cottonwood groves seem to be a favored nesting location in Nebraska.

Great Egret, *Ardea alba*
An, Bl, Bo, Br, Ch, Cu, Gar, Gr, Gre, Grf, Hol, Ke, Li, Mc, Mo, Ro, Wh

Status. The great egret is an occasional to locally uncommon spring and fall migrant or summer visitor. It is most common in eastern counties but has been observed throughout the Sandhills. Possible or probable recent nesting has been reported from Brown, Cherry, Garden, Logan, and Loup Counties (Mollhoff, 2016). Breeding Bird Surveys between 1966 and 2015 indicate the species collectively underwent a survey-wide population increase (0.91% annually) during that period.

Migration. Sixty-two initial or only spring records are from March 26 to June 1, with a median of April 29. Half of the records fall within the period April 16–May 10. Ten final spring sightings are from April 6 to June 8, with a median of May 9. Twenty-one total fall records are from August 2 to October 21, with a median of September 1. Of 95 total records, the largest number (34) are for May, followed by April (30), August (10), and September (8).

Habitats. Great egrets are associated with streams, swamps, and lake borders and are usually found near trees during the nesting season.

Snowy Egret, *Egretta thula*
An, Bo, Br, Ch, **Gar**, Gre, Ke, Li, Lo, Mo, Ro, Sh, Wh

Status. The snowy egret is an occasional vagrant or summer visitor throughout Nebraska, including the Sandhills. Breeding Bird Surveys between 1966 and 2015 indicate the species collectively underwent a survey-wide population increase (0.65% annually) during that period. The only confirmed breeding comes from Crescent Lake NWR, Garden County, from June 1989 (Silcock and Jorgensen, various dates).

Migration. Twenty-four total spring records are from April 13 to June 10, with a median of May 7. Ten total fall records are from July 30 to October 1, with a median of August 17. Of 34 total records, the largest number are for May (17), followed by April (6) and August (4).

Habitats. Nonbreeding birds occur over a wide array of aquatic habitats that support fish. During the breeding season, fairly sheltered habitats with shrubby or low tree growth are favored. Nesting often occurs among breeding groups of other heron species.

Little Blue Heron, *Egretta caerulea*
Ch, Ke

Accidental. The little blue heron is a rare spring and fall visitor, observed May 5–13 and June 4–September 5 at Lake McConaughy, Keith County (Brown, Dinsmore, and Brown, 2012). It was also recorded in Cherry County on September 8, 1990 (Silcock and Jorgensen, various dates). Richard Rosche considered this species "always the rarest" of the southern herons in Nebraska (Silcock and Jorgensen, various dates).

Reddish Egret, *Egretta rufescens*
Ke

Accidental. One reddish egret was seen September 27 to October 5, 2000, at Lake McConaughy, Keith County (Brown, Dinsmore, and Brown, 2012).

Cattle Egret, *Bubulcus ibis*
An, Bl, Bo, Br, **Ch**, Cu, **Gar**, Gre, **Grf**, **Hol**, **Ke**, Li, Lo, Log, **Mc**, Wh

Status. The cattle egret is an uncommon spring and fall migrant, first reported in Nebraska in 1965. Sandhills nesting has been documented for Keith (*Nebraska Bird Review* 63: 89), Cherry, and McPherson Counties (Mollhoff, 2001, 2016). Possible or probable recent nesting has been reported from Lincoln, Logan, and Rock Counties (Mollhoff, 2016). Breeding Bird Surveys between 1966 and 2015 indicate the species underwent a population decline (1.38% annually) during that period.

Migration. Twenty-one total spring records range from April 12 to June 3, with a median of May 9. Eleven total fall records are from July 23 to October 20, with a median of August 29. Of 32 total records, the largest number (11) are for May, followed by April (8) and August (5).

Great blue heron, adult foraging. *Photo by J. Kren.*

Habitats. Migrants are associated with upland meadows and pastures. Since this species found its way to America from Africa via the West Indies, it has spread widely. Feeding on insects disturbed by foraging cattle on the American plains is seemingly little different from feeding around the feet of zebras and wildebeest on the savannas of East Africa.

Green Heron, *Butorides virescens*
An, Bl, Bo, Br, **Ch**, Cu, **Gar**, Grf, Hol, **Ke**, **Li**,
Lo, Sh, Th, Wh

Status. The green heron is a common migrant and a summer resident, probably breeding over all of the Sandhills. Possible or probable recent nesting has been reported from Blaine, Custer, Holt, Logan, Loup, Rock, Sheridan, Thomas, and Wheeler counties (Mollhoff, 2016). Breeding Bird Surveys between 1966 and 2015 indicate the species underwent a national population decline (1.77% annually) during that period. Until recently it has also been called the "green-backed heron" and "little green heron," in part because of some Latin American populations of uncertain taxonomy.

Migration. The range of 93 initial spring sightings is from March 10 to June 7, with a median of April 27. Half of the records fall within the period April 15–May 6. The range of 50 final fall sightings is from July 23 to November 9, with a median of September 18. Half of the records fall within the period September 4–25.

Habitats. Migrating birds occur almost anywhere small fish (such as minnows) can be captured. Breeding usually occurs near trees, but some nesting is in marshlands well away from tree cover.

Black-crowned Night-Heron, *Nycticorax nycticorax*
An (H), **Ar**, Bl, **Br**, **Ch**, **Gar**, Gr, Ho, **Hol**, Ke,
Li, **Mc**, Mo, **Ro**, **Sh**

Status. The black-crowned night-heron is a common migrant throughout Nebraska that breeds locally in suitable habitats throughout most of the state except perhaps the driest portions of western Nebraska. Breeding Bird Surveys between 1966 and 2015 indicate the species collectively underwent a survey-wide population increase (0.84% annually) during that period, and Nebraska underwent an estimated 1.00 percent rate of annual decline.

Migration. Eighty initial spring sightings range from March 29 to June 9, with a median of April 25. Half of the records fall within the period April 18–May 10. Fifty-four final fall sightings are from July 22 to November 15, with a median of September 6. Half of the records fall within the period August 18–September 29.

Habitats. This night-heron is a highly adaptable species, found in a wide array of aquatic habitats, with nesting occurring in swamps, marshes, and sometimes even city parks or orchards where water is nearby.

Yellow-crowned Night-Heron, *Nyctanassa violacea*
An, Bo, Br, Hol, Ke, Li

Status. The yellow-crowned night-heron is an uncommon spring and fall migrant and occasional summer visitor in Nebraska, mainly in the eastern half of the state and the Sandhills.

Migration. Forty-three total spring sightings range from April 2 to June 10, with a median of May 6. Half of the records fall within the period April 29–May 14. Twelve total fall records are from August 1 to October 24, with a median of September 5.

Habitats. Nonbreeding birds occupy a wide range of aquatic habitats, but in Nebraska the birds are often found along tree-lined rivers. Juvenile birds sometimes stray into city parks or ponds.

Family Threskiornithidae (Ibises and Spoonbills)

White Ibis, *Eudocimus albus*
Ke

Accidental. An adult white ibis was observed May 17, 2000, on Keystone Lake, Keith County (Brown, Dinsmore, and Brown, 2012).

Glossy Ibis, *Plegadis falcinellus*
An, Ch, Ke

Rare. More than 50 spring records have accumulated for the glossy ibis, including the Sandhills region,

Black-crowned night-heron, adult in breeding plumage. *Photo by J. Kren.*

through 2011, mostly since 2004. Immatures and nonbreeders have been reported for Nebraska, and breeding has occurred in the Rainwater Basin. Records extend from April to August. Apparent hybrids with the white-faced ibis have also been seen.

White-faced Ibis, *Plegadis chihi*
An, Ar, Bo, Br, **Ch**, Cu, **Gar**, **Gr**, Grf, Ke, Li, Lo, Mo, **Sh**, Th

Status. The white-faced ibis is an increasingly common spring migrant and breeding summer visitor throughout Nebraska. Local Sandhills breeding has occurred in Garden and Cherry Counties, and possible or probable recent nesting was reported from Arthur, Garfield, Lincoln, Logan, Loup, McPherson, and Thomas Counties (Mollhoff, 2001, 2016). Breeding Bird Surveys between 1966 and 2015 indicate the species underwent a population increase (2.40% annually) during that period, and Nebraska underwent an estimated 14.66 percent rate of annual increase.

Migration. Thirty-two total records range from April 9 to October 14. The largest number of sightings are for May (14), followed by April (9), with two records each for June, August, September, and October.

Habitats. Nonbreeding birds may occur in almost any wet or moist habitat, including marshes, flooded fields, wet meadows, and other areas that have shallow water for foraging. Nesting usually occurs in shallow marshes with extensive emergent vegetation.

Family Cathartidae (New World Vultures)

Turkey Vulture, *Cathartes aura*
An, Ar, Bl, Bo, **Br**, **Ch**, Cu, Gar, Gr, Gre, Grf, Ho, Hol, Ke, Li, Lo, Log, Mc, Mo, Ro, **Sh**, Th, Wh

Status. The turkey vulture is an uncommon to common spring and fall migrant in the Sandhills and a little-documented summer resident. It is a local breeder along some of the major river systems (Republican, Missouri, and Niobrara) and in the Pine Ridge area, but there are few actual published records. Mollhoff (2000, 2016) reported only six confirmed nestings during the early *Breeding Bird Atlas*ing years and five in the later years. Breeding Bird Surveys between 1966 and 2015 indicate the species collectively underwent a survey-wide population increase (2.25% annually) during that period, and Nebraska underwent an unbelievable estimated 14.56 percent rate of annual increase.

Migration. Ninety initial spring sightings are from January 12 to June 10, with a median of April 14. Half of the records fall within the period April 1–24. Nineteen final spring sightings are from April 11 to June 10, with a median of May 18. Eleven initial fall sightings are from July 20 to September 25, with a median of September 6. Thirty-five final fall sightings are from August 6 to December 30, with a median of September 26. Half of the records fall within the period September 16–October 4.

Habitats. Migrants or nonbreeders are found widely over open plains, sandhills, or other areas offering visual foraging. At the northern end of its range, during the breeding season, the species is mostly associated with brushy woodlands adjoining open grasslands or croplands. Cliffs, crevices, abandoned buildings (barns or farmhouses), or some other type of cavity are needed for nesting sites. Once associated largely with the remote deserts of the West, the turkey vulture has become yet another urbanized species. Many now roost nightly during summer in the groves of small Sandhills towns such as Mullen, or even in church belfries. The birds move out to the country during the day to scavenge for carrion along roadsides.

Family Pandionidae (Ospreys)

Osprey, *Pandion haliaetus*
An, Ch, Cu, Gar, Gr, Gre, Grf, Hol, **Ke**, Li, Lo, Log, Mo, Sh, Th, Wh

Status. The osprey is an uncommon to occasional spring and fall migrant in the Sandhills, probably most common eastwardly, where more large rivers and reservoirs exist. Sandhills nesting has occurred since 2008 on various nesting platforms, such as those near Keystone, Keith County (*Nebraska Bird Review* 76: 57; 80: 91). The birds are now regular spring and fall migrants at Lake

McConaughy and other larger reservoirs in the state. Breeding Bird Surveys between 1966 and 2015 indicate the species had a population increase (2.34% annually) during that period.

Migration. The range of 102 initial spring sightings is from January 1 to May 25, with a median of April 21. Half of the records fall within the period April 12–May 1. Twenty-one final spring sightings are from April 7 to May 27, with a median of May 5. Twenty-two initial fall sightings are from August 28 to November 30, with a median of September 15. Half of the records fall within the period September 14–24. Seventeen final fall sightings are from September 17 to December 26, with a median of October 9.

Habitats. While on migration, this species occurs along rivers, lakes, and reservoirs that support fishes and have fairly clear water for foraging.

Family Accipitridae (Hawks, Eagles and Kites)

White-tailed Kite, *Elanus leucurus*
Gar, Li

Accidental. Three records of the white-tailed kite exist from two Sandhills counties. One is from Garden County on August 19, 1981, and two more are from Lincoln County on July 1, 2008, and June 22–July 2, 2009 (Silcock and Jorgensen, various dates).

Golden Eagle, *Aquila chrysaetos*
An, Ar, Bl, Ch, **Gar**, Gr, Grf, Ho, Hol, Ke, **Li**,
Log, Lo, **Mo**, **Sh**, Th, Wh

Status. The golden eagle is an uncommon migrant and winter resident throughout Nebraska, becoming more common westwardly, and a permanent resident in western Nebraska, especially in the Pine Ridge region. Older Sandhills breeding observations are from Sheridan, Morrill, Garden, and Lincoln Counties, according to Nebraska Game and Parks Commission records. Breeding Bird Surveys between 1966 and 2015 indicate the species collectively underwent a survey-wide population decline (0.13% annually)

Migration. This species is evidently a resident in western Nebraska and a winter visitor elsewhere, and thus the records are not susceptible to ready statewide analysis. Late winter sightings seem to follow closely the temporal pattern of the bald eagle.

Habitats. Throughout most of the year, this species is associated with arid, open country, often with buttes, mountains, or canyons that offer remote nesting sites and large areas of grassland vegetation for foraging. In winter it is sometimes found near rivers or reservoirs but not nearly to the extent that is true of the bald eagle. Breeding Bird Surveys of golden eagles in Nebraska suggest that they are still fairly widely distributed in the western counties, with no special areas of concentration. This is not surprising, since jackrabbits and cottontails are probably important parts of the diet, but there is no attraction to localized sources of fish.

Northern Harrier, *Circus hudsonius*
An, **Ar**, Bl, Bo, **Br**, Ch, Cu, **Gar**, Gr, Gre, Grf, Ho,
Hol (H), **Ke**, **Li**, Lo, Log, Mc, Mo, Ro, **Sh**, **Th**, Wh

Status. The northern harrier is a common migrant and permanent resident throughout Nebraska. Although during cold winters most birds may leave the state, in most areas and years the species can be regarded as a resident. It is probably most common as a breeder in the Sandhills. Possible or probable breeding has recently been reported from Cherry, Custer, Garden, Grant, Hooker, Holt, McPherson, Morrill, Rock, and Thomas Counties (Mollhoff, 2016). A nest was found and chicks banded in Arthur County in 1993. The harrier breeds locally almost throughout the Great Plains states and is a regular throughout during migration. Breeding Bird Surveys between 1966 and 2015 indicate the species collectively underwent a survey-wide population decline (0.21%) annually, and Nebraska underwent an estimated 0.12 percent rate of annual increase.

Migration. Thirty-nine initial spring sightings range from January 1 to June 2, with a median of March 13. The wide spread of the records suggest this species is a resident over much of the state. Thirty-six final fall records are from September 14 to December 31, with a median of December 9.

Habitats. The northern harrier occurs in open habitats such as native grasslands, prairie marshes, and wet meadows. Nesting is done in grassy or woody vegetation ranging from upland grasses and shrubs to emergent vegetation in water more than two feet deep.

Sharp-shinned Hawk, *Accipiter striatus*
An, Ar, Bl, Bo, **Br**, Ch, Cu, Gar, Gr, Grf, Ho, Hol, Ke, Li, Lo, Log, Mc, Mo, Ro, Sh, Th, Wh

Status. The sharp-shinned hawk is an uncommon to occasional winter visitor and spring migrant throughout Nebraska. The only recent breeding records are for the northwest (Sioux County and the Niobrara River valley and Brown County), but the species may also nest along the Missouri River's forested valley. Possible recent Sandhills nesting was reported from Cherry, Holt, and Loup Counties (Mollhoff, 2016) Breeding Bird Surveys between 1966 and 2015 indicate the species collectively underwent a survey-wide population increase (0.92%) annually.

Migration. A total of 142 initial spring records range from January 1 to June 1, with a median of March 29. Half the records fall within the two periods January 1–9 and March 17–April 27, indicating that this species is probably a winter visitor and early spring migrant. Forty-one initial fall records are from July 26 to December 30, with a median of September 16. Half of the records fall within the period September 3–19. Thirty-five final fall sightings are from August 20 to December 31, with a median of November 10.

Habitats. Throughout the year, this species is associated with fairly dense forests, especially mixed woods with some coniferous trees. During winter it often enters wooded yards and hides near bird feeders to wait for possible prey. In Lincoln, nearly equal numbers of sharp-shinned and Cooper's hawks are present during winter months.

Cooper's Hawk, *Accipiter cooperii*
An, Ar, Bo, Br, **Ch**, Cu, **Gar**, Gr, Grf, Ho, Hol, Ke, Li, Lo, Log, Mo, Ro, Sh, Th, Wh

Status. The Cooper's hawk is an uncommon winter visitor and spring migrant throughout the Sandhills and a local permanent resident. Possible and probable recent nestings have also been reported from Blaine, Brown, Garfield, Holt, Lincoln, Loup, Rock, and Sheridan Counties (Mollhoff, 2016). Breeding Bird Surveys between 1966 and 2015 indicate the species collectively underwent a survey-wide population increase (2.24% annually), a trend supported by Christmas Bird Count records in recent years.

Migration. A total of 164 initial spring sightings range from January 1 to June 10, with a median of March 16. Half of the records fall within the two periods January 1–9 and March 13–April 26, suggesting that the species is a winter visitor and early spring migrant. Thirty-four initial fall records are from August 7 to December 27, with a median of September 16. Half of the records fall within the period September 4–October 1. Thirty-five final fall sightings are from September 8 to December 31, with a median of October 30.

Habitats. Throughout the year, this species is associated with mature forests, especially hardwood forests such as the Niobrara River valley, but it also breeds farther east, such as in Lincoln's city parks.

Northern Goshawk, *Accipiter gentilis*
An, Cu, Gar, Ke, Li

Status. The northern goshawk is an occasional winter visitor and spring migrant nearly statewide but especially in the Sandhills. It is probably less common now than historically, but there have been observations from Cherry and Custer Counties, according to older Nebraska Game and Parks Commission records.

Migration. Forty-eight spring records range from January 1 to June 1, with a median of March 15. Half of the records fall within the two periods January 1–11 and April 14–May 16, suggesting this species is both a winter visitor and late spring migrant. Twenty-two total fall records are from September 16 to December 31, with half of the records occurring within the two periods September 21–October 17 and December 25–31.

Habitats. Throughout the year, this species is rarely found far from wooded to heavily forested areas.

Bald Eagle, *Haliaeetus leucocephalus*
An, Ar, Bl, **Bo**, **Br**, **Ch**, **Cu**, **Gar**, Gre, **Grf**, Ho, **Hol**, **Ke**, **Li**, **Lo**, Log, **Mc**, Mo, Ro, **Sh**, Th, **Wh**

Status. The bald eagle is an uncommon spring and fall migrant and locally common winter resident in Nebraska, especially along the major rivers and reservoir areas, where nesting also occurs in the majority of the state's counties. Although it once bred regularly in eastern Nebraska, the first known modern-era nesting attempt was in 1973 in Cedar County (*Nebraska Bird Review* 41: 76). More than

200 nests have been active during recent surveys (Birds of Nebraska–Online). Breeding Bird Surveys between 1966 and 2015 indicate the species collectively underwent a survey-wide population increase (5.18% annually). Bald eagle winter populations in Nebraska have greatly increased in recent years; now an average of more than 1,000 birds winter within the state. Lake Ogallala is especially favored, with up to 300 or more birds sometimes present. Usually about 25 to 30 percent of these birds are immatures, suggesting that favorable reproduction is occurring. Even larger numbers (up to about 800) have been seen at Calamus Reservoir at the time of ice breakup and the exposure of vast numbers of winter-killed fish, especially gizzard shad (*Dorosoma*).

Migration. Sixty-five initial fall sightings range from September 16 to December 31, with a median of November 29. Half of the records fall within the period November 16–December 16. Eighty-eight final spring sightings are from January 8 to May 12, with a median of March 19. Half of the records fall within the period March 17–April 2.

Habitats. During winter, bald eagles in Nebraska use ice-free areas of larger tree-lined rivers and reservoirs where fishes are abundant or hunter-wounded waterfowl are common. Perching and nesting sites are often in tall cottonwoods near water. Adults are more likely to attack live waterfowl, whereas juveniles are more likely to scavenge from available carcasses.

Mississippi Kite, *Ictinia mississippiensis*
Ho, **Ke**, Li

Status. The Mississippi kite is rare in the Sandhills. Since 1991 Sandhills breeding attempts have occurred regularly in the city of Ogallala, Keith County (*Nebraska Bird Review* 63: 89; 65: 88–89, 164). Breeding Bird Surveys between 1966 and 2015 indicate the species collectively underwent a survey-wide population increase (0.55%) annually.

Migration. Eight total spring records are from April 15 to May 30, with a mean of May 15. Four fall records are for September 9 (two), 11, and 19. Fall records in Kansas extend to late October.

Habitats. This species is associated with scrub and open woodlands near water. Parks and golf courses are also used for nesting by these birds.

The Ogallala nestings have been in large trees in a residential area. Breeding by this attractive little kite has occurred for two decades in Ogallala but has spread only to a few new nesting locations, in spite of several broods that have been reared successfully there. The breeding range in Kansas has slowly advanced northward, so additional nesting locations in Nebraska should be expected.

Red-shouldered Hawk, *Buteo lineatus*
An, Br, Gar, Li

Rare. The red-shouldered hawk has several reports from four Sandhills counties. Three birds were seen at Crescent Lake NWR, Garden County, on May 13, 1978; May 11, 1980; and March 29, 1995. A bird was reported in Lincoln County on May 11, 2012, and August 27, 2011, and at Niobrara Valley Preserve, Brown County, on May 28, 2019. Some older records are from Lincoln County, in October 1934 and 1937, and from Antelope County in October 1898.

Broad-winged Hawk, *Buteo platypterus*
An, Bo, Br, Cu, Gar, Ke, **Li**, Sh

Status. The broad-winged hawk is an uncommon spring and fall migrant in eastern Nebraska and an occasional summer resident in the Missouri River's forested valley and the panhandle. Breeding Bird Surveys between 1966 and 2015 indicate the species had a population increase (0.9% annually) during that period. Like the red-shouldered hawk, this little woodland-nesting buteo has regionally declined in population and shows little sign of recovery. It is a highly migratory species, and like the Swainson's hawk is perhaps exposed to pesticides on its neotropical wintering grounds.

Migration. Excluding a single January record, the range of 82 initial spring sightings is from March 4 to June 6, with a median of April 26. Half of the records fall within the period April 17–May 1. Nineteen final spring sightings are from April 12 to June 8, with a median of May 15. Eleven initial fall sightings are from August 8 to October 3, with a median of September 12. Sixteen final fall sightings are from August 25 to November 19, with a median of October 5.

Habitats. This species is associated with mature deciduous forests, especially those near water, during the breeding season. Migrant birds are sometimes seen in flocks ("kettles") over open country.

Swainson's Hawk, *Buteo swainsoni*
An, **Ar**, **Bl**, **Bo**, Br, **Ch**, Cu, **Gar**, Gr, Gre, Grf, Ho, Hol, **Ke**, **Li**, Lo, **Log**, **Mc**, Mo, **Ro**, **Sh**, Th, Wh

Status. The Swainson's hawk is a common to uncommon spring and fall migrant and summer resident almost statewide, especially in the Sandhills; the eastern limit of regular breeding is probably west of a line from Gage to Burt Counties. Possible or probable breeding has been reported from most Sandhills counties (Mollhoff, 2016). The largest numbers occur during the fall migration period in late September, but none overwinter. West of about Kearney most of the buteos seen from roadsides are likely to be Swainson's hawks, whereas east of Grand Island red-tailed hawks make up nearly all the summer buteos. Breeding Bird Surveys between 1966 and 2015 indicate the species underwent a population increase (0.72% annually) during that period, and Nebraska underwent an estimated 1.64 percent rate of annual increase.

Migration. Ninety-three initial spring sightings are from January 1 to June 8, with a median of April 18. Half of the records fall within the period April 3–May 3. Sixty-five final fall sightings are from August 4 to December 27, with a median of September 26. Half of the records fall within the period September 14–October 1.

Habitats. While this species occurs in Nebraska, it is associated with open country, especially high plains and sandhills that have only scattered trees for nesting sites. This plains-adapted, largely rodent- and insect-eating hawk is still quite common in western Nebraska, although in recent years mass poisoning by pesticides on wintering areas in South America has done great regional damage to populations.

Zone-tailed Hawk, *Buteo albonotatus*
Ke

Accidental. A single Keith County report of a zone-tailed hawk was that of an individual near Cedar Point Biological Station on April 25, 2007 (Brown, Dinsmore, and Brown, 2012).

Red-tailed Hawk, *Buteo jamaicensis*
An, **Ar**, Bl, Bo, **Br**, **Ch**, **Cu**, **Gar**, Gr, **Gre**, **Grf**, Ho, **Hol**, **Ke**, **Li**, **Lo**, **Log**, Mc, **Mo**, **Ro**, **Sh**, Th, **Wh**

Status. The red-tailed hawk is an uncommon summer or permanent resident statewide, but more common eastwardly, and a common spring and fall migrant. Possible or probable breeding has been reported from most Sandhills counties (Mollhoff, 2016). It is a breeder and migrant throughout the Great Plains states. Breeding Bird Surveys between 1966 and 2015 indicate the species has undergone a population increase (1.7% annually) during that period, and Nebraska underwent an estimated 3.58 percent rate of annual increase.

Not all red-tailed hawks have rusty tails. First-year birds have a barred brown tail, and the Harlan's race, *B. j. harlani*, often has a grayish tail with little or no rufous tinting. The pale Plains-breeding Krider's hawk (*B. j. krideri*) often has a pinkish tail and is more likely to be an infrequent semi-albinistic variant of the eastern race *borealis* than a recognizable geographic subspecies. Typical Harlan's hawks are frequent wintering migrants in Nebraska, composing up to nearly 20 percent of the eastern winter population and an even higher percentage of western birds (Brown, Dinsmore, and Brown, 2012). They are believed to originate from breeding grounds in northwestern Canada or Alaska's Yukon River valley.

Migration. Thirty-two initial spring sightings of all morphs range from January 1 to May 21, with a median of March 22 and a nearly random temporal distribution, indicating that the species is essentially a permanent resident. Twenty-three final fall sightings are from September 29 to December 31, with a median of November 26. Migrants from breeding grounds farther north also move through the state during September and October

Swainson's hawk, adult with avian prey. *Photo by P. Johnsgard.*

and again in March and April, and the Harlan's morph is mostly present from October to March.

Habitats. A combination of extensive open habitat for visual hunting and scattered clumps or groves of tall trees for nesting provide the year-round needs for this species. The red-tailed hawk is the most familiar of Nebraska's buteo hawks and was listed as one of the ten most common breeding birds of Nebraska by Mollhoff (2016). Nesting is done in tall hardwoods near the edges of woodlands, and the birds are highly effective predators of rodents, rabbits, and snakes, such as bull snakes.

Ferruginous Hawk, *Buteo regalis*
Ar, Bl, Bo, Br, **Ch**, Cu, Gar, Gr, Gre, Ho, Hol, Ke, **Li**, Lo, Log, Mc, Mo, Sh, Th, Wh

Status. The ferruginous hawk is an uncommon to occasional permanent resident in the Sandhills. It is apparently migratory and a breeding summer resident in northwestern Nebraska but elsewhere is a permanent resident or winter visitor. Regular breeding once occurred west of a line from Dundy to Keya Paha Counties, and there are fairly recent records of breeding from Cherry and Lincoln Counties. Breeding Bird Surveys between 1966 and 2015 indicate the species underwent a slight population increase (0.61% annually) during that period. This is one of the very few grassland birds that has apparently managed to avoid the sharp declines in population during recent decades (Johnsgard, 2001b).

Migration. Seventy initial spring sightings range from January 1 to May 25, with a median of March 1. The wide spread of the records (half falling between January 17 and April 12) suggest that the species is essentially residential in Nebraska. Twenty final fall records are likewise widely spread between August 26 and December 31.

Habitats. While in Nebraska, this species is normally found in grassland habitats that have scattered trees or steep buttes or bluffs for nesting sites. This majestic buteo is almost the size of an eagle, and like the golden eagle it is able to prey very effectively on prairie dogs (a favorite) and rabbits. It has a broad gape that allows it to swallow small rodents whole.

Rough-legged Hawk, *Buteo lagopus*
An, Ar, Bl, Bo, Br, Cu, Gar, Gr, Gre, Grf, Ho, Hol, Ke, Li, Lo, Log, Mc, Mo, Ro, Sh, Th, Wh

Status. The rough-legged hawk is an uncommon migrant and winter visitor statewide, becoming more common westwardly. It also occurs throughout the entire Great Plains region.

Migration. Eighty-five initial fall records range from September 30 to December 30, with a median of November 2. Half of the records fall within the period October 9–November 22. A total of 73 final spring sightings range from January 8 to May 20, with a median of March 26. Half of the records fall within the period March 10–April 12.

Habitats. Open prairies, plains, and other grassland habitats are used while on migration and during wintering in the Plains states.

Tytonidae (Barn Owls)

Barn Owl, *Tyto alba*
An, Ch, Cu, **Ga**, **Ke**, **Li**, Sh

Status. The barn owl is an uncommon permanent resident statewide but is probably more common in the Sandhills. Breeding Bird Surveys between 1966 and 2015 indicate the species underwent a population increase (0.61% annually) during that period.

Habitats. Open to semi-open habitats, where small rodents are abundant and where hollow trees, old buildings, or caves are available to provide roosting and nesting sites are used by this species. Rats are a favored prey species, but many other rodents are also consumed. Barn owls are rodent catchers without peer, and the presence of a pair at a farm or ranch may account for the disappearance of several thousand mice or rats per year. They are thus highly valuable birds, although farmers often seem unaware of their presence or, if aware, may actually try to kill them. Near Cedar Point Biological Station in Keith County, the nesting birds concentrate on pocket mice and kangaroo rats for prey but in turn are preyed upon by great horned owls.

Ferruginous hawk, adult with prairie rattlesnake

Family Strigidae (Typical Owls)

Eastern Screech-Owl, *Megascops asio*
An, Ar, **Bl**, Bo, **Br**, **Ch**, Cu, Gar, Gr, Gre, Grf, Hol, Ke, **Li**, **Lo**, Log, Mc, Mo, Ro, **Sh**, Th, Wh

Status. The eastern screech-owl is a common permanent resident in wooded areas throughout the state but is rare or absent from treeless areas. Possible or probable recent breeding was reported from Antelope, Arthur, Garden, Holt, Loup, Rock, and Thomas Counties (Mollhoff, 2016). There are no Nebraska records of the western species *M. kennicottii*. Breeding Bird Surveys between 1966 and 2015 indicate the species underwent a national population decline (1.27% annually) during that period.

Habitats. This widespread species occurs in a variety of wooded habitats, including farmyards, cities, orchards, and other human-made habitats, as well as in forests and woodlands. It is probably more common in cities than in heavy woodlands, where it is preyed upon by larger owls. Screech-owls often go unnoticed in places where they are common; the whinny-like call these birds utter is not very owl-like, and they hide during daylight hours in tree cavities. In eastern Nebraska about 90 percent of the birds are gray morph plumage types, with the remainder rufous or intermediate in plumage color; farther west the rufous morph is even rarer. Eastwardly, the rufous morph is progressively more common and is thought to be better camouflaged in the floristically diverse eastern deciduous forests, whereas the gray morph is visually better camouflaged in the less colorful coniferous forests to the west and north (Johnsgard 2002b).

Great Horned Owl, *Bubo virginianus*
An, **Ar**, Bl, Bo, **Br**, Ch, Cu, **Gar**, **Gr**, Gre, Grf, **Ho**, **Hol**, **Ke**, **Li**, Lo, Log, Mc, **Mo**, Ro, **Sh**, Th, Wh

Status. The great horned owl is an uncommon permanent resident statewide but probably most common in the heavily wooded major river valleys and the Pine Ridge region. It is locally common in the Sandhills, where it breeds in old raptor nests and uses old earthen barn owl cavities in cutbanks. Possible or probable breeding is also reported from most Sandhills counties, except Blaine and Logan Counties (Mollhoff, 2016). Breeding Bird Surveys between 1966 and 2015 indicate the species underwent an estimated 0.81 percent rate of annual decline, and Nebraska underwent an estimated 0.59 percent rate of annual decline.

Habitats. This highly adaptable and widespread species occurs in a variety of habitat types ranging from dense forests to city parks and farm woodlands and even nonwooded environments in rocky canyons and gullies. Second only to the eastern screech-owl, it is one of the state's two most abundant and widespread owls, with few if any more powerful enemies.

Snowy Owl, *Bubo scandiacus*
An, Bo, Br, Ch, Grf, Hol, Ke, Li, Ro

Status. The snowy owl is an occasional winter visitor, not present every winter but sporadically occurring almost anywhere in the state. Only during occasional winters do snowy owls enter Nebraska in any numbers; this probably occurs during high population of lemmings in the Arctic, when the excessive numbers of young birds must wander south to find adequate food. More than 200 were reported in Nebraska during the major invasion of 2011–12 (*Nebraska Bird Review* 80: 72–76).

Migration. This winter visitor shows a range in 18 initial fall sightings from November 6 to December 29, with a median of December 4. Twenty-three final spring sightings are from January 3 to April 30, with a median of February 5.

Habitats. Wintering birds are usually associated with open fields, plains, marshes, and grassy lowlands, often perching on haystacks or other somewhat elevated sites. The birds are highly conspicuous where snow is absent from the landscape, and many snowy owls are then shot by ignorant hunters. Most of the birds arrive in near-starving condition, and probably few survive to return back north the following spring.

Great horned owl, adult incubating. *Photo by P. Johnsgard.*

Burrowing Owl, *Athene cunicularia*
An, Ar, Bl, **Ch**, Cu, **Gar**, Gr, Gre, Hol, **Ke**, Li, **Lo**, Log, Mc, Mo, **Ro**, **Sh**, Th

Status. The burrowing owl is a common to uncommon spring and fall migrant and summer resident in western and central Nebraska, especially in the panhandle region where tunneling rodents provide nesting cavities. Possible or probable recent breeding was reported from Arthur, Brown, and Logan Counties (Mollhoff, 2016). Breeding Bird Surveys between 1966 and 2015 indicate the species underwent a national population decline (0.98% annually) during that period, and Nebraska underwent an estimated 0.85 percent rate of annual decline. Partly because of state laws that require the control of prairie dogs on private land, the numbers of both prairie dogs and burrowing owls have plummeted in recent decades, and there are only a few places left in Nebraska (such as Fort Niobrara NWR) where these fascinating little owls can be readily observed. Prairie dogs are not common in the Sandhills except on lowland sites that have organic-rich soils able to support tunnel systems without collapsing, so burrowing owls are more likely to be found in grassy lowland meadows than on uplands.

Migration. The range of 119 initial spring sightings is from March 10 to June 10, with a median of April 24. Half of the records fall within the period April 13–May 9. Forty-three final fall sightings are from July 21 to November 9, with a median of September 16. Half of the records fall within the period August 30–September 30.

Habitats. This species is normally associated with heavily grazed grasslands, especially those that support colonies of large rodents such as prairie dogs, whose abandoned burrows are used for nesting. Normally colonial, scattered nestings may also occur by individual pairs where suitable excavations or natural cavities are available. Unlike most owls, the birds are daytime feeders, and they also are mostly insect eaters, at least while they are in Nebraska. Johnsgard (2006) and Desmond (1991) described the symbiotic relationships between prairie dogs and burrowing owls in Nebraska.

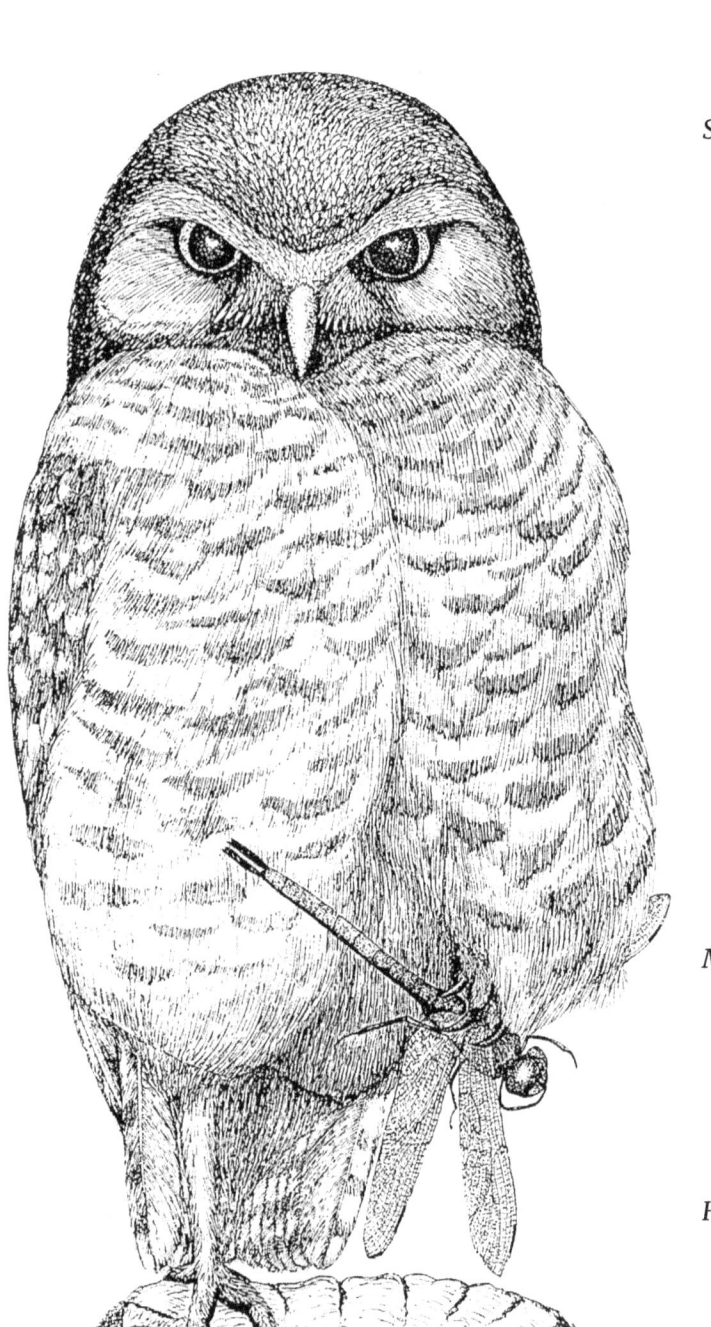

Burrowing owl, adult with darner dragonfly

Burrowing owl, adult. *Photo by P. Johnsgard.*

Barred Owl, *Strix varia*
An, Bo, Hol, Li

Status. The barred owl is very rare in the Sandhills region. It is an uncommon permanent resident in southeastern Nebraska, becoming rarer westwardly and absent from the western half of the state except along a few well-wooded forest corridors. Breeding Bird Surveys between 1966 and 2015 indicate the species underwent a national population increase (1.63% annually) during that period.

Habitats. Throughout the year, this species is found in dense riverbottom woods, which in Nebraska are typically hardwoods; however, coniferous forests are also used when they are available.

Long-eared Owl, *Asio otus*
An, Bo, Br, Ch, **Ke**, Lo, Mc, **Sh**, Th

Status. The long-eared owl is a permanent resident in wooded areas (such as major river valleys) throughout the state, uncommon in the east and becoming rarer westwardly. It is local in the Sandhills.

Migration. Twenty-four spring sightings range from January 2 to May 14, with a median of March 9. Nineteen fall sightings are from July 21 to December 31, with a median of November 24. These limited data suggest that the species is a summer resident and a late fall and early spring migrant, with frequent overwintering.

Habitats. Throughout the year, this species is associated with wooded areas, including riverbottom forests, parks, orchards, and woodlots. Both coniferous and hardwood woodlands are utilized, with the former apparently preferred, such as in mature and dense shelterbelts.

Short-eared Owl, *Asio flammeus*
An, Ch, Cu, Gar, Hol, Ke, Li, Lo, Mc, Sh

Status. The short-eared owl is a permanent resident throughout Nebraska, more common during summer in the Sandhills and other natural grasslands. Probable recent nesting has been reported from Garden and Sheridan Counties (Mollhoff, 2016). During winter the population is apparently supplemented by migrants from farther north. Breeding Bird Surveys between 1966 and 2015 indicate the species underwent a national population decline (0.89% annually) during that period, and Nebraska underwent an estimated 4.08 percent rate of annual decline.

Migration. Thirty-five spring sightings range from January 8 to June 6, with a median of March 12. Twenty-nine fall sightings are from July 20 to December 31, with a median of November 30. The data are very similar to those of the long-eared owl, suggesting that the species is a summer resident and a late fall and early spring migrant, with frequent overwintering.

Habitats. Throughout the year, this species is found in open, grass-dominated environments, and in Nebraska the Sandhills and other natural grasslands are favored habitats. Nesting usually occurs in grassy cover, with several pairs often nesting fairly close to one another in a loose colonial situation.

Northern Saw-whet Owl, *Aegolius acadicus*
An, **Ch**, **Gar**, Ke, Li, Sh, **Th**

Status. The northern saw-whet owl is an uncommon to rare winter visitor, at least in eastern Nebraska and perhaps statewide. But a newly fledged juvenile was found as a roadkill in Antelope County in late May 2002 (*Nebraska Bird Review* 70: 63). Nesting has recently been proven to occur in Garden and Cherry Counties, and territorial birds have been reported from Sheridan, Lincoln, and Keith Counties (Mollhoff, 2016).

Migration. Ten fall records are from July 29 to December 22, with a median of November 8. Seven spring records are from January 1 to May 16, with a median of February 20. These and other limited data suggest that the species is primarily a winter visitor. In northwestern Nebraska it is reportedly a rare summer resident, arriving as early as April 18 (Rosche, 1982).

Habitats. Although normally associated with rather dense woods, especially cedar groves in Nebraska, this species sometimes appears in unexpected locations during migration. In the Black Hills of South Dakota, it breeds in pine and spruce forests, and the same is true in the Pine Ridge region, where only ponderosa pines are present.

KINGFISHERS · WOODPECKERS

Family Alcedinidae (Kingfishers)

Belted Kingfisher, *Megaceryle alcyon*
An, **Bl**, Bo, **Br**, Ch, Cu, Gar, Gr, Gre, Grf, **Ho**, Hol, **Ke**, **Li**, Lo, Log, Mo, Ro, **Sh**, **Th**, Wh

Status. The belted kingfisher is a common spring and fall migrant and summer resident statewide in suitable habitats and an uncommon winter resident where open water persists. Probable recent nesting was reported from Antelope, Boone, Cherry, Garden, Garfield, Holt, Loup, Rock, and Wheeler Counties (Mollhoff, 2016). Breeding Bird Surveys between 1966 and 2015 indicate the species underwent a national population decline (1.5% annually) during that period.

Migration. Forty-three initial spring sightings range from January 2 to May 10, with a median of March 20. Half of the records fall within the period February 14–April 10. Forty-seven final fall sightings are from July 26 to December 31, with a median of November 15. The concentration of fall records toward the end of the year (nearly half occurring in December) suggest that the species overwinters frequently.

Habitats. Throughout the year, this species occurs near water areas that support populations of fish, amphibians, and other aquatic life. Nests are excavated in nearly vertical earth exposures in bluffs, roadcuts, eroded stream banks, and the like. The belted kingfisher is Nebraska's only representative of this large and diverse family of mostly fish-eating birds (although the smallest kingfishers are largely insectivorous and the largest are omnivorous).

Family Picidae (Woodpeckers)

Lewis's Woodpecker, *Melanerpes lewis*
Ch (Valentine NWR), Gr (NOU website checklist), Ke, Lo, **Sh**

Status. Lewis's woodpecker is a rare summer resident in the Pine Ridge region and an extremely rare breeder in Sheridan County. During fall, winter, and spring it sometimes occurs elsewhere in northwestern Nebraska.

Red-headed Woodpecker, *Melanerpes erythrocephalus*
An, Ar, **Bl**, **Bo**, Br, **Ch**, **Cu**, **Gar**, Gr, Gre, **Grf**, Ho, **Hol**, **Ke**, **Li**, **Lo**, **Log**, Mc, Mo, **Ro**, **Sh**, Th, **Wh**

Status. The red-headed woodpecker is a common spring and fall migrant and summer resident nearly statewide but more common eastwardly. It is distinctly migratory and only very infrequently overwinters in the state. Breeding Bird Surveys between 1966 and 2015 indicate the species underwent a national population decline (2.35% annually) during that period, and Nebraska underwent an estimated 1.33 percent rate of annual decline. Possible or probable recent nesting has been reported from most Sandhills counties (Mollhoff, 2016).

Migration. Ninety-eight initial spring sightings are from January 2 to June 9, with a median of May 7. Half of the records fall within the period April 28–May 17. The range of 106 final fall sightings is from August 8 to December 31. Half of the records fall within the period September 8–October 3. Less than 10 percent of the fall records are for December, suggesting that this species only rarely overwinters. Presumably its relatively high dependence on aerial insects accounts for this species' migration tendencies, as compared with most other more adaptable Nebraska woodpeckers.

Acorn Woodpecker, *Melanerpes formicivorus*
Hol

Accidental. A single bird was observed at a feeder at Chambers, Holt County, between May 19 and 22, 1996 (Silcock and Jorgensen, various dates).

Red-bellied Woodpecker, *Melanerpes carolinus*
An, Ar, Bl, Bo, Br, Ch, Gar, **Gre**, Grf, Ho, HoL, **Ke**, **Li**, Lo, Log, Mo, Ro, Sh, Th, Wh

Status. The red-bellied woodpecker is a common permanent resident in eastern Nebraska, extending westward along the major river systems, at least in the Sandhills to the Valentine area of Cherry County in the Niobrara valley and to Garden County in the Platte valley. Possible recent nesting has been reported from Antelope, Boone, Brown, Cherry, Custer, Garden, Holt, and Rock Counties (Mollhoff, 2016). Breeding Bird Surveys between

1966 and 2015 indicate the species underwent a population increase (1.02% annually) during that period and is increasing in Nebraska, with an estimated 5.12 percent annual upward rate.

Habitats. Throughout the year, this species occupies somewhat open stands of coniferous or hardwood forests, often riverbottom forests. It also frequents orchards, gardens, and similar urban or suburban areas.

Yellow-bellied Sapsucker, *Sphyrapicus varius*
An, Br, Ch, Cu, Grf, Hol, Ho, Ke, Li, Lo, Wh

Status. The yellow-bellied sapsucker is an uncommon spring and fall migrant in eastern Nebraska, becoming rarer westwardly. It is an occasional to uncommon winter visitor, perhaps statewide.

Migration. Thirty-four initial fall sightings are from September 1 to December 30, with a median of October 3. Twenty-five final fall sightings are from October 9 to December 31, with a median of December 18. Sixteen initial springs sightings are from January 1 to May 28, with a median of March 14. Fourteen final spring sightings are from January 9 to May 21, with a median of March 23. These data would suggest that this species is a very late fall migrant, frequently overwintering in the state, and remaining in Sandhills counties for a rather variable period in spring.

Habitats. While in Nebraska this species is associated with various woodlands, especially those containing poplars or aspens, which are favored foraging trees. However, it also drills foraging holes in birches, maples, cottonwoods, apple trees, and junipers but only infrequently in such hardwoods as oaks and hackberries. Yellow-bellied sapsuckers are among the few woodpeckers that would rather drink the sugar-rich sap of trees than capture insects, and they are very efficient at excavating equally spaced holes in relatively soft-wooded trees such poplars and birches to extract sap. Sapsucker-drilled trees often attract other sugar-loving species too, such as hummingbirds and flying squirrels.

Red-naped Sapsucker, *Sphyrapicus nuchalis*
Br, Gar, Ke

Very rare. An individual red-naped sapsucker was observed at Lake Ogallala, Keith County, October 26–November 2, 2000 (Brown, Dinsmore, and Brown, 2012). Two other records are from Brown County, September 15–16, 2018, and Garden County, where a male was photographed at Ash Hollow State Historical Park on March 23, 2020 (Silcock and Jorgensen, various dates).

Downy Woodpecker, *Dryobates pubescens*
An, Ar, Bl, **Bo**, **Br**, **Ch**, **Cu**, Gar, Gr, Gre, Grf, Ho, **Hol**, **Ke**, Li, **Lo**, Log, Mc, Mo, Ro, **Sh**, Th, Wh

Status. The downy woodpecker is a common permanent resident statewide, occupying essentially the same habitats as the hairy woodpecker, but it is somewhat more common than that species. Possible nesting was also reported from Antelope, Blaine, Garden, Hooker, Lincoln, Logan, Rock, and Thomas Counties (Mollhoff, 2016). Breeding Bird Surveys between 1966 and 2015 indicate the species underwent a national population increase (0.03% annually) during that period, and Nebraska underwent an estimated 0.27 percent rate of annual increase.

Habitats. Throughout the year, this species is found in dense or open forests but also in cities in parks, gardens, and the like. Besides foraging in smaller trees and the smaller branches of large trees, it also sometimes visits shrubs and tall weeds. Downy woodpeckers are perhaps the commonest of Nebraska's woodpeckers, and the nesting holes they drill provide potential nesting sites for many other cavity-dependent birds, such as bluebirds, tree swallows, chickadees, and nuthatches. In locations where it competes with hairy woodpeckers, the downys concentrate their foraging on smaller branches and twigs, or even on shrubs or weeds that are able to support their weight. Woodpeckers probably help protect many tree species from boring beetle infestations, and so they fully deserve our protection.

Hairy Woodpecker, *Dryobates villosus*
An, Ar, Bl, Bo, Br, **Ch**, Cu, Gar, Gre, Grf, Ho, Hol, Ke, Li, Lo, Log, Mc, Mo, **Ro**, **Sh**, **Th**, Wh

Status. The hairy woodpecker is a common permanent resident statewide in suitable wooded habitats. Possible and probable recent nestings have also been reported from Blain, Brown, Custer, Garden, Holt, Keith, Lincoln, Loup, Thomas, and Wheeler

Counties (Mollhoff, 2016). Breeding Bird Surveys between 1966 and 2015 indicate the species underwent a slight population increase (0.81% annually) during that period.

Habitats. Throughout the year, this species prefers fairly extensive areas of coniferous or deciduous forest, or streamside groves of trees. Although sometimes seen in urban areas, the species more commonly remains in mature forests, especially hardwood forests, where it forages on the trunks and larger branches. Hairy woodpeckers have substantially longer and more robust beaks than do downy woodpeckers, so they can drill deeper into wood. They also excavate somewhat larger nest cavities, which eventually get used by other cavity-nesting species. Records from the Nebraska breeding bird atlasing project suggest that the hairy woodpecker is about half as common as the downy woodpecker in Nebraska (Mollhoff, 2016). The hairy's distribution in the state may be more closely associated with the larger river valleys, where large trees are more abundant.

Northern Flicker, *Colaptes auratus*
An, **Ar**, **Bl**, Bo, **Br**, **Ch**, **Cu**, **Gar**, Gr, **Gre**, **Grf**, Ho, **Hol**, **Ke**, **Li**, **Lo**, Log, Mc, Mo, **Ro**, **Sh**, Th, **Wh**

Status. The northern flicker is a common permanent resident statewide. In eastern Nebraska the population is predominantly of the yellow-shafted race or hybrids, with typical red-shafted types found only in extreme western Nebraska (Short, 1961). Possible and probable recent nestings have been also reported from most Sandhills counties (Mollhoff, 2016). Probably most of the Nebraska population is influenced by hybridization; many intermediate-appearing birds can be seen in the Sandhills region. Breeding Bird Surveys between 1966 and 2015 indicate the species underwent a national population decline (1.33% annually) during that period.

Habitats. Throughout the year this species occupies diverse habitats, including relatively open woodlands, orchards, woodlots, and urban environments. Dense forests are apparently avoided, and much foraging is done by probing in the ground. To a greater degree than other Nebraska woodpeckers, this is an ant-eating species, and because of that flickers often forage in fields well away from woodlands. Although essentially sedentary, some movement out of the state occurs during most winters.

Family Falconidae (Falcons and Caracaras)

American Kestrel, *Falco sparverius*
An, Ar, **Bl**, Bo, **Br**, **Ch**, Cu, **Gar**, Gr, Gre, Grf, Ho, **Hol**, Ke, **Li**, **Lo**, **Log**, Mc, **Ro**, **Sh**, Th, **Wh**

Status. The American kestrel is a common permanent resident statewide. It is less common in winter and more abundant during spring and fall, so substantial migration must occur. Possible and probable recent nestings have also been reported from most Sandhills counties (Mollhoff, 2016). Breeding Bird Surveys between 1966 and 2015 indicate the species underwent a national population decline (1.39% annually) during that period.

Migration. Twenty-nine spring records and 22 fall records are widely scattered, suggesting that the species is largely residential in Nebraska.

Habitats. Open country with elevated perching sites such as telephone lines or scattered trees are used throughout the year, and nesting is usually done in tree hollows near large areas of grasslands or croplands. These falcons often choose old woodpecker cavities for nest sites but also nest in artificial cavities. Once called the "sparrow hawk" because of their small size, kestrels feed largely on grasshoppers and other large insects during summer but turn to small mammals and other prey in cold weather.

Merlin, *Falco columbarius*
An, Bl, Bo, Br, Ch, Cu, Gar, Grf, Gr, Gre, Hol, Ho, Ke, Li, Log, Lo, Mc, Mo, Ro, Sh, Th, Wh

Status. The merlin is an uncommon migrant and winter visitor statewide, and an extremely rare summer resident in the Pine Ridge area. Breeding Bird Surveys between 1966 and 2015 indicate the species underwent a national population increase (2.63% annually) during that period.

Migration. Ninety-nine initial spring sightings range from January 1 to June 6, with a median of March 19. Half of the records fall within the two periods January 1–20 and March 30–April 24, suggesting that the species is primarily a winter visitor and spring migrant. Forty-eight fall records extend from August 16 to December 31, with a median of October 23. The largest number of fall records are for December (21), followed by September (15) and October (7).

Habitats. Open country with elevated perches such as telephone lines or scattered trees are used throughout the year, and nesting is typically in scattered trees or groves near large areas of grasslands, croplands, or badlands.

Gyrfalcon, *Falco rusticolus*
Gar, Ch, Ke, Li, Mo, Th

Status. The gyrfalcon is a rarely seen but probably regular winter visitor in the Sandhills. There are Sandhills county sight records from Keith County (1947), Lincoln County (1975), and Garden County (1979) (Brogie, 1997). It is a rare or accidental winter migrant in the Lake McConaughy region (Brown, Dinsmore, and Brown, 2012). There have also been periodic Sandhills captures of gyrfalcons by falconers.

Migration. Eight total records for this rare species range from November 27 to March 3: three records for January, two for December, and one each for November, February, and March.

Habitats. Open plains and prairies are used during migration and while wintering. This is the bird most prized by falconers for their sport; gyrfalcons have been trained to kill birds as large as great bustards (*Otis tarda*) and will readily attack pheasants or large waterfowl. In the Sandhills, sharp-tailed grouse are apparently major prey. The species exhibits a broad array of color morphs, ranging from nearly pure white to dusky gray. The paler-plumaged birds are from high-latitude Arctic breeding populations.

Peregrine Falcon, *Falco peregrinus*
An, Bl, Ch, Gar, Grf, Ke, Li, Log, Ro, Sh

Status. The peregrine falcon is a rare to occasional migrant and winter visitor statewide and a recent local breeder. Recovery programs in Omaha and Lincoln have produced several successful nestings in both locations during recent years, and Sandhills sightings are uncommon. Breeding Bird Surveys between 1966 and 2015 indicate the species underwent a national population increase (2.77% annually) during that period.

Migration. A total of 97 initial spring sightings range from January 1 to May 17, with a median of March 20. Half of the records fall within two periods January 1–20 and April 21–May 11, suggesting that the species is a winter visitor and spring migrant. Twenty total fall records extend from July 26 to December 26, with a median of September 22. The largest number of fall records (8) is for September, but the sample is too small to suggest a peak period.

Habitats. During migration this species is most likely to be found in open, grassland habitats, but it sometimes enters cities while hunting pigeons, and city-nesting peregrines are also efficient pigeon hunters. In Lincoln, peregrines breeding on the capitol have even been seen hunting at night, using light from the capitol dome to locate roosting prey.

Prairie Falcon, *Falco mexicanus*
An, Bl, Bo, Br, **Ch**, Cu, **Gar**, Gr, **Ke**, Li, Lo, Log, Mc, Mo, Ro, **Sh**, Th, Wh

Status. The prairie falcon is an occasional to rare permanent resident in western Nebraska, with sightings throughout the Sandhills region. It is a rare and local breeder in the panhandle, with Sandhills nesting records for Cherry, Garden, Keith, and Sheridan Counties. Breeding Bird Surveys between 1966 and 2015 indicate the species underwent a national population increase (1.05% annually) during that period.

Migration. A total of 135 initial spring sightings range from January 1 to May 22, with a median of January 30. Half of the records fall within the period January 1–30, suggesting that the species is primarily a resident and winter visitor, with no obvious secondary peak of spring migration. Forty-five fall records extend from July 21 to December 31, with a median of November 13 and no obvious fall peak in records. There is a progressively smaller number of monthly records from December backward to July.

Habitats. This species is associated with large expanses of open grasslands or sagebrush scrub, with nearby cliffs, bluffs, or rocky outcrops for nesting.

Prairie falcon with young and a green-winged teal

Family Tyrannidae (Tyrant Flycatchers)

Olive-sided Flycatcher, *Contopus cooperi*
An, Bo, Br, Cu, Gre, Ke, Li, Sh

Status. The olive-sided flycatcher is an uncommon to occasional spring and fall migrant in eastern Nebraska. Farther west and in the Sandhills region the species is less common, but it probably migrates statewide.

Migration. Sixty-eight initial spring sightings range from April 3 to June 4, with a median of May 18. Half of the records fall within the period May 10–26. Sixteen final spring sightings are from May 10 to June 8, with a median of May 24. Thirteen initial fall sightings are from August 24 to September 9, with a median of September 2. Twelve final fall sightings are from September 1 to September 29, with a median of September 20.

Habitats. Migrants are found in wooded areas where there are trees with prominent dead upper branches; they sometimes also perch on telephone wires in open country.

Western Wood-Pewee, *Contopus sordidulus*
Ar, **Ch**, **Gar**, Gr, **Ke**, Li, Log, Mo, **Sh**, Th

Status. The western wood-pewee is a common spring and fall migrant and summer resident in western and northwestern Nebraska; the Sandhills breeding range probably extends east to at least Garden County. Possible nesting was also reported from Lincoln County (Mollhoff, 2016). Hybridization possibly occurs in areas of contact with *C. virens*. Singing has been heard east to Brown and Keya Paha Counties in the Niobrara River valley (*Nebraska Bird Review* 71: 119, 76: 195), and both species occur in Keith County along the North Platte River valley (*Nebraska Bird Review* 76: 105). Breeding Bird Surveys between 1966 and 2015 indicate the species underwent a national population decline (1.37% annually) during that period.

Migration. Sixty-four initial spring sightings range from March 20 to June 10, with a median of May 21. Half of the records fall within the period May 13–26. Thirty-three final fall sightings are from July 8 to October 9, with a median of September 4. Half of the records fall within the period August 22–September 12.

Habitats. In the Black Hills, and probably in the Pine Ridge region, this species is mostly associated with open mature pine forests. Generally the birds use habitats dominated by conifers, but they also use mixed woodlands and generally occupy drier areas than do eastern wood-pewees. Although the two wood-pewees differ in the color of their lower mandibles and have slightly differing plumage hues, it is probably easier to recognize this species by its distinctive somewhat raspy *pee-err* vocalization.

Eastern Wood-Pewee, *Contopus virens*
An, **Br**, **Ch**, Cu, Grf, **Hol**, **Ke**, Li, **Lo**, **Ro**, Sh, Wh

Status. The eastern wood-pewee is a common spring and fall migrant and summer resident in eastern Nebraska, extending west locally in the Sandhills at least as far as Cherry and Keith Counties along river systems. Possible recent nesting has also been reported from Antelope, Custer, and McPherson Counties (Mollhoff, 2016).

Migration. Seventy-seven initial spring sightings range from March 20 to June 10, with a median of May 10. Half of the records fall within the period May 3–21. Sixty-one final fall sightings are from July 29 to October 12, with a median of September 10. Half of the records fall within the period August 31–September 18. Breeding Bird Surveys between 1966 and 2015 indicate the species underwent a national population decline (1.60% annually) during that period.

Habitats. While in Nebraska this species is generally associated with deciduous forests, including floodplain and river bluff forests, but it also occurs in woodlots, orchards, and suburban areas with tree plantings. Over most of Nebraska the wood-pewees seen are most likely to be the eastern species, whose song is a distinctive *pee-a-wee*. However, in the panhandle and western Niobrara River valley, birders should be on the alert for possible western wood-pewees.

Yellow-bellied Flycatcher, *Empidonax flaviventris*
Bo, Gar, Ke

Very rare. The yellow-bellied flycatcher is reported as a rare spring Sandhills transient in May and June. A single August sighting was made at Cedar Point Biological Station, Keith County (Brown, Dinsmore, and Brown, 2012). The latest fall record from Lake Ogallala, Keith County, is from September 3, 2019. Another single record is from Crescent Lake NWR, Garden County, on June 3, 2001, and a specimen was collected in Albion, Boone County, on September 13, 1982 (Silcock and Jorgensen, various dates).

Acadian Flycatcher, *Empidonax virescens*
Ch, Ke

Accidental. Four Acadian flycatchers banded at Cedar Point Biological Station, Keith County, in late May 1994 were identified as this species by wing measurements (Brown, Dinsmore, and Brown, 2012). A specimen was collected in Cherry County on May 29, 1932 (Silcock and Jorgensen, various dates).

Alder Flycatcher, *Empidonax alnorum*
An, Ch, Cu, Ke

Status. The alder flycatcher apparently is a regular but occasional migrant in Nebraska, at least in spring. The small proportion of sightings attributed to this species since it was separated from *E. traillii* suggest that it must be quite infrequent by comparison. However, it has been reported to possibly breed in southeastern South Dakota, so it should be looked for in Nebraska. Breeding Bird Surveys between 1966 and 2015 indicate the alder/willow flycatcher complex underwent a national population decline (1.2% annually) during that period. Brown et al. (1996) considered the alder flycatcher a common migrant in the general Keith County area May 22–June 2; an amazing 62 were banded there over four years during spring and fall (Silcock and Jorgensen, various dates).

Migration. Eight initial spring sightings attributed to this species range from May 8 to May 29, with a mean of May 21. Six final spring sightings are from May 24 to June 18, with a mean of June 7. Six fall sightings range from July 20 to September 16, with a mean of August 19.

Habitats. Migrants probably use the same habitats as does the willow flycatcher, namely shrubbery and small trees near openings of grassland or water. While breeding it generally occupies the more northerly and easterly forested areas, compared with the more open and arid habitats of the willow flycatcher. This flycatcher is too little known in Nebraska to say much about it. However, 92 of 203 "Traill's flycatchers" banded in the Platte River valley by Dr. William Scharf were identified as alders. Thus, the species may be a much more regular migrant through Nebraska than is now appreciated.

Willow Flycatcher, *Empidonax traillii*
An, **Bl**, Bo, **Br**, **Ch**, Cu, Gar, Gre, Grf, **Ho**, **Hol**, **Ke**, **Li**, **Lo**, **Log**, **Mc**, **Ro**, Sh, **Th**, Wh

Status. The willow flycatcher is a common spring and fall migrant and uncommon to rare summer resident in eastern Nebraska. Breeding extends west at least to Cherry, Thomas, and Keith Counties in the Sandhills and to Sheridan County in the panhandle. Possible nesting was also reported from most Sandhills counties except Arthur and Grant Counties (Mollhoff, 2016). Breeding Bird Surveys between 1966 and 2015 indicate the alder/willow flycatcher complex underwent a national population decline (1.48% annually) during that period.

Migration. Seventy-eight initial spring sightings range from April 17 to June 10, with a median of May 15. Half of the records fall within the period May 9–25. Sixteen final fall sightings range from July 26 to September 21, with a median of September 2. Half of the records fall within the period August 29–September 7.

Habitats. In Nebraska this species uses edge habitats, such as thickets or groves of small trees and shrubs surrounded by grasslands and the edges of gallery forests along rivers. Probably this bird is the most common and widespread of Nebraska's *Empidonax* species, although in appearance it is extremely similar to the alder flycatcher.

Least Flycatcher, *Empidonax minimus*
An, Bo, Br, Ch, Cu, Gar, Grf, Gr, Hol, Ke, Li, Mo, Sh, Th

Status. The least flycatcher is a common spring and fall migrant statewide and possibly an extremely rare summer resident. Territorial birds have been reported in Brown County. Thus, northern Nebraska possibly constitutes part of the breeding range, but there were no confirmed breedings during the atlasing years (Mollhoff, 2001, 2016). Breeding Bird Surveys between 1966 and 2015 indicate the species underwent a national population decline (1.71% annually) during that period.

Migration. The range of 100 initial spring sightings is from April 7 to June 9, with a median of May 8. Half of the records fall within the period May 3–11. Sixteen final spring sightings are from May 3 to June 3, with a median of May 14. Twenty-four fall sightings range from July 29 to October 1, with a median of September 5. Half of the records fall within the period August 30–September 12.

Habitats. While in Nebraska this species occupies floodplain forests in grassland areas, scattered grovelands, shelterbelts, and urban parks or gardens. This flycatcher is the smallest of the Nebraska *Empidonax* species, but in the field this size difference is not apparent.

Dusky Flycatcher, *Empidonax oberholseri*
Ke, Mo

Accidental. There are three Sandhills records of the dusky flycatcher from two counties: a bird at Mud Springs, Morrill County, on September 11, 2000, and two documented records from Lake McConaughy, Keith County, on April 30, 2018, and October 8, 2019 (Silcock and Jorgensen, various dates).

Hammond's Flycatcher, *Empidonax hammondii*
Gar, Ke, Li

Very rare. Single Hammond's flycatchers have been seen during September at Lake Ogallala and Ash Hollow State Historical Park, Keith and Garden Counties (Brown, Dinsmore, and Brown, 2012). Two records are from Crescent Lake NWR, Garden County, from May 13, 2006, and May 30, 2009. A single record is from Lincoln County on September 27, 2018 (Silcock and Jorgensen, various dates).

Cordilleran Flycatcher, *Empidonax occidentalis*
Ch (Valentine NWR checklist), Gar (Crescent Lake NWR checklist), **Sh**

Status. The Cordilleran flycatcher is an occasional or local migrant and summer resident in northwestern Nebraska. It has also been observed in Garden, McPherson, and Sheridan Counties. This species probably breeds throughout the Pine Ridge, east to Metcalf Wildlife Management Area, Sheridan County, where nest building was observed on July 20, 2011—which is the easternmost breeding location known to date (Silcock and Jorgensen, various dates).

Migration. Five fall records are all in the period August 9–September 10 (*Nebraska Bird Review* 65: 167).

Habitats. While breeding, this species is associated with forested canyons and mountain slopes, but on migration it may occur in deciduous trees along streambeds, oak-lined gullies, and other wooded habitats.

Eastern Phoebe, *Sayornis phoebe*
An, **Bl**, Bo, **Br**, **Ch**, **Cu**, Gar, Gre, **Grf**, Ho, **Hol**, Ke, **Li**, **Lo**, Log, Mc, **Ro**, **Sh**, **Th**, **Wh**

Status. The eastern phoebe is a common spring and fall migrant and summer resident in woodlands of eastern Nebraska, extending west locally in the Sandhills to Thomas, Lincoln, and Garden Counties along the major river valleys. Possible nesting was also reported from Hooker and Keith Counties (Mollhoff, 2016). Breeding Bird Surveys between 1966 and 2015 indicate this species underwent a national population increase (0.22% annually) during that period.

Migration. The range of 169 initial spring sightings is from March 20 to June 10, with a median of April 16. Half of the records fall within the period March 28–April 29. Sixty-seven final fall sightings range from August 4 to October 25, with a median of September 26. Half of the records fall within the period September 5–October 6.

Habitats. During summer, this species is usually found near water in woodlands or partially wooded areas, including farmsteads. Farm buildings, bridges, and other locations that provide artificial or natural ledges protected from above are used for nest sites.

Say's Phoebe, *Sayornis saya*
An, Ar, Bl, Bo, **Br**, **Ch**, Cu, **Gar**, Grf, Ho, **Ke**, **Li**, Log, Lo, Mc, Mo, **Sh**, Th, Wh

Status. Say's phoebe is a common spring and fall migrant and summer resident in western Nebraska, including the Sandhills region. Possible nesting has also been reported from Hooker County (Mollhoff, 2016). Breeding Bird Surveys between 1966 and 2015 indicate the species underwent a population increase (1.24% annually) during that period.

Migration. The range of 129 initial spring sightings is from March 20 to June 10, with a median of April 16. Half of the records fall within the period April 5–24. Fifty-two final fall sightings range from July 29 to October 29, with a median of September 14. Half of the records fall within the period September 8–20.

Habitats. In Nebraska this species is found in fairly open and dry habitats, including rocky canyons, badlands, and ranchlands. The species is independent of surface water, but in common with the eastern phoebe, it often nests under bridges or on the horizontal ledges of other human-made structures. In Keith County around Cedar Point Biological Station both the eastern and Say's phoebes occur, but they do not appear to interact and rarely nest in the same immediate area.

Vermilion Flycatcher, *Pyrocephalus rubinus*
Ke, Li

Accidental. A recent photographic record of a vermilion flycatcher is from Keith County, near Keystone, on April 29, 2011. Three older records are from Lincoln County: a male was present near North Platte between October and December 1954, another individual was at North Platte on November 4, 1960, and one without specific location information was reported May 27, 1976 (Silcock and Jorgensen, various dates).

Great Crested Flycatcher, *Myiarchus crinitus*
An, Bl, Bo, **Br**, **Ch**, Cu, Gar, Gre, Grf, **Hol**, **Ke**, Li, Lo, Log, **Ro**, Sh, Th, Wh

Status. The great crested flycatcher is a common spring and fall migrant and summer resident in eastern Nebraska, mainly along the larger river valleys but extending west locally to Sioux County in the north; Garden, Keith and Deuel Counties along the North Platte and South Platte Rivers; and Dundy County in the Republican River valley. Possible and probable recent Sandhills nestings have also been reported from Boone, Brown, Custer, Garden, Garfield, Loup, Sheridan, and Thomas Counties (Mollhoff, 2016). Breeding Bird Surveys between 1966 and 2015 indicate the species underwent a population decline (0.03% annually) during that period.

Migration. The range of 130 initial spring sightings is from March 30 to June 9, with a median of April 30. Half of the records fall within the period May 2–15. Sixty-six final fall sightings are from July 22 to October 3, with a median of September 6. Half of the records fall within the period August 30–September 12.

Habitats. During the breeding season, this species occurs in rather extensive hardwood forests, including riverbottom forests, and especially those with fairly open canopies. Unlike most flycatchers, the great crested flycatcher nests in cavities, such as old woodpecker holes.

Cassin's Kingbird, *Tyrannus vociferans*
Ch, Gar, Ke, Mo, Sh

Status. Cassin's kingbird is an occasional spring and fall migrant in the Sandhills. The species breeds locally in Nebraska's panhandle region. Possible nesting was reported from Garden County (Mollhoff, 2016).

Migration. Eight initial spring sightings range from April 27 to May 30, with a mean of May 2. Twelve last fall sightings range from August 22 to September 28, with a median of September 17.

Habitats. To a greater degree than the western kingbird, this species is associated with dry open country, such as plains and semideserts, with only scattered tall trees. However, the Cassin's overlaps widely with the western kingbird and probably competes locally with it.

Western Kingbird, *Tyrannus verticalis*
An, Ar, Bl, Bo, Br, Cu, Gar, Gr, Gre, Grf, Ho, Hol, Ke, Li, Lo, Log, Mc, Mo, Ro, Sh, Th, Wh

Status. The western kingbird is a common spring and fall migrant and summer resident almost statewide and a very common summer breeder in the Sandhills. Breeding Bird Surveys between 1966 and 2015 indicate the species underwent a national population increase (0.6% annually) during that period.

Migration. The range of 117 initial spring sightings is from April 30 to May 26, with a median of May 5. Half of the records fall within the period May 1–10. The range of 125 final fall sightings is from July 26 to October 10, with a median of September 3.

Half of the records fall within the period August 24–September 10.

Habitats. While in Nebraska this species seems to occupy the same habitats as does the eastern kingbird, including a variety of edge environments such as shelterbelts, orchards, woodland margins, and tree-lined residential districts.

Eastern Kingbird, *Tyrannus tyrannus*
An, **Ar**, **Bl**, **Bo**, Br, **Cu**, **Gar**, **Gr**, Gre, Grf, **Ho**, **Hol**, **Ke**, **Li**, **Lo**, **Log**, **Mc**, **Mo**, **Ro**, **Sh**, **Th**, **Wh**

Status. The eastern kingbird is a common spring and fall migrant and summer resident statewide, including the Sandhills, where it is generally considerably less common than the western kingbird. Breeding Bird Surveys between 1966 and 2015 indicate the species underwent a national population decline (1.28% annually) during that period.

Migration. Seventy-three initial spring sightings range from March 24 to May 29, with a median of May 3. Half of the records fall within the period May 1–7. The range of 126 final fall sightings is from August 4 to October 14, with a median of September 9. Half of the records fall within the period September 1–16.

Habitats. While in Nebraska this species occupies open areas that have scattered trees or tall shrubs and forest edges or hedgerows. It is one of the ten most common breeding birds of Nebraska (Mollhoff, 2016).

Scissor-tailed Flycatcher, *Tyrannus forficatus*
An, Bl, Gr, Ke, Li, Mo

Status. The scissor-tailed flycatcher is a very rare spring and fall migrant in the Sandhills.

Migration. Seventeen initial spring sightings range from April 19 to June 10, with a median of May 2. Half of the records fall within the period April 29–May 3. Eight final fall sightings are from July 23 to October 5, with a mean of September 14.

Habitats. During the summer this species is found in open to semi-open habitats with a scattering of trees or other elevated perching sites, and in woodlands with edges or openings for foraging. Nesting usually occurs in isolated trees or on tall structures, such as utility poles or windmills, rather than in groves or heavy cover.

Family Laniidae (Shrikes)

Loggerhead Shrike, *Lanius ludovicianus*
An, **Ar**, Bl, Bo, **Br**, **Ch**, **Cu**, **Gar**, **Gr**, Gre, Grf, **Ho**, Hol, **Ke**, Li, Lo, **Log**, **Mc**, Mo, Ro, **Sh**, Th, Wh

Status. The loggerhead shrike is a declining and increasingly uncommon to occasional spring and fall migrant and summer resident throughout the Sandhills. Possible and probable recent nestings have been reported from most Sandhills counties except Thomas and Wheeler Counties (Mollhoff, 2016). A few birds overwinter in some years, but apparently the population is essentially migratory. Breeding Bird Surveys between 1966 and 2015 indicate the species underwent a marked national population decline (2.78% annually) during that period. The once common Nebraska Sandhills population now seems to be part of that decline.

Migration. The range of 95 initial spring sightings is from January 2 to May 28, with a median of April 4. Half of the records fall within the period March 17–April 21. Ninety-eight final fall sightings are from July 26 to December 30, with a median of September 19. Half of the records occur August 26–October 1.

Habitats. Outside of the breeding season, these birds occupy the same open country that northern shrikes utilize, and during the nesting period they are also associated with open habitat with scattered or clustered shrubs or small trees. The Nebraska Sandhills seem to represent perfect habitat for these birds; scattered Russian olive trees are favorite nesting sites, and the open country provides excellent viewing of the surroundings.

Northern Shrike, *Lanius borealis*
An, Bl, Bo, Br, Ch, Cu, Gar, Grf, Gr, Gre, Hol, Ho, Ke, Li, Log, Lo, Mc, Mo, Ro, Sh, Th, Wh

Status. The northern shrike is an uncommon winter resident throughout the Sandhills. It rarely overlaps in seasonal occurrence with the loggerhead shrike.

Migration. The range of 44 initial fall sightings is from August 28 to December 26, with a median of November 9. Half of the records fall within the period October 23–November 28. Twenty-four final spring sightings range from January 7 to April 24, with a median of March 11. Half of the records fall within the period February 23 to March 25.

Habitats. Migrants and wintering birds are found on open plains or prairies that have scattered trees or telephone posts for perches.

Family Vireonidae (Vireos)

White-eyed Vireo, *Vireo griseus*
Bo, Ch, Ke

Very rare. Two fall (September and October) records and one spring (May) record exist for the white-eyed vireo at Cedar Point Biological Station, Keith County (Brown, Dinsmore, and Brown, 2012). Two additional records are from Boone County on May 8, 1983, and northeast Cherry County on June 10, 2016 (Silcock and Jorgensen, various dates).

Bell's Vireo, *Vireo bellii*
An, Bl, Bo, **Br**, **Ch**, Cu, **Gar**, Gr, Gre, Grf, Hol, **Ke**, **Li**, **Lo**, **Log**, Mc, Mo, Sh, **Th**, Wh

Status. Bell's vireo is a common spring and fall migrant and summer resident in the eastern and central Sandhills, breeding locally west at least to Cherry County. Possible and probable recent nestings have also been reported from most Sandhills counties except Arthur, Grant, and Sheridan Counties (Mollhoff, 2016). Breeding Bird Surveys between 1966 and 2015 indicate the species underwent a population increase (0.63% annually) during that period.

Migration. The range of 114 initial spring sightings is from March 30 to June 10, with a median of May 13. Half of the records fall within the period May 6–20. Sixty-four final fall sightings range from July 24 to October 20, with a median of September 8. Half of the records fall within the period August 25–September 17.

Habitats. In Nebraska this prairie-adapted vireo is widespread in thickets near streams or rivers and in second-growth scrub, forest edges, and brush patches.

Loggerhead shrike, adult on yucca

Yellow-throated Vireo, *Vireo flavifrons*
An, **Gar**, Grf, Hol, Ke, Lo, Ro

Status. The yellow-throated vireo is an uncommon spring and fall migrant in eastern counties and an uncommon summer resident in the forested valley of the Missouri River and west in the Sandhills along various tributaries to at least Garfield County. Breeding Bird Surveys between 1966 and 2015 indicate this species had a population increase (0.98% annually) during that period.

Migration. Eighty initial spring sightings range from March 24 to June 3, with a median of May 7. Half of the records fall within the period April 30–May 13. Twenty-seven final fall sightings range from July 21 to October 26, with a median of September 9. Half of the records fall within the period August 30–September 16.

Habitats. Migrants and breeding birds are associated with mature, moist deciduous forests, especially riverbottom forests and shady slopes, and they infrequently occur in wooded residential areas.

Cassin's Vireo, *Vireo cassinii*
Gar (NOU list), Gr (NOU list), Ke, Mc

Status. The Cassin's vireo is a fall migrant in western Nebraska and a very rare migrant in the Sandhills. Because of the recent taxonomic splitting of this form from the blue-headed vireo, there has been little information on the status of this species in Nebraska.

Blue-headed Vireo, *Vireo solitarius*
An, Bo, Br, Ch, Ke

Status. The blue-headed vireo is an uncommon spring and fall migrant in eastern Nebraska, becoming rare westwardly but reported at least as far as Keith and Cherry Counties. Breeding Bird Surveys between 1966 and 2015 indicate the species underwent a population increase (2.86% annually) during that period.

Migration. Seventy-seven initial spring sightings (as reported for the originally constituted solitary vireo) range from April 18 to June 10, with a median of May 9. Half of the records fall within the period May 3–16. Fourteen final spring sightings range from May 7 to June 7, with a median of May 18. Eighteen initial fall sightings range from July 22 to October 6, with a median of September 11. Half of the records fall within the period September 3–16. Twenty final fall sightings are from September 22 to November 3, with a median of October 1.

Habitats. Migrating birds occupy riverbottom cottonwood forests and other deciduous wooded habitats, where the birds usually forage among the larger branches. It breeds in swampy coniferous forests.

Plumbeous Vireo, *Vireo plumbeus*
Gar (NOU county list), Gr, Ke

Status. The plumbeous vireo is a very rare fall migrant in the Sandhills.

Migration. No good Nebraska migration data for this rather recently recognized species exists. The few available fall dates are for September.

Habitats. While this species is breeding, pine forests and scrubby oak woodlands are favored habitats in the Black Hills and Colorado.

Warbling Vireo, *Vireo gilvus*
Ar, **Bl**, **Bo**, **Br**, Ch, Cu, **Gar**, Gr, Gre, **Grf**, Ho, **Hol**, **Ke**, **Li**, **Lo**, **Log**, Mc, **Ro**, **Sh**, **Th**, **Wh**

Status. The warbling vireo is a common spring and fall migrant throughout the Sandhills. Possible nesting has been reported from most Sandhills counties except Grant County (Mollhoff, 2016). Breeding Bird Surveys between 1966 and 2015 indicate the species underwent a population increase (0.85% annually) during that period.

Migration. The range of 112 initial spring sightings is from April 30 to June 10, with a median of May 8. Half of the records fall within the period May 1–14. Seventy-nine final fall sightings range from July 26 to October 4, with a median of September 9. Half of the records fall within the period August 30–September 16.

Habitats. During the summer this species occurs in open stands of deciduous trees, including streamside vegetation, groves, scrubby hillsides, and residential areas. Tall streamside trees such as cottonwoods are favored nesting sites.

Loggerhead shrike, adult. *Photo by P. Johnsgard.*

Philadelphia Vireo, *Vireo philadelphicus*
An, Bo, Br, Gar, Ke

Status. The Philadelphia vireo is an uncommon spring and fall migrant in eastern Nebraska, west less often in the Sandhills to at least Garden County.

Migration. Fifty-two initial spring sightings range from April 23 to June 4, with a median of May 13. Half of the records fall within the period May 5–19. Eleven final spring sightings are from May 10 to June 10, with a median of May 24. Thirteen initial fall sightings range from July 30 to September 25, with a median of August 25. Twelve final fall sightings are from September 1 to October 21, with a median of September 21.

Habitats. Migrants are associated with open second-growth woodlands, old burned-over wooded areas and clearings, and streamside or lakeside thickets.

Red-eyed Vireo, *Vireo olivaceus*
An, Bo, **Br**, **Ch**, Cu, Gar, Gre, Grf, Hol, Ke, Li, **Lo** (H), Ro, Sh, **Th**, Wh

Status. The red-eyed vireo is a common spring and fall migrant in riverine woodlands throughout the Sandhills. Possible and probable recent nestings have also been reported from Antelope, Garfield, Garden, Holt, Keith, Lincoln, Logan, Loup, Rock, and Wheeler Counties (Mollhoff, 2016). Breeding Bird Surveys between 1966 and 2015 indicate the species underwent a population increase (0.75% annually) during that period.

Migration. The range of 129 initial spring sightings is from March 20 to June 10, with a median of May 14. Half of the records fall within the period May 9–22. Eighty final fall sightings range from July 23 to October 20, with a median of September 7. Half of the records fall within the period August 25–September 5.

Habitats. While in Nebraska these birds are usually found in mature deciduous forests, especially those with rather open canopies and fairly large trees.

Family Corvidae (Crows, Jays, and Magpies)

Canada (Gray) Jay, *Perisoreus canadensis*
Sh

Accidental. The only documented Sandhills record of a Canada jay is from Antioch, Sheridan County, February 2–26, 1930 (Silcock and Jorgensen, various dates).

Pinyon Jay, *Gymnorhinus cyanocephalus*
Gar (NOU list), Ke, Mo, Sh

Status. The pinyon jay is a vagrant or very rare permanent resident of the western Sandhills counties (probably Sheridan and Morrill Counties). Vagrants may appear elsewhere in the state (e.g., Keith, Lincoln, and Garfield Counties) during winter months. Breeding Bird Surveys between 1966 and 2003 indicate the species underwent a national population decline (3.69% annually) during that period.

Migration. The pinyon jay is probably a permanent resident in northwestern Nebraska. Vagrants sometimes appear in other parts of the state during late winter or spring.

Habitats. In the Black Hills, and probably also in the Pine Ridge, this species is found in pine forests where the soil is fairly dry and the trees are small and scattered.

Steller's Jay, *Cyanocitta stelleri*
Gar, Ke, Li, Sh

Rare. Several old April, May, August, and October records for Steller's jay are from Keith, Lincoln, Garden, and Sheridan Counties (Silcock and Jorgensen, various dates). A more recent record is of two birds at Cedar Point Biological Station in May 2000 (Brown, Dinsmore, and Brown, 2012).

Blue Jay, *Cyanocitta cristata*
An, Ar, Bl, Bo, **Br**, Ch, Cu, **Gar**, Gr, Gre, **Grf**, Ho, **Hol**, **Ke**, **Li**, Lo, Log, Mc, Mo, Ro, Sh, Th, **Wh**

Status. The blue jay is a common permanent resident throughout the Sandhills. Breeding Bird Surveys between 1966 and 2015 indicate the species underwent a national population decline (0.7%

annually) during that period. Possible and probable recent nestings have also been reported from most Sandhills counties (Mollhoff, 2016).

Habitats. Throughout the year this species is widely distributed in forests, parks, suburbs, cities, and almost anywhere a combination of trees and grasslands occur. It is somewhat more adapted to city life than is the Steller's jay and is likely to dominate bird feeders during food shortages, especially when family-sized groups of possessive jays are resident in a neighborhood.

Clark's Nutcracker, *Nucifraga columbiana*
An, Ke, Li

Very rare. Records of Clark's nutcracker come from three Sandhills counties: a single bird was recorded at Lake McConaughy, Keith County, on November 1, 1998; a single bird in Lincoln County, on August 30, 2004; and a single bird near Orchard, Antelope County, on September 9, 2007 (Silcock and Jorgensen, various dates).

Black-billed Magpie, *Pica hudsonia*
An, Bl, Bo, **Br**, **Ch**, Cu, Gar, Gr, **Gre**, Grf, Ho, **Hol**, **Ke**, **Li**, **Lo**, Mo, Ro, Sh, Th, Wh

Status. The black-billed magpie is a previously common permanent resident throughout the Sandhills. Possible nesting has been reported from Lincoln County (Mollhoff, 2016). This species becomes rarer eastwardly in Nebraska and has declined rapidly since the early 2000s, when the West Nile virus greatly reduced its population. Breeding Bird Surveys between 1966 and 2015 indicate the species underwent a national population decline (0.49% annually) during that period.

Habitats. Throughout the year this magpie normally frequents wooded canyons, river-bottom forests, and forest edges but ranges out into more arid environments wherever there are thickets of shrubs or small trees that provide nest sites.

American Crow, *Corvus brachyrhynchos*
An, Ar, **Bl**, Bo, Br, **Ch**, Cu, Gar, Gr, Gre, Grf, Ho, **Hol**, Ke, **Li**, **Lo**, Log, **Mc**, Mo, Ro, **Sh**, Th, Wh

Status. The American crow is a common spring and fall migrant and summer resident throughout the Sandhills. Possible and probable recent nestings have also been reported from most Sandhills counties except Grant County (Mollhoff, 2016). Numbers are greatly increased in winter by migrants from farther north, so the species is usually present throughout the year. Breeding Bird Surveys between 1966 and 2015 indicate the species underwent a population increase (0.66% annually) during that period, although during the early 2000s the population was seriously affected by West Nile disease.

Habitats. Throughout the year this species occurs in a wide variety of forests, wooded river bottoms, suburban areas, orchards, parks, and woodlots.

Common Raven, *Corvus corax*
Ch

Extirpated. By the late 1800s the common raven was extirpated from Nebraska. However, recent sight records from Cherry County suggest occasional vagrants might occur in the Sandhills. This species was placed in the Accidental III category (supported by 1 or 2 documentations) in Nebraska by the Nebraska Ornithologists' Union (Brogie, 2017).

Family Alaudidae (Larks)

Horned Lark, *Eremophila alpestris*
An, Ar, Bl, Bo, Br, Ch, Cu, Gar, Gr, Gre, Grf, Ho, Ke, Li, Lo, Log, Mc, Mo, Ro, Sh, Th, Wh

Status. The horned lark is a common to abundant spring and fall migrant and summer resident throughout the Sandhills and a common winter visitor as well. Several subspecies are present in the state at various times of the year. Breeding Bird Surveys between 1966 and 2015 indicate the species underwent a national population decline (2.46% annually) during that period.

Habitats. A variety of low-stature open habitats are used by this species throughout the year, but in Nebraska it is mostly found in natural grasslands and cultivated fields. The sparse grasslands of the Sandhills are probably a nearly optimum habitat. Few if any other species of songbirds are as common as the horned lark in the Nebraska Sandhills.

Family Hirundinidae (Swallows)

Bank Swallow, *Riparia riparia*
An, Ar, Bl, Bo, Br, **Ch**, Cu, **Gar**, Gr, **Gre**, **Grf**, Ho, Hol, **Ke**, **Li**, **Lo**, Log, Mc, Mo, Ro, **Sh**, **Th**, Wh

Status. The bank swallow is a common but locally distributed spring and fall migrant throughout the Sandhills and a local breeder. Rare, irregular, or local breeding occurs in most Sandhills counties (Silcock and Jorgensen, various dates). Breeding Bird Surveys between 1966 and 2003 indicate the species underwent a national population decline (5.33% annually) during that period.

Migration. The range of 104 initial spring sightings is from March 20 to June 8, with a median of May 6. Half of the records fall within the period April 28–May 6. Sixty-five final fall sightings range from July 31 to October 29, with a median of September 8. Half of the records fall within the period August 23–September 15.

Habitats. While in Nebraska this species occurs in a variety of open habitats, especially grasslands and croplands, but is typically found near water. It is dependent on suitable potential nest sites in the form of vertical banks of clay, sand, or gravel that can be excavated by the birds. Bank swallows are local nesters in the state, requiring rather large areas of barren, often clay-based, roadcuts to support a breeding colony. (The nearly vertical clay-like banks of loess that are common beside roads along the Missouri River valley provide the perfect nesting situation for these birds.)

Tree Swallow, *Tachycineta bicolor*
An, **Ar**, Bl, Bo, **Br**, **Ch**, Cu, **Gar**, Gr, Gre, **Grf**, Ho, **Hol**, Ke, **Li**, **Lo**, **Log**, **Mc**, Mo, **Ro**, **Sh**, Th, **Wh**

Status. The tree swallow is a common spring and fall migrant throughout the Sandhills and a common breeder. Possible and probable recent nestings have also been reported from most Sandhills counties (Mollhoff, 2016). Breeding Bird Surveys between 1966 and 2003 indicate the species underwent a national population decline (1.38% annually) during that period.

Migration. The range of 86 initial spring sightings is from March 20 to June 8, with a median of April 29. Half of the records fall within the period April 14–May 11. Twenty-eight final fall sightings are from July 25 to October 27, with a median of September 17. Half of the records fall within the period August 26–October 7.

Habitats. During summer this species occurs in open woodlands, usually fairly close to water. Woodpecker holes in dead trees, especially aspens and willows, are favorite nesting sites. Tree swallows have benefited greatly from the bluebird nest box program in Nebraska (and elsewhere) and have expanded their breeding range into treeless areas of the state accordingly.

Violet-green Swallow, *Tachycineta thalassina*
Ch, Gar, Ke, Sh

Status. The violet-green swallow is a very rare spring and fall migrant or vagrant in the Sandhills.

Migration. Thirty-eight initial spring sightings range from April 17 to June 10, with a median of May 13. Half of the records fall within the period May 5–19. Four final fall sightings are from August 20 to September 5, with a mean of August 27.

Habitats. During summer, this species is found in open forests such as ponderosa pine forests or poplar woodlands, but it sometimes also extends into urban areas, occasionally nesting in birdhouses. Old woodpecker holes are the usual nesting sites in forested areas.

Northern Rough-winged Swallow, *Stelgidopteryx serripennis*
An, Ar, Bl, Bo, Ch, Gar, Gr, Gre, Grf, Ho, Hol, Ke, Li, Lo, Log, Mc, Mo, Ro, Sh, Th, Wh

Status. The northern rough-winged swallow is a common spring and fall migrant and summer resident throughout the Sandhills. Breeding Bird Surveys between 1966 and 2015 indicate the species underwent a population decline (1.53% annually) during that period.

Migration. The range of 136 initial spring sightings is from March 2 to May 29, with a median of April 28. Half of the records fall within the period April 18–May 6. Seventy-two final fall sightings are from July 21 to October 15, with a median of September

Horned lark, adult. *Photo by P. Johnsgard.*

3. Half of the records fall within the period August 23–September 15.

Habitats. This swallow is an open-country species, often found near rivers or creeks that have exposed vertical banks of clay or other materials that can be excavated to provide nest sites. Unlike the colonial bank swallow, this species is a solitary nester. Rough-winged swallows are among the most common swallows in eastern Nebraska, especially near streams that have steep-sided mud banks. They also nest in natural cavities or rocky outcrops, although perhaps less frequently, and have even been found to accept horizontally installed drainpipes as nesting cavities.

Purple Martin, *Progne subis*
An, Bo, Br, **Ch, Cu, Gar**, Gre, Grf, Hol, **Ke**, Li, Log, Ro, Sh

Status. The purple martin is an uncommon and increasingly rare spring and fall migrant and summer resident throughout the Sandhills. Breeding Bird Surveys between 1966 and 2015 indicate the species underwent a national population decline (0.91% annually) during that period. Small populations bred regularly in the North Platte valley west as far as the Lake McConaughy area, Keith County, around 1977–79. Lewellen, in Garden County, was long considered the "westernmost regular nesting site in Nebraska," although there are no recent reports from that area. Westernmost current (2017) breeding is at Ogallala and Lake McConaughy, Keith County, where nesting birds have been present since at least 2004. There are no records west of Ogallala in the South Platte River valley of Nebraska (Silcock and Jorgensen, various dates.

Migration. The range of 143 initial spring sightings is from March 8 to June 5, with a median of April 10. Half of the records fall within the period March 27–April 15. The range of 101 final fall sightings is from July 22 to October 15, with a median of August 30. Half of the records fall within the period August 20–September 15.

Habitats. Purple martins are widespread in urban, suburban, and rural habitats, usually fairly near water and always where suitable nesting cavities are available. Typically these are in birdhouses, but the birds sometimes also nest in clusters of gourds or even in unused woodpecker holes or crevices in old buildings.

Barn Swallow, *Hirundo rustica*
An, Ar, Bl, Bo, Ch, Gar, Gr, Gre, Grf, Ho, Hol, Ke, Li, Lo, Log, Mc, Mo, Ro, Sh, Th, Wh

Status. The barn swallow is a common spring and fall migrant and summer resident throughout the Sandhills. Breeding Bird Surveys between 1966 and 2015 indicate the species had a national population decline (1.19% annually) during that period.

Migration. The range of 155 initial spring sightings is from March 9 to June 10, with a median of April 23. Half of the records fall within the period April 18–30. The range of 119 final fall sightings is from August 5 to October 6, with a median of September 30. Half of the records fall between September 19 and October 6.

Habitats. Widespread during the summer, this species occupies open forests, farmlands, suburbs, and rural areas, usually nesting on or inside buildings that have horizontal beams available for nesting sites. It is typically colonial, sometimes nesting near or among cliff swallows. It is one of the ten most common breeding birds of Nebraska (Mollhoff, 2016).

Cliff Swallow, *Petrochelidon pyrrhonota*
An, Ar, **Bl, Ch, Gar**, Gr, **Gre, Grf**, Ho, **Hol, Ke, Li, Lo, Log, Mc, Mo, Ro, Sh, Th, Wh**

Status. The cliff swallow is a common to locally abundant spring and fall migrant and summer resident throughout the Sandhills. Breeding Bird Surveys between 1966 and 2015 indicate the species underwent a population increase (1.72% annually) during that period.

Migration. The range of 125 initial spring sightings is from March 22 to June 10, with a median of April 28. Half of the records fall within the period April 29–May 18. The range of 101 final fall sightings is from July 22 to October 30, with a median of September 4. Half of the records fall within the period August 20–September 15.

Habitats. This species occurs over open areas of farmland and towns, near cliffs, around bridges, and in other areas where mud supplies and potential

Cliff swallow, pair at nest. *Photo by P. Johnsgard.*

nest sites on vertical and overhanging surfaces exist. Cliff swallows are highly social and colonial nesters, often nesting in the same locations year after year. Brown and Brown (1996) exhaustively monographed this species' biology and social behavior, and documented the advantages (benefits) and disadvantages (costs) of their high degree of sociality.

Cave Swallow, *Petrochelidon fulva*
Gar, Ke

Accidental. Several adult and juvenile cave swallows have been found among cliff swallow colonies in the vicinity of Cedar Point Biological Station, Keith County, and Ash Hollow State Historical Park, Garden County (Brown, Dinsmore, and Brown, 2012).

Family Paridae (Chickadees and Titmice)

Black-capped Chickadee, *Poecile atricapillus*
An, Ar, Bl, **Bo**, **Br**, **Ch**, Cu, **Gar**, Gr, Gre, Grf, Ho, **Hol**, **Ke**, **Li**, Lo, Log, Mc, Mo, **Ro**, **Sh**, **Th**, Wh

Status. The black-capped chickadee is a common permanent resident throughout the Sandhills. Possible and probable recent nestings have also been reported from Antelope, Custer, Garfield, Loup, and Wheeler Counties (Mollhoff, 2016). Breeding Bird Surveys between 1966 and 2003 indicate the species underwent a population increase (0.61% annually) during that period.

Habitats. Throughout the year this species is found in deciduous and coniferous forests as well as orchards and woodlots. Nesting often occurs in edge situations or open areas of forests, but during the winter period the birds frequently appear at residential feeding stations, especially where suet is available.

Mountain Chickadee, *Poecile gambeli*
Gar (NOU website checklist), Ke, Mo

Status. The mountain chickadee is a very rare winter visitor in the Sandhills region.

Migration. Records for this rare winter vagrant extend from October 5 to May 23. The largest number of records are for October (5), November (4), and December (4), followed by February (2) and April (2).

Habitats. This species is normally associated with montane coniferous forests throughout the year, but winter vagrants sometimes appear at residential feeding stations.

Tufted Titmouse, *Baeolophus bicolor*
Ch

Accidental. A single record of a tufted titmouse is from Valentine NWR, Cherry County, on May 25, 2006 (Silcock and Jorgensen, various dates).

Family Sittidae (Nuthatches)

Red-breasted Nuthatch, *Sitta canadensis*
An, Ar, **Bl**, Bo, **Br** (H), **Ch**, Cu, Gar, Gr, Gre, Grf, Ho, Hol, Ke, Li, Log, Lo, Mo, Ro, Sh, **Th**, Wh

Status. The red-breasted nuthatch is a common winter visitor in the Sandhills region. Possible and probable recent nestings have also been reported from Garden, Brown, and Rock Counties (Mollhoff, 2016). There is a 1980 nesting record for the McKelvie (Nebraska) National Forest, Cherry County, and a historic record from Brown County. Breeding Bird Surveys between 1966 and 2015 indicate the species underwent a population increase (0.72% annually) during that period.

Migration. Seventy-two initial fall sightings range from August 10 to December 31, with a median of October 9. Half of the records fall within the period September 18–October 17. Thirty-nine final spring sightings are from January 4 to June 8, with a median of April 3. Half of the records fall within the period March 3–April 23.

Habitats. Except for the Panhandle region, where this species probably breeds in coniferous forests, this bird is likely to be found in conifer plantations and mixed woodlands—and sometimes also at eastern bird feeding stations during winter.

White-breasted Nuthatch, *Sitta carolinensis*
An, Ar, Bl, Bo, **Br**, **Ch**, Cu, Gar, Gr, Gre, Grf, Ho, **Hol**, **Ke**, **Li**, Lo, Log, Mo, Ro, Sh, Th, **Wh**

Status. The white-breasted nuthatch is an uncommon permanent resident throughout the Sandhills. Possible and probable recent nestings have also been reported from Custer, Garfield, Logan, Loup, Thomas, and Wheeler Counties (Mollhoff, 2016). Breeding Bird Surveys between 1966 and 2015 indicate the species underwent a population increase (1.71% annually) during that period.

Habitats. In Nebraska this species is generally associated with fairly mature floodplain forests during the breeding season, while during the rest of the year it is more widespread and often visits residential feeding stations, especially where suet is provided. The long, sharp beak of nuthatches adapts them for probing in the crevices of tree bark, feeding on some of the same insects that woodpeckers consume. The name "nuthatch" is derived from an older and more descriptive name, "nut-hack."

Pygmy Nuthatch, *Sitta pygmaea*
Ch, Ke, Lo, **Sh**, **Th**

Status. The pygmy nuthatch is probably a rare winter visitor and rare permanent resident of the Sandhills region. Studies first proved its nesting in Sheridan County (*Nebraska Bird Review* 65: 150–58). It also nests in McKelvie National Forest, Cherry County, and the Bessey Ranger District of Nebraska National Forest, Thomas County.

Habitats. Throughout the year this species is generally associated with ponderosa pines, especially those growing in open, parklike situations. In the winter, vagrants may appear along cottonwood-lined rivers, often in small flocks.

Family Certhiidae (Creepers)

Brown Creeper, *Certhia americana*
An, Ar, Bo, **Br**, Ch, Cu, Gar, Gre, Grf, Hol, Ke, Li, Lo, Mc, Sh, Th

Status. The brown creeper is a common winter visitor and possible local breeder in wooded areas of the Sandhills. Breeding Bird Surveys between 1966 and 2015 indicate the species underwent a population increase (0.55% annually) during that period.

Migration. Ninety-two initial fall sightings range from August 5 to December 30, with a median of October 17. Half of the records fall within the period September 17–October 17. Forty-four final spring sightings are from January 8 to May 29, with a median of March 22. Half of the records fall within the period March 3–April 23. In a few areas the species breeds and can be considered a permanent resident.

Habitats. While breeding, these birds are associated with fairly mature deciduous or coniferous forests, but in the winter the birds move to woodland streams, wooded parks, suburbs, and the like. The nests are hidden behind loose bark and are very difficult to locate, which accounts for the scanty nesting records.

Family Troglodytidae (Wrens)

Rock Wren, *Salpinctes obsoletus*
An, Ch, Cu, **Gar**, **Ke**, **Li**, **Log**, Mo, **Sh** (H), Th

Status. The rock wren is an uncommon breeder and spring and fall migrant in rocky habitats within the Sandhills region. Possible recent nesting has been reported from Cherry, Hooker, and Lincoln Counties (Mollhoff, 2016). Breeding Bird Surveys between 1966 and 2015 indicate the species underwent a population decline (0.65%) annually during that period.

Migration. Eighty-three initial spring sightings range from April 2 to June 9, with a median of May 2. Half of the records fall within the period April 22–May 13. Thirty-three final fall sightings are from August 18 to October 29, with a median of October 27. Half of the records fall within the period September 17–October 6.

Habitats. In Nebraska this species occupies eroded slopes and badlands, rocky outcrops, cliff walls, talus slopes, and similar generally arid environments. Few locations within the Sandhills offer these habitats.

House Wren, *Troglodytes aedon*
An, **Ar**, **Bl**, **Bo**, **Br**, **Ch**, **Cu**, **Gar**, Gr, **Gre**, **Grf**, **Ho**, **Hol**, **Ke**, **Li**, **Lo**, **Log**, Mc, **Mo**, **Ro**, **Sh**, **Th**, **Wh**

Status. The house wren is a common spring and fall migrant and summer resident throughout the Sandhills. Breeding Bird Surveys between 1966 and 2015 indicate the species underwent a population increase (1.26% annually) during that period.

Migration. The range of 136 initial spring sightings is from March 10 to May 24, with a median of April 24. Half of the records fall within the period April 19–May 2. The range of 131 final fall sightings is from July 24 to October 22, with a median of September 26. Half of the records fall within the period September 10–October 7.

Habitats. Originally associated with deciduous forests and open woods, this species is now also adapted to cities and frequently nests in birdhouses. However, it is also abundant in riverbottom forests, cottonwood groves, and wooded hillsides or canyons.

Winter Wren, *Troglodytes hiemalis*
An, Ch, Gar, Ho, Hol, Ke, Li, Lo, Log, Th

Status. The winter wren is an uncommon spring and fall migrant and winter resident in the Sandhills region.

Migration. The range of 38 initial fall sightings is from August 30 to December 26, with a median of October 16. Half of the records fall within the period January 21–May 29, with a median of April 13. Half of the records fall within the period April 5–23.

Habitats. While in Nebraska this inconspicuous species is usually found among dense ravine thickets along streams but sometimes also in suburban gardens, parks, and other habitats.

Sedge Wren, *Cistothorus platensis*
An, Bo, Br, Ch, Gre, Grf, Hol, Ke, Li, Lo, Ro, Th, Wh

Status. The sedge wren is an uncommon spring and fall migrant in the Sandhills. Possible and probable recent nestings have also been reported from Brown, Garfield, Holt, Keith, Lincoln, Rock, and Wheeler Counties (Mollhoff, 2016). Breeding Bird Surveys between 1966 and 2015 indicate the species underwent a population increase (0.40% annually) during that period.

Migration. Twenty-five initial spring sightings range from April 16 to June 3, with a median of May 8. Half of the records fall within the period May 1–12. Seventeen final fall sightings are from July 29 to October 22, with a median of September 28. Half of the records fall within the period September 11–October 9. Many birds seem to arrive in Nebraska during midsummer and begin nesting at that time. Sedge wrens are common breeders in southeastern Nebraska, where they arrive and begin to sing in early May. Then, in July or August a new song cycle begins, leading some to speculate that these are late-arriving birds, perhaps from farther north, where they may have been unsuccessful breeders. A similar late summer migration might occur in marsh wrens (*Nebraska Bird Review* 76: 107).

Habitats. In Nebraska and the northern plains, sedge wrens breed in wet meadows, typically those dominated by sedges and tall grasses, and breed less often in the emergent vegetation of marshes as well as retired croplands and hayfields.

Marsh Wren, *Cistothorus palustris*
An, Ar, Bl, Br, **Ch**, Cu, **Gar**, **Gr**, Gre, Grf, **Ho**, **Hol**, **Ke**, **Li**, Lo, Log, Mo, **Ro**, **Sh**, **Wh**

Status. The marsh wren is a common spring and fall migrant statewide and locally common summer resident throughout the Sandhills. Possible and probable recent nestings have also been reported from Arthur, Blain, Brown, Garfield, Logan, Loup, and McPherson Counties (Mollhoff, 2016). Two song types (eastern and western) occur in the state, with the dividing line passing southeast through O'Neill approximately along the Elkhorn River valley (*Nebraska Bird Review* 64: 99), or along the eastern edge of the Sandhills (Mollhoff, 2001). Breeding Bird Surveys between 1966 and 2015 indicate the species underwent a population increase (1.71% annually) during that period.

Migration. Seventy-eight initial spring sightings range from March 13 to June 9, with a median of May 5. Half of the records fall within the period April 26–May 15. Thirty-two final fall sightings are from August 9 to November 22, with a median of October 2. Half of the records fall within the period September 8–October 10.

Habitats. During the breeding season these birds are primarily found in freshwater marshes that have extensive tall emergent vegetation, such as bulrushes and cattails. The marsh wrens of Nebraska pose a problem in evolution with two distinct song types occurring in the state; perhaps the two types represent "sibling species" that seem to differ only in their vocalizations but act biologically as distinct species.

Carolina Wren, *Thryothorus ludovicianus*
Ch, Cu, Ke, Li, Wh

Status. The Carolina wren is a rare permanent resident in the Sandhills region. A notable confirmed nesting occurred in Cherry County during the early atlasing years (Mollhoff, 2001).

Migration. Seventy-two initial spring sightings range from January 1 to June 4, with a median of March 1. Nearly half occur in the month of January. Seven final fall sightings range from August 29 to December 31, with a mean of October 21. The data suggest that the species is primarily a permanent resident within its limited Nebraska breeding range and is a vagrant elsewhere.

Habitats. During the breeding season and probably also the rest of the year, this species occupies riverbottom forests, forest edges, cutover forests, and cultivated areas with brush heaps as well as suburban parks and gardens. It is more closely associated with bottomland forests in Nebraska than is the Bewick's wren or house wren, but the three species all overlap in their ecological distributions.

Bewick's Wren, *Thryomanes bewickii*
An, Ch, Ke, Li

Status. Bewick's wren is a rare spring and fall migrant and very rare or extirpated summer resident in the Sandhills. An early report of breeding in Lincoln County seems questionable.

Migration. Forty-four initial spring sightings range from March 26 to May 28, with a median of April 24. Half of the records fall within the period April 9–May 8. Nine final fall sightings range from August 11 to October 3, with a mean of September 20.

Habitats. Habitats used during the breeding season include open woodlands, brushy habitats, farmsteads, and towns. In Colorado the birds are mostly associated with dry canyons and scrubby forests, but farther east they overlap with house wrens in their habitats.

Family Cinclidae (Dippers)

American Dipper, *Cinclus mexicanus*
Ch, Hol

Accidental. The American dipper is reported from two Sandhills counties: Holt County during December 1969 and Cherry County, at the Niobrara River 8 to 10 miles east of Valentine, on May 1, 1977 (Silcock and Jorgensen, various dates).

Family Polioptilidae (Gnatcatchers)

Blue-gray Gnatcatcher, *Polioptila caerulea*
An, Bo, Br, Ch, **Gar**, Hol, Ke, Mo

Status. The blue-gray gnatcatcher is a common spring and fall migrant and summer resident in most of Nebraska except the Sandhills, where it is an occasional migrant or possible summer resident. Possible nesting was reported from Sheridan County (Mollhoff, 2016). Breeding Bird Surveys between 1966 and 2015 indicate the species underwent a population increase (0.38% annually) during that period.

Migration. Eighty-five initial spring sightings range from March 30 to June 6, with a median of May 2. Half of the records fall within the period April 23–May 10. Seven fall sightings are from July 26 to September 22, with a mean of September 1.

Habitats. Breeding occurs in the deciduous bottomland forests of eastern Nebraska. The western race, *P. c. amoenissima*, often uses scrubby woodlands for breeding in western Nebraska.

Family Regulidae (Kinglets)

Golden-crowned Kinglet, *Regulus satrapa*
An, Bo, Br, Ch, Cu, Gar, Gre, Grf, Hol, Ke, Li, Lo, Sh, Th, Wh

Status. The golden-crowned kinglet is a common to uncommon fall to spring migrant throughout the Sandhills.

Migration. Seventy-five initial fall sightings range from August 13 to December 30, with a median of

October 19. Half of the records fall within the period October 10–29. Fifty-nine final fall sightings are from November 6 to December 31, with a median of December 26, suggesting that the species should be normally considered a winter resident. Fifty-three final spring records are from January 9 to May 29, with a median of April 10. Half of the records fall within the period April 3–26.

Habitats. While in Nebraska this species occupies a wide variety of woodlands, forests, and scrubby habitats, including both coniferous and hardwood but especially the former.

Ruby-crowned Kinglet, *Regulus calendula*
An, Ar, Bl, Bo, Br, Ch, Cu, Gar, Gr, Gre, Grf, Ho, Hol, Ke, Li, Lo, Log, Mc, Mo, Ro, Sh, Th, Wh

Status. The ruby-crowned kinglet is a common to uncommon spring and fall migrant throughout the Sandhills.

Migration. Seventy-four initial spring sightings range from January 12 to May 28, with a median of April 13. Half of the records fall within the period April 1–22. Forty-nine final spring sightings are from April 7 to May 22, with a median of May 10. Seventy-five initial fall sightings are from August 7 to December 10, with a median of September 23. Half of the records fall within the period September 10–October 7. Sixty-nine final fall records are from August 16 to December 31, with a median of October 28. Less than a fourth of the final fall records are for December, suggesting that the species only rather rarely overwinters in Nebraska.

Habitats. While in Nebraska this species occurs in a wide variety of forested and shrubby habitats, including gardens and parks. It occurs in both deciduous and coniferous vegetation, showing no apparent preference for either.

Family Turdidae (Thrushes)

Eastern Bluebird, *Sialia sialis*
Ar, **Bl**, **Br**, **Ch**, Cu, **Gar**, Gr, **Grf**, Ho, **Hol**, **Ke**, **Li**, **Lo**, **Log**, Mc, Mo, **Ro**, **Sh**, **Th**, **Wh**

Status. The eastern bluebird is an uncommon spring and fall migrant throughout the Sandhills and a local breeder. Possible nesting was reported from Hooker County (Mollhoff, 2016).

Migration. The range of 123 initial spring sightings is from January 1 to June 8, with a median of March 23. Half of the records fall within the period March 1–April 25, and more than 10 percent of the records are for January. Seventy-four final fall sightings are from August 14 to December 31, with a median of November 5. Half of the records are within the period October 8–27, and nearly a third are for December. The seasonal data indicate this species occasionally overwinters in Nebraska.

Habitats. During summer this species frequents open hardwood forests, especially those adjacent to grasslands. Forest edges, shelterbelts, city parks, farmsteads, and similar habitats are also used by breeding birds and migrants.

Mountain Bluebird, *Sialia currucoides*
Ke, Li

Status. The mountain bluebird is a common migrant in western Nebraska, becoming rarer in the Sandhills, and with breeding records limited to the panhandle region. At Cedar Point Biological Station, Keith County, it is a spring and fall transient and winter resident from mid-October to mid-April.

Migration. Eighty-four initial spring sightings are from January 1 to May 25, with a median of March 11. Half of the records fall within the period February 28–March 2. Thirty-five final fall sightings are from July 21 to December 31, with a median of October 16. Half of the records fall within the period October 8–27.

Habitats. During the breeding season this species occupies open woodlands, especially open pine forest stands, burned or cutover areas, and aspen clumps. While on migration it often occurs in flocks in open country, perching on roadside fences or telephone wires. The birds seem to be more gregarious than eastern bluebirds, which generally migrate in very small groups or even singly. A hybrid from Dawes County has been reported (Wilson et al., 1986), but hybrids between the mountain and eastern bluebirds are rare.

Townsend's Solitaire, *Myadestes townsendi*
An, Bl, Ch, Cu, Gar, Gr, Grf, Ke, Li, Lo, Log, Mc, Mo, Ro, Sh, Th, Wh

Status. Townsend's solitaire is an uncommon to locally common spring and fall migrant throughout the Sandhills.

Migration. Fifty initial fall sightings are from August 23 to December 5, with a median of September 26. Half of the records fall within the period September 17–October 1. Forty-five final spring sightings are from January 10 to May 25, with a median of March 20. Half of the records fall within the period February 9–April 7. The species is sometimes seen during summer in northwestern Nebraska and perhaps rarely breeds there, but it essentially must be considered a winter visitor in Nebraska.

Habitats. Breeding habitats of this species are rather dense coniferous forests in mountainous areas. During migration the birds are often found on wooded slopes rich in juniper berries.

Veery, *Catharus fuscescens*
Ch, Ke, Li

Status. The veery is a very rare spring and fall migrant throughout the Sandhills.

Migration. The range of 108 initial spring sightings is from March 10 to June 4, with a median of May 15. Half of the records fall within the period May 10–21. Eighteen final spring sightings are from May 9 to May 29, with a median of May 18. Seven fall sightings range from August 28 to September 23, with a mean of September 13.

Habitats. Migrating birds are found in dense and damp bottomland deciduous forests close to flowing water.

Gray-cheeked Thrush, *Catharus minimus*
An, Bo, Br, Ch, Ke, Th

Status. The gray-cheeked thrush is an occasional spring and fall migrant throughout the Sandhills.

Migration. The range of 100 initial spring sightings is from March 20 to June 6, with a median of May 9. Half of the records fall within the period May 4–13. Forty-one final spring sightings are from May 6 to June 5, with a median of May 17. Five initial fall sightings are from September 2 to October 22, with a mean of October 1.

Habitats. This thrush arrives during spring in Nebraska at the same time as the Swainson's thrush. They occupy the same woodland habitats, namely heavy shrubbery and shady deciduous woodlands, often near creeks or rivers. Both are secretive species that only infrequently sing while migrating.

Swainson's Thrush, *Catharus ustulatus*
An, Ar, Bo, **Br** (H), Ch, Cu, Gar, Gr, Hol, Ke, Li, Lo, Log, Mc, Mo, Ro, Sh, Th

Status. Swainson's thrush is a common spring and fall migrant throughout the Sandhills. A 1900 breeding record of uncertain validity came from Brown County (Bates, 1900).

Migration. The range of 141 initial spring sightings is from April 9 to May 30, with a median of May 6. Half of the records fall within the period May 1–11. Seventy-four final spring sightings are from April 20 to June 9, with a median of May 27. Fifty-one initial fall sightings are from July 29 to October 14, with a median of September 8. Half of the records fall within the period September 3–16. Fifty-one final fall sightings are from September 11 to December 1, with a median of September 28.

Habitats. While on migration this species occupies riverbottom forests, shelterbelts, and parks or shade trees in towns. During breeding it is associated with cool and dense coniferous forests that have a fairly open understory that allows for easy ground foraging.

Hermit Thrush, *Catharus guttatus*
An, Bl, Ch, Grf, Ke, Li, Sh

Status. The hermit thrush is an occasional spring and fall migrant throughout the Sandhills.

Migration. Except for one January record, the range of 94 initial spring sightings is from March 9 to June 3, with a median of April 20. Half of the records fall within the period April 10–May 2. Twenty-six final spring sightings are from April 10 to May 26, with a median of April 26. Fourteen initial fall sightings are from September 4 to December 31, with a median of October 6. Twelve final fall sightings are from September 11 to December 14 with a median of October 16.

Habitats. Migrants are found in dense to semi-open areas of woodland, shrubbery, and vine-draped tangles, but they occasionally move into more open areas. Fairly heavy deciduous woodlands are the favored habitat in eastern Nebraska.

Wood Thrush, *Hylocichla mustelina*
Br (H), Ch, Hol, Ke, **Li**, **Lo**

Status. The wood thrush is a rare spring and fall migrant throughout the Sandhills. There is a historical breeding record from Brown County and more recent reports from Lincoln and Logan Counties. Breeding Bird Surveys between 1966 and 2015 indicate the species underwent a national population decline (2.2% annually) during that period.

Migration. The range of 120 initial spring sightings is from April 1 to June 10, with a median of May 10. Half of the records fall within the period May 5–19. Thirty-one final fall sightings are from July 23 to October 6, with a median of September 10. Half of the records fall within the period September 5–23.

Habitats. Migrants and breeding birds are associated with mature, shady forests, especially deciduous woods, and also with wooded parks and gardens. The birds prefer breeding habitats with a dense understory, running water nearby, and tall trees for singing perches. Wood thrushes somewhat resemble improperly plumaged robins; they are about the same size, have a distinctly robinlike profile and behavior, and lay eggs that are robin's-egg blue, like those of the robin, veery, and hermit thrush. The adaptive value of such egg coloration remains speculative.

American Robin, *Turdus migratorius*
An, **Ar**, **Bl**, **Bo**, **Br**, **Ch**, **Cu**, **Gar**, **Gr**, **Gre**, **Grf**, **Ho**, **Hol**, **Ke**, **Li**, **Lo**, **Log**, **Mc**, **Mo**, **Ro**, **Sh**, **Th**, **Wh**

Status. The American robin is an abundant spring and fall migrant and common summer resident statewide. Overwintering is frequent in some years and localities. Breeding occurs nearly throughout the Great Plains states, except for the extreme southwestern areas where it is only a migrant. Breeding Bird Surveys between 1966 and 2015 indicate the species underwent a population increase (0.12% annually) during that period.

Migration. Forty-five initial spring sightings are from January 1 to May 26, with a median of February 20. Half of the records fall within the period February 2–March 4. Fifty-four final fall sightings are from September 1 to December 31, with a median of November 19. Half of the records fall within the period October 20–December 14. Over a third of the records are for December, indicating that the species commonly overwinters in Nebraska.

Habitats. Although this species was originally associated with open woodlands, it is probably most common in cities, suburbs, parks, gardens, and farmlands. It is one of the ten most common breeding birds of Nebraska (Mollhoff, 2016).

Varied Thrush, *Ixoreus naevius*
Ke, Li, Mc

Status. The varied thrush is a very rare vagrant in the Sandhills, with records from only Keith, Lincoln, and McPherson Counties.

Migration. Four fall records for this rare vagrant are from October 1 to December 4, and three spring records are from February 18 to April 10.

Habitats. This species is normally associated with coniferous montane forests, but migrants move into more open woodlands on migration and during winter, sometimes wandering widely.

Family Mimidae (Mockingbirds, Thrashers, and Catbirds)

Gray Catbird, *Dumetella carolinensis*
An, **Bl**, Br, Ch, Cu, **Gar**, Gr, Gre, Grf, Ho, **Hol**, **Ke**, **Li**, **Lo**, **Log**, Mo, Ro, Sh, Th, **Wh**

Status. The gray catbird is a common spring and fall migrant and summer resident throughout the Sandhills. Possible recent nesting was reported from Brown, Cherry, Garfield, Rock, Sheridan, and Thomas Counties (Mollhoff, 2016). Breeding Bird Surveys between 1966 and 2015 indicate the species underwent a population decline (1.01% annually) during that period.

Migration. The range of 134 initial spring sightings is from March 20 to June 5, with a median of May 11. Half of the records fall within the period May 5–17. The range of 128 final fall sightings is from July 22 to December 11, with a median of September 24. Half of the records fall within the period September 16–October 2.

Habitats. Breeding habitats include thickets, woodland

edges, shrubby marsh borders, orchards, parks, and similar brushy habitats.

Northern Mockingbird, *Mimus polyglottos*
An, Ar, Br, Ch, Cu, Gar, Gre, Grf, Ho, Hol, Ke, Li, Lo, Log, Mc, Mo, Ro, Sh

Status. The northern mockingbird is an uncommon to occasional spring and fall migrant and summer resident throughout the Sandhills. Possible and probable recent nestings have also been reported from Arthur, Brown, Cherry, Garden, Holt, Lincoln, Logan, Loup, McPherson, Rock, and Sheridan Counties (Mollhoff, 2016).

Migration. The range of 132 initial spring sightings is from January 1 to June 10, with a median of May 2. Half of the records fall within the period April 21–May 13, and about 6 percent of the records are for January. Sixty-one final fall sightings are from July 22 to December 31, with a median of September 11. Half of the records fall within the period August 15–October 13, and nearly 10 percent of the records are for December. The data suggest that the species overwinters occasionally.

Habitats. A variety of habitats, ranging from open woodlands, forest edges, and farmlands to parks and cities are utilized, but treeless plains and heavy forests are avoided.

Brown Thrasher, *Toxostoma rufum*
An, Ar, Bl, **Bo**, **Br**, **Ch**, **Cu**, **Gar**, Gr, **Gre**, **Grf**, Ho, **Hol**, **Ke**, **Li**, **Lo**, **Log**, Mc, **Mo**, Ro, **Sh**, Th, **Wh**

Status. The brown thrasher is a common spring and fall migrant and summer resident throughout the Sandhills. Possible and probable recent nestings have also been reported from most Sandhills counties (Mollhoff, 2016). Breeding Bird Surveys between 1966 and 2015 indicate the species underwent a population decline (1.04% annually) during that period.

Migration. The range of 134 initial spring sightings is from January 1 to June 2, with a median of April 26. Half of the records fall within the period April 19–May 4. The range of 164 final fall records is from July 22 to December 31, with a median of September 28. Half of the records fall within the period September 13–October 11. More than 10 percent of the records are for December, suggesting that the species occasionally overwinters.

Habitats. During summer this species frequents open brushy woods, scattered patches of brush and small trees in open environments, shelterbelts, woodlands, and shrubby residential areas.

Curve-billed Thrasher, *Toxostoma curvirostre*
Ch, Gar, Li, Lo

Rare. Reports of curve-billed thrashers have come from four Sandhills counties. A specimen was collected at North Platte, Lincoln County, on May 2, 1936. A single bird was observed at Valentine NWR, Cherry County, July 8–10, 2006; at Calamus Reservoir, Loup County, February 19–April 17, 2016; and at Crescent Lake NWR, Garden County, May 14, 2017 (Silcock and Jorgensen, various dates).

Sage Thrasher, *Oreoscoptes montanus*
Ch (NOU website checklist), Gar (Crescent Lake NWR checklist), Mo, Sh

Status. The sage thrasher is a very rare migrant and a locally rare summer resident in the Pine Ridge region (Rosche, 1982). Vagrants have also been observed in Lincoln, Garden, and Sheridan Counties.

Migration. Three initial spring sightings are from March 23 to April 21, with a mean of April 17. Seven final fall sightings are from August 24 to October 12, with a mean of September 16.

Habitats. During the breeding season, this species is closely associated with sage-dominated grasslands and similar shrubby arid lands. On migration it has a broader distribution, occurring in open prairies and also in ponderosa pine woodlands.

Family Bombycillidae (Waxwings)

Bohemian Waxwing, *Bombycilla garrulus*
An, Bo, Br, Ch, Gar, Grf, Ke, Li, Mo, Sh

Status. The Bohemian waxwing is an increasingly rare winter visitor in Nebraska, irregular in geographic and yearly occurrence. Only during unusually cold winters do Bohemian waxwings now visit Nebraska, usually wintering farther north.

Migration. The range of 11 initial fall sightings is from September 25 to December 27, with a median of November 20. Nineteen final spring sightings range from January 2 to May 22, with a median of February 28.

Habitats. Migrants are associated with fruit-bearing trees in woodlands, shelterbelts, and urban parks or gardens, often in association with cedar waxwings.

Cedar Waxwing, *Bombycilla cedrorum*
An, Ar, Bl, Bo, Br, Ch, Cu, **Gar**, Gr, Gre, Grf, Ho, Hol, **Ke**, Li, Lo, Log, Mc, Mo, Ro, Sh, Th, Wh

Status. The cedar waxwing is a common spring and fall migrant and a local breeder throughout the Sandhills. Possible and probable recent nestings have also been reported from most Sandhills counties, except Arthur, Grant, Hooker, McPherson, and Morrill Counties (Mollhoff, 2016). Breeding Bird Surveys between 1966 and 2015 indicate the species underwent a population increase (0.07% annually) during that period.

Migration. The range of 54 initial spring sightings is from January 2 to May 20, with a median of February 24. Half of the records fall within the period February 1–April 23. Forty-five initial fall sightings are from July 20 to December 28, with a median of October 4. Fifty-eight final fall sightings are in December, suggesting that the species rather frequently overwinters in the state.

Habitats. Outside the breeding season this species occurs in flocks that concentrate in fruit-bearing trees, such as hackberries and mountain ash, and tall shrubs, such as pyracantha, junipers, and sumac. Breeding usually occurs in semi-open deciduous woodlands, including floodplain forests, upland woodlands, and sometimes parks, farmsteads, or residential areas.

Family Sturnidae (Starlings)

European Starling, *Sturnus vulgaris*
An, Ar, Bl, Bo, Br, Ch, Cu, Gar, Gr, Gre, Grf, Ho, Hol, Ke, Li, Lo, Log, Mc, Mo, Ro, Sh, Th, Wh

Status. The European starling is an introduced and common to abundant permanent resident throughout the Sandhills, with numbers supplemented during fall and winter by migrants. Breeding Bird Surveys between 1966 and 2015 indicate the species underwent a population decline (1.46% annually) during that period. No nest cavities of this species were examined during the second atlasing period of the Breeding Bird Atlas project, but nesting was confirmed in 316 of 557 survey blocks (57 percent) (Mollhoff, 2016). By comparison there were confirmed nestings in 224 of 443 blocks (50.2 percent) during the first survey (Mollhoff, 2001).

Habitats. This unwelcome species is found virtually everywhere throughout the year but is especially associated with human habitations, such as cities, suburbs, and farms, and with mature woodlands that have woodpecker holes or other tree cavities for nest sites.

Family Passeridae (Old World Sparrows)

House Sparrow, *Passer domesticus*
An, Ar, Bl, Bo, Br, Ch, Cu, Gar, Gr, Gre, Grf, Ho, Hol, Ke, Li, Lo, Log, Mc, Mo, Ro, Sh, Th, Wh

Status. The house sparrow is an abundant introduced permanent resident throughout the Sandhills. Breeding Bird Surveys between 1966 and 2015 indicate the species had a national population decline (3.64% annually) during that period.

Habitats. This species is always associated with humans, breeding in cities, suburbs, and around farm buildings. Nesting occurs in almost any kind of cavity or crevice, including those provided by buildings, dense vines growing against walls, tree cavities, old swallow nests, and other diverse locations. This familiar species is slowly becoming less numerous, as it is encountering competition from the house finch, declining numbers of farms, and increasingly fewer farms that keep livestock, with which house sparrows are often associated.

Family Motacillidae (Pipits)

American Pipit, *Anthus rubescens*
An, Ar, Bl, Br, Ch, Cu, Gar, Gr, Gre, Grf, Ho, Hol, Ke, Li, Lo, Log, Mc, Ro, Sh, Th

Status. The American pipit is a common spring and fall migrant throughout the Sandhills. Breeding Bird Surveys between 1966 and 2015 indicate the species had a national population decline (3.8% annually) during that period.

Migration. The range of 125 initial spring sightings is from January 1 to May 21, with a median of April 23. Half of the records fall within the period April 13–May 5. Eleven final spring sightings are from April 17 to May 23, with a median of April 28. Eighteen initial fall sightings are from August 24 to October 29, with a median of October 2. Sixteen final fall sightings are from September 14 to December 31, with a median of October 26. Probably overwintering is quite rare, judging from the limited number of late fall records.

Habitats. Migrating birds are found in open plains, fields, and bare shorelines; they generally favor moist to wet environments over dry.

Sprague's Pipit, *Anthus spragueii*
An, Gar, Ke

Very rare. Two Sprague's pipits were seen at Clear Creek, Keith County, in late April 1995 and 2000 (Brown, Dinsmore, and Brown, 2012). Two additional records of this migrant species are from Antelope County on March 17, 1963, and Garden County on October 4, 2009 (Silcock and Jorgensen, various dates).

Family Fringillidae (Boreal Finches)

Evening Grosbeak, *Coccothraustes vespertinus*
Ch, Gar, Ke, Li, Mo, Sh, Th

Status. The evening grosbeak is an irregular and increasingly rare winter visitor throughout the Sandhills. Breeding Bird Surveys between 1966 and 2015 indicate the species underwent a national population decline of 1.4 percent annually during that period.

Migration. Thirty-four initial fall sightings are from September 3 to December 31, with a median of November 9. Half of the records fall within the period October 19–November 29. Fifty-two final spring sightings are from January 5 to May 28, with a median of April 25. Half of the records fall within the period April 21–May 20.

Habitats. While in Nebraska this species is usually associated with streamside woodlands that have seed-bearing deciduous trees; it sometimes also appears at bird-feeding stations. This large, massive-billed finch is especially fond of sunflower seeds and can easily crack any hard seeds it encounters.

Gray-crowned Rosy-Finch, *Leucosticte tephrocotis*
Ga, Ke, Li

Very rare. There are two January and February records for the gray-crowned rosy-finch for Ogallala, Keith County, and Oshkosh, Garden County (Brown, Dinsmore, and Brown, 2012). A single bird was recorded in Lincoln County on December 6, 1983 (Silcock and Jorgensen, various dates).

House Finch, *Haemorhous mexicanus*
An, Ar, Bo, Br, Ch, Cu, **Gar**, Gr, Gre, Grf, Ho, Hol, **Ke, Li**, Lo, Log, Mc, Mo, Ro, Sh, Th, Wh

Status. The house finch is a locally common permanent resident throughout the Sandhills. Possible and probable recent nestings have also been reported from most Sandhills counties, except Arthur, Grant, and McPherson Counties (Mollhoff, 2016). Breeding Bird Surveys between 1966 and 2015 indicate the species underwent a population increase (0.12% annually) during that period.

Habitats. This species is associated with open woods, river-bottom thickets, scrubby vegetation, ranchlands, and (in Nebraska) suburbs and towns. House finches historically occurred in western Nebraska but arrived in eastern Nebraska in the late 1980s from western Iowa. The entire eastern population derives from a few birds released in New York City during the 1940s, when commercial pet dealers dumped their illegally captive birds in order to escape arrest and prosecution.

The Sandhills population might have come from either or both of these sources.

Purple Finch, *Haemorhous purpureus*
An, Bl, Bo, Br, Ch, Cu, Gar, Gre, Grf, Hol, Ke, Li, Lo, Log, Ro, Sh, Th, Wh

Status. The purple finch is an uncommon migrant and winter visitor in the Sandhills.

Migration. Thirty-seven initial fall sightings range from August 14 to December 26, with a median of October 27. Half of the records fall within the period October 15–November 6. Forty-nine final spring sightings are from January 2 to June 5, with a median of April 23. Half of the records fall within the period April 16–May 8.

Habitats. Nonbreeding purple finches are associated with woodland streams. They sometimes also appear at bird feeders during winter.

Cassin's Finch, *Haemorhous cassinii*
Gar, Ke, Sh

Status. Very rare. The Cassin's finch is reported as an irregular early winter visitor in the Lake Ogallala vicinity, Keith County, with records from November to January and March (Brown, Dinsmore, and Brown, 2012). It has also been reported from Sheridan County (NOU website checklist). A single bird was netted in Garden County during July 24–25, 1979 (Silcock and Jorgensen, various dates). Breeding Bird Surveys between 1966 and 2015 indicate the species collectively underwent a survey-wide population decline of 2.5 percent annually during that period.

Migration. The only fall records are for October 26 and 27. Thirteen winter and spring records range from January 1 to May 14, with a median of April 12. Half of the records fall between March 30 and May 3. Kansas records are nearly all from September 22 to April 28 but mainly extend from October to March (Thompson et al., 2011).

Habitats. Normally associated with open coniferous forests during winter, this finch usually forages on the ground for seeds.

Common Redpoll, *Acanthis flammea*
An, Ch, Gar, Ho, Hol, Ke, Li, Lo, Mo, Sh, Wh

Status. The common redpoll is an occasional winter visitor throughout the Sandhills. It is locally common during some winters but absent in others.

Migration. Twenty initial fall sightings range from August 8 to December 30, with a median of November 26. Thirty final spring sightings are from January 10 to May 30, with a median of March 17. Half of the records fall between March 7 and March 26.

Habitats. While in Nebraska this species is associated with conifers, deciduous thickets, and weedy fields; it also sometimes visits bird feeders.

Red Crossbill, *Loxia curvirostra*
An, Bl, Bo, Br, **Ch, Cu**, Gar, Gr, Hol, **Ke**, Li, Sh, Th, Wh

Status. The red crossbill is an irregular winter visitor and migrant throughout the Sandhills in wooded habitats. The birds breed locally or rarely in the Bessey Ranger District of the Nebraska National Forest but are probably uncommon only in the panhandle region. Breeding Bird Surveys between 1966 and 2015 indicate the species underwent a population decline (0.83% annually) during that period.

Migration. Thirty-one initial fall sightings range from July 26 to December 29, with a median of November 12. Half of the records fall within the period October 28–December 14. Forty-four final spring sightings are from January 1 to June 2, with a median of April 1. Half of the records fall within the period March 19–May 19.

Habitats. During the breeding season this species is primarily associated with coniferous forests. Migrants and wintering birds are also largely confined to conifer plantings or forests, but sometimes flocks may also be found foraging in stands of sunflowers or ragweeds. Red crossbills periodically appear in eastern Nebraska, especially around coniferous plantations, where they can pry seeds out of cones using their unique beak tips, which are twisted screwdriver-like to open the seed-containing bracts. Different populations around the country vary in beak shape, flight call, and alarm call, suggesting there may be several "sibling species" now considered as a single species. The form most common in Nebraska (*L. c. benti*) is adapted to feeding on the seeds of ponderosa pine (*Nebraska Bird Review* 78: 62).

White-winged Crossbill, *Loxia leucoptera*
Ar, Bo, Br

Status. The white-winged crossbill is a very rare and irregular winter visitor and spring migrant throughout the Sandhills.

Migration. Three fall records are from October 16 to November 24. Twenty-two spring sightings range from January 1 to June 14, with a median of March 6. Half of the records fall within the period February 4–April 20.

Habitats. This crossbill species is associated with coniferous forests or plantations throughout the year, especially pines.

Pine Siskin, *Spinus pinus*
An, Ar, Bl, Bo, Br, Ch, Cu, Gar, Gr, Gre, Grf, Ho, Hol, **Ke**, Li, Lo, Log, Mc, Mo, Ro, Sh, **Th**, W

Status. The pine siskin is an irregular but sometimes common migrant and winter visitor and an occasional summer resident throughout the Sandhills. Regular breeding is limited to the Pine Ridge area, but sporadic nestings have occurred widely in the state, following cold springs (*Wilson Bulletin* 41: 77). Probable nesting occurred in the vicinity of Cedar Point Biological Station, Keith County, because both juveniles and adults with brood patches were mist-netted and banded there (Brown et al., 1996).

Migration. Sixty initial fall sightings range from July 25 to December 31, with a median of October 16. Half of the records fall within the period October 1–November 18. Thirty-five final spring sightings range from January 19 to June 9, with a median of May 12. Half of the records fall within the period May 8–June 1.

Habitats. Nonbreeding birds occur in both wooded and treeless areas, often in small flocks that feed on weed seeds. Breeding can occur in diverse settings from rural to suburban or urban, in conifers and deciduous trees, including evergreen plantings, ornamental shrubs (such as lilacs), and vines.

Lesser Goldfinch, *Spinus psaltria*
Ga, Grf, Ke

Very rare. A single lesser goldfinch was seen at Cedar Point Biological Station in June 1998 (Brown, Dinsmore, and Brown, 2012). Three reports are from Crescent Lake NWR, Garden County: May 25–June 9, 2008; June 12, 2009; and May 27–29, 2010 (Silcock and Jorgensen, various dates). This species is also listed for Garfield County on the NOU website checklist.

American Goldfinch, *Spinus tristis*
An, Ar, Bl, Bo, **Br**, Ch, **Cu**, Gar, Gr, Gre, Grf, Ho, Hol, **Ke**, **Li**, Lo, **Log**, Mc, Mo, Ro, **Sh**, **Th**, Wh

Status. The American goldfinch is a common permanent resident throughout the Sandhills. Winter populations vary from year to year. Possible and probable recent nestings have been reported from most Sandhills counties (Mollhoff, 2016). Breeding Bird Surveys between 1966 and 2015 indicate the species underwent a population decline (0.17% annually) during that period.

Habitats. During the fall and winter, flocks of this species may often be found foraging in fields of tall weeds, such as ragweeds and sunflowers. Breeding usually occurs in rather open grazing country, farmyards, swamps, weedy fields, and other open habitats where thistles and cattails (the down of which is used for nest lining and the seeds for feeding the young) are abundant.

Family Calcariidae (Longspurs and Snow Buntings)

Lapland Longspur, *Calcarius lapponicus*
An, Ar, Bo, Br, Ch, Cu, Gar, Gr, Gre, Hol, Ke, Li, Lo, Log, Mc, Mo, Ro, Sh

Status. The Lapland longspur is a locally common migrant and winter visitor throughout the Sandhills. It is probably the commonest of the longspurs in Nebraska during winter.

Migration. Fifty-six initial fall sightings are from September 25 to December 31, with a median of

November 12. Half of the records fall within the period October 25–November 21. Forty-four final spring records are from January 3 to May 10, with a median of February 27. Half of the records fall within the period February 24–March 23.

Habitats. Migrants and wintering birds occur in open grassy plains, stubble fields, overgrazed pastures, and similar grassy or low-stature habitats.

Chestnut-collared Longspur, *Calcarius ornatus*
Ar, Ch, Gar, Gr, Hol, Ke, Mc, Mo, Sh, Wh

Status. The chestnut-collared longspur is an uncommon migrant and winter visitor throughout the Sandhills and a summer resident in the northwestern corner of the state southeastwardly to Sheridan County and perhaps northern Cherry County.

Migration. Thirty initial spring sightings in northwestern Nebraska are from March 18 to June 3, with a median of April 12. Sixteen final fall sightings are from September 22 to October 22, with a median of October 8. Like the thick-billed longspur, the migration pattern of this species is extremely difficult to estimate in Nebraska, since in various regions it may be a summer resident, a spring and fall migrant, or a winter visitor.

Habitats. Migrants and wintering birds occur on open plains and grassy fields, including those at airports. Breeding usually occurs on short-grass or cut mixed-grass prairies and less frequently in the low meadow zones around ponds and in disturbed grasslands such as grazed pasturelands.

Smith's Longspur, *Calcarius pictus*
An, Cu, Sh

Very rare. Sandhills reports of the Smith's longspur are from three counties: Custer County on November 12, 1966; Sheridan County on September 27, 1981; and Antelope County on March 21, 2016 (Silcock and Jorgensen, various dates).

Thick-billed Longspur, *Rhynchophanes mccownii*
(Previously McCown's Longspur)
Ch, Gar, Ke, Sh

Status. The thick-billed longspur is an occasional migrant and winter visitor throughout the Sandhills.

Migration. Twenty-six initial spring sightings in northwestern Nebraska are from March 16 to May 21, with a median of April 3. Six final fall sightings are from September 5 to November 26, with a mean of October 1. Elsewhere in the state this species is a spring and fall migrant, and sometimes a winter visitor, so its migration status statewide is impossible to summarize easily.

Habitats. Migrants inhabit shortgrass plains, pasturelands, and plowed fields. Breeding occurs in short-grass and mixed-grass prairies, stubble fields, and newly sprouted grain fields.

Snow Bunting, *Plectrophenax nivalis*
An, Ar, Bo, Br, Ch, Grf, Gr, Ke, Lo, Mo, Ro, Sh, Wh

Status. The snow bunting is an uncommon winter visitor throughout the Sandhills, appearing only very irregularly and probably mainly in northern counties. Numbers in Nebraska appear to be declining in association with global warming.

Migration. Eleven initial fall sightings are from October 19 to December 24, with a median of November 16. Thirty-one final spring sightings are from January 1 to March 23, with a median of February 10.

Habitats. Migrants and wintering birds are associated with open plains and snow-covered fields.

Family Passerellidae (New World Sparrows and Towhees)

Cassin's Sparrow, *Peucaea cassinii*
Ch, Gar, **Ke**, Li

Status. The Cassin's sparrow is a rare and irregular spring and fall migrant and very rare summer resident in the Sandhills. The species has been reported from a number of counties, and singing males have been seen in Keith and Garden Counties (Brown et al., 1996; Brown, Dinsmore, and Brown, 2012). The species is irruptive, periodically moving north to breed, but it is normally restricted to the southern and western portions of the Great Plains region. In 2011 a major influx came into Nebraska during a drought in the Southwest (*Nebraska Bird Review* 78: 960).

Grasshopper sparrow, adult on annual sunflower head

Grasshopper Sparrow, *Ammodramus savannarum*
An, **Ar**, Bl, Bo, Br, Ch, Cu, Gar, Gr, Gre, Grf, Ho, Hol, Ke, Li, Lo, Log, Mc, Mo, Ro, Sh, Th, Wh

Status. The grasshopper sparrow is a common spring and fall migrant and summer resident throughout the Sandhills. Breeding Bird Surveys between 1966 and 2015 indicate the species underwent a national population decline (2.4% annually) during that period, one of the most rapid rates of population decline among grassland birds.

Migration. The range of 85 initial spring sightings is from March 14 to June 10, with a median of May 6. Half of the records fall within the period April 27–May 15. Sixty-seven final fall sightings range from July 26 to November 6, with a median of September 9. Half of the records fall within the period August 12–September 29.

Habitats. Migrants and breeding birds occur in mixed-grass prairies, pasturelands, short-grass prairies, sage prairies, and, to a limited extent, tall-grass prairies. Areas that have grown up to shrubs are avoided, but scattered trees in grassland are sometimes used for song perches. The birds feed largely on grasshoppers during their time in Nebraska, which might help account for their unusually sturdy beak.

Black-throated Sparrow, *Amphispiza bilineata*
Ke, Li

Accidental. A single black-throated sparrow was seen near Keystone, Keith County, May 26, 1984 (Brown, Dinsmore, and Brown, 2012).

Lark Sparrow, *Chondestes grammacus*
An, **Ar**, Bl, Bo, Br, Ch, Cu, Gar, Gr, Gre, Grf, Ho, Hol, Ke, Li, Lo, Log, Mc, Mo, Ro, Sh, Th, Wh

Status. The lark sparrow is a common spring and fall migrant and a common summer resident in grasslands throughout the Sandhills. Breeding Bird Surveys between 1966 and 2015 indicate the species underwent a national population decline (0.78% annually) during that period.

Migration. The range of 125 initial spring sightings is from April 5 to June 10, with a median of May 5. Half of the records fall within the period April 28–May 13. Seventy-six final fall sightings range from July 23 to November 13, with a median of September 3. Half of the records fall within the period August 22–September 18.

Habitats. While in Nebraska this species occupies natural grasslands or weedy fields that adjoin or include scattered trees, shrubs, and weeds.

Lark Bunting, *Calamospiza melanocorys*
An, **Ar**, Bl, **Ch**, **Cu**, **Gar**, **Gr**, Gre, Ho, Hol, Ke, Li, Lo, Log, **Mc**, Mo, Ro, **Sh**, Th, Wh

Status. The lark bunting is a common spring and fall migrant and summer resident throughout the Sandhills. Possible and probable recent nestings have been also reported from Blaine, Brown, Holt, Hooker, Keith, Lincoln, Logan, and Rock Counties (Mollhoff, 2016). Breeding Bird Surveys between 1966 and 2015 indicate the species underwent a national population decline (2.9% annually) during that period. Outside the breeding season it is highly gregarious, and it is colonial even during the nesting period. Near Cedar Point Biological Station in Keith County, it may be very common one year only to be gone the following and then to return again some years later. Perhaps local precipitation or irrigation patterns cause its periodic appearance and subsequent disappearance.

Migration. The range of 104 initial spring sightings is from April 8 to June 10, with a median of May 10. Half of the records fall within the period May 4–16. Sixty-five final fall sightings are from July 20 to October 13, with a median of August 30. Half of the records fall within the period August 20–September 8.

Habitats. While in Nebraska this species is usually found in mixed-grass or short-grass prairies and sage-dominated areas, but it also occurs in areas of taller grasses with scattered shrubs and along weedy roadsides, in retired croplands, and in fields of alfalfa or clover.

Grasshopper sparrow, adult male singing. *Photo by P. Johnsgard.*

Chipping Sparrow, *Spizella passerina*
An, Ar, Bl, Bo, **Br**, Ch, Cu, Gar, Gr, **Grf**, Ho, **Hol**, Ke, **Li**, **Lo**, Log, Mc, Mo, Ro, **Sh**, **Th**, Wh

Status. The chipping sparrow is a common spring and fall migrant and a common summer resident throughout the Sandhills. Possible and probable recent nestings have been reported from Blaine, Cherry, Custer, Garden, Grant, Hooker, Keith, Logan, McPherson, and Rock Counties (Mollhoff, 2016). Breeding Bird Surveys between 1966 and 2015 indicate the species underwent a population decline (0.50% annually) during that period.

Migration. The range of 100 initial spring sightings is from January 14 to June 3, with a median of April 23. Half of the records fall within the period April 6–May 2. Ninety-nine final fall records range from July 23 to December 20, with a median of October 2. Half of the records fall within the period September 17–October 16.

Habitats. While in Nebraska this species is associated with the margins of deciduous forests, parks, gardens, residential areas, farmsteads, orchards, and other open areas with nearby or scattered trees and few or no shrubs.

Clay-colored Sparrow, *Spizella pallida*
An, Ar, Bl, Bo, Br, Ch, Cu, Gar, Grf, Gr, Gre, Hol, Ho, Ke, Li, Log, Lo, Mc, Mo, Ro, Sh, Th, Wh

Status. The clay-colored sparrow is a common spring and fall migrant throughout the Sandhills. Breeding Bird Surveys between 1966 and 2015 indicate the species underwent a population decline (1.14% annually) during that period.

Migration. The range of 124 initial spring sightings is from March 3 to May 29, with a median of May 3. Half of the records fall within the period April 28–May 8. Eighty-nine final spring sightings range from April 24 to June 1, with a median of May 16. Forty-one initial fall sightings are from July 23 to November 2, with a median of September 9. Half of the records fall within the period August 30–September 18. Thirty-nine final fall sightings are from August 27 to December 18, with a median of October 8.

Habitats. Migrants occur in thickets and weed patches among grassland. Breeding birds move to similar habitats, which provide a mixture of medium-stature grasses and scattered shrubs or low trees, or disturbed lands such as cutover or burned woodlands.

Field Sparrow, *Spizella pusilla*
An, Ar, **Bl**, Bo, Br, **Ch**, Cu, Gar, Gr, **Gre**, Grf, Ho, Hol, **Ke**, **Li**, **Lo**, Log, Mc, Mo, Ro, **Th**, **Wh**

Status. The field sparrow is a common spring and fall migrant and a locally common summer visitor throughout the Sandhills. Possible and probable recent nestings have also been reported from Antelope, Boone, Brown, Garfield, Holt, Hooker, Keith, Logan, Rock, and Thomas Counties (Mollhoff, 2016). Breeding Bird Surveys between 1966 and 2015 indicate the species underwent a population decline (2.33% annually) during that period.

Migration. Eighty-one initial spring sightings range from February 11 to June 6, with a median of April 20. Half of the records fall within the period April 4–May 6. Eighty-three final fall sightings are from August 1 to December 26, with a median of October 6. Half of the records fall within the period September 23–October 25.

Habitats. During the breeding season this species occurs in brushy but open woodlands, forest edges, brushy ravines or draws, sagebrush flats, abandoned hayfields, forest clearings, and similar open habitats that have scattered shrubs or low trees. It is similar to the chipping sparrow in its habitat but depends more on shrubs and less on trees for nesting.

Brewer's Sparrow, *Spizella breweri*
Ch (H), Ke, Mo, Sh

Status. Brewer's sparrow is a very rare spring and fall migrant in the Sandhills region.

Migration. Twenty-seven initial spring sightings range from April 18 to May 21, with a median of May 5. Half of the records fall within the period April 29–May 12. Fifteen final fall records range from August 18 to October 12, with a median of September 7.

Habitats. This sparrow species while in Nebraska is associated with open scrublands, especially short-grass plains with sagebrush, rabbitbrush, or other semiarid shrubs.

Lark sparrow, breeding adult. *Photo by P. Johnsgard.*

Fox Sparrow, *Passerella iliaca*
An, Ch, Hol, Ke, Wh

Status. The fox sparrow is an occasional spring and fall migrant throughout the Sandhills.

Migration. Fifty-three initial spring sightings are from January 4 to June 4, with a median of March 30. Half of the records fall within the period March 17–April 18. Twenty-two final spring sightings are from April 1 to April 23, with a median of April 10. Thirty-one initial fall records are from August 2 to November 11, with a median of October 11. Half of the records fall within the period October 5–17. Twenty-eight final fall sightings are from August 18 to December 31, with a median of November 11.

Habitats. Migrants are usually associated with brushy woodlands, streamside thickets, and sometimes residential shrubbery.

American Tree Sparrow, *Spizelloides arborea*
An, Ar, Bl, Bo, Br, Ch, Cu, Gar, Gr, Gre, Grf, Ho, Hol, Ke, Li, Lo, Log, Mc, Mo, Ro, Sh, Th, Wh

Status. The American tree sparrow is a common migrant and winter visitor in grasslands and brushy habitats throughout the Sandhills.

Migration. The range of 127 initial fall sightings is from September 3 to December 31, with a median of October 21. Half of the records fall within the period October 12–November 2. Sixty-five final spring sightings range from January 24 to May 27, with a median of April 6. Half of the records fall within the period March 27–April 22.

Habitats. During migration and winter periods, this species is found in flocks among thickets, brushy areas, and shrubby or weedy grasslands.

Dark-eyed Junco, *Junco hyemalis*
An, Ar, Bl, Bo, Br, Ch, Cu, Gar, Gr, Grf, Ho, **Hol** (H), Ke, Li, Lo, Log, Mc, Mo, Ro, Sh, Th, Wh

Status. The dark-eyed junco is a common migrant and winter visitor throughout the Sandhills. The nominate slate-colored race, *J. h. hyemalis*, is common statewide and is the most common of the many confusing plumage variants. The Oregon phenotype (consisting of several intergrading races, including the so-called "pink-sided," *J. h. mearnsi*) is fairly common throughout the state, and the gray-headed race, *J. h. caniceps*, is an irregular and occasional winter visitor in western Nebraska, sometimes occurring as far east as Antelope County. The slightly larger "white-winged" race, *J. h. aikeni* (which has whitish tips to some of the larger wing coverts), is a breeder in the Black Hills and adjacent Pine Ridge and mainly winters within the panhandle. Last, a little-studied plumage variant called the Cassiar junco (*J. h. cismontanus*) has been increasingly reported in the state. Except perhaps for the white-winged race, all of these variants are likely to be encountered in the Sandhills. Breeding Bird Surveys between 1966 and 2015 indicate the species underwent a national population decline (1.30% annually) during that period.

Migration. The range of 105 initial fall sightings is from September 1 to December 31, with a median of October 6. Half of the records fall within the period September 26–October 15. Seventy-five final spring sightings are from January 1 to May 20, with a median of April 15. Half of the records fall within the period March 27–April 25. Four initial fall sightings of *J. h. caniceps* are from September 21 to October 21, with a mean of October 3. Twenty final spring sightings are from January 1 to May 18, with a median of March 23.

Habitats. Migrants and wintering birds are widely distributed in woodlands, suburbs, and residential areas, where they forage on the ground and often visit feeding stations. Breeding in the Black Hills occurs in coniferous forests, aspen groves, and deciduous woodlands in hollows, canyons, and gulches; similar habitats are probably used in the Pine Ridge region. One of the commonest of Nebraska's wintering sparrows, the dark-eyed junco is one of the most frequently seen species at winter bird-feeding stations. A review of bird-feeder abundance in Nebraska indicates that, in descending sequence, the four most abundant species are northern cardinal, dark-eyed junco, black-capped chickadee, and house finch.

White-crowned Sparrow, *Zonotrichia leucophrys*
An, Ar, Bl, Bo, Br, Ch, Cu, Gar, Gr, Gre, Grf, Ho, Hol, Ke, Li, Lo, Log, Mc, Ro, Sh, Th, Wh

Status. The white-crowned sparrow is a common spring and fall migrant throughout the Sandhills and a locally common winter visitor.

Migration. Ninety-eight initial fall sightings range from August 25 to December 29, with a median of October 3. Half of the records fall within the period September 21–October 16. Eighty-two final spring sightings are from February 1 to May 27, with a median of May 15. Half of the records fall within the period May 2–8.

Habitats. Migrants are associated with thickets, woodland edges, and weedy areas. They sometimes move to farmyards and feeding stations in winter.

Harris's Sparrow, *Zonotrichia querula*
An, Ar, Bl, Bo, Br, Ch, Cu, Gar, Gr, Gre, Grf, Ho, Hol, Ke, Li, Lo, Log, Mc, Ro, Sh, Th, Wh

Status. The Harris's sparrows is a common spring and fall migrant throughout the Sandhills.

Migration. The range of 115 initial fall sightings is from August 13 to December 31, with a median of October 14. Half of the records fall within the period October 4–22. Ninety-five final spring sightings are from February 8 to June 10, with a median of May 12. Half of the records fall within the period May 9–16.

Habitats. Migrants and wintering birds occur in rural, suburban, or urban areas that have shrubs, low trees, and tall weedy plants, often near streamside woodland edges or thickets.

White-throated Sparrow, *Zonotrichia albicollis*
An, Ar, Bl, Bo, Ch, Cu, Gar, Gr, Gre, Grf, Ho, Hol, Ke, Lo, Log, Mc, Ro, Sh, Th, Wh

Status. The white-throated sparrow is a common spring and fall migrant throughout the Sandhills and a locally common winter visitor.

Migration. Sixty-five initial fall sightings range from September 18 to November 25, with a median of October 3. Half of the records fall within the period September 25–October 5. Fifty-two final spring sightings are from February 2 to June 4, with a median of May 12. Half of the records fall within the period May 6–17.

Habitats. Migrants are associated with woodland edges, thickets, weedy fields, and sheltered areas near water; they sometimes come to feeding stations during winter.

Vesper Sparrow, *Pooecetes gramineus*
An, Ar, Bl, Bo, Br, **Ch**, Cu, **Gar**, Gr, Gre, Ho, **Hol**, Ke, **Li**, **Lo**, **Mc**, Mo, Ro, **Sh**, **Th**, Wh

Status. The vesper sparrow is a common spring and fall migrant and breeder throughout the Sandhills. Possible and probable recent nestings have also been reported from Antelope, Blaine, Brown, Garden, Grant, Holt, Hooker, and Rock Counties (Mollhoff, 2016). Breeding Bird Surveys between 1966 and 2015 indicate the species underwent a population decline (0.85% annually) during that period.

Migration. Eighty initial spring sightings are from March 4 to May 24, with a median of April 18. Half of the records fall within the period April 13–27. Eighty-three final fall sightings range from August 13 to November 24, with a median of October 9. Half of the records fall within the period September 26–October 18.

Habitats. Migrants and breeding birds frequent overgrown fields, prairie edges, and similar habitats where grasslands join or are mixed with shrubs and scattered low trees.

LeConte's Sparrow, *Ammospiza leconteii*
An, Bo, Br, Ch, Cu, Gar

Status. LeConte's sparrow is an inconspicuous but regular and probably uncommon spring and fall migrant in the Sandhills, west to at least Cherry County.

Migration. Fifty-four initial spring sightings are from April 1 to June 7, with a median of April 29. Half of the records fall within the period April 21–May 8. Thirteen final spring sightings are from April 17 to May 19, with a median of May 2. Twenty-one initial fall sightings are from July 25 to October 15, with a median of September 22. Seventeen final fall sightings are from July 26 to November 9, with a median of October 20.

Habitats. Migrants are found in wet meadows and marshy edges with sedges, cattails, and deep grasses.

Nelson's Sparrow, *Ammospiza nelsoni*
An, Ch, Sh

Status. Nelson's sparrow is an inconspicuous and seemingly very rare spring and fall migrant in the eastern Sandhills, west to at least Cherry and Sheridan Counties.

Migration. Five spring sightings are from March 29 to May 30, with a mean of May 5. Three of the records are for the month of May. Nine fall records are from September 7 to October 21, with a mean of September 30. Five of the records are for the month of October.

Habitats. Migrants are found along the wet edges of marshes and sloughs, usually in wetter habitats than those used by LeConte's sparrow.

Baird's Sparrow, *Centronyx bairdii*
Cu, Gar, Ke, Mc, Th

Rare. Individual Baird's sparrows have been seen on two occasions at the Clear Creek Wildlife Management Area marshes, Keith County, during May and September (Brown, Dinsmore, and Brown, 2012). The other Sandhills records are from Custer County on September 9, 1994; Bessey Ranger District, Nebraska National Forest, Thomas County, on September 9, 2002; and McPherson County on September 16, 2017. One Baird's sparrow was banded at Crescent Lake NWR, Garden County, on October 15, 1980 (Silcock and Jorgensen, various dates).

Savannah Sparrow, *Passerculus sandwichensis*
An, Ar, Bl, Bo, Br, Ch, Cu, Gar, Gr, Gre, Grf, Ho, Hol, Ke, Li, Lo, Log, Mc, Mo, Ro, Sh, Th, Wh

Status. The savannah sparrow is a common spring and fall migrant statewide and a rare or local summer resident in the Sandhills. Sandhills breeding seems to be limited to the western and northern parts of this region. Breeding Bird Surveys between 1966 and 2015 indicate the species underwent a population decline (1.36% annually) during that period.

Migration. The range of 69 initial spring sightings is from March 17 to June 5, with a median of April 22. Half of the records fall within the period April 15–29. Thirty-eight final spring sightings are from April 10 to May 30, with a median of May 10. Thirty-nine initial fall sightings range from July 28 to October 9, with a median of September 19. Half of the records fall within the period September 5–28. Thirty-nine final fall sightings are from October 2 to November 22, with a median of October 19.

Habitats. Migrants are usually found in open grasslands, lightly grazed pastures, and brushy edges. Breeding occurs in wet-meadow zones of wetlands and in tallgrass to mixed-grass prairies.

Song Sparrow, *Melospiza melodia*
An, Ar, Bl, Bo, Br, Ch, **Cu**, **Gar**, Gr, Gre, **Grf**, Ho, Hol, Ke, Li, **Lo**, Log, **Mc**, Mo, Ro, **Sh**, Th, **Wh**

Status. The song sparrow is a common spring and fall migrant and uncommon winter visitor throughout the Sandhills. Breeding is probably limited mostly to the eastern parts of the Sandhills. Possible and probable recent nestings have also been reported from Antelope, Blaine, Boone, Brown, Cherry, Holt, Keith, Lincoln, Logan, Rock, Sheridan and Thomas Counties (Mollhoff, 2016). Breeding Bird Surveys between 1966 and 2015 indicate the species underwent a population decline (0.76% annually) during that period.

Migration. Forty-five initial spring sightings are from January 1 to June 6, with a median of April 8. Forty-five final spring sightings are from January 12 to June 3, with a median of April 30. Seventy-six initial fall sightings are from August 2 to November 2, with a median of September 30. Forty-four final fall sightings are from October 6 to December 31, with a median of December 20. The data suggest that this species commonly overwinters in Nebraska and that its migration tendencies are very poorly defined.

Habitats. Migrants and wintering birds occur in weedy areas, thickets, and streamside woodland edges. Breeding occurs in similar habitats, including forest margins, shrubby swamps, the brushy edges of ponds, shelterbelts, and farmsteads.

Lincoln's Sparrow, *Melospiza lincolnii*
An, Ar, Bl, Br, Ch, Cu, Gar, Gr, Gre, Grf, Ho, Hol, Ke, Li, Lo, Log, Mc, Mo, Ro, Sh, Th, Wh

Status. Lincoln's sparrow is a common spring and fall migrant throughout the Sandhills. Breeding Bird Surveys between 1966 and 2015 indicate the species underwent a population decline (0.36% annually) during that period.

Migration. Ninety-four initial spring sightings are from January 2 to May 29, with a median of April 26. Half of the records fall within the period April 19–May 7. Sixty-two final spring sightings are

New World Sparrows and Towhees

Prairie passerine birds, including (A) savannah sparrow, (B) clay-colored sparrow, (C) lark bunting male, (D) grasshopper sparrow, and (E) horned lark

from April 20 to May 31, with a median of May 13. Forty-eight initial fall sightings are from September 2 to October 12, with a median of September 15. Half of the records fall within the period September 7–17. Twenty-five final fall sightings are from September 20 to December 29, with a median of October 19.

Habitats. Migrants are associated with streamside thickets, thick weedy areas, and other rather dense grassy or weedy areas close to water; they occur less frequently in residential shrubbery.

Swamp Sparrow, *Melospiza georgiana*
An, Ar, Bl, **Bo**, **Br**, Ch, Cu, **Gar**, Grf, Gr, Gre, Hol, Ke, **Li**, **Lo**, Log, **Ro**, **Sh**, Th, **Wh**

Status. The swamp sparrow is a spring and fall migrant throughout the Sandhills and a local summer resident in central Nebraska marshes, including in Antelope, Boone, Brown, Garden, Loup, Rock, Sheridan, and Wheeler Counties. Possible and probable recent nestings have also been reported from Cherry, Custer, Garfield, Holt, and Logan Counties (Mollhoff, 2016). Breeding Bird Surveys between 1966 and 2015 indicate the species underwent a population increase (0.93% annually) during that period.

Migration. Thirty-three initial spring sightings are from March 30 to June 6, with a median of April 23. Half of the records fall within the period April 10–30. Fourteen final spring sightings are from April 13 to May 25, with a median of May 7. Nineteen initial fall sightings are from July 21 to October 21, with a median of September 30. Thirteen final fall sightings are from October 2 to December 29, with a median of October 24.

Habitats. Migrants are found in marshy areas, and during the breeding season nesting occurs in marshes or other wetlands that have such vegetation as cattails, phragmites, and shrubs or small trees. This species is a semicolonial nester whose habitat needs seemingly limit it to only a few known nesting locations in Nebraska, primarily the Sandhills marshes.

Green-tailed Towhee, *Pipilo chlorurus*
Ke, Li, Mc

Very rare. Four mostly older records of the green-tailed towhee are from Keith County on May 3, 1955; Logan County on May 31, 1963; McPherson County on June 6, 1982; and Lincoln County on June 4, 1985 (Silcock and Jorgensen, various dates).

Spotted Towhee, *Pipilo maculatus*
An, Ar, Bl, Bo, **Br**, **Ch**, Cu, **Gar**, Gr, Gre, Grf, Ho, Hol, **Ke**, **Li**, Lo, Mc, Mo, **Ro**, **Sh**, Th, **Wh**

Status. Collectively, the spotted and eastern towhees are common spring and fall migrants and summer residents throughout the Sandhills. Breeding is very local in the Sandhills but extends from the Colorado and Wyoming borders (mainly *P. maculatus* phenotypes) east in the Platte River valley, where the population is composed of mainly *P. erythropthalmus* phenotypes in northeastern and southeastern Nebraska. Possible and probable recent nestings have also been reported from Blaine, Boone, Garfield, Holt, Hooker, Loup, and Thomas Counties (Mollhoff, 2016). Breeding Bird Surveys between 1966 and 2015 indicate the species underwent a population decline (0.03% annually) during that period.

Migration. Sixty-nine initial spring sightings range from February 7 to May 30, with a median of April 22. Half of the records fall within the period April 10–30. Ninety-three final fall records are from July 24 to December 31, with a median of October 15. Half of the records fall within the period September 30–October 31. Nearly 20 percent of the records are for December, suggesting that overwintering is fairly frequent.

Habitats. While in Nebraska these towhees occur in brushy fields, thickets, woodland edges or openings, second-growth forests, and city parks or suburbs with trees and tall shrubbery. The zone of hybridization between these dubious species is especially wide in Nebraska; farther south in Kansas there is a geographic break between breeding habitats that makes the situation there less confusing. Many of the summering birds along the Platte and North Platte Rivers are apparent hybrids (*Auk* 76: 326–38; Brown et al., 1996).

Eastern Towhee, *Pipilo erythropthalmus*
An, Bo, Br, Ch, Cu, Grf, Hol, Ke, Li, Lo, Ro, Th, Wh

Status. See the account for the spotted towhee. Unlike the spotted towhee, the eastern towhee rarely winters in Nebraska, except in the extreme southeast. Possible and probable recent nestings have also been reported from Garfield, Holt, Keith, Lincoln, Rock, and Thomas Counties (Mollhoff, 2016). Breeding Bird Surveys between 1966 and 2015 indicate the eastern towhee underwent a national population decline (1.34% annually) during that period.

Family Icteriidae (Chats)

Yellow-breasted Chat, *Icteria virens*
An, Bl, Br, **Ch**, Cu, **Gar**, Gr, Gre, Grf, Ho, Hol, **Ke**, Li, Lo, Mo, Ro, Sh, Th, Wh

Status. Previously a common spring and fall migrant and summer resident throughout the Sandhills, the yellow-breasted chat is now increasingly uncommon. Possible and probable recent nestings have been reported from Blaine, Brown, Grant, Holt, Hooker, Lincoln, Loup, Rock, Sheridan, Thomas, and Wheeler Counties (Mollhoff, 2016). Breeding Bird Surveys between 1966 and 2015 indicate the species underwent a national population decline (0.62% annually) during that period. In Nebraska, the greatest declines have occurred in eastern populations.

Migration. The range of 120 initial spring sightings is from April 23 to June 7, with a median of May 15. Half of the records fall within the period May 10–21. The range of 63 final fall sightings is from July 21 to October 16, with a median of September 9. Half of the records fall within the period August 21–September 23.

Habitats. Breeding birds usually favor ravine or streamside thickets, especially those with small trees and tall shrubs, as well as forest edges, dense stands of tree saplings, and clumps of shrubs in overgrazed pastures.

Family Icteridae (Blackbirds, Orioles, and Meadowlarks)

Yellow-headed Blackbird,
Xanthocephalus xanthocephalus
An, Ar, Bl, Bo, **Br**, **Ch**, Cu, **Gar**, Gr, Gre, Grf, Ho, Hol, Ke, **Li**, Lo, Log, **Mc**, Mo, **Ro**, **Sh**, Th, Wh

Status. The yellow-headed blackbird is a common to abundant spring and fall migrant statewide and a locally common summer resident in permanent marshes throughout the Sandhills. Possible and probable recent nestings have also been reported from Arthur, Garfield, Grant, Hooker, Keith, Logan, Loup, Thomas, and Wheeler Counties (Mollhoff, 2016). Breeding Bird Surveys between 1966 and 2015 indicate the species underwent a population decline (0.06% annually) during that period.

Migration. The range of 103 initial spring sightings is from January 1 to June 5, with a median of April 21. Half of the records fall within the period April 11–May 1. Eighty-two final fall sightings range from July 23 to December 28, with a median of September 18. Half of the records fall within the period September 4–30.

Habitats. During the breeding season this species occurs in deep marshes, the marsh zones of lakes or shallow impoundments, and other locations that have extensive stands of cattails, bulrushes, or phragmites. It is often found breeding in association with red-winged blackbirds, utilizing the deeper portions of the marsh. Migrants are sometimes seen flying or perching with groups of red-winged blackbirds, but more often they remain separate from them.

Bobolink, *Dolichonyx oryzivorus*
An, Ar, Bl, Bo, Br, **Ch**, Cu, **Gar**, **Gr**, Gre, Grf, **Hol** (H), **Ke**, **Li**, Lo, **Log**, Mc, Mo, **Ro**, **Sh**, Th, Wh

Status. The bobolink is a spring and fall migrant throughout the Sandhills—fairly common in central Nebraska but less common in the eastern and western areas—and a summer resident throughout most of the state, west in the Sandhills at least to Garden County. Possible and probable recent nestings have also been reported from Arthur, Blaine, Boone, Brown, Garfield, Holt, Hooker,

Keith, Lincoln, Logan, Loup, McPherson, Rock, Sheridan, Thomas, and Wheeler Counties (Mollhoff, 2016). Breeding Bird Surveys between 1966 and 2015 indicate the species underwent a national population decline (2.06% annually) during that period.

Migration. The range of 116 initial spring sightings is from March 20 to June 20, with a median of May 16. Half of the fall records fall within the period July 29–August 20.

Habitats. While in Nebraska this species is usually found in ungrazed to lightly grazed mixed-grass to tallgrass prairies, wet meadows, retired croplands, and occasionally small-grain croplands.

Eastern Meadowlark, *Sturnella magna*
An, Ar, Bl, Ch, Cu, **Gar**, Gr, Grf, Ho, Hol, Ke, Li, Lo, **Log**, Mc, Mo, Ro, **Sh**, Th, **Wh**

Status. The eastern meadowlark is a common spring and fall migrant in eastern Nebraska, becoming rarer westwardly, and a local summer resident in the Sandhills. It sometimes overwinters in the state. Possible and probable recent nestings have also been reported from Boone, Cherry, Grant, Holt, Keith, Lincoln, Logan, McPherson, Rock, and Sheridan Counties (Mollhoff, 2016). The species is a fairly common breeder east of a line from Gage to Thurston Counties, and there is local breeding along river courses and wet meadows as far west as Morrill County in the Sandhills region. It is common throughout the western Sandhills. Breeding Bird Surveys between 1966 and 2015 indicate the species underwent a national population decline (3.28% annually) during that period.

Migration. Fifty-nine initial spring sightings range from January 1 to May 30, with a median of April 8. Half of the records fall within the period March 17–May 6. Thirty final fall sightings are from August 2 to December 31, with a median of October 10. Half of the records fall within the period September 20–November 20.

Habitats. Breeding birds are associated with tallgrass prairies, meadows, and open croplands of small grain as well as weedy orchards and similar open, grass-dominated habitats. At the western edge of its range in the Sandhills and along the Platte River it is limited to low and rather moist habitats around marshes and in wet meadows. Although national populations of the eastern meadowlark have decreased by more than 50 percent since 1966, the birds are still fairly common in easternmost Nebraska. In these areas the eastern species can usually be found on meadows near water and the western species on drier hillsides.

Western Meadowlark, *Sturnella neglecta*
An, Ar, Bl, Bo, Br, Ch, Cu, Gar, Gr, Gre, Grf, Ho, Hol, Ke, Li, Log, Mc, Mo, Ro, Sh, Th, Wh

Status. The western meadowlark is a common spring and fall migrant and a common summer resident throughout the Sandhills. Breeding Bird Surveys between 1966 and 2015 indicate the species underwent a national population decline (1.29% annually) in that period.

Migration. Sixty-one initial spring sightings range from January 1 to May 26, with a median of March 4. Half of the records fall within the period February 9–March 21. Forty-three final fall sightings are from August 20 to December 31, with a median of October 28. Half of the records fall within the period October 10–November 21. The western meadowlark is an earlier spring and later fall migrant than is the eastern meadowlark and is more prone to overwintering than that species.

Habitats. In Nebraska this species is associated with tallgrass and mixed-grass prairies, hayfields, wet meadows, the weedy borders of croplands, retired croplands, and to a limited extent with short-grass and sage-dominated plains, where it is limited to moister situations. The overall range of the western meadowlark is much greater than that of the eastern, and it has not suffered as much from land-use changes. It is one of the ten most common breeding birds of Nebraska (Mollhoff, 2016).

Orchard Oriole, *Icterus spurius*
An, Ar, Bl, Bo, Br, Ch, Cu, Gar, Gr, Gre, Grf, Ho, Hol, Ke, Li, Log, Mc, Mo, Ro, Sh, Th, Wh

Status. The orchard oriole is a common spring and fall migrant and a common summer resident throughout the Sandhills. Breeding Bird Surveys between 1966 and 2015 indicate the species underwent a

Yellow-headed blackbird, territorial male displaying. *Photo by J. Kren.*

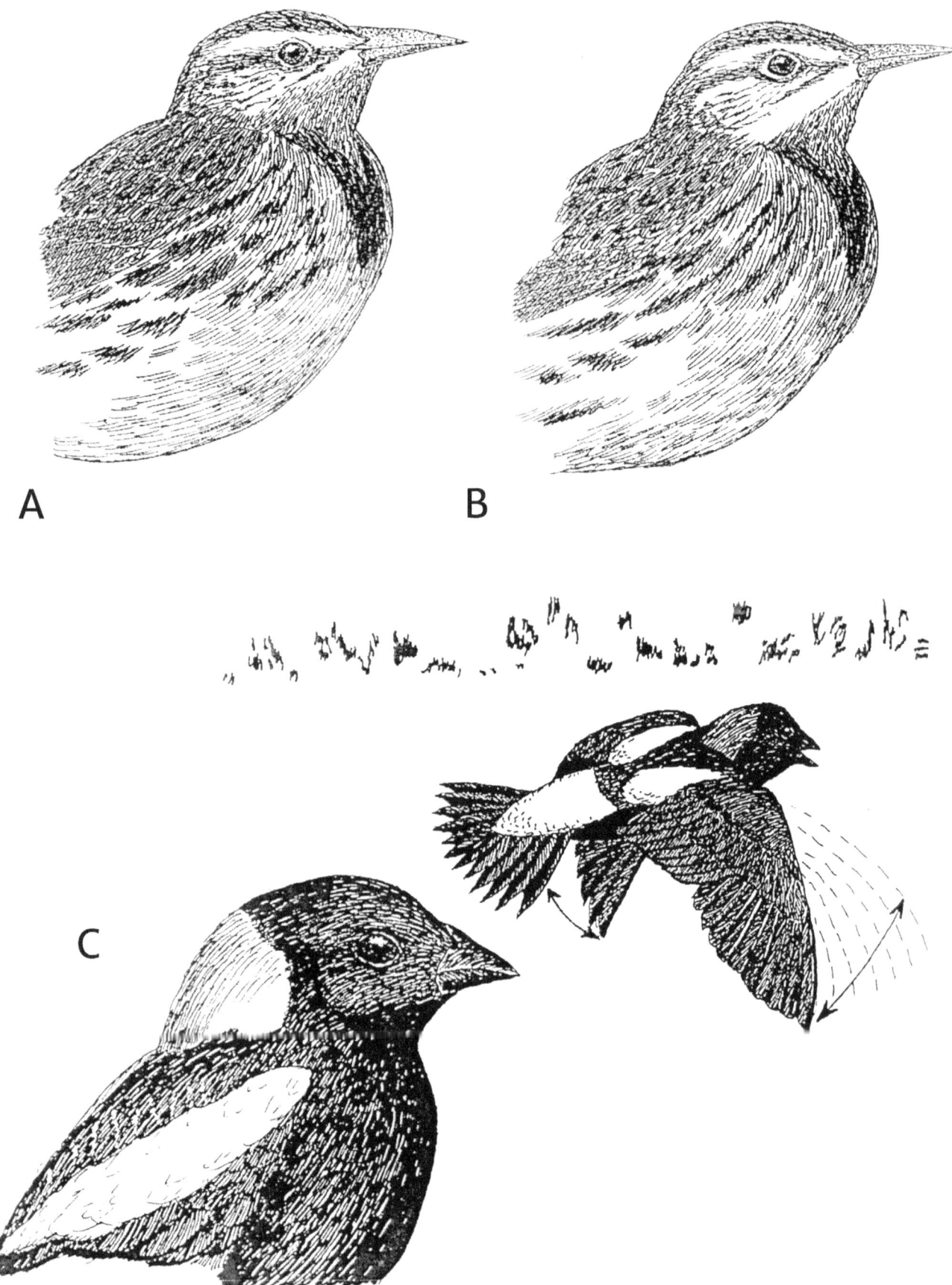

(A) Eastern meadowlark and (B) western meadowark, and (C) bobolink male and song-flight

national population decline (0.87% annually) during that period.

Migration. The range of 188 initial spring sightings is from March 24 to June 10, with a median of May 9. Half of the records fall within the period May 3–14. The range of 115 final fall sightings is from July 21 to October 9, with a median of August 24. Half of the records fall within the period August 14–September 5.

Habitats. During the breeding season this species occupies lightly wooded river bottoms, scattered trees in open country, shelterbelts, farmsteads, orchards, and residential areas. Relatively open rather than closed woodlands are preferred, and areas of low junipers or even grasslands may be used, especially if nearby nest sites are available. It is one of the ten most common breeding birds of Nebraska (Mollhoff, 2016). At Cedar Point Biological Station they are much more abundant than Baltimore and Bullock's orioles and more thoroughly studied (Clawson, 1980; Scharf and Kren, 1996). All of these orioles are prone to nest in trees occupied by nesting kingbirds, since they evidently gain some protection from the highly territorial and protective kingbirds.

Bullock's Oriole, *Icterus bullockii*
Ar, Ch, **Gar**, Ke, Li, Mo, Sh

Status. Collectively, the Bullock's and Baltimore orioles are common spring and fall migrants and summer residents throughout the Sandhills. The eastern taxon (Baltimore oriole) is present over most of Nebraska during summer, but in the panhandle counties many of the birds are of the western (Bullock's oriole) phenotype, or are apparent hybrids (Sibley and Short, 1964; Brown et al., 1996). Breeding Bird Surveys between 1966 and 2015 indicate the Bullock's oriole underwent a national population decline of 0.66 percent annually during that period.

Migration. The range of 192 initial spring sightings (both taxa combined) is from April 16 to June 5, with a median of May 6. Half of the records fall within the period May 1–10. The range of 136 final fall sightings is from July 26 to October 25, with a median of September 7. Half of the records fall within the period September 2–13.

Habitats. During the breeding season this species occupies wooded river bottoms, upland forests, shelterbelts, and partially wooded residential areas and farmsteads. In extreme western Nebraska river-bottom stands of cottonwoods and willows are the usual habitat of *bullockii*-type birds or apparent hybrids.

Baltimore Oriole, *Icterus galbula*
An, **Ar**, **Bl**, Bo, **Br**, Ch, Cu, Gr, Gre, Grf, Ho, **Hol**, **Ke**, **Li**, **Lo**, Log, **Mc**, Mo, **Ro**, Sh, Th, **Wh**

Status. See the Bullock's oriole account. Many of the orioles that breed along the North Platte River valley are apparent hybrids of the Baltimore and Bullock's species (Sibley and Short, 1964), so it is difficult to map the breeding ranges of these two orioles accurately in western Nebraska. From the 1950s until 1995 they had been regarded as a single species owing to extensive hybridization, but in 1995 they were "split" taxonomically, as evidence accumulated that the rate of hybridization was declining and they were not as close genetically as once assumed (Corbin and Sibley, 1977). Possible and probable recent Baltimore oriole nestings have also been reported from most Sandhills counties (Mollhoff, 2016). Breeding Bird Surveys between 1966 and 2015 indicate the Baltimore oriole underwent national population declines during that period of 1.49 percent annually.

Migration. See the Bullock's oriole account.

Habitats. See the Bullock's oriole account.

Red-winged Blackbird, *Agelaius phoeniceus*
An, **Ar**, **Bl**, Bo, **Br**, Ch, Cu, **Gar**, Gr, Gre, Grf, Ho, **Hol**, **Ke**, **Li**, **Log**, **Mc**, Mo, **Ro**, Sh, Th, **Wh**

Status. The red-winged blackbird is an abundant spring and fall migrant statewide and a common to abundant summer resident throughout the Sandhills. It overwinters fairly frequently, while large numbers of migrants pass through the state every spring and fall. Breeding Bird Surveys between 1966 and 2015 indicate the species underwent a national population decline (0.93% annually) during that period.

Migration. The range of 90 initial spring sightings is from January 1 to May 26, with a median of March 3. Half of the records fall within the period February 17–March 17. Eighty final fall sightings range from August 8 to December 31, with a median of

Adult male Baltimore oriole (top), Bullock's oriole (bottom), and two hybrid phenotypes

November 21. Half of the records fall within the period November 3–December 21.

Habitats. Breeding occurs on a wide range of habitats, from deep marshes or the emergent zones of lakes and impoundments through progressively drier habitats such as wet meadows, ditches, brushy patches in prairie, hayfields, and weedy croplands or roadsides. Migrants often are seen in flocks with other blackbird species, feeding in fields or elsewhere; roosting, however, is typically done in wet areas rather than residential locations. The redwinged blackbird is one of Nebraska's most abundant birds (nationally, it numbers in the hundreds of millions) and also one of the most attractive. It is one of the five most common breeding birds of Nebraska (Mollhoff, 2016). Like several other grassland-nesting birds, it is geatly affected by the brown-headed cowbird; few of its nests in Nebraska survive without being parasitized (Kren, 1996; Johnsgard, 1997a).

Brown-headed Cowbird, *Molothrus ater*
An, Ar, Bl, Bo, Br, Ch, Cu, Gar, Gr, Gre, Grf, Ho, Hol, Ke, Li, Lo, Log, Mc, Mo, Ro, Sh, Th, Wh

Status. The brown-headed cowbird is a common to abundant spring and fall migrant and a common summer resident throughout the Sandhills. It also sometimes overwinters. Breeding occurs throughout the entire Great Plains states region. Breeding Bird Surveys between 1966 and 2015 indicate the species underwent a national population decline (0.66% annually) during that period.

Migration. Eighty-three initial spring sightings range from January 6 to May 26, with a median of April 17. Half of the records fall within the period April 2–May 1. Eighty-five final fall sightings are from August 1 to December 31, with a median of October 7. Half of the records fall within the period September 11–November 27. Nearly 20 percent of the records are for December, which suggests some overwintering may occur.

Habitats. Breeding by this socially parasitic species usually occurs in woodland edges, brushy thickets, and other habitats where low and scattered trees are interspersed with grasslands. Migrants are often found in fields among cattle. Prairie and edge-nesting host species are most often parasitized, including the song sparrow, indigo bunting, and field sparrow, but some woodland-nesting birds such as the wood thrush are also vulnerable. Brown-headed cowbirds are very serious brood parasites for many species of Nebraska's songbirds, with dickcissels, yellow warblers, redwinged blackbirds, and northern cardinals being among the species most frequently exploited (Johnsgard, 1997a). Newly hatched cowbirds do not eject the eggs or young of its host species from the nest but by their constant begging manage to get the majority of the food brought to the nest, often causing starvation of the host's own chicks. The cowbird is one of the ten most common breeding birds of Nebraska (Mollhoff, 2016).

Rusty Blackbird, *Euphagus carolinus*
An, Bo, Br, Ch, Cu, Gar, Gre, Ke, Li, Lo, Sh, Wh

Status. The rusty blackbird is an uncommon and increasingly rare spring and fall migrant throughout the Sandhills. It frequently overwinters in the state. The species migrates through the entire Great Plains states region. Breeding Bird Surveys between 1966 and 2015 indicate the species underwent a national population decline (3.6% annually) during that period.

Migration. Forty-five initial spring sightings range from January 1 to May 19, with a median of March 22. Twenty-one final spring sightings range from January 5 to May 23, with a median of April 14. Twenty-five initial fall sightings are from August 10 to December 17, with a median of November 3. Twenty-one final fall sightings are from October 4 to December 31, with a median of December 26. The large proportion of final sightings in late December suggest that this species overwinters rather frequently in Nebraska.

Habitats. Migrants and wintering birds are usually found in deciduous woodlands near streams rather than in the open marshlands, grasslands, and croplands favored by other species of blackbirds in Nebraska.

Brewer's Blackbird, *Euphagus cyanocephalus*
An, Ar, Bl, Bo, Br, Ch, Cu, Gar, Gr, Gre, Ho, Hol, Ke, Li, Log, Mc, Mo, Ro, Sh, Th, Wh

Status. Brewer's blackbird is a common spring and fall migrant throughout the Sandhills, overwintering in the state infrequently. Breeding Bird Surveys between 1966 and 2015 indicate the species

underwent a population decline (2.25% annually) during that period.

Migration. Sixty-three initial spring sightings range from January 1 to May 25, with a median of April 12. Half of the records fall within the period March 22–April 24. Forty-five final fall sightings are from September 1 to December 31, with a median of November 5. The proportion of late December records is much smaller than for the rusty blackbird, suggesting that overwintering is rather rare in this species.

Habitats. Migrants are usually seen in pastures, barnyards, and grainfields, often in the company of other kinds of blackbirds. During the breeding season the birds favor low-stature grasslands (such as mowed roadsides or burned areas near railroads), residential areas, and farmsteads. Areas that have a combination of grassy habitats, scattered shrubs or small trees, and nearby water are especially favored.

Common Grackle, *Quiscalus quiscula*
An, Ar, Bl, Bo, Br, Ch, Cu, Gar, Gr, Gre, Grf, Ho, Hol, Ke, Li, Lo, Log, Mc, Mo, Ro, Sh, Th, Wh

Status. The common grackle is a common to abundant spring and fall migrant and summer resident throughout the Sandhills and an occasional winter resident. Breeding Bird Surveys between 1966 and 2015 indicate the species underwent a national population decline (1.75% annually) during that period.

Migration. Eighty-two initial spring sightings range from January 22 to June 7, with a median of March 26. Half of the records fall within the period March 16–April 6. Ninety final fall records are from August 9 to December 30, with a median of October 28. Half of the records fall within the period September 30 to December 3. Nearly half of the records are for December, so overwintering may occur fairly frequently. Like the other "blackbirds," this grackle is especially abundant during fall migration, when vast mixed-species flocks appear during late September and October on their way southward.

Habitats. During the breeding season this species frequents woodland edges or areas partially planted to trees, such as residential areas, parks, farmsteads, shelterbelts, and the like. Tall shrub thickets near croplands or marshlands are also used. Migrants are often seen in large flocks in residential and rural areas. Common grackles are egg stealers and nestling eaters, so they sometimes cause some damage to the reproductive efforts of other nesting songbirds. They are one of the ten most common breeding birds of Nebraska (Mollhoff, 2016).

Great-tailed Grackle, *Quiscalus mexicanus*
An, **Bo**, Br, Ch, **Cu**, **Gar**, **Gr**, Gre, Grf, Hol, Ke, **Li**, Lo, Log, Mo, Ro, **Sh**, Th

Status. The great-tailed grackle is an uncommon but increasingly regular and now locally common spring and fall migrant and a local summer resident throughout the Sandhills. The species was first found breeding in the state in 1976, when nesting occurred in Adams and Douglas Counties (*Nebraska Bird Review* 45: 18). Possible and probable recent nestings have also been reported from Garfield, Keith, Logan, and Wheeler Counties (Mollhoff, 2016). Breeding Bird Surveys between 1966 and 2003 indicate the species underwent a population increase (1.99% annually) during that period.

Migration. Five initial spring sightings are from March 31 to May 14, with a mean of April 21. Most breeding birds depart by the end of August; the latest fall record is November 27.

Habitats. Breeding occurs in a wide variety of habitats, but these usually include both open ground and nearby water, so this species is common in irrigated croplands. It is regrettable that great-tailed grackles have made their way into Nebraska because they are efficient predators of eggs and young of other species of songbirds. Yet, they are interesting to watch and are not nearly so destructive to other species as brown-headed cowbirds.

Red-winged blackbird, territorial male displaying. *Photo by P. Johnsgard.*

Family Parulidae (New World Warblers)

Ovenbird, *Seiurus aurocapilla*
An, Bl, Bo, Br, **Ch**, Cu, Gar, Ho, Hol, Ke, Li, Lo, Mc, **Ro**, Sh, Th, Wh

Status. The ovenbird is an uncommon to common spring and fall migrant throughout the Sandhills and a locally common summer resident, mainly in the Niobrara River valley west to at least Cherry County. Possible and probable recent nestings have also been reported from Brown, Garfield, Holt, and Sheridan Counties (Mollhoff, 2016). Breeding Bird Surveys between 1966 and 2015 indicate the species underwent a population decline (0.07% annually) during that period.

Migration. The range of 140 initial spring sightings is from April 21 to June 2, with a median of May 13. Half of the records fall within the period May 7–18. Forty final fall records are from July 25 to October 11, with a median of September 11. Half of the records fall within the period September 3–18.

Habitats. In summer these birds are mostly limited to well-drained bottomland deciduous forests and mature and shaded upland forests.

Worm-eating Warbler, *Helmitheros vermivorum*
Gar, Ke

Accidental. There are three May and July records of the worm-eating warbler at Cedar Point Biological Station, Keith County (Brown, Dinsmore, and Brown, 2012). It is also listed on the Crescent Lake NWR, Garden County, bird checklist.

Northern Waterthrush, *Parkesia noveboracensis*
An, Ch, Gar, Ke, Li, Lo, Sh

Status. The northern waterthrush is an uncommon spring and fall migrant throughout the Sandhills.

Migration. The range of 135 initial spring sightings is from April 10 to May 27, with a median of May 7. Half of the records fall within the period May 2–11. Twenty-six final spring sightings are from May 3 to May 21, with a median of May 14. Eight initial fall sightings are from August 10 to September 10, with a mean of August 29. Seven final fall sightings range from September 9 to October 12, with a mean of September 22.

Habitats. While in Nebraska this species is associated with deciduous forests or woodlands near streams. The birds often forage on the ground and near water.

Golden-winged Warbler, *Vermivora chrysoptera*
An, Ch, Ke, Th

Status. The golden-winged warbler is a rare and local spring and fall migrant in eastern Nebraska, with vagrants reaching Logan, Keith, and Cherry Counties.

Migration. Eight spring sightings range from May 5 to May 25, with a mean of May 15. There are fall records for September 6 and 7.

Habitats. Migrating and breeding birds are usually found in second-growth woodlands or scrubby thickets and overgrown pastures.

Blue-winged Warbler, *Vermivora cyanoptera*
Br, Ch, Ke, Th

Very rare. One May record of the blue-winged warbler is from Cedar Point Biological Station, Keith County (Brown, Dinsmore, and Brown, 2012). The species is also listed for Cherry County on the NOU county checklist. Two older records are from Brown County on May 22, 1971, and Thomas County, May 17–18, 1980 (Silcock and Jorgensen, various dates).

Black-and-White Warbler, *Mniotilta varia*
An, Bo, **Br**, **Ch**, Gar, Hol, Ke, Lo, Log, Mo, Ro, Sh, **Th**

Status. The black-and-white warbler is a common spring and fall migrant throughout the Sandhills and a local and uncommon summer resident in the forested valley of the Niobrara River, reaching Brown, Cherry, and Rock Counties. Possible and probable recent nestings have been reported from Brown, Cherry, and Rock Counties (Mollhoff, 2016). Breeding Bird Surveys between 1966 and 2015 indicate the species underwent a population decline (0.86% annually) during that period.

Migration. Ninety-two initial spring sightings range from March 25 to June 10, with a median of May 4. Half of the records fall within the period April 25–May 9. Forty final fall sightings are from August 21 to October 6, with a median of September

12. Half of the records fall within the period September 4–20.

Habitats. On migration this species occurs in deciduous woodlands along rivers and streams, and in parks and residential areas. Nesting usually is in semi-open upland stands of deciduous or coniferous forest, especially those that have immature or scrubby trees, and hillside or ravine groves with thin understories. Foraging is done in a creeper-like fashion on tree trunks and larger branches.

Prothonotary Warbler, *Protonotaria citrea*
Ch, Ke

Accidental. One May record of three individual prothonotary warblers is from Cedar Point Biological Station, Keith County (Brown, Dinsmore, and Brown, 2012). This warbler is also listed for Cherry County on the NOU county checklist.

Tennessee Warbler, *Leiothlypis peregrina*
An, Bl, Bo, Br, Ch, Cu, Gar, Hol, Ke, Li, Lo, Mo, Sh, Th

Status. The Tennessee warbler is a common spring and fall migrant throughout the Sandhills, becoming uncommon westwardly.

Migration. Ninety-five initial spring sightings range from April 1 to June 4, with a median of May 8. Half of the records fall within the period May 4–14. Forty-seven final spring sightings are from April 30 to June 9, with a median of May 23. Thirty-one initial fall sightings are from August 19 to October 22, with a median of September 8. Half of the records fall within the period August 28–September 15. Twenty-seven final fall sightings range from September 9 to October 27, with a median of October 5.

Habitats. Migrants are associated with deciduous woodlands and forests, where they usually forage in the upper portions of rather tall trees.

Orange-crowned Warbler, *Leiothlypis celata*
An, Ar, Bl, Bo, Br, Ch, Cu, Gar, Gr, Gre, Grf, Ho, Hol, Ke, Li, Lo, Log, Mc, Mo, Ro, Sh, Th, Wh

Status. The orange-crowned warbler is a common spring and fall migrant throughout the Sandhills.

Migration. The range of 112 initial spring sightings is from April 8 to May 30, with a median of April 30. Half of the records fall within the period April 25–May 5. Seventy-four final spring sightings are from April 25 to May 30, with a median of May 13. Sixty-one initial fall sightings are from August 11 to October 12, with a median of September 19. Half of the records fall within the period September 14–28. Sixty final fall sightings are from September 11 to November 6, with a median of October 15.

Habitats. Migrants are associated with deciduous forests, woodlands, and brushy thickets. They also forage in stands of tall sunflowers and ragweeds and shrubs, often fairly close to the ground.

Nashville Warbler, *Leiothlypis ruficapilla*
An, Bo, Br, Ch, Cu, Gar, Grf, Hol, Ke, Li, Lo, Sh, Th

Status. The Nashville warbler is a common spring and fall migrant throughout the Sandhills; it perhaps becomes less common westwardly.

Migration. Eighty-one initial spring sightings range from March 29 to June 3, with a median of May 7. Half of the records fall within the period May 1–13. Thirty-four final spring sightings are from April 30 to June 2, with a median of May 14. Forty-one initial fall sightings are from July 28 to September 27, with a median of September 10. Half of the records fall within the period September 3–15. Forty final fall records are from September 13 to October 30, with a median of October 8.

Habitats. Migrants are associated with second-growth woodlands that have a brushy undercover. Foraging occurs in tall weeds as well as on shrubs and low trees.

Connecticut Warbler, *Oporornis agilis*
Ch, Hol, Ke, Li, Mc, Th

Status. The Connecticut warbler is a rare to occasional spring and fall migrant in the Sandhills, rarely occurring as far west as Cherry, Lincoln, and McPherson Counties.

Migration. Twenty spring records range from April 25 to June 6, with a median of May 18. Half of the records fall within the period May 10–19. Ten initial fall sightings are from September 1 to October 11, with a median of September 30. This is one of the few warblers that seems to be more common in fall than during spring.

Habitats. Generally associated with low woodlands having brushy tangles, these birds usually forage on or near the ground.

MacGillivray's Warbler, *Geothlypis tolmiei*
Bo, Br, Ch, Gar, Ke, Mc, Sh

Status. MacGillivray's warbler is a rare spring and fall migrant in western Nebraska. Most of the records are from the panhandle, but at least five are from McPherson County.

Migration. Twenty-eight spring sightings range from May 5 to June 2, with a median of May 15. Half of the records fall within the period May 10–17. Thirteen fall records range from August 21 to October 10, with a median of September 6. Half of the records fall within the period August 29–September 16.

Habitats. This species is usually associated with dense undergrowth near streams, but migrants also are found on hillside brush and in dense stands of weeds, such as thistle and sunflowers.

Mourning Warbler, *Geothlypis philadelphia*
Bo, Br, Ch, Gar, Li, Sh

Status. The mourning warbler is an uncommon to occasional spring and fall migrant in the Sandhills, becoming rarer westwardly but reported west to Lincoln and Sheridan Counties.

Migration. Eighty-seven initial spring sightings range from March 20 to May 30, with a median of May 19. Half of the records fall within the period May 15–23. Nineteen final spring sightings are from May 18 to June 10, with a median of May 28. Eighteen initial fall sightings are from September 1 to October 20, with a median of September 8. Eighteen final fall sightings are from September 26 to October 24, with a median of October 7.

Habitats. Breeding birds are usually found in dense undergrowth along streams, but during migration the birds often inhabit various thickets and tall weedy areas, usually foraging rather close to the ground.

Kentucky Warbler, *Geothlypis formosa*
An, Ke, Li, Th

Status. The Kentucky warbler is a rare spring and fall migrant in eastern Nebraska, with a few scattered records for the Sandhills.

Migration. Forty-six initial spring sightings range from April 30 to June 2, with a median of May 10. Half of the records fall within the period May 5–14. Twelve fall records range from July 21 to October 7, with a median of August 29.

Habitats. During the breeding season and while on migration, this species is found in shrubby, moist ravines and bottomlands. Winter habitat similarly consists of tropical lowland forest and second growth.

Common Yellowthroat, *Geothlypis trichas*
An, **Ar**, Bl, **Bo**, Br, **Ch**, Cu, **Gar**, **Gr**, Gre, Grf, Ho, **Hol**, **Ke**, **Li**, **Lo**, Log, Mc, Mo, Ro, **Sh**, Th, Wh

Status. The common yellowthroat is a common to abundant spring and fall migrant and summer resident throughout the Sandhills. Possible and probable recent nestings have also been reported from most Sandhills counties (Mollhoff, 2016). Breeding Bird Surveys between 1966 and 2015 indicate the species had a national population decline (1.02% annually) in that period.

Migration. The range of 107 initial spring sightings is from April 5 to June 10, with a median of May 7. Half of the records fall within the period May 2–13. The range of 114 final fall sightings is from July 20 to October 29, with a median of September 13. Half of the records fall within the period August 30–October 3.

Habitats. While in Nebraska this species is found near moist or aquatic sites, especially the tall grasses, emergent vegetation, and shrubs or trees along shorelines. Occasionally it also extends to upland shrub thickets, retired croplands, weedy residential areas, and overgrown orchards.

Hooded Warbler, *Setophaga citrina*
Gar, Grf, Ke, Li

Rare. A single hooded warbler was netted and photographed at Crescent Lake NWR, Garden County, on May 2, 1981. Two birds were banded near Cedar Point Biological Station, Keith County, on May 16, 1994, and May 20, 1996. A bird was photographed in Lincoln County on May 1, 2013, and another in Garfield County on May 16, 2014 (Silcock and Jorgensen, various dates).

Common yellowthroat, breeding adult male. *Photo by J. Kren.*

American Redstart, *Setophaga ruticilla*
An, Bo, **Br** (H), Ch, Cu, Gar, Gr, Grf, Hol, Ke, Li, Lo, Log, Mc, Ro, Sh, **Th**

Status. The American redstart is a common spring and fall migrant throughout Nebraska and a local summer resident in eastern counties, with breeding probably across the entire Niobrara River valley, extending locally into the Sandhills, including the Bessey Ranger District in the Nebraska National Forest. Possible and probable recent nestings have also been reported from Brown, Cherry, Holt, and Rock Counties (Mollhoff, 2016). Breeding Bird Surveys between 1966 and 2015 indicate the species underwent a population decline (0.28% annually) during that period.

Migration. The range of 131 initial spring sightings is from April 10 to June 3, with a median of May 12. Half of the reports fall within the period May 7–16. Ninety final fall sightings range from August 11 to October 19, with a median of September 10. Half of the records fall within the period September 3–17.

Habitats. Breeding usually occurs in moist bottomland woods, usually deciduous and especially young or second-growth stands, and near the margins of openings in mature forests. Probably the breeding range of this species in Nebraska is slowly expanding, as riparian forests along the Platte and other eastward-flowing rivers have gradually matured.

Cape May Warbler, *Setophaga tigrina*
Ar, Ke, Sh

Very rare. There is one August record of a Cape May warbler at Cedar Point Biological Station, Keith County (Brown, Dinsmore, and Brown, 2012). It is also listed on the Arthur County checklist of the NOU. A spring record is from Smith Lake, Sheridan County, May 18, 2004 (Silcock and Jorgensen, various dates).

Cerulean Warbler, *Setophaga cerulea*
Ke, Sh

Accidental. There is one May record of a cerulean warbler at Cedar Point Biological Station, Keith County (Brown, Dinsmore, and Brown, 2012). An older record is of a male collected along the Niobrara River near Rushville, Sheridan County, on June 6, 1964 (Silcock and Jorgensen, various dates).

Northern Parula, *Setophaga americana*
An, Bo, Br, Ch, Gar, Ke, Sh

Status. The northern parula is an uncommon spring and fall migrant in eastern Nebraska; migrants occur west in the Sandhills to at least Garden and Sheridan Counties.

Migration. Thirty-four spring sightings are from April 2 to May 27, with a median of May 5. Half of the records fall within the period April 20–May 14. Nine fall records are from August 24 to October 2, with a mean of September 12.

Habitats. During summer this warbler species is restricted to swampy woods, especially those rich in Spanish moss in the south or old man's beard lichen in the north. On migration they also occur in parks, orchards, and along roadsides.

Magnolia Warbler, *Setophaga magnolia*
An, Bo, Br, Ch, Gar, Gr, Ke, Sh

Status. The magnolia warbler is an uncommon spring and fall migrant in eastern Nebraska; migrants occur west in the Sandhills to at least Garden and Sheridan Counties.

Migration. The range of 121 initial spring sightings is from April 20 to June 4, with a median of May 15. Half of the records fall within the period May 10–19. Fifteen final spring sightings are from May 14 to June 4, with a median of May 19. Thirteen initial fall sightings range from August 25 to October 5, with a median of September 9. Twelve final fall sightings are from September 9 to October 24, with a median of October 1.

Habitats. Migrant birds are associated with a wide array of deciduous and coniferous habitats, but they are often in rather thick woods, foraging 20 to 30 feet above the ground.

Bay-breasted Warbler, *Setophaga castanea*
Bo, Br, Ch, Gar, Ke, Lo, Th

Status. The bay-breasted warbler is an uncommon spring and fall migrant in eastern Nebraska; migrants occur west in the Sandhills to at least Garden and Cherry Counties.

Migration. Forty-one initial spring sightings range from April 29 to May 27, with a median of May 17. Half of the records fall within the period May 11–19. Eleven final spring sightings are from May 12 to May 28, with a median of May 19. Seven initial fall sightings are from September 4 to September 20, with a mean of September 14. Seven final fall sightings are from September 17 to October 14, with a mean of September 22.

Habitats. During migration this species is found in a variety of wooded habitats.

Blackburnian Warbler, *Setophaga fusca*
An, Bo, Br, Ch, Gar, Ke

Status. The Blackburnian warbler is an uncommon spring and fall migrant in eastern Nebraska; migrants occur west in the Sandhills to at least Garden and Cherry Counties.

Migration. Seventy-six initial spring sightings range from April 5 to June 4, with a median of May 14. Half of the records fall within the period May 10–20. Sixteen final spring sightings are from May 8 to June 8, with a median of May 17. Ten initial fall sightings range from August 20 to September 30, with a median of September 3. Ten final fall sightings are from September 1 to October 9, with a median of October 3.

Habitats. Migrating birds are usually found in tall trees, foraging near their tops, and in hardwood or coniferous forests.

Yellow Warbler, *Setophaga petechia*
An, Ar, Bl, Bo, Br, **Ch**, Cu, **Gar**, Gr, **Gre**, Grf, Ho, **Hol**, **Ke**, **Li**, **Lo**, **Log**, Mc, Mo, Ro, **Sh**, Th, Wh

Status. The yellow warbler is a common spring and fall migrant and summer resident throughout the Sandhills. Possible and probable recent nestings have also been reported from most Sandhills counties (Mollhoff, 2016). It is probably the commonest breeding warbler in the Sandhills region. Breeding Bird Surveys between 1966 and 2015 indicate the species underwent a population decline (0.61% annually) during that period.

Migration. The range of 126 initial spring sightings is from March 20 to May 30, with a median of May 7. Half of the records fall within the period May 1–11. The range of 120 final fall sightings is from July 23 to November 6, with a median of September 3. Half of the records fall within the period August 21–September 16.

Habitats. During the breeding season these birds prefer rather wet habitats, such as brushy edges of swamps, marshes, or creeks, but they also nest commonly in roadside thickets, hedgerows, orchards, and forest edges, avoiding both heavy forests and grassy environments that lack both trees and shrubs.

Chestnut-sided Warbler, *Setophaga pensylvanica*
An, Bo, Br, Ch, Ke, Lo

Status. The chestnut-sided warbler is an uncommon spring and fall migrant in eastern Nebraska; migrants occur west in the Sandhills to at least Keith and Cherry Counties.

Migration. Sixty-one initial spring sightings are from April 25 to June 4, with a median of May 15. Half of the records fall within the period May 12–19. Nineteen final spring sightings are from May 6 to June 4, with a median of May 23. Six initial fall sightings are from August 17 to September 19, with a mean of September 2. Seven final fall sightings are from September 1 to October 16, with a mean of September 26.

Habitats. Migrants are usually found in thickets along woodland edges. When breeding the species occurs in low shrubbery, briar thickets, forest clearings or edges, overgrown pastures, and similar low-stature habitat.

Blackpoll Warbler, *Setophaga striata*
Bo, Br, Ch, Cu, Gar, Hol, Ke, Li, Lo, Mo, Sh

Status. The blackpoll warbler is a common spring and fall migrant in eastern Nebraska; migrants occur west in the Sandhills to at least Garden and Sheridan Counties.

Migration. The range of 120 initial spring sightings is from April 9 to June 2, with a median of May 12. Half of the records fall within the period May 8–18. Forty-seven final spring sightings are from May 1 to May 30, with a median of May 20. Seven initial fall sightings are from August 28 to September 22, with a mean of September 9. Seven final fall sightings are from September 1 to October 21, with a mean of September 26.

Habitats. During migration this species is usually found in tall deciduous trees, such as cottonwoods, and generally in streamside forests.

Black-throated Blue Warbler, *Setophaga caerulescens*
Gar, Ke, Lo, Mc, Sh

Status. The black-throated blue warbler is a rare spring and fall migrant in eastern Nebraska. Migrants have been observed at least as far west in the Sandhills as Garden and Sheridan Counties.

Migration. Nine spring records range from April 23 to May 24, with a mean of May 10. Twenty-seven fall records range from August 5 to October 20, with a median of September 23. Half of the records fall within the period September 19–October 5. The species is apparently more common in fall than during spring, as is true of many passerine species.

Habitats. While on migration this species tends to occur in low shrubby areas, such as woodlands, parks, and residential gardens.

Palm Warbler, *Setophaga palmarum*
An, Ch, Ke, Li, Sh

Status. The palm warbler is an uncommon spring and fall migrant in eastern Nebraska; migrants have been reported from as far west in the Sandhills as Sheridan County.

Migration. Sixty-three initial spring sightings range from April 16 to June 2, with a median of May 5. Half of the records fall within the period May 1–9. Ten final spring sightings are from April 19 to May 24, with a median of May 9. Ten fall records range from September 2 to November 10, with a median of October 5. Half of the records fall within the period October 1–6.

Habitats. This warbler species is generally associated with brushy fields, open wooded areas, or wooded edges and clearings in woods, where the birds can forage on the ground.

Pine Warbler, *Setophaga pinus*
Cu, Ke, Li

Status. The pine warbler is a very rare migrant or vagrant in eastern Nebraska. Sandhills records are from as far west as Keith County.

Migration. Ten spring sightings range from April 17 to May 27, with a median of May 13. Four fall records are from September 7 to September 22, with a mean of September 13.

Habitats. Migrants are associated with a wide variety of forests, especially pine, but they also utilize deciduous forests and orchards.

Yellow-rumped Warbler, *Setophaga coronata*
An, Ar, Bo, Br, Ch, Cu, Gar, Gr, Gre, Ho, Hol, Ke, Li, Lo, Log, Mo, Ro, Sh, Th, Wh

Status. The yellow-rumped warbler is a common to abundant spring and fall migrant statewide and a local summer resident in the Pine Ridge region, east at least to Dawes County.

Migration. The range of 75 initial spring sightings is from February 14 to May 24, with a median of April 23. Half of the records fall within the period April 12–29. Fifty-three final spring sightings are from April 27 to May 29, with a median of May 14. Eighty initial fall sightings are from August 10 to November 1, with a median of September 28. Half of the records fall within the period September 20–October 3. Seventy-seven final fall sightings are from September 10 to December 18, with a median of October 22.

Habitats. This warbler species is widespread in wooded habitats during migration, arriving well before tree leaves appear and often wintering as far north as southern Oklahoma, where it forages on juniper berries. Breeding birds occupy coniferous forests, usually nesting in scattered trees, open plantings, or streamside thickets rather than dense mature forests. In the eastern part of the state most birds are of the white-throated (myrtle) plumage type, whereas in the panhandle the majority are of the yellow-throated (Audubon's) race.

Grace's Warbler, *Setophaga graciae*
Gar

Accidental. Nebraska's first reported Grace's warbler was found at the headquarters complex at Crescent Lake NWR, Garden County, on May 4, 2008 (Silcock and Jorgensen, various dates).

Prairie Warbler, *Setophaga discolor*
Br, Ch, Gar, Ke, Th

Accidental. One May record of a prairie warbler is from Oshkosh, Garden County (Brown, Dinsmore, and Brown, 2012). Other records are from Niobrara Valley Preserve, Brown County, May 26–June 1, 1982; Bessey Ranger District, Nebraska National Forest, Thomas County, on July 5, 1997; Niobrara River in eastern Cherry County, on May 28, 2007; and Lake McConaughy, Keith County, on April 30, 2018 (Silcock and Jorgensen, various dates).

Black-throated Gray Warbler, *Setophaga nigrescens*
Ch (Valentine NWR checklist), Gar, Gr, Mc

Status. The black-throated gray warbler is a rare vagrant. It has been observed during May and August in Cherry, Garden, and McPherson Counties.

Habitats. This warbler species is normally associated with dry slopes, thickets, and oak or pine woodlands.

Townsend's Warbler, *Setophaga townsendi*
Gar, Gr, Ke, Sh

Status. Townsend's warbler is a very rare vagrant with a few scattered records in the Sandhills region.

Migration. Six spring records date from April 25 to May 17, with a mean of May 7. Six fall sightings are from August 30 to September 17, with a mean of September 9.

Habitats. This species is often associated with low oak, juniper, or pine woodlands while on migration but is found in tall coniferous forests during the breeding season.

Hermit Warbler, *Setophaga occidentalis*
Ga

Accidental. One hermit warbler was recorded at Crescent Lake NWR, Garden County, on May 21, 2010 (Silcock and Jorgensen, various dates).

Black-throated Green Warbler, *Setophaga virens*
Bl, Bo, Br, Hol, Ke, Mc, Sh

Status. The black-throated green warbler is an uncommon spring and fall migrant in eastern Nebraska; migrants have been reported as far west as Lincoln and McPherson Counties.

Migration. Fifty-four initial spring sightings range from April 18 to June 4, with a median of May 9. Half of the records fall within the period May 3–15. Six final spring sightings are from May 9 to May 24, with a mean of May 16. Sixteen initial fall sightings are from August 30 to October 2, with a median of September 18. Sixteen final fall sightings are from September 12 to October 21, with a median of October 5.

Habitats. This species is associated with a wide variety of deciduous or coniferous woodlands on migration but is most often seen in second growth forest, especially in willows and elms.

Canada Warbler, *Cardellina canadensis*
Bo, Br, Ch, Ke, Mc, Sh, Th

Status. The Canada warbler is an occasional spring and fall migrant in eastern Nebraska; migrants have been reported as far west as McPherson and Sheridan Counties.

Migration. Twenty-eight spring sightings range from April 28 to June 6, with a median of May 20. Half of the records fall within the period May 17–25. Fourteen initial fall sightings range from August 10 to October 2, with a median of September 1. Thirteen final fall sightings are from September 3 to October 8, with a median of September 16.

Habitats. Migrants are usually found in brushy areas near streams but sometimes also range well up into trees at a considerable distance from water.

Wilson's Warbler, *Cardellina pusilla*
An, Ar, Bl, Bo, Br, Ch, Cu, Gar, Gr, Hol, Ke, Li, Lo, Mc, Mo, Sh, Th

Status. Wilson's warbler is a common spring and fall migrant in eastern Nebraska, but migrants are uncommon throughout the Sandhills.

Migration. The range of 101 initial spring sightings is from April 14 to June 4, with a median of May 12. Half of the records fall within the period May 5–16. Thirty-six final spring sightings range from April 28 to May 30, with a median of May 19. Sixty-nine initial fall sightings range from August 9 to September 26, with a median of September 1. Half of the records fall within the period August 26 to

September 7. Sixty-nine final fall records are from September 2 to October 22, with a median of September 26.

Habitats. Migrants are usually found in brushy areas near streams.

Family Cardinalidae (Cardinals, Tanagers, and Grosbeaks)

Summer Tanager, *Piranga rubra*
Br, Cu, Gar, Ke, Li, Th

Status. The summer tanager is an uncommon spring and fall migrant and summer resident in southeastern Nebraska, with migrants or vagrants occasionally seen farther west in the Sandhills region to Lincoln and Garden Counties. Possible nesting has been reported from Brown County (Mollhoff, 2016).

Migration. Twenty-nine initial spring sightings range from April 25 to May 31, with a median of May 15. Half of the records fall within the period May 12–20. Two late fall sightings are for September 5 and 15.

Habitats. Like the scarlet tanager, this species favors mature deciduous forests, especially bottomland forests in Nebraska, where they often nest in tall oak trees. Elsewhere it nests in mixed and sometimes open coniferous forests, and in general it may favor slightly lower and more open woodlands than does the scarlet tanager.

Scarlet Tanager, *Piranga olivacea*
An, **Br**, Ch, Hol, Ke, Ro

Status. The scarlet tanager is an uncommon spring and fall migrant in eastern Nebraska, becoming rare westwardly, with migrants rarely occurring as far west in the Sandhills region as Keith and Garden Counties. It is a summer resident in the Niobrara River valley west to at least Cherry County. Possible and probable recent nestings have also been reported from Brown, Garden, Holt, and Rock Counties (Mollhoff, 2016). Breeding Bird Surveys between 1966 and 2015 indicate the species underwent a population decline (0.22% annually) during that period.

Migration. The range of 132 initial spring sightings is from April 5 to June 10, with a median of May 10. Half of the records fall within the period May 5–15. Twenty-three final fall records are from July 21 to October 3, with a median of August 23. Half of the records fall within the period August 5–September 16.

Habitats. In Nebraska this species is restricted primarily to mature hardwood forests in river valleys, hill slopes, and valleys; less frequently it is found in city parks and mature orchards.

Western Tanager, *Piranga ludoviciana*
Gar (NOU list), Ke, Li, Lo, Mo, Sh

Status. The western tanager is an uncommon spring and fall migrant and summer resident in the Pine Ridge region, extending east in the Niobrara River valley to at least Sheridan County, and far enough to come into contact occasionally with the scarlet tanager (*Nebraska Bird Review* 29: 19).

Migration. Sixty-three initial spring sightings range from May 3 to June 8, with a median of May 19. Half of the records fall within the period May 13–24. Twenty-two final fall records are from August 14 to October 10, with a median of September 15. Half of the records fall within the period September 4–23.

Habitats. In the Black Hills and Pine Ridge regions, this species is mainly associated with pine forests and secondarily with deciduous forests along rivers, gulches, and canyons.

Northern Cardinal, *Cardinalis cardinalis*
An, Bl, **Bo**, **Br**, Ch, Cu, **Gar**, Gre, **Grf**, Ho, **Hol**, **Ke**, Li, Lo, Log, Mc, Mo, Ro, Sh, **Th**, Wh

Status. The northern cardinal is a common permanent resident in eastern Nebraska, becoming uncommon to occasional in western Nebraska. It breeds west at least to Garden County along the North Platte River but is apparently absent from the western Sandhills. Possible and probable recent nestings have also been reported from most Sandhills counties except Arthur and Grant Counties (Mollhoff, 2016). Breeding Bird Surveys between 1966 and 2015 indicate the species underwent a population increase (0.32% annually) during that period.

Habitats. Throughout the year this species is associated with forest edges or brushy forest openings, parks and residential areas planted to shrubs and low trees, second-growth woods, and river-bottom gallery forests in grasslands.

Rose-breasted Grosbeak, *Pheucticus ludovicianus*
An (H), **Br** (H), Ch, Cu, Gar, Grf, **Hol** (H), **Ke**, Li, Lo, **Log**, Mo, Sh, Th, Wh

Status. The rose-breasted grosbeak is a common spring and fall migrant and summer resident in eastern Nebraska. It breeds west to Holt and Garfield Counties, with the western limits confused by hybridization with the black-headed grosbeak. Possible and probable recent nestings have also been reported from Antelope, Boone, Brown, Custer, Garfield, Holt, Lincoln, Loup, Rock, and Sheridan Counties (Mollhoff, 2016). Breeding Bird Surveys between 1966 and 2003 indicate the species underwent a national population decline (0.86% annually) during that period.

Migration. The range of 134 initial spring sightings is from April 10 to June 3, with a median of May 7. Half of the records fall within the period May 1–10. Seventy-one final fall sightings are from July 23 to November 22, with a median of September 10. Half of the records fall within the period August 23–September 24.

Habitats. During the breeding season this species occurs in relatively open deciduous forests on floodplains, slopes, and bluffs. A dense understory is apparently not so important to this species as it is to the black-headed grosbeak. Rose-breasted grosbeaks hybridize fairly frequently with black-headed grosbeaks in the western Platte River valley, which produces some very strange-looking birds (West, 1962).

Black-headed Grosbeak, *Pheucticus melanocephalus*
An, Ar, Bl, Bo, Ch, Cu, Gar, Gr, Gre, Grf, Hol, **Ke**, Li, Lo, Log, Mo, Ro, Sh, Th, Wh

Status. The black-headed grosbeak is a common spring and fall migrant and summer resident in the Sandhills and western Nebraska. It breeds eastward locally to at least Rock and Garfield Counties, but the eastern limits are affected by hybridization with the rose-breasted grosbeak (*Auk* 79: 399–424; *Wilson Bulletin* 85: 230–36). Possible and probable recent nestings have been reported from Brown, Cherry, Garfield, Holt, Hooker, Rock, Sheridan, and Thomas Counties (Mollhoff, 2016). Breeding Bird Surveys between 1966 and 2015 indicate the species underwent a population increase (0.72% annually) during that period.

Migration. The range of 114 initial spring sightings is from April 23 to June 8, with a median of May 14. Half of the records fall within the period May 10–19. Thirty-six final fall sightings are from July 20 to September 30, with a median of August 29. Half of the records fall within the period August 20–September 8.

Habitats. While in Nebraska this species occupies relatively open stands of deciduous forest in floodplains or uplands, especially those with well-developed understories. It also occurs in orchards, brushy woodlands, and parks or suburbs with many trees.

Blue Grosbeak, *Passerina caerulea*
An, Ar, Bl, Bo, **Br**, **Ch**, **Cu** (H), Gar, Gr, **Gre**, Grf, Ho, **Hol**, **Ke**, **Li**, Lo, **Log**, Mc, Mo, Ro, **Sh**, **Th**, Wh

Status. The blue grosbeak is an uncommon spring and fall migrant and local summer resident throughout the Sandhills. Possible and probable recent nestings have been reported from most Sandhills counties (Mollhoff, 2016). Breeding Bird Surveys between 1966 and 2015 indicate the species had a population increase (0.81% annually) in that period.

Migration. The range of 129 initial spring sightings is from April 18 to June 10, with a median of May 20. Half of the records fall within the period May 16–24. Eighty-eight final fall sightings are from July 20 to October 13, with a median of August 27. Half of the records fall within the period August 12–September 6.

Habitats. During the breeding season this species prefers weedy pastures, old fields with scattered saplings, forest edges, streamside thickets, and hedgerows. Like the dickcissel, it is frequently parasitized by brown-headed cowbirds in these habitats.

Lazuli Bunting, *Passerina amoena*
Ch, Gar, **Ke**, Li, Lo, Mo, Sh, Th

Status. The lazuli bunting is an uncommon spring and fall migrant and summer resident in western Nebraska, including the Sandhills. Breeding is generally limited to an area west of a line from Keith County to eastern Cherry County. Range limits are confused by hybridization with the indigo bunting (*Auk* 76: 433–63; *Wilson Bulletin* 87: 145–77). Possible nesting was reported from Cherry, Garden, Holt, Sheridan, and Thomas Counties (Mollhoff, 2016). Breeding Bird Surveys between 1966 and 2015 indicate the species underwent a population increase (0.21% annually) during that period.

Migration. The range of 113 initial spring sightings is from March 18 to June 9, with a median of May 16. Half of the records fall within the period May 10–20. Twenty final fall sightings are from July 21 to September 30, with a median of August 25. Half of the records fall within the period August 19–30.

Habitats. During the breeding season this species occupies the same habitats as does the indigo bunting, namely successional habitats offering a diversity of shrubs, low trees, and herbaceous vegetation; however, it probably prefers lower, shrubbier, and drier vegetation than does the indigo bunting.

Indigo Bunting, *Passerina cyanea*
An, Ar, Bo, **Br**, Ch, Cu, Gar, Gre, Grf, **Hol**, **Ke**, Li, Lo, Log, Mo, Ro, Sh, Th, Wh

Status. The indigo bunting is an uncommon spring and fall migrant and summer resident throughout the Sandhills. Breeding is generally limited to an area west of a line from Keith County to eastern Cherry County. Eastern limits are confused by hybridization with the lazuli bunting (Baker and Boylan, 1999). Possible and probable recent nestings have also been reported from Antelope, Blaine, Boone, Cherry, Custer, Garfield, Lincoln, Loup, Rock, and Thomas Counties (Mollhoff, 2016). Breeding Bird Surveys between 1966 and 2015 indicate the species underwent a population decline (0.73% annually) during that period.

Migration. The range of 113 initial spring sightings is from March 18 to June 9, with a median of May 16. Half of the records fall within the period May 10–20. Twenty final fall sightings are from July 21 to September 30, with a median of August 25. Half of the records fall within the period August 19–30.

Habitats. During the breeding season this species occupies virtually the same habitats as does the lazuli bunting, namely successional habitats offering a diversity of shrubs, low trees, and herbaceous vegetation.

Painted Bunting, *Passerina ciris*
Ke, Li

Accidental. An older Sandhills record is of a male painted bunting reported in Lincoln County on June 4, 1973, and a recent one is of a female seen at Cedar Point Biological Station, Keith County, on April 26, 2019 (Silcock and Jorgensen, various dates).

Dickcissel, *Spiza americana*
An, **Ar**, **Bl**, **Bo**, **Br**, **Ch**, Cu, **Gar**, Gr, Gre, Grf, Ho, **Hol**, **Ke**, **Li**, **Lo**, **Log**, Mc, Mo, **Ro**, Sh, **Th**, Wh

Status. The dickcissel is a spring and fall migrant and summer resident throughout the Sandhills. Possible and probable recent nestings have also been reported from most Sandhills counties (Mollhoff, 2016). Breeding Bird Surveys between 1966 and 2015 indicate the species underwent a national population decline (0.36% annually) during that period, and a decline of 1.04 percent annually in Nebraska.

Migration. The range of 199 initial spring sightings is from April 16 to June 10, with a median of May 16. Half of the records fall within the period May 6–24. The range of 105 final fall sightings is from July 21 to October 30, with a median of August 22. Half of the records fall within the period August 10–September 2.

Habitats. While in Nebraska this species is associated with grasslands that have a combination of tall grasses, forbs, and shrubs, and with various croplands, especially alfalfa, clover, and timothy. Although generally abundant in eastern Nebraska, it is heavily parasitized by brown-headed cowbirds (Johnsgard, 1997a). Dickcissels are still very common over much of Nebraska, but their numbers have greatly declined nationwide. In part this decline has resulted from poisoning by pesticides on their wintering grounds in South America.

Refuges, Preserves, and Other Natural Areas in the Sandhills Region

P. A. Johnsgard

Note: What follows is a nearly complete list of the Sandhills region's many wildlife management areas (WMAs), all of which are free to access, and the region's state recreation areas (SRAs), which require daily or annual entry permits. National wildlife refuges (NWRs) are also included (Maps 6 and 7). Location information given here may be inadequate for finding some sites; having a good atlas such as DeLorme's *Nebraska Atlas & Gazetteer* is highly recommended. Maps that show many of these locations can also be found in Johnsgard (2011b). The Nebraska Game and Parks Commission (NGPC) annually publishes its *Public Access Atlas* with 49 maps (scale 5 miles per inch) that cover the entire state and show the locations of nearly 400 state, federal, and nonprofit sites that offer public access for outdoor activities such as hunting, fishing, and trapping. It is available free at NGPC offices and various tourism locations or may be obtained online at http://outdoornebraska.gov/publicaccessatlas/. It may also be viewed as a digital flipbook or as single map sheets in Adobe PDF format.

Principles for Safe and Courteous Sandhills Driving

Do not drive or park on wet sand.
Do not park on bare sand on upslopes.
Do not drive fast on sand—it is slippery.
Have food, fluids, and flashlight in the car.
Keep your car well filled with gasoline.
Check the weekend hours and the status of gas stations in small towns.
Call ahead to get motel accommodations (few are available).
Have a GPS device, cell phone, and a detailed road atlas.
A compass and tow rope are sometimes very useful.

General Social and Appropriate Birding Behavior

Wave to all approaching vehicles. Drivers will stop to help if you signal; ranchers are the friendliest people in Nebraska.
Do not drive over or collect snakes and turtles. Nearly all are protected by state law.
Do not disturb breeding birds, especially threatened and colonial species.
Avoid contact with poison ivy (*Toxicodendron*) in woodlands and sandbur (*Cenchrus*) in weedy grasslands. Stinging nettle (*Urtica*) is also common in wooded areas.
Avoid sunburn and overheating. Keep a supply of water handy.

The Northern and Other Sandhills

Brown County

Brown County is a Niobrara River valley and Sandhills county with about 8,000 acres of surface water. The county's area is 1,221 square miles, and it averages 2.4 people per square mile. It contains three SRAs, seven WMAs, and its entire northern border is bounded by the Niobrara River. The headwaters of the Calamus River are located here.

American Game Association Marsh WMA. Area 160 acres. A large Sandhills marsh and surrounding grassland. During wet years there are at least 120 acres of marshland. Wetland birds include several ducks, great blue heron, black-crowned night-heron, American bittern, sora and Virginia rails, swamp sparrow, and yellow-headed and red-winged blackbirds. Located 1 mile east and 19 miles south of Johnson. Lat, long: 42.3078, −100.06539. http://outdoornebraska.gov/longlake/

Bobcat WMA. Area 893 acres. Consists of coniferous woods along Plum Creek canyon and some Sandhills grasslands. Located 12 miles north of Ainsworth. Lat, long: 42.72726, −99.87732.

Long Lake SRA. Area 80 acres, with 50 acres of wetland. A Sandhills lake and smaller marshes among

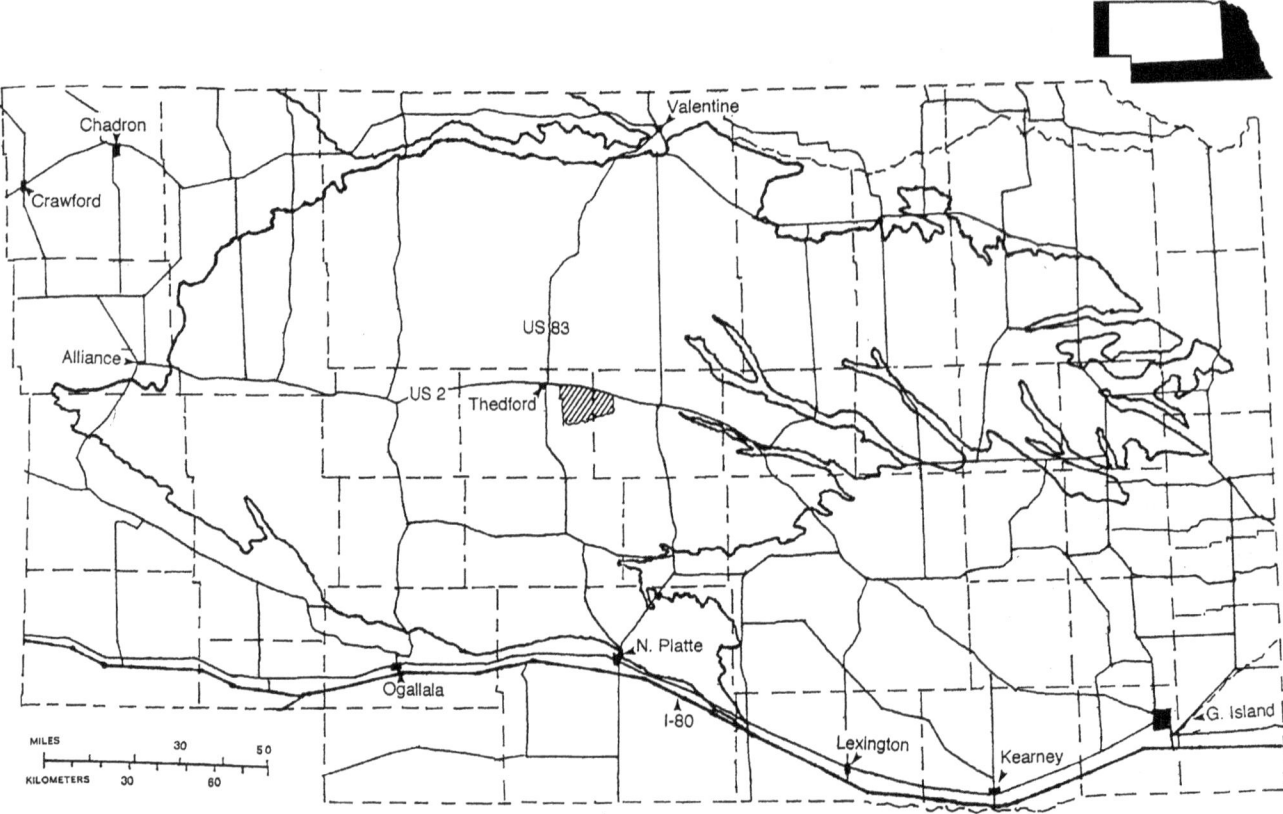

Map 6. Major roads and highways in the Nebraska Sandhills. The locations of larger towns and the Bessey Ranger District of the Nebraska National Forest (hatched) are also shown. From Johnsgard, 1995.

the headwaters of the Calamus River. Located 20 miles south of Johnson. State park entry permit required (phone 402-684-2921). Lat, long: 42.29292, −100.10351.

Long Pine SRA and WMA. Area of SRA 160 acres. Mostly coniferous woods along Long Pine Creek, a small but beautiful stream. Located south of US Hwy. 20, one mile west of Long Pine. State park entry permit required (phone 402-684-2921). Lat, long: 42.54651, −99.7109. http://outdoornebraska.gov/longpine/

Long Pine WMA is located in the same vicinity but lies north of Hwy. 20 and also has riparian habitats along Long Pine Creek. Lat, long: 42.55361, −99.70319.

Pine Glen WMA. Area 960 acres. Creek-bottom woods, mixed grasslands, and wooded canyon habitats. Located 7 miles west and 6.5 miles north of Bassett. Lat, long: 42.67304, −99.69679.

Plum Creek WMA. Area 1,320 acres. Two miles of Plum Creek riparian frontage and Sandhills prairie. From Johnston drive west 1.5 miles on US Hwy. 20, then south 1.5 miles via county road. Lat, long: 42.54543, −100.10433.

School Land WMA and Keller Park SRA. Area of combined WMA/SRA 836 acres (WMA 640 acres, SRA 196 acres). Native prairie, wooded canyons, and five small ponds (totaling 10 acres) near Dune Creek. Located 7 miles north and 4 miles east of Ainsworth (School Land WMA), or 12 miles north of US Hwy. 20 on US Hwy. 183 (Keller Park SRA). State park entry permit required for Keller Park SRA (phone 402-684-2921). Lat, long: 42.65846 −99.78476. http://outdoornebraska.gov/kellerpark/

South Pine WMA. Area 420 acres, including 152 acres of marsh. Located 11.5 miles south of Long Pine. Lat, long: 42.36858, −99.72682.

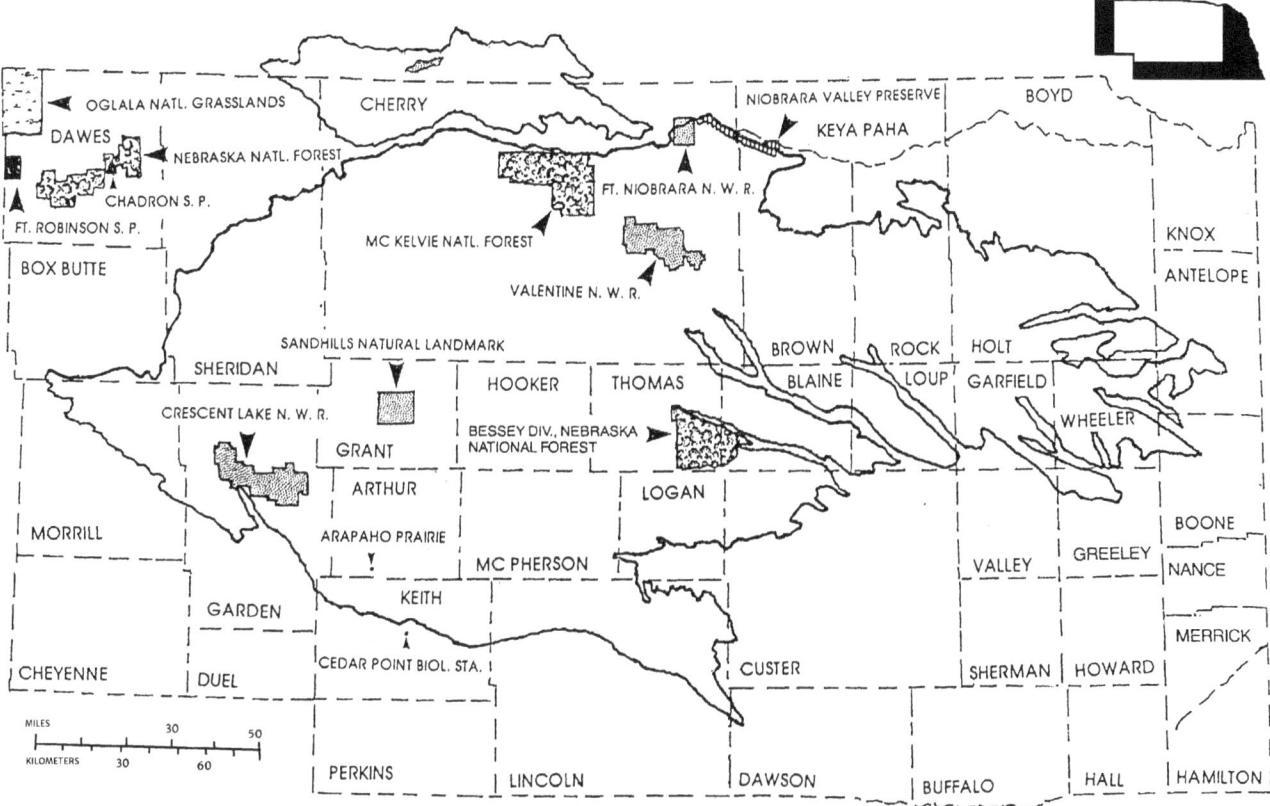

Map 7. Locations of counties plus selected wildlife refuges, preserves, parks, and other protected areas in the Nebraska Sandhills. From Johnsgard, 1995.

South Twin Lake WMA. Area 160 acres. A 60-acre Sandhills lake and grasslands. Located 19 miles south and three miles west of Johnson, via a sand road, or 11 miles south of Long Pine. Lat, long: 42.3137, −100.11954.

Willow Lake WMA (Brown County). Area 511 acres. A 450-acre Sandhills lake and 61 acres of wet meadows. (The Brown County designation distinguishes this site from the Willow Lake located in Valentine National Wildlife Refuge, Cherry County.) Located 24 miles south of Johnson. Lat, long: 42.23678, −100.0813.

Cherry County

Cherry County is a Sandhills and Niobrara River valley county and mostly consists of Sandhills habitat with about 41,000 acres of surface wetlands, mostly freshwater marshes, and several fens. This largest of Nebraska's counties contains 5,718 square miles (averaging 0.96 people per square mile). It includes a major national wildlife refuge, one national forest, one state park, one state recreation area, and ten wildlife management areas. Its entire east-west length is crossed by the Niobrara River, and the spring-fed headwaters of the Snake, North Loup, Middle Loup, and Dismal Rivers are all located here.

Ballard's Marsh WMA. Area 1,561 acres. A large Sandhills marsh and adjoining grasslands. Located 18 miles south of Valentine. Lat, long: 42.59624, −100.54873.

Big Alkali Lake WMA. Area about 900 acres. An 842-acre Sandhills lake and adjacent wet meadows. Located 15 miles south and 3 miles west of Valentine. Lat, long: 42.63914, −100.60673.

Chat Canyon WMA. Area 460 acres, including 2.25 miles of Niobrara River shoreline. Located about 10 miles southeast of Nenzel via county roads (south 4 miles, east 2 miles, then south 4 miles; use an atlas and look for pronghorns). The south side of the WMA is directly across the Niobrara River from the

115,000-acre Samuel R. McKenzie National Forest. This recently (2013) established WMA is a mixture of a steep wooded canyon of mixed hardwood forest, wetlands, and grasslands, and is jointly operated by the Nebraska Forest Service and Nebraska Game and Parks Commission. Ponderosa pines grow in the canyons that support a small (hunted) elk population, a rare endemic race of the eastern wood rat, wild turkey, sharp-tailed grouse, and many songbirds, including the regionally declining yellow-breasted chat. More than 90 bird species were found here by the authors and the former owner of the property during a May trip. This beautiful and undeveloped canyon site was described in detail by Fowler (2015).

Cottonwood Lake SRA. Area 180 acres. A 60-acre Sandhills lake and adjacent wet meadows. From Merriman, drive 0.5 mile east on US Hwy. 20 and then 0.5 mile south. State park entry permit required (phone 308-684-3428). Lat, long: 42.91593, −101.67505. http://outdoornebraska.gov/cottonwood/

Cottonwood-Steverson Lake WMA. Area 2,919 acres, including three lakes. Cottonwood, Steverson, and Home Valley Lakes are in the headwaters area of the North Loup River. Steverson Lake (about 500 acres) is the largest, Cottonwood Lake (about 230 acres) is the deepest Sandhills lake at 20 feet, and Home Valley Lake (about 200 acres) is the smallest. The western end of Steverson Lake has a wetland fen with associated cold-climate relict plants and breeding swamp sparrows. Several other fens also occur in the vicinity. Located about 28 miles north of Hyannis on state Hwy. 61. Lat, long: 42.41736, −101.6975.

Merritt Reservoir SRA. Area 6,147 acres, with 3,000 water acres. A Sandhills reservoir on the Snake River. Located 28 miles southwest of Valentine on state Hwy. 97. Adjoins Samuel R. McKenzie National Forest. Park permit required (phone 402-376-3320). Lat, long: 42.60838, −100.89559. http://outdoornebraska.gov/merrittreservoir/

Samuel R. McKelvie National Forest. Area 115,000 acres. Sandhills grasslands planted with 2,200 acres of coniferous forest south of the Niobrara River. The only wetlands are in the Lord Lakes area east of the headquarters. Located 18 miles south of Nenzel via county road S16-F. The Forest Service's main east-west "road" in this area is mostly a sandy trail that requires using a four-wheel-drive vehicle. Address: Samuel R. McKelvie National Forest, 125 N. Main St., Chadron, NE 69337 (phone 308-533-2257 or 308-432-0300).

Valentine NWR. Area 71,516 acres. Nebraska's largest national wildlife refuge, consisting mostly of Sandhills prairie, with sand dunes and intervening interdune depressions that contain many shallow marshes and six large lakes. The refuge checklist of 272 species includes 100 wetland species, including 31 shorebirds, 24 waterfowl, 10 gulls and terns, 5 grebes, and 4 rails. Probable or known wetland breeders include 11 waterfowl (including trumpeter swans) and 3 grebes. Other notable wetland breeders are the least bittern, white-faced ibis, cattle egret, willet, upland sandpiper, long-billed curlew, black and Forster's terns, marsh wren, and swamp sparrow. Free-access prairie-chicken and sharp-tailed grouse blinds are available on a first-come-first-serve basis. Some of the sandy roads connecting the lakes on the refuge are recommended only for adventurous persons with a good deal of self-confidence and who are driving vehicles with four-wheel drive. Although mostly outside the refuge, the road leading west from Hackberry Lake through Kennedy to state Hwy. 97 and then south through Wamaduze Valley to Brownlee is worth driving to see the many small and attractive wetlands near the road. Located 22 miles south of Valentine off Hwy. 83 (phone 402-376-1889). https://www.fws.gov/refuge/valentine/

Custer County

Custer County is a Sandhills and Loup River valley county, with about 2,500 acres of surface water, mostly associated with the Loup River valley. The county's area is 2,576 square miles (averaging 4.2 people per square mile). It contains two state recreation areas and one wildlife management area, and is crossed diagonally by the South and Middle Loup Rivers.

Arcadia Diversion Dam WMA. Area 925 acres. Riparian woods along the Middle Loup River. Located 8.5 miles northwest of Arcadia. Lat, long: 41.49138, −99.23107.

Pressey WMA. Area 1,640 acres. South Loup River valley lowlands, plus hills and steep canyons. Jon Farrar (2004) listed 38 birds as a "sampler" of the area's bird life, of which most are riparian forest species, along with some more typical wetland species, such as the wood duck, great blue heron, and northern harrier. Located five miles north of Oconto. Lat, long: 41.18373, −99.70866.

Garfield County

Garfield County is a Sandhills county with about 6,000 acres of surface water, nearly all reservoir acreage. The county's area is 570 square miles (averaging 3.5 people per square mile). It contains one WMA/SRA and is crossed diagonally by the Calamus and North Loup Rivers.

Calamus Reservoir SRA/WMA. Area 11,370 acres. A 5,123-acre reservoir on the Calamus River, extending into Loup County. This lake is a major foraging and migration stopover area for hundreds of American white pelicans and double-crested cormorants. The upper end is swamplike with submerged and standing snags, which attract hundreds of bald eagles during the period of ice breakup in spring. Located seven miles northwest of Burwell, on state Hwy. 96. A state park entry permit is required for the SRA (phone 308-346-5666). Lat, long: 41.87433, −99.28328. http://outdoornebraska.gov/calamus/

Grant County

Grant County is a Sandhills county with about 3,500 acres of surface water. It contains three state wildlife management areas. The county's area is 776 square miles (averaging 0.8 people per square mile). The Ogallala aquifer is more than 500 feet deep throughout the entire county, but the county has no rivers, and the tallest dune (over 400 feet) in the entire Sandhills region occurs in northern Grant County.

Avocet Lake WMA. Area about 600 acres. A large roadside Sandhills marsh that typically supports breeding coots, eared grebes, and American avocets. Trumpeter swans and black-necked stilts are often seen here. Located two miles east of Hyannis (junction of US Hwy. 2 and state Hwy. 81). Although lacking public access, Doc Lake, 12 miles east of Hyannis near Whitman, can easily be observed from Hwy. 2. Doc Lake often has a pair of nesting trumpeter swans as well as a diversity of waterfowl and other wetland birds.

De Fair Lake WMA. Area about 400 acres. A typical Sandhills marsh. Located two miles east of Hyannis and south on state Hwy. 81 for three miles. Lat, long: 41.96298, −10 1.71131.

Frye Lake WMA. Area about 600 acres. A typical Sandhills lake. Located 1 mile north and 1.5 miles east of Hyannis. Lat, long: 42.02011, −101.74465.

Holt County

Holt County is a Sandhills and Niobrara River valley county with more than 12,000 acres of surface water, mostly typical Sandhills wetlands. The county's area is 2,413 square miles (averaging 4.2 people per square mile). It contains one state recreation area and three wildlife management areas, and its entire northern border is bounded by the Niobrara River.

Atkinson Lake SRA. Area 54 acres, including a 14-acre Elkhorn River reservoir. Located at the northwest edge of Atkinson. State park entry permit required (phone 402-935-5313). Lat, long: 42.5386, −99.00032.

Goose Lake WMA. Area 349 acres. A Sandhills lake surrounded by grasslands and wooded uplands. Located 4 miles west of US Hwy. 281 and 2 miles north of the Wheeler County boundary, or 23 miles south and 4 miles east of O'Neill (phone 402-370-3374). Lat, long: 42.11046, −98.5641.

Redbird WMA. Area 433 acres. Mostly woods along Louse Creek, plus upland grasslands. Located one mile south of the US Hwy. 281 bridge over the Niobrara River. Lat, long: 42.7559, −98.43152.

Rock County

Rock County is a Niobrara River valley and Sandhills county with about 11,000 acres of surface water, mostly Sandhills wetlands. The county's area is 1,009 square miles (averaging 1.3 people per square mile). It contains few wildlife preserves, although the John and Louise Seier National Wildlife Refuge (west of Rose) is under development and there is one state wildlife management area. Rock County's entire northern border is bounded by the Niobrara River, and the headwaters of the Elkhorn River are located here.

Hutton Niobrara Ranch Wildlife Sanctuary. Area 4,919 acres, including several miles of Niobrara River frontage. Meadows and pastures at the head of Willow Creek are present as well as spring-fed streams and wet meadows. No bird list is available yet, but grassland and meadow species such as long-billed curlew, sharp-tailed grouse, and bobolink are among the nesters. Sandhill cranes have also nested here. Located about 15 miles northeast of Bassett. Two guest houses are available for short stays. Drive north five miles, east six miles, and then north again four miles on county roads to reach the Hutton guest house; see the sanctuary website for more detailed driving directions and information on possible stays (https://www.niobrarasanctuary.org/). Owned by Audubon of Kansas (phone 785-537-4385, https://www.audubonofkansas.org/index.cfm).

John W. and Louise Seier NWR. Area 2,400 acres. A Sandhills national wildlife refuge 25 miles south of Bassett and west of Rose. Mostly grassland, with about 400 acres of wetlands. Two small creeks pass through the refuge. Under development and not yet open to the public. https://www.fws.gov/refuge/john_w_and_louise_seier/

Twin Lakes WMA (Rock County). Area 113 acres, including 83 acres of Sandhills lakes. From Bassett, drive 15 miles south, 3 miles east, and 3 more miles south. Lat, long: 40.83408, −96.9534.

Thomas County

Thomas County is a Sandhills county with about 1,500 acres of surface water. The county's area is 713 square miles (averaging 1.0 person per square mile). It contains one (human-planted) national forest and is crossed by the Middle Loup, Dismal, and South Loup Rivers. The Ogallala aquifer is more than 500 feet deep throughout nearly the entire county.

Bessey Ranger District, Nebraska National Forest. Area 90,465 acres. Planted conifers in this forest provide habitat for species as diverse as the great horned owl, black-capped chickadee, chipping sparrow, and red crossbill. Deciduous riparian thicket areas along the Middle Loup and Dismal Rivers attract several woodpeckers, both towhees, and the brown thrasher and Baltimore oriole. The local bird list exceeds 200 species. Common poorwills can often be heard at night and sometimes seen along sandy roadsides in car headlights. At least four woodland warblers nest here, including the yellow and black-and-white warblers, American redstart, and ovenbird. The common yellowthroat and yellow-breasted chat are local breeders. Three vireos (Bell's, warbling, and red-eyed) also nest here. Jon Farrar (2004) listed 65 birds as a "sampler" of the area's bird life, nearly all of which are grassland, forest, and forest-edge species, as well as a few typical wetland species, such as the great blue heron and belted kingfisher. Prairie-chicken and sharp-tailed grouse blinds are available for first-come-first-serve public use (the sharp-tailed grouse blind is usually better). Located two miles west of Halsey on state Hwy. 2 and then south on Spur 86B. Address: Bessey Ranger District, US Forest Service, PO Box 39, Halsey, NE 69142 (phone 308-533-2257). https://www.fs.usda.gov/nebraska

Wheeler County

Wheeler County is an eastern Sandhills county, with 1,300 acres of surface water. The county's area is 575 square miles (averaging 1.4 people per square mile). It contains one state recreation area and is crossed diagonally by Beaver Creek.

Pibel Lake Recreation Area. Area 72 acres, including a 24-acre Sandhills lake designated for fishing and recreation. Located seven miles east and two miles south of Erickson. Free camping is permitted; operated by the Lower Loup Natural Resources District. Lat, long: 41.75817, −98.53155. https://www.llnrd.org/recreation.html

The Loup/Platte Sandhills

Between the Loup and central Platte Rivers, a narrow strip of isolated Sandhills topography extends from eastern Buffalo County to eastern Platte County, and is most conspicuously present in Merrick County. Wetlands in this region have been extensively destroyed or drained and are now largely limited to a 70-square-mile area south of Genoa (Nance County). These wetlands are mostly small sites averaging less than five acres and vary from temporary ponds to semipermanent wetlands (LaGrange, 2005).

Merrick County

Merrick County is a Platte River valley county with about 600 acres of surface water. The county's area is 485 square miles (averaging 16.7 people per square mile). Its entire east-west width is bounded on the south by the Platte River. Tourist accommodations are at Genoa (in adjoining Nance County), which at one time was the tribal headquarters of the Pawnees after they were confined to a reservation and before they were removed to Oklahoma in 1879.

Sunny Hollow WMA. Area 169 acres. Mostly grassy upland, with two marshes and a dugout wetland. Located four miles south and one mile west of Genoa. Lat, long: 41.37685, −97.73845.

The Western Alkaline Sandhills

This remarkable region in the Sandhills known as the Western Alkaline Sandhills is notable for the high levels of alkalinity that are found in its numerous wetlands. About 85 percent of the region's hyperalkaline wetlands are located in Sheridan, northern Garden, and northeastern Morrill Counties. For example, Sand Lake in Garden County has been reported to have a salt concentration of 136,000 milligrams per liter!

The heart of the hyperalkaline wetlands region centers around Antioch, a nearly abandoned settlement about 15 miles east of Alliance, where the wetlands are rich in sodium and potassium carbonates. Potash Lake is a hyperalkaline wetland located at the eastern edge of Antioch, and many other salt-rimmed wetlands are visible along the county road north of Antioch. These vegetation-free wetlands often attract American avocets, phalaropes, black-necked stilts, and other shorebirds. Similar hyperalkaline wetlands may be seen from Antioch east to Lakeside, where a large wetland is located along state Hwy. 250 at the northeast edge of town. The sandy road that is accessed east of Lakeside (the last gas stop for about 50 miles) crosses the alkaline lake region that extends south to Crescent Lake National Wildlife Refuge. North from Lakeside, via state Hwy. 250, the variably alkaline wetland region extends for about 20 miles. The same is true along state Hwy. 27 going north from Ellsworth and the county road going north from Antioch. All these wetlands are located on private property but many can be observed from public roadsides.

Garden County

Garden County is a Sandhills county with more than 22,000 acres of surface water, mostly freshwater or alkaline Sandhills wetlands. The county's area is 1,705 square miles (averaging 1.1 people per square mile). Northern Garden County south to Crescent Lake National Wildlife Refuge is the geographic center of the Sandhills alkaline to hyperalkaline wetland region. The county contains one national wildlife refuge and one wildlife management area, and its entire east-west width is crossed by the North Platte River.

Crescent Lake NWR. Area 45,818 acres. There are about 20 wetland complexes on this enormous Sandhills national wildlife refuge; the wetlands total 8,251 acres and make up almost 20 percent of the refuge. The refuge bird list includes 273 species, with many wetland species. At least 32 species of waterfowl have been reported here, and 14 are known or suspected breeders. Three grebes (western, eared, and pied-billed) are also breeders. Other wetland breeders include the double-crested cormorant, great blue heron, black-crowned night-heron, sora and Virginia rails, and black and Forster's terns. The common yellowthroat and marsh wren are abundant, and both the white-faced ibis and black-necked stilt have bred periodically. The marshes and shallow lakes in this large and remote refuge vary greatly as to their relative alkalinity. Border Lake, at the western edge of the refuge, marks the eastern boundary of hypersaline water conditions; the Wilson's phalarope and American avocet are common breeders here. Located 28 miles north of Oshkosh; no gas station or motel accommodations are closer to the refuge. Phone: 308-762-4893 or 308-635-7851. https://www.fws.gov/refuge/crescent_lake/

Morrill County

Morrill County is a North Platte River valley and high plains county, with almost 5,000 acres of surface water. The county's area is 1,424 square miles (averaging 3.3 people per square mile). It contains one state recreation area and one wildlife management area, and its entire east-west width is crossed by the North Platte River.

Chet and Jane Fleisbach WMA. (Previously known as Facus Springs WMA.) Area 422 acres. This wetland site east of Chimney Rock National Monument is one of the few remaining alkaline marshes in the North Platte River valley. Sandhill cranes have bred here repeatedly in recent years. Other known or probable wetland nesters include the cinnamon teal, American avocet, Wilson's phalarope, and Wilson's snipe. Located two miles south and three miles east of Bayard. Lat, long: 41.6922, −103.26333.

Sheridan County

Sheridan County is a northern Panhandle county with more than 20,000 acres of surface wetlands, some of which are highly alkaline Sandhills marshes. The county's area is 2,441 square miles (averaging 2.1 people per square mile). It contains one state recreation area and two wildlife management areas, and its entire east-west width is crossed diagonally by the Niobrara River.

Smith Lake WMA. Area 640 acres. A 222-acre Sandhills lake is surrounded by cattail marsh, wet meadows, grasslands, and woods. This lake was well described (under the fictitious name "Pine Lake") by Stephen Jones in his book *The Last Prairie: A Sandhills Journal*. He observed 145 bird species there, including 51 probable or possible breeders. Known wetland breeders include the wood duck, ruddy duck, northern harrier, long-billed curlew, swamp sparrow, and bobolink. The marbled godwit is also a rare or perhaps occasional nester here. Jon Farrar (2004) listed 40 birds as a "sampler" of the area's bird life, of which 18 are typical wetland species, such as the bald eagle, piping plover, and spotted sandpiper. Many other attractive but privately owned and increasingly alkaline wetlands may be seen farther south along state Hwy. 260 in Sheridan and Garden Counties. Located 21 miles south of Rushville. Lat, long: 42.40563, −102.45414.

Walgren Lake SRA. Area 130 acres. A 50-acre impoundment in an otherwise poorly watered region, which includes open water, wet meadows, and uplands. Located three miles south and two miles east of Hay Springs. State park entry permit required (phone 308-763-2940). Lat, long: 42.63765, −102.62868. https://outdoornebraska.gov/walgrenlake/

Lake McConaughy and Vicinity

Keith County

Keith County's area is 1,061 square miles (averaging 7.5 people per square mile). The county is notable in having more than 37,000 acres of surface water (nearly all reservoirs), nearly 6,000 acres of wooded habitats, and over 420,000 acres of Sandhills grasslands or ranchlands. Tourist accommodations are at Keystone, Lemoyne, Ogallala, and Paxton.

Clear Creek WMA. Area 6,100 acres. This WMA includes the west end of Lake McConaughy and the North Platte River inflow area, part of which is posted as a refuge. The low meadows support nesting bobolinks and probably breeding Wilson's snipes, and the tall tree groves support many breeding passerines. White pelicans are common throughout summer, and least bitterns have been sighted. Although a local bird list has not been developed, this is one of the state's best birding areas, but mosquitoes can be a major problem during summer. Barn owl nest cavities usually can be seen in the cutbanks at the turn-off from the main highway; nests in the Sandhills are usually in such excavated sites rather than in old buildings. Rosche (1994) has described this area and its birds very well. It is the state's only known nesting area for Clark's grebe.

Lake McConaughy SRA and vicinity. Area 6,492 acres. This SRA occupies much of the north side of the Lake McConaughy reservoir, the largest body of water in Nebraska, and is highly popular with campers and fishermen. Some small developed areas on the south side are also included in the SRA. This general area has the largest bird list of any location in the state, including about 360 species, with 104 known breeders, 17 additional possible breeders, and about 200 transients (Brown, Dinsmore, and Brown, 2012). The large water area attracts vast numbers of migrant waterfowl, grebes (especially western grebes), gulls (including many rarities), and shorebirds. A good spotting scope is needed to cover this vast reservoir from the top of Kingsley Dam, but many of the waterfowl congregate near the spillway during winter or toward the western end in summer (see "Clear Creek Wildlife Management Area"). Large numbers of bald eagles also build up in winter, attracted by dead fish and the large wintering duck and goose populations; a viewing blind below Kingsley Dam is available for free use during the eagle-watching period of October to May (peak in January). Large numbers of cliff swallows nest in the rocky outcrops along the dam; rock wrens and great horned owls nest on higher canyon slopes. Well over 100 miles of shoreline are present along the lake, with the southern shoreline being rocky and steep. Ash Hollow State Historical Park is located west of the lake on US Hwy. 26; it has a history-oriented visitor center and more than two miles of hiking trails. The northern shore of Lake McConaughy is sandy and supports an important population of nesting piping plovers as well as some least terns. Classified as a Nebraska Important Bird Area. An entry permit is required; the area is a major tourist attraction for fishermen, boaters, and campers (phone 308-284-8800). http://outdoornebraska.gov/lakemcconaughy/

Kingsley Dam and Lake Ogallala SRA. Area 339 acres. Kingsley Dam offers a good vantage point for birds both on the deeper end of Lake McConaughy and on the shallower and much smaller Lake Ogallala located at the eastern base of the dam. Lake Ogallala (and its eastern end, which is often called Keystone Lake) receives the spillway water from Lake McConaughy, and its level fluctuates greatly, making it unsuitable for aquatic nesting birds. However, it is very attractive to migrant ducks, ospreys, Caspian terns, cliff swallows, American white pelicans, double-crested cormorants, several vagrant gull species and other summering birds, and is used by Canada geese, ducks, gulls, and numerous bald eagles in winter (100 species have been recorded during Audubon Christmas Bird Counts). An eagle-watching blind is available during peak periods, when 200 to 300 eagles are sometimes present. It is available from late December through early March, Thursdays and Fridays, 8 a.m. to noon; Saturdays and Sundays, 8 a.m. to 4 p.m. The northern shoreline of Lake Ogallala has deciduous wooded habitats with a rich array of nesting passerines, but lake fluctuations also associated with irrigation diversion limit nesting success for aquatic species. The eastern end of Lake Ogallala has an irrigation diversion dam, below which the North Platte River passes through open riverine woodlands with many breeding songbirds (and lots of poison ivy). Lake Ogallala State Recreation Area is classified as a Nebraska Important Bird Area. A state entry permit is required (phone 308-284-2332 or 308-284-8800 for eagle-viewing or general information). Address: 1475 NE-61, Ogallala, NE 69153. http://outdoornebraska.gov/lakeogallala/

Cedar Point Biological Station (CPBS). This teaching and research facility is located along the south shore of Lake Ogallala. Although an extension of the University of Nebraska and a summer field station, and thus not open to the public, ornithological research here has made its avifauna the best known of any area in the state (Brown, Dinsmore, and Brown, 2012). Ornithology courses have been taught here on a regular basis since 1976, and long-term monographic studies on the costs and benefits of sociality in the cliff swallow by Charles and Mary Brown are of national significance (Brown and Brown, 1996). Extensive bird-banding took place at CPBS between 1992 and 1996 (Brown et al., 1996). The CPBS Bird Checklist, which includes both Lake McConaughy and the Lake Ogallala–Keystone areas, contains 365 species.

Suggested Birding Routes in the Western and Central Nebraska Sandhills

1. From Oshkosh, Garden County, north, via NE Rd. 181, to Lakeside, Sheridan County. Total distance 56 miles.

This is perhaps the best birding trip in the western Sandhills, especially from May until mid-June. Along the sandy road from Oshkosh north to Crescent Lake (23 miles), you will encounter numerous western meadowlarks, lark buntings, horned larks, and several species of sparrows, especially grasshopper sparrows and lark sparrows, usually singing from fenceposts. Stop at Blue Creek (which flows through one of Ted Turner's many ranches) and look for upland sandpipers, bobolinks, marsh wrens, cliff and barn swallows (nesting under the bridge), and some shorebirds, such as spotted sandpipers. Western meadowlarks will accompany you until you reach the large and beautiful Crescent Lake at the southern end of the refuge. On it and other wetlands you will encounter numerous species of ducks, grebes, American white pelicans, and shorebirds in the vegetation along the shores and long-billed curlews flying over your head. Large flocks of migrating Wilson's phalaropes and sandpipers pass through in May. You might want to stop at the refuge headquarters for access to the only toilets (available 24 hours/day) and a drinkable water supply. While stopped, search the trees for migrating warblers, thrushes, sparrows, and other species. When you reach Goose Lake (about 0.8 mile north of headquarters), where eared grebes and double-crested cormorants often breed, turn right on Rd. 181. From here to Lakeside (about 26 miles), besides seeing numerous species and large numbers of shorebirds and ducks, you might encounter flocks of white-faced ibises and possibly lone American bitterns and burrowing owls, the latter sometimes nesting close to the road. On shallow weed-edged wetlands you might find marsh wrens, cinnamon teal, and soras.

2. From Lakeside south to Goose Lake, Garden County (28 miles). Total distance 54 miles. From Goose Lake to Border Lake, and from Border Lake to Antioch (26 miles). Total distance about 70 miles. See map 8.

Turn south about a mile west of Lakeside from US Hwy. 2. This sandy and poorly marked road will take you to Goose Lake at Crescent Lake National Wildlife Refuge. During this part of your journey you might encounter such typical Sandhills species as long-billed curlews, sharp-tailed grouse, burrowing owls, Swainson's and ferruginous hawks, and prairie-chickens. If you turn west at Goose Lake, you will pass many small wetlands rich in aquatic birds. In stands of emergent plants on Island Lake there will probably be white-faced ibises, yellow-headed blackbirds, and marsh wrens. Eventually you will reach Border Lake, near the refuge's western border, which often has cinnamon teal, avocets, and Wilson's phalaropes. This is a good place to turn around. Alternatively, you can turn north on a county road about a mile west of Border Lake and drive about 20 miles to Hwy. 2 and Antioch. No wetlands are near this road, but curlews can often be seen. Besides birds, there is a good chance of seeing pronghorns (*Antilocapra americana*) and mule deer (*Odocoileus hemionus*) anywhere in the refuge's vicinity. Be aware that the trip will probably require an entire day. Alliance and Oshkosh (and possibly Ellsworth) are the nearest towns with motel accommodations.

3. From Ellsworth, Sheridan County, via US Hwy. 2 to Antioch, Sheridan County. Total distance 15 miles. Also, Hwy. 27 north from Ellsworth for about 15 miles and return. See map 9.

Highway 2 provides a wonderful birding experience, especially if you prefer to stay on an asphalt road. Fortunately, there is a wide shoulder along the highway, so you can easily get well off the road. There are numerous shallow marshes on both sides of the highway with many species of ducks and shorebirds. You will probably see black-crowned night-herons, American bitterns, white-faced ibises, American avocets, black-necked stilts, and yellow-headed blackbirds. The birds are usually not disturbed by the traffic, which is very low on weekend mornings.

Suggested Birding Routes

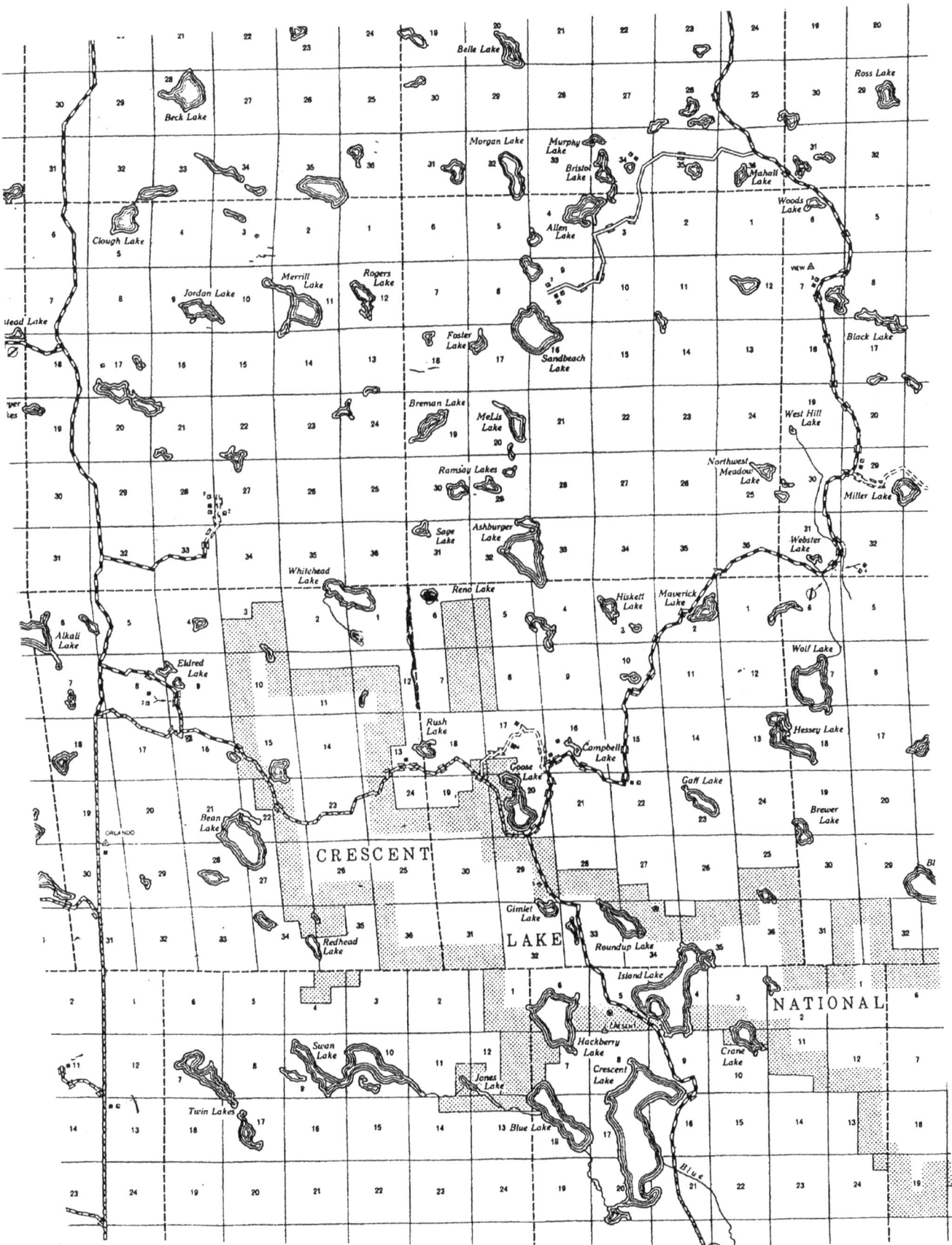

Map 8. Crescent Lake National Wildlife Refuge and northern approaches. Nebraska Department of Roads map.

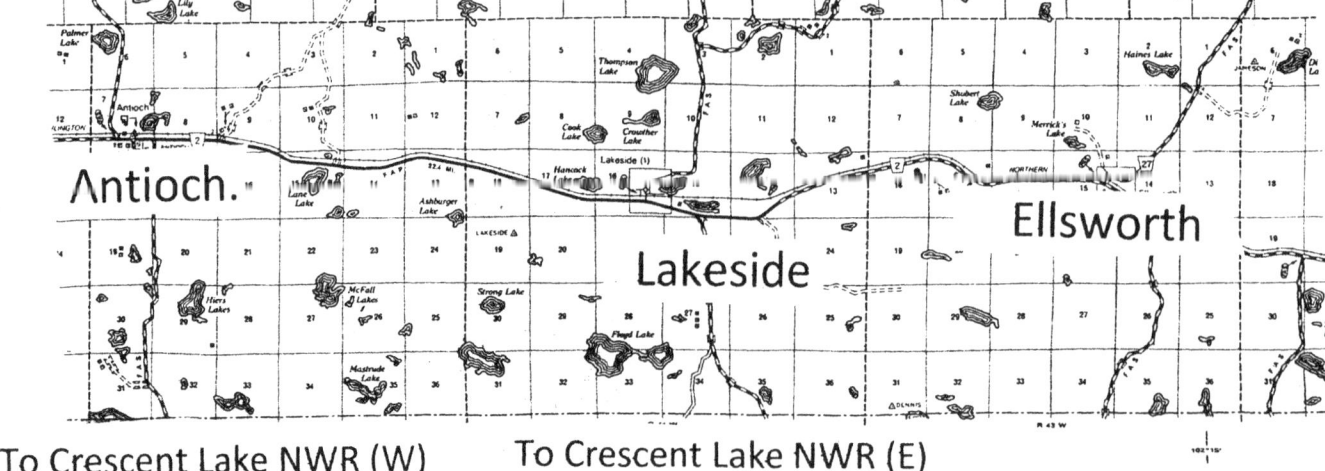

Map 9. Vicinities of Antioch and Lakeside, showing suggested birding routes. Dotted lines indicate secondary routes leading to Alliance (left) and connecting two suggested routes (right). Adapted from a Nebraska Department of Roads map.

Suggested Birding Routes

Adventurous drivers with a detailed county road map or atlas might choose to go north from Antioch for about seven miles and then turn northwest onto an unmarked county road that will take you past several wetlands, such as Jess and Wickson Lakes, and eventually turn west to connect with Hwy. 81 about seven miles north of Alliance via Carhenge. Hwy. 27 north from Ellsworth has some good wetlands for the first 15 miles, after which the wetlands peter out and it would be good to turn around and return.

4. From Lakeside, Sheridan County, north via Hwy. 250 to Smith Lake WMA. Total 26 miles. Possible alternative routes are to Alliance (left dotted line) or to return to Hwy. 2 (right dotted line) on sandy ranch roads. See map 9.

Hwy. 250 is a very nice stretch of a rather narrow state highway (almost no shoulder) with beautiful shallow marshes on both sides. At the eastern edge of Lakeside, you will find a lake with perhaps numerous ruddy ducks and eared grebes, white-faced ibises, and American avocets along the shoreline vegetation, all often close to the highway. As you continue north on the highway, you will see a beautiful marsh on your left, where you should watch for long-billed curlews, upland sandpipers, willets, American bitterns, and cattle egrets. Various species of ducks, often including a good number of northern pintails, might be seen on the small lakes on both sides. Swainson's hawks regularly nest in the scattered trees along the highway. The first four miles along the road are wonderful for finding dozens of species of birds.
    Sidetrip #1: About seven miles along, a sandy ranch road to the west leads to some lake-sized marshes and ranches, and after about seven miles connects with Hwy. 27 and a seven-mile drive south back to Alliance.
    Sidetrip #2: After driving north about 13 miles on Hwy. 250 from Lakeside, a ranch road (sandy trail) to the east extends four miles to connect with a north-south ranch road (both possibly requiring four-wheel drive) that extends south past a series of alkaline wetlands and for about 11 miles and turns west to connect with Hwy. 250 about 4 miles north of Lakeside. Smith Lake WMA, about 25 miles north of Lakeside on Hwy. 250, is a bird-rich destination and provides primitive camping opportunities. Its plants and animals were lovingly described by Stephen Jones (2000) (see the Sheridan County preserves in the "Refuges" section).

5. Around Hyannis, Grant County, and north 30 miles via Hwy. 61 to Cottonwood-Steverson Lake WMA, Cherry County. Total round trip about 60 miles.

Before you leave Hyannis on Hwy. 2, check Beem Lake (also called East Hyannis Lake) on the eastern edge of Hyannis. Besides black terns, American white pelicans, and various species of ducks, you will probably see a nesting pair of trumpeter swans at adjacent Avocet WMA. Before turning north on Hwy. 61, examine the ditch on the north side of Hwy. 2 for wood ducks. Also, the trees at the local cemetery are worthy of searching for migrating birds. About a mile north of Hyannis, take a right turn and drive a mile to see Frye Lake WMA, a 240-acre lake popular with fishermen. Take Hwy. 61 north about 30 miles to Cottonwood-Steverson Lake WMA (2,900 acres, with 660 acres of water) and Home Valley Lake immediately to the north. This is a nice drive with some lakes mostly on the west side as well as some botanically interesting fens. (See the Cherry County preserves in the "Refuges" section for information on Cottonwood-Steverson Lake WMA.)

6. From Valentine, Cherry County, south via Hwy. 83 to Valentine NWR, and return. Total distance 20 miles, round trip about 50 miles, plus within-refuge driving.

The huge Valentine National Wildlife Refuge (71,516 acres), in the heart of the northern Sandhills, consists of native prairie, lakes, and wetlands and supports a diversity of about 270 species of birds. Trumpeter swans are regular nesters, as are many other waterfowl. Little has changed in this part of the Sandhills from historic times, and some of the roads fit nicely into that time frame. Several larger lakes have wooded edges and good fish populations. Valentine NWR has been designated an Important Bird Area (IBA) by the National Audubon Society. (See also the Cherry County preserves in the "Refuges" section.)

7. Ogallala to Kingsley Dam, Lake McConaughy, and vicinity via Hwy. 61 and west via Hwy. 92 to Clear Creek WMA. Round trip about 50 miles.

This is a prime Nebraska birding area, with the highest diversity of bird species in both the Sandhills and the entire state. It regularly tallies the largest number of birds of any Nebraska area during Audubon Christmas Bird Counts. After about a ten-mile drive on Hwy. 61 from Interstate 80 through the town of Ogallala (beware a well-known speed trap at the north end of town), you will reach the North Platte River valley, Lake McConaughy, Lake Ogallala, and Kingsley Dam, where you can find dozens of passerines and nonpasserines, with rock wrens singing from nearby canyons and often Swainson's hawks nesting in low trees near the highway. The southern end of the Sandhills reaches the north shore of Lake McConaughy, forming a wide, sandy beach where least terns and piping plovers (and sometimes also snowy plovers) nest. Below the dam's spillway, gulls, mergansers, and sometimes loons gather on Lake Ogallala to feed on disabled fish that have been expelled through the dam's "rooster tail" water-release system. Clear Creek WMA, at the west end of Lake McConaughy (about 25 miles via Hwy. 92) is an excellent woodland, wet meadow, and wetland birding area. Motel accommodations are available at Lewellen and Oshkosh. (See the Keith County preserves in "Refuges" for more information about Clear Creek WMA, Lake McConaughy, Kingsley Dam and Lake Ogallala, and Cedar Point Biological Station.)

There are thus still places in Nebraska where one can lie back on a fragrant bed of last-year's bluestem in early April, with the half-intoxicating odor of freshly germinating grass invading one's nose, and the shrill but majestic music of cranes almost constantly overhead, with occasional harmonies added by arctic-bound if nearly invisible geese. There is then a true sense of belonging to and being a part of the land, and one can only give an unspoken prayer that such treasures will still be there for those of the next generation to savor and love. At such times one will realize that, although there may be places with higher mountains than Nebraska, with magnificent rock-bound coastlines, or with misty cloud forests, it really doesn't matter. This is our spiritual home, our own self-chosen Nirvana, our prairie-born paradise, the natural surviving legacy of long-forgotten winds, immense amounts of water, now-vanished glacial ice, and unfathomable eons of time. It has been freely bestowed upon us, either to keep or to destroy. May we choose to keep it.

—*The Nature of Nebraska*

References

General Surveys

Bentall, R. 1989. Streams. Pp. 93–114, in *An Atlas of the Sand Hills* (A. Bleed and C. Flowerday, eds.). Resource Atlas No. 5. Lincoln: Conservation and Survey Division, Institute of Agriculture and Natural Resources, University of Nebraska–Lincoln. 238 pp.

Dreeszen, V. 1984. Overview of Nebraska and the Sandhills. Pp. 1–15, in *The Sandhills of Nebraska—Yesterday, Today and Tomorrow*. Proceedings of 1984 Water Resources Seminar Series. Nebraska Water Resources Center, Institute of Agriculture and Natural Resources, University of Nebraska–Lincoln.

Ginsberg, M. H. 1984. Physical characteristics of the Sandhills: Hydrology. Pp. 37–43, in *The Sandhills of Nebraska—Yesterday, Today and Tomorrow*. Proceedings of 1984 Water Resources Seminar Series. Nebraska Water Resources Center, Institute of Agriculture and Natural Resources, University of Nebraska–Lincoln.

Johnsgard, P. A. 1995. *This Fragile Land: A Natural History of the Nebraska Sandhills*. University of Nebraska Press, Lincoln. 256 pp.

Keech, C., and R. Bentall. 1971. *Dunes on the Plains: The Sandhills Region of Nebraska*. Lincoln, NE: Resource Report No. 4. Conservation and Survey Division. University of Nebraska–Lincoln. 18 pp.

Martin, D. L. 1984. Possible changes in the Sandhills: Ground and surface water quality and other environmental impacts. Pp. 109–120, in *The Sandhills of Nebraska—Yesterday, Today and Tomorrow*. Proceedings of 1984 Water Resources Seminar Series. Nebraska Water Resources Center, Institute of Agriculture and Natural Resources, University of Nebraska–Lincoln.

Whitcomb, R. F. 1989. Nebraska Sand Hills: The last prairie. Pp. 57–69, in *Prairie Pioineers: Ecology, History and Culture: Proceedings of the Eleventh North American Prairie Conference*, August 7–11, 1988, Lincoln, Nebraska.

Geology, Physiography, and Wetlands

Ahlbrandt, T S., J. B. Swinehart, and D. G. Marones. 1983. The dynamic Holocene dune fields of the Great Plains and Rocky Mountain basins. Pp. 379–406, in *Eolian Sediments and Processes* (M. E. Brookfield and T. S. Ahlbrandt, eds.). Amsterdam: Elsevier Science Publishers.

Bittenger, M. W., and E. B. Green. 1980. *You Never Miss the Water Till . . . (The Ogallala Story)*. Littleton, CO: Water Resources Publications. 134 pp.

Bleed, A., and C. Flowerday, eds. 1989. *An Atlas of the Sand Hills*. Resource Atlas No. 5. Lincoln: Conservation and Survey Division, Institute of Agriculture and Natural Resources, University of Nebraska–Lincoln. 238 pp.

Bleed, A., and M. Ginsberg. 1989. Lakes and Wetlands. Pp. 115–122, in *An Atlas of the Sand Hills* (A. Bleed and C. Flowerday, eds.). Resource Atlas No. 5. Lincoln: Conservation and Survey Division, Institute of Agriculture and Natural Resources, University of Nebraska–Lincoln. 238 pp.

Buckwalter. D. W. 1983. *Monitoring Nebraska's Sandhills Lakes*. Lincoln, NE: Conservation Survey Division Resource Report No. 10.

Doubková, M., and G. M. Heneby. 2005. Assessing land surface dynamics across the Nebraska Sand Hills using advanced microwave scanning radiometer (AMSR-E) data products. Pecora 16 "Global Priorities in Land Remote Sensing," October 23–27, 2005, Sioux Falls, SD. 8 pp.

Fleming, A., L. M. Delserone, and E. M. Nowick. 2012. The Ogallala Aquifer in Nebraska: Gray literature (1891–2010). *Journal of Agricultural and Food Information* 13(3): 213–239.

Gilbert, M. C., M. W. Freel, and A. J. Bieber. 1980. Remote sensing and field evaluation of wetlands in the Sandhills of Nebraska. Omaha, NE: US Army Corps of Engineers Report. 65 pp.

Ginsberg, M. H. 1984. Physical characteristics of the Sandhills: Hydrology. Pp. 37–43, in *The Sandhills of Nebraska—Yesterday, Today and Tomorrow*. Proceedings of 1984 Water Resources Seminar Series. Nebraska Water Resources Center, Institute of Agriculture and Natural Resources, University of Nebraska–Lincoln.

———. 1985. Nebraska's sandhills lakes—a hydrogeologic overview. *Water Resources Bulletin* 21(4): 573–578.

Hayford, B., and D. Baker. 2012. Lakes of the Nebraska Sandhills. *Lakeline* 31: 26–30.

Hiskey, R. M. 1981. The trophic dynamics of an alkaline-saline Nebraska Sandhills lake. PhD dissertation. University of Nebraska–Lincoln.

Johnsgard, P. A. 2012. *Nebraska's Wetlands: Their Wildlife and Ecology*. Water Survey Paper No. 78. Lincoln: Conservation and Survey Division, Institute of Agriculture and Natural Resources, University of Nebraska–Lincoln. 202 pp.

LaBaugh, J. W. 1986. Limnological characteristics of selected lakes in the Nebraska Sandhills, USA, and their relation to chemical characteristics of adjacent ground water. *Journal of Hydrology* 86(3/4): 279–298.

LaGrange, T. G. 2005. *Guide to Nebraska Wetlands and Their Conservation Needs*. 2nd ed. Lincoln, NE: Nebraska Game and Parks Commission. 57 pp. www.nebraskawetlands.com

Lawson, M. P., C. Rundquist, R. C. Balling, Jr., R. S. Cerveny, and L. P. Queen. 1985. *Variability in the Surface Area of Sand Hills Lakes and Its Relationship to Precipitation and Groundwater Levels*. Lincoln: Department of Geography Occasional Papers No. 7, University of Nebraska.

Loope, D. B., and J. B. Swinehart. 2000. Thinking like a dune field: Geologic history in the Nebraska Sand Hills. *Great Plains Research* 10: 5–35.

Martin, D. L. 1984. Possible changes in the Sandhills: Ground and surface water quality and other environmental impacts. Pp. 109–120, in *The Sandhills of Nebraska—Yesterday, Today and Tomorrow*. Proceedings of 1984 Water Resources Seminar Series. Nebraska Water Resources Center, Institute of Agriculture and Natural Resources, University of Nebraska–Lincoln.

McCarraher, D. B. 1960. Sandhills lake survey. Job completion report. Lincoln: Nebraska Game and Parks Commission.

———. 1969. *Nebraska's Sandhills Lakes: Their Characteristics and Fisheries Management Problems*. Lincoln: Nebraska Game and Parks Commission.

———. 1977. *Nebraska's Sandhills Lakes*. Lincoln: Nebraska Game and Parks Commission. 67 pp.

McMurtrey, M. S., R. Craig, and G. Schildmann. 1972. *Nebraska Wetland Survey*. Lincoln: Nebraska Game and Parks Commission. 78 pp.

Novacek, J. M. 1989. The water and wetland resources of the Nebraska Sandhills. Pp. 340–384, in *Northern Prairie Wetlands* (A. van der Valk, ed.). Ames: Iowa State University Press. 400 pp.

Omernik, J. M. 1987. Ecoregions of the conterminous United States. Map (scale 1:7,500,000). *Annals of the Association of American Geographers* 77(1): 118–125.

———. 1995. Ecoregions: A spatial framework for environmental management. Pp. 49–62, in *Biological Assessment and Criteria: Tools for Water Resource Planning and Decision Making* (W. S. Davis and T. P. Simon, eds.). Boca Raton, FL: Lewis Publishers.

Opie, J. 2000. *Ogallala: Water for a Dry Land*. 2nd ed. Lincoln: University of Nebraska Press. 504 pp.

Rundquist, D. C. 1983. *Wetland Inventories of Nebraska's Sandhills. Resource Report No. 9*. Lincoln: Conservation and Survey Division, Institute of Agriculture and Natural Resources, University of Nebraska–Lincoln. 46 pp.

Smith, H. T. U. 1965. Dune morphology and chronology in central and western Nebraska. *Journal of Geology* 73: 557–578.

Swinehart, J. B. 1984. Physical characteristics of the Sandhills: Geology. Pp. 32–36, in *The Sandhills of Nebraska—Yesterday, Today and Tomorrow*. Proceedings of 1984 Water Resources Seminar Series. Nebraska Water Resources Center, Institute of Agriculture and Natural Resources, University of Nebraska–Lincoln.

Wilhite, D. A., and K. G. Hubbard. 1998. Climate. Pp. 17–28, in *An Atlas of the Sand Hills*. 3rd ed. (A. S. Bleed and C. A. Flowerday, eds.). Lincoln: Conservation and Survey Division, Institue of Agriculture and Natural Resources, University of Nebraska–Lincoln. 12 pp.

Wolfe, C. 1984. Physical characteristics of the Sandhills: Wetlands, fisheries, and wildlife. Pp. 54–61, in *The Sandhills of Nebraska—Yesterday, Today and Tomorrow*. Proceedings of 1984 Water Resources Seminar Series. Nebraska Water Resources Center, Institute of Agriculture and Natural Resources, University of Nebraska–Lincoln.

Botany, Zoology, and Ecology

Bogan, M. A. 1995. *A Biological Survey of the Fort Niobrara and Valentine National Wildlife Refuges*. Ft. Collins, CO: Midcontinent Ecological Service Center, National Biological Service, US Department of the Interior.

Bogan, M. A., M. Jennings, and F. Knopf. 1995. A portrait of faunal and floral change in the Sandhills of northern Nebraska. Pp. 6–24, in *A Biological Survey of the Fort Niobrara and Valentine National Wildlife Refuges* (M. A. Bogan, ed.) Fort Collins, CO: Midcontinent Ecological Science Center, National Biological Service, US Department of the Interior.

Chapman, S. S., et al. 2001. *Ecoregions of Nebraska and Kansas* (color poster and map). Reston, VA: US Geological Survey.

Cox, M. K., and W. L. Franklin. 1988. Faunal survey of the birds, mammals, and reptiles at Scotts Bluff National Monument. *Iowa Cooperative Fish and Wildlife Research Unit Annual Report* 53: 26–28.

———. 1989. Terrestrial vertebrates of Scotts Bluff National Monument, Nebraska. *Great Basin Naturalist* 49: 597–613.

Fowler, E. 2015. Preserving a Niobrara gem. *NEBRASKAland*, April, pp. 50–55. (Chat Canyon WMA)

Hartman J. C. 2015. A desert in disguise: The resilience of the Nebraska Sandhills. PhD dissertation. University of Nebraska–Lincoln.

Henzlik, R. E. 1960. A study of the animal ecology of a man-made forest in the Nebraska Sandhills. PhD dissertation. University of Nebraska–Lincoln. 211 pp.

Hrabik, R. A. 1998. Fishes. Pp. 143–154, in *An Atlas of the Sand Hills*. 3rd ed. (A. S. Bleed and C. A. Flowerday, eds.). Resource Atlas No. 5. Lincoln: Conservation and Survey Division, Institute of Agriculture and Natural Resources, University of Nebraska–Lincoln. 238 pp.

Ingwersen, M. B. 1998. A study of the floristic composition, zonation, and abiotic parameters of three fens in the Sand Hills of Nebraska. PhD dissertation. University of South Dakota, Vermillion.

Johnsgard, P. A. 2001. *The Nature of Nebraska: Ecology and Biodiversity*. Lincoln: University of Nebraska Press. 402 pp.

———. 2003. *Great Wildlife of the Great Plains*. Lawrence: University Press of Kansas. 309 pp.

———. 2004. *Prairie Dog Empire: A Saga of the Shortgrass Prairie*. Lincoln: University of Nebraska Press. 142 pp.

———. 2007a. *A Guide to the Natural History of the Central Platte Valley of Nebraska*. School of Biological Sciences, University of Nebraska–Lincoln. UNL Digital Commons. 156 pp. https://digitalcommons.unl.edu/biosciornithology/40/

———. 2007b. *A Guide to the Tallgrass Prairies of Eastern Nebraska and Adjacent States*. School of Biological Sciences, University of Nebraska–Lincoln. UNL Digital Commons. 158 pp. https://digitalcommons.unl.edu/biosciornithology/39/

———. 2007c. *The Niobrara: A River Running through Time*. Lincoln: University of Nebraska Press. 373 pp.

———. 2008. *The Platte: Channels in Time*. 2nd ed. Lincoln: University of Nebraska Press. 176 pp. http://digitalcommons.unl.edu/biosciornithology/39/

———. 2018. *A Naturalist's Guide to the Great Plains*. Lincoln: University of Nebraska–Lincoln Digital Commons and Zea Books. 161 pp. https://digitalcommons.unl.edu/zeabook/63/

———. 2019. *Wyoming Wildlife: A Natural History*. Lincoln: University of Nebraska–Lincoln Digital Commons and Zea Books. 242 pp. https://digitalcommons.unl.edu/zeabook/73/

———. 2020. *Wildlife of Nebraska: A Natural History*. Lincoln: University of Nebraska Press. 528 pp.

Jones, S. R. 2000. *The Last Prairie: A Sandhills Journal*. New York: McGraw-Hill. 244 pp.

Jones, S. R., and R. C. Cushman. 2004. *The North American Prairie*. Boston: Houghton Mifflin.

Kantak, G. E., and S. P. Churchill. 1993. The Niobrara Valley Preserve: An inventory of a biogeographical crossroads. *Transactions of the Nebraska Academy of Sciences* 20: 1–12. http://digitalcommons.unl.edu/tnas/121

Kaul, R. 1998. Plants. Pp. 127–142, in *An Atlas of the Sand Hills*. 3rd ed. (A. S. Bleed and C. A. Flowerday, eds.). Resource Atlas No. 5. Lincoln: Conservation and Survey Division, Institutue of Agriculture and Natural Resources, University of Nebraska–Lincoln. 238 pp.

Kaul, R. B., D. Sutherland, and S. Rolfsmeier. 2012. *The Flora of Nebraska*. 2nd ed. Lincoln: Conservation and Survey Division, School of Natural Resources, University of Nebraska–Lincoln. 966 pp.

Kaul, R. B., G. E. Kantak, and S. P. Churchill. 1988. The Niobrara River valley, a postglacial migration corridor and refugium of forest plants and animals in the grasslands of central North America. *The Botanical Review* 54: 44–81.

Knopf, F. L., and F. B. Samson. 1997. Conservation of grassland vertebrates. Pp. 273–289, in *Ecology and Conservation of Great Plains Vertebrates* (F. L. Knopf and F. B. Samson, eds.). New York: Springer-Verlag. 320 pp.

Knue, J. 1992. *Nebraska Wildlife Viewing Guide*. Helena, MT: Falcon Press, 96 pp.

Krapu, G. L. (ed.). 1996. *The Platte River Ecology Study: Special Research Report*. Jamestown, ND: Northern Prairie Wildlife Research Station. 186 pp.

Maier, C. R. 1993. The Niobrara River Valley—A crossroads of nature. *Research Symposium: Environmental and Natural Resources of the Nebraska River Basin* (R. Kuzelka, ed.). Oct. 14–15, 1993, Ainsworth, Nebraska. Lincoln: Water Center/Environmental Programs, University of Nebraska–Lincoln. 5 pp.

McClure, H. E. 1966. Some observations of vertebrate fauna of the Nebraska Sandhills, 1941 through 1943. *Nebraska Bird Review* 34: 2–15.

Nichols, J. T. 1984. Physical characteristics of the Sandhills: Vegetation. Pp. 74–79, in *The Sandhills of Nebraska—Yesterday, Today and Tomorrow*. Proceedings of 1984 Water Resources Seminar Series. Nebraska Water Resources Center, Institute of Agriculture and Natural Resources, University of Nebraska–Lincoln.

Oberholser, H. C., and W. L. McAtee. 1920. *Waterfowl and Their Food Plants in the Sandhill Region of Nebraska*. Washington, DC: US Department of Agriculture Bulletin No. 794.

Panella, M. J. 2010. *Nebraska's At-Risk Wildlife*. Lincoln: Wildlife Division, Nebraska Game and Parks Commission. 196 pp.

Pool, R. J. 1914. A study of the vegetation of the Sandhills of Nebraska. *Minnesota Botanical Studies* 4(3): 189–312.

Pound, R., and F. C. Clements. 1898. *Phytogeography of Nebraska*. Lincoln, NE: Jacob North. 329 pp.

Schneider, R., K. Stoner, G. Steinauer, M. Panella, and M. Humpert, eds. 2011. *The Nebraska Natural Legacy Project: State Wildlife Action Plan*. 2nd ed. Lincoln: Nebraska Game and Parks Commission. 344 pp.

Stone, E. N., and W. T. Bagley. 1961. *The Forest Resources of Nebraska*. Release 4. Fort Collins, CO: USDA Forest Service Rocky Mountain Range and Experiment Station.

Steinauer, E., and E. Scudder. [undated]. *The Niobrara Valley Preserve, Crossroads of Nature: Animal Species List*. Johnstown, NE: The Nature Conservancy. 22 pp.

Steinauer, G. 1992. Sandhills fens. *NEBRASKAland* 70(6): 16–32.

Steinauer, G., and S. B. Rolfsmeier. 2003. *Terrestrial Natural Communities of Nebraska*. Lincoln: Nebraska Game and Parks Commission. 162 pp.

Stubbendieck, J., and K. L. Kottas. 2005. *Common Grasses of Nebraska: Prairies, Rangelands, Pasturelands*. University of Nebraska–Lincoln Extension Bulletin EC05-170. UNL Department of Agronomy and Horticulture, Institute of Agriculture and Natural Resources. 123 pp. https://digitalcommons.unl.edu/extensionhist/4786/

———. 2007. *Common Forbs and Shrubs of Nebraska: Prairies, Rangelands, Pasturelands.* University of Nebraska–Lincoln Extension Bulletin EC07-118. UNL Department of Agronomy and Horticulutre, Institute of Agriculture and Natural Resources. 178 pp. https://digitalcommons.unl.edu/extensionhist/4799/

Wehrman, K. C. 1961. A study of the transition zone between the Loess Hills and the Sand Hills in central Nebraska. MS thesis. University of Nebraska–Lincoln.

Birds

American Ornithologists' Union (AOU). 1998. *The A.O.U. Check-list of North American Birds.* 7th ed. Washington, DC: AOU. With annual supplements through 2019 (see Chesser et al., 2019).

Austin, O. L., ed. 1968. *Life Histories of North American Cardinals, Grosbeaks, Buntings, Towhees, Finches, Sparrows and Allies.* Washington, DC: Smithsonian Institution Press. 602 pp.

Baicich P. J, and C. J. O. Harrison. 1997. *A Guide to the Nests, Eggs and Nestlings of North American Birds.* 2nd ed. New York: Academic Press. 346 pp.

Baker, M. C., and J. T. Boylan. 1999. Singing behavior, mating associations and reproductive success in a population of hybridizing lazuli and indigo buntings. *Condor* 181: 493–503.

Banko, W. E. 1960. *The Trumpeter Swan: Its History, Habits, and Population in the United States.* North American Fauna No. 63. Washington, DC: US Department of the Interior, Fish and Wildlife Service. 214 pp.

Bates, J. M. 1900. Additional notes and observations of the birds of northern Nebraska. *Proceedings of the Nebraska Ornithologists' Union* 1: 15–18.

Beed, W. E. 1934. Summer bird life of the Niobrara Game Preserve. *Nebraska Bird Review* 2: 119–120.

Bergin, T. 1987. A multivariate hierarchical examination of habitat selection in *Tyrannis verticalis*. MS thesis. University of Nebraska–Lincoln.

Bicak, T. K. 1977. Some eco-ethological aspects of a breeding population of long-billed curlews (*Numenius americanus*) in Nebraska. MA thesis. University of Nebraska Omaha.

BNA Online (Birds of North America Online) and Birds of the World Online. See https://birdsoftheworld.org/bow/species/

Bock, C. E., and W. C. Scharf. 1994. A nesting population of Cassin's sparrows in the Sandhills of Nebraska. *Journal of Field Ornithology* 65: 472–475.

Bomberger, M. B. 1982. Aspects of the breeding biology of Wilson's phalarope in western Nebraska. MS thesis. University of Nebraska–Lincoln.

———. 1984. Nesting habitat of Wilson's phalarope in western Nebraska. *Wilson Bulletin* 96: 126–128.

Brogie, M. A. 1997. 1996 (eighth) report of the NOU Records Committee. *Nebraska Bird Review* 65(3): 115–126.

———. 2017. The official list of the birds of Nebraska. *Nebraska Bird Review* 85: 179–197.

Brogie, M. A., and M. J. Mossman. 1983. Spring and summer birds of the Niobrara Valley Preserve area, Nebraska. *Nebraska Bird Review* 51: 44–51.

Brown, C. R, and M. B. Brown. 1996. *Coloniality in the Cliff Swallow.* Chicago: University of Chicago Press.

———. 2001. *Birds of the Cedar Point Biological Station.* Lincoln, NE: Occasional Papers of the Cedar Point Biological Station No. 1. 36 pp.

Brown, C. R, M. B. Brown, P. A. Johnsgard, J. Kren, and W. C. Scharf. 1996. Birds of the Cedar Point Biological Station area, Keith and Garden counties, Nebraska: Seasonal occurrence and breeding data. *Transactions of the Nebraska Academy of Sciences* 29: 91–108.

Brown, M. B., and P. A. Johnsgard. 2013. *Birds of the Central Platte River Valley and Adjacent Counties.* Lincoln: Conservation and Survey Division, Institute of Agriculture and Natural Resources, University of Nebraska–Lincoln. 182 pp. https://digitalcommons.unl.edu/zeabook/15/

Brown, M. B., S. Dinsmore, and C. R. Brown. 2012. *Birds of Southwestern Nebraska.* Lincoln: Conservation and Survey Division, Institute of Agriculture and Natural Resources, University of Nebraska–Lincoln. 151 pp.

Bruner, L. 1902. A comparison of the bird life found in a sandhills region of Holt County in 1883–84 and in 1901. *Proceedings of the Nebraska Ornithologists' Union* 3: 58–63.

Busby, W. H., and J. L. Zimmerman. 2001. *Kansas Breeding Bird Atlas.* Lawrence: University Press of Kansas.

Butterfield, J. D. 1969. Nest-site requirements of the lark bunting in Colorado. MS thesis. Colorado State University, Fort Collins.

Canterbury, J. L., P. A. Johnsgard, and H. F. Dunning. 2013. *Birds and Birding in Wyoming's Bighorn Mountains Region.* Lincoln: University of Nebraska–Lincoln Digital Commons and Zea Books. 260 pp. https://digitalcommons.unl.edu/zeabook/18/

Chesser, R. T., K. J. Burns, C. Cicero, J. L. Dunn, A. W. Kratter, I. J. Lovette, P. C. Rasmussen, J. V. Remsen, Jr., D. F. Stotz, and K. Winker. 2019. Sixtieth Supplement to the American Ornithological Society's *Check-list of North American Birds*. *The Auk: Ornithological Advances* 136(3): 1–23. https://doi.org/10.1093/auk/ukz042

Chupp, N. 1952. Nesting observations on certain Sandhills lakes. *Nebraska Bird Review* 20: 49–50.

Clawson, S. D. 1980. Comparative ecology of the northern oriole and the orchard oriole in western Nebraska. MS thesis. University of Nebraska–Lincoln.

Corbin, K. W., and C. G. Sibley, 1977. Rapid evolution in orioles of the genus *Icterus*. *Condor* 79: 335–342.

Creighton, P. D. 1971. *Nesting of the Lark Bunting in North-central Colorado.* US International Biological Program, Grassland Biome Technical Report No. 68. Fort Collins: Colorado State University. 17 pp.

Currier, P. J., G. R. Lingle, and J. G. VanDerwalker. 1985. *Migratory Bird Habitat on the Platte and North Platte Rivers in Nebraska*. Grand Island, NE: Whooping Crane Habitat Maintenance Trust. 177 pp.

Delphey, P. J., and J. J. Dinsmore. 1993. Breeding bird communities of recently restored and natural prairie potholes. *Wetlands* 13: 200–206.

Desmond, M. J. 1991. Ecological aspects of burrowing owl nesting strategies in the Nebraska panhandle. MS thesis. University of Nebraska–Lincoln. 114 pp.

Desmond, M. J., and J. A. Savidge. 1996. Factors influencing burrowing owl nest densities and numbers in western Nebraska. *American Midland Naturalist* 136: 143–148.

Desmond, M. J., J. A. Savidge, and R. M. Eskridge. 2000. Correlations between burrowing owl and black-tailed prairie dog declines: A 7-year analysis. *Journal of Wildlife Management* 64: 1067–1075.

Dinan, L. R., J. G. Jorgensen, and M. Bomberger. 2018. *Secretive Marshbird Abundance, Distribution and Habitat Use in Nebraska, 2016–2017*. Lincoln: Nebraska Game and Parks Commission. 55 pp.

Ducey, J. E. 1984. Location and habitat size of lakes in the Nebraska Sandhills utilized by trumpeter swans. *Nebraska Bird Review* 52: 19–22.

———. 1988. *Nebraska Birds: Breeding Status and Distribution*. Omaha, NE: Simmons-Boardman Books. 148 pp.

———. 1989. Birds of the Niobrara River valley. *Transactions of the Nebraska Academy of Sciences* 17: 37–60.

———. 2000. *Birds of the Untamed West: The History of Birdlife in Nebraska, 1750 to 1875*. Omaha, NE: Making History Press.

Dugger, B. D., and K. M. Dugger. 2002. Long-billed curlew (*Numenius americana*). In: *The Birds of North America*, no. 628 (A. Poole and F. Gill, eds.). Philadelphia: Academy of Natural Sciences, and Washington, DC: American Ornithologists' Union. 28 pp.

Dunham, D. W. 1966. Territorial and sexual behavior in the rose-breasted grosbeak. *Zeitschrift fur Tierpsychologie* 23: 438–451.

Emlen, S. T., J. D. Rising, and W. L. Thompson. 1975. A behavioral and morphological study of sympatry in the indigo and lazuli buntings of the Great Plains. *Wilson Bulletin* 87: 145–179.

Faanes, C. E., and G. R. Lingle. 1995. *Breeding Birds of the Platte Valley of Nebraska*. Jamestown, ND: Northern Prairie Wildlife Research Center.

Fairbairn, S. E., and J. J. Dinsmore. 2001. Local and landscape-level influences on wetland bird communities of the Prairie Pothole Region of Iowa, USA. *Wetlands* 21: 41–47.

Farrar, J. 2004. Birding Nebraska. *NEBRASKAland* (special issue) 82(1). 178 pp.

Farrar, J., ed. 1985. Birds of Nebraska. *NEBRASKAland* (special issue) 63(1). 146 pp.

Faulkner D. W. 2012. *Birds of Wyoming*. Greenwood Village, CO: Roberts. 403 pp.

Fellows, S. D., and S. L. Jones. 2009. Status Assessment and Conservation Action Plan for the Long-billed Curlew (*Numenius americanus*). Washington, DC: US Department of the Interior, Fish and Wildlife Service, Biological Technical Publication, FWS/BTP-R6012-2009.

Greer, R. D., and S. H. Anderson. 1989. Relationships between population demography of McCown's longspurs and habitat resources. *Condor* 91: 609–619.

Gregory, C. 2010. Long-billed curlew: Mysterious bird of the Sandhills. *NEBRASKAland* 88(4): 32–37.

Griebel, R. L., S. L. Winter, and A. A. Steuter. 1998. Grassland birds and habitat structure in Sandhills prairie managed for cattle or bison plus fire. *Great Plains Research* 8: 255–268.

Hammerstrom, F. 1986. *Harrier: Hawk of the Marshes*. Washington, DC: Smithsonian Institution Press.

Hancock, J., and H. Elliott. 1978. *The Herons of the World*. New York: Harper and Row. 304 pp.

Harms, T. M., and S. J. Dinsmore. 2012. Density and abundance of secretive marsh birds in Iowa. *Waterbirds* 35: 208–216.

———. 2013. Habitat associations of secretive marsh birds in Iowa. *Wetlands* 33: 561–571.

Hemesath, L. M. 1991. Species richness and nest productivity of marsh birds on restored prairie potholes in northern Iowa. MS thesis. Iowa State University, Ames.

Higgins, K. F., and L. M. Kirsch. 1975. Some aspects of the breeding biology of the upland sandpiper in North Dakota. *Wilson Bulletin* 87: 96–102.

Houston, C. S., and D. E. Bowen, Jr. 2001. Upland sandpiper (*Bartramia longicauda*). In: *The Birds of North America*, no. 580 (A. Poole and F. Gill, eds.). Philadelphia: Academy of Natural Sciences, and Washington, DC: American Ornithologists' Union. 32 pp.

Johnson, D. H., L. D. Igl, J. A. Shaffer, and J. P. DeLong, eds. 2019. *The Effects of Management Practices on Grassland Birds*. US Geological Survey Professional Paper 1842. https://doi.org/10.3133/pp1842

Johnsgard, P. A. 1973. *Grouse and Quails of North America*. Lincoln: University of Nebraska Press. 553 pp. http://digitalcommons.unl.edu/bioscigrouse/1

———. 1975. *Waterfowl of North America*. Bloomington: Indiana University Press. 573 pp.

———. 1979. *Birds of the Great Plains: Breeding Species and Their Distribution*. Lincoln: University of Nebraska Press. (See also 2009 edition supplement and revised maps, http://digitalcommons.unl.edu/bioscibirdsgreatplains/1/.)

———. 1980a. Copulatory behavior in the American bittern. *Auk* 97: 868–869.

———. 1980b. Where have all the curlews gone? *Natural History* 89(8): 30–33. http://digitalcommons.unl.edu/biosciornithology/23

———. 1981. *The Plovers, Sandpipers, and Snipes of the World.* Lincoln: University of Nebraska Press. 492 pp.

———. 1983. *The Cranes of the World.* Bloomington: Indiana University Press. 256 pp.

———. 1987. *Diving Birds of North America.* Lincoln: University of Nebraska Press. 286 pp.

———. 1990. *Hawks, Eagles, and Falcons of North America: Biology and Natural History.* Washington, DC: Smithsonian Institution Press. 403 pp.

———. 1991. *Crane Music: A Natural History of American Cranes.* Washington, DC: Smithsonian Institution Press.

———. 1993. *Cormorants, Darters and Pelicans of the World.* Washington, DC: Smithsonian Institution Press. 445 pp.

———. 1994. *Arena Birds: Sexual Selection and Behavior.* Washington, DC: Smithsonian Institution Press. 330 pp.

———. 1997a. *The Avian Brood Parasites: Deception at the Nest.* New York: Oxford University Press. 409 pp.

———. 1997b. *The Hummingbirds of North America.* 2nd ed. Washington, DC: Smithsonian Institution Press. 277 pp.

———. 2000. A century of ornithology in Nebraska: A personal view. Pp. 347–371, in *Contributions to the History of North American Ornithology, Volume II* (W. E. Davis and J. A. Jackson, eds.). Boston: Nuttall Ornithological Club. http://digitalcommons.unl.edu/biosciornithology/26

———. 2001b. *Prairie Birds: Fragile Splendor in the Great Plains.* Lawrence: University Press of Kansas. 331 pp.

———. 2002a. *Grassland Grouse and Their Conservation.* Washington, DC: Smithsonian Institution Press. 157 pp.

———. 2002b. *North American Owls: Biology and Natural History.* 2nd ed. Washington, DC: Smithsonian Institution Press, 298 pp.

———. 2006. The howdy owl and the prairie dog. *Birding* 38(1): 40–44.

———. 2007. A dozen squaretails and a sharpy. *Nebraska Life*, March April, 2007, 80 86.

———. 2011a. *A Nebraska Bird-Finding Guide.* Lincoln: University of Nebraska–Lincoln Digital Commons and Zea Books. 166 pp. https://digitalcommons.unl.edu/zeabook/5/

———. 2011b. *The Sandhill and Whooping Cranes: Ancient Voices over the America's Wetlands.* Lincoln: University of Nebraska Press. 155 pp.

———. 2012a. *Wetland Birds of the Central Plains: South Dakota, Nebraska and Kansas.* Lincoln: University of Nebraska–Lincoln Digital Commons and Zea Books. 276 pp. http://digitalcommons.unl.edu/zeabook/8

———. 2012b. *Wings over the Great Plains: Bird Migrations in the Central Flyway.* Lincoln: University of Nebraska–Lincoln Digital Commons and Zea Books. 249 pp. http://digitalcommons.unl.edu/zeabook/13

———. 2014. What are blue Ross's geese? *Nebraska Bird Review* 82(2): 81–85. https://digitalcommons.unl.edu/nebbirdrev/1346/

———. 2015a. *Birding Nebraska's Central Platte Valley and Rainwater Basin.* Lincoln: University of Nebraska–Lincoln Digital Commons and Zea Books. 54 pp. http://digitalcommons.unl.edu/zeabook/36

———. 2015b. *A Chorus of Cranes: The Cranes of North America and the World.* Boulder: University Press of Colorado. 242 pp.

———. 2015c. *Global Warming and Population Responses among Great Plains Birds.* Lincoln: University of Nebraska–Lincoln Digital Commons and Zea Books. https://digitalcommons.unl.edu/zeabook/26/

———. 2016a. Bittern surprise. *Birdwatching* 32(2): 36–39.

———. 2016b. *The North American Geese: Their Biology and Behavior.* Lincoln: University of Nebraska Digital Commons and Zea Books. 159 pp. http://digitalcommons.unl.edu/zeabook/44/

———. 2016c. *The North American Grouse: Their Biology and Behavior.* Lincoln: University of Nebraska–Lincoln Digital Commons and Zea Books. 183 pp. https://digitalcommons.unl.edu/zeabook/41/

———. 2016d. *The North American Sea Ducks: Their Biology and Behavior.* Lincoln: University of Nebraska–Lincoln Digital Commons and Zea Books. 256 pp. http://digitalcommons.unl.edu/zeabook/50/

———. 2016e. *Swans: Their Biology and Natural History.* Lincoln: University of Nebraska–Lincoln Digital Commons and Zea Books. 114 pp. http://digitalcommons.unl.edu/zeabook/38/

———. 2017a. *The North American Perching and Dabbling Ducks: Their Biology and Behavior.* Lincoln: University of Nebraska–Lincoln Digital Commons and Zea Books. 228 pp. http://digitalcommons.unl.edu/zeabook/53/

———. 2017b. *The North American Quails, Partridges, and Pheasants.* Lincoln: University of Nebraska–Lincoln Digital Commons and Zea Books. 131 pp. http://digitalcommons.unl.edu/zeabook/58/

———. 2017c. *The North American Whistling-Ducks, Pochards, and Stifftails.* Lincoln: University of Nebraska–Lincoln Digital Commons and Zea Books. 188 pp. http://digitalcommons.unl.edu/zeabook/54/

———. 2018. *The Birds of Nebraska.* 2nd digital ed. Lincoln: University of Nebraska–Lincoln Digital Commons and Zea Books. 307 pp. https://digitalcommons.unl.edu/zeabook/65/

———. 2020a. *Audubon's Lillian Annette Rowe Sanctuary: A Refuge, a River, and a Migration.* Lincoln, NE: Infusion Media. 205 pp.

———. 2020b. *The North American Swans: Their Biology and Conservation.* Lincoln: University of Nebraska–Lincoln Digital Commons and Zea Books. 164 pp. https://digitalcommons.unl.edu/zeabook/89/

Johnsgard, P. A , and J. Dinan. 2005. Habitat associations of Nebraska birds. *Nebraska Bird Review* 73(1): 20–25. https://digitalcommons.unl.edu/nebbirdrev/1104/

Johnsgard, P. A., and M. Carbonell. 1996. *Ruddy Ducks and Other Stifftails: Their Behavior and Biology*. Norman: University of Oklahoma Press. 284 pp.

Johnsgard, P. A., ed. 1999. *Proceedings of the Centennial Meeting, Nebraska Ornithologists' Union, Lincoln, Nebraska, May 14–16, 1999*. Lincoln: Nebraska Ornithologists' Union. 76 pp.

Jones, J. O. 1990. *Where the Birds Are: A Guide to All 50 States and Canada*. New York: Willliam Morrow.

Jones, S. L., C. S. Nations, S. D. Fellows, and L. L. McDonald. 2008. Breeding abundance and distribution of long-billed curlews (*Numenius americanus*) in North America. *Waterbirds* 31: 1–14.

Jorgensen, J. 2006. The Long-billed Curlew (*Numenius americanus*) in Nebraska: Status, Trends and Conservation Needs. Final report [unpublished manuscript]. Lincoln: Nebraska Game and Parks Commission.

Jorgensen, J. G. 2012. *Birds of the Rainwater Basin, Nebraska*. Lincoln: Nebraska Game and Parks Commission. (See also http://outdoornebraska.gov/rainwaterbasin/.)

———. 2015. First nesting record and status review of the glossy ibis in Nebraska. *Nebraska Bird Review* 83: 139–148. https://digitalcommons.unl.edu/nebbirdrev/1380/

Kangarise, C. M. 1979. Breeding biology of Wilson's phalarope in North Dakota. *Bird-Banding* 50: 12–22.

Kantrud, H. A., and R. E. Stewart. 1984. Ecological distribution and crude density of breeding birds on prairie wetlands. *Journal of Wildlife Management* 48: 426–437.

Kilham, L. 1968. Reproductive behavior of white-breasted nuthatches. I. Distraction display, bill-sweeping, and nest hole defense. *Auk* 85(3): 477–492.

———. 1972. Reproductive behavior of white-breasted nuthatches. II. Courtship. *Auk* 89(1): 115–129.

Kingery, H., ed. 1998. *Colorado Breeding Bird Atlas*. Denver: Colorado Division of Wildlife. 600 pp.

Klataske, R. D. 1966. Mourning dove nesting success and nest site selection in a Sandhill region of Nebraska. *Nebraska Bird Review* 34: 71–75. https://digitalcommons.unl.edu/nebbirdrev/703/

Kren, J. 1996. Proximate and ultimate mechanisms of red-winged blackbird (*Agelaius phoeniceus*) responses to interspecific brood parasitism. PhD dissertation. University of Nebraska–Lincoln.

Kroodsma, R. L. 1970. North Dakota species pairs. I. Hybridization in buntings, grosbeaks and orioles. II. Species' recognition behavior of territorial male rose-breasted and black-headed grosbeaks (*Pheucticus*). PhD dissertation. North Dakota State University, Fargo.

Labedz, T. 1989. Birds. Pp. 161–180, in *An Atlas of the Sand Hills* (A. Bleed and C. Flowerday, eds.). Resource Atlas No. 5. Lincoln: Conservation and Survey Division, Institute of Agriculture and Natural Resources, University of Nebraska–Lincoln. 238 pp.

Lederer, R. J. 1977. Winter feeding territories in the Townsend's solitaire. *Bird-Banding* 48: 11–18.

Lincer, J. L., and K. Steenhof, eds. 1997. *The Burrowing Owl, Its Biology and Management, Including the Proceedings of the First International Burrowing Owl Symposium*. Raptor Research Report No. 9. The Raptor Research Foundation.

Lingle, G. R. 1994. *Birding Crane River: Nebraska's Platte*. Grand Island, NE: Harrier Publishing.

Lingle, G. R., and G. L. Krapu. 1986. Winter ecology of bald eagles in south-central Nebraska. *Prairie Naturalist* 18: 65–78.

Lumsden, H. G. 1965. *Displays of the Sharptail Grouse*. Technical Series Research Report No. 66. Maple: Ontario Department of Lands and Forests.

MacWhirter, R. B., and K. L. Bildstein. 1996. Northern harrier (*Circus cyaneus*). In: *The Birds of North America*, no. 210 (A. Poole and F. Gill, eds.). Philadelphia: Academy of Natural Sciences, and Washington, DC: American Ornithologists' Union. 32 pp.

McNicholl, M. K., P. E. Lowther, and J. A. Hall. 2001. Forster's tern (*Sterna forsteri*). In: *The Birds of North America*, no. 595 (A. Poole and F. Gill, eds.). Philadelphia: Academy of Natural Sciences, and Washington, DC: American Ornithologists' Union. 24 pp.

Meyeriecks, A. J. 1960. *Comparative Behavior of Four Species of North American Herons*. Publications of the Nuttall Ornithological Club No. 2. 158 pp.

Mohler, L. L. 1946. Notes on the breeding and nesting of the long-billed curlew. *Nebraska Bird Review* 14(2): 31–33. https://digitalcommons.unl.edu/nebbirdrev/892/

Mollhoff, W. J. 2001. *The Nebraska Breeding Bird Atlas*. Lincoln: Nebraska Game and Parks Commission. 233 pp.

———. 2016. *The Second Nebraska Breeding Bird Atlas*. Lincoln: Bulletin of the University of Nebraska State Museum Volume 29. 304 pp.

———. 2018. Northern saw-whet owl (*Aegolius acadicus*) nest box project: The first seven years. *Nebraska Bird Review* 86: 168–174.

Newman, O. A. 1970. Cowbird parasitism and nesting success of lark sparrows in southern Oklahoma. *Wilson Bulletin* 82: 304–309.

Oberholser, H. C., and W. L. McAtee. 1920. *Waterfowl and Their Food Plants in the Sandhill Region of Nebraska*. Washington, DC: US Department of Agriculture Bulletin 794. 79 pp.

Ortega, C. P. 2000. *Cowbirds and Other Brood Parasites*. Tucson: University of Arizona Press. 371 pp.

Panella, M. J. 2010. *Nebraska's At-risk Wildlife*. Lincoln: Nebraska Game and Parks Commission. 196 pp.

Peer, D., S. K. Robinson, and J. R. Herkert. 2000. Egg rejection by cowbird hosts in grasslands. *Auk* 117: 892–901.

Peterson, R. A. 1995. *The South Dakota Breeding Bird Atlas*. Aberdeen: South Dakota Ornithologists' Union.

Poole, A., ed. [Various dates]. *The Birds of North America Online*. Ithaca, NY: Cornell University, Laboratory of Ornithology.

Ratti, J. T., A. M. Rocklage, J. H. Giudice, E. O. Garton, and D. P. Golner. 2001. Comparison of avian communities on restored and natural wetlands in North and South Dakota. *Journal of Wildlife Management* 65: 676–684.

Rich, T. C., C. J. Beardmore, H. Berlanga, P. J. Blancher, M. S. W. Bradstreet, G. S. Butcher, D. W. Demerest, E. H. Dunn, W. C. Hunter, E. E. Inig-Elias, J. A. Kennedy, A. M. Martell, A. O. Punjabi, D. N. Pashley, K. V. Rosenburg, C. M. Rusta, J. S. Wendt, and T. C. Will. 2004. *North American Landbird Conservation Plan*. Ithaca, NY: Partners in Flight and Cornell University Laboratory of Ornithology. 84 pp.

Rising, J. D. 1970. Morphological variation and evolution in some North American orioles. *Systematic Zoology* 19: 315–351.

———. 1983. The Great Plains hybrid zones. *Current Ornithology* 1: 131–157.

Rosche, R. C. 1982. *Birds of Northwestern Nebraska and Southwestern South Dakota*. Chadron, NE: Published by the author. 100 pp.

———. 1994. *Birds of the Lake McConaughy Area and the North Platte Valley, Nebraska*. Chadron, NE: Published by the author. 115 pp.

Rosche, R. C., and P. A. Johnsgard. 1984. Birds of Lake McConaughy and the North Platte River valley, Oshkosh to Keystone. *Nebraska Bird Review* 52(2): 26–35. https://digitalcommons.unl.edu/nebbirdrev/1199/

Ryan, M. R., R. B. Renken, and J. J. Dinsmore. 1984. Marbled godwit habitat selection in the northern prairie region. *Journal of Wildlife Management* 48: 1206–1218.

Sauer, J. R., D. K. Niven, J. E. Hines, D. J. Ziolkowski, Jr., K. L. Pardieck, J. E. Fallon, and W. A. Link. 2017. *The North American Breeding Bird Survey, Results and Analysis, 1966–2015. Version 2.07.2017*. Laurel, MD: USGS Patuxent Wildlife Research Center. https://www.mbr-pwrc.usgs.gov/bbs/spec15.html

Scharf, W. C. 2005. New westward breeding records for eastern towhees in central Nebraska. *Nebraska Bird Review* 73: 26–28.

Scharf, W. C., and J. Kren. 1996. Orchard Oriole (*Icterus spurius*). The Birds of North America Online (A. Poole, ed.). Ithaca: Cornell Lab of Ornithology.

Scharf, W. C., J. Berigan, and J. Kren. 1993. Pine siskins in breeding condition along the North Platte River, Keith County, Nebraska, 1993. *Nebraska Bird Review* 61(4): 144–145. https://digitalcommons.unl.edu/nebbirdrev/482/

Scharf, W. C., J. Kren, P. A. Johnsgard, and L. R. Brown. 2008. *Body Weights and Species Distributions of Birds in Nebraska's Central and Western Platte Valley*. University of Nebraska–Lincoln Digital Commons, Papers in Ornithology. https://digitalcommons.unl.edu/biosciornithology/43/

Schneider, R., K. Stoner, G. Steinauer, M. Panella, and M. Humpert. 2018. *The Nebraska Natural Legacy Project: State Wildlife Action Plan*. 2nd ed. Lincoln: Nebraska Game and Parks Commission.

Schwilling, M. D. 1962. Species and nesting density of birds in grassland habitats near Burwell, Nebraska, in 1960. *Nebraska Bird Review* 30(1): 9–11. https://digitalcommons.unl.edu/nebbirdrev/911/

Sharpe, R. S. 1969. Evolutionary relationships and comparative behavior of prairie chickens. PhD dissertation. University of Nebraska–Lincoln.

Sharpe, R. S., and R. R. Payne. 1966. Nesting birds of Crescent Lake National Wildlife Refuge. *Nebraska Bird Review* 34(2): 31–34. https://digitalcommons.unl.edu/nebbirdrev/701/

Sharpe, R. S., W. R. Silcock, and J. G. Jorgensen. 2001. *The Birds of Nebraska: Their Distribution and Temporal Occurrence*. Lincoln: University of Nebraska Press. 513 pp.

Short, L. L., Jr. 1961. Notes on bird distribution in the central plains. *Nebraska Bird Review* 29(1): 2–22. https://digitalcommons.unl.edu/nebbirdrev/907/

———. 1965. Hybridization in the flickers (*Colaptes*) of North America. *Bulletin of the American Museum of Natural History* 129: 309–428.

Shreiber, J. A. 1994. Structure of breeding-bird communities on natural and restored Iowa wetlands. PhD dissertation. Iowa State University, Ames.

Sibley, C. G., and D. A. West. 1959. Hybridization in the rufous-sided towhees of the Great Plains. *Auk* 76: 326–338.

Sibley, C. G., and L. L. Short, Jr. 1959. Hybridization in the buntings (*Passerina*) of the Great Plains. *Auk* 76: 443–463.

———. 1964. Hybridization in the orioles of the Great Plains. *Condor* 66: 130–150.

Silcock, R., and J. Jorgensen. [Various dates]. Birds of Nebraska–Online. https://birds.outdoornebraska.gov/

Sisson, L. H. 1970. Distribution and selection of sharp-tailed grouse dancing grounds in the Nebraska Sandhills. *Proceedings of the 8th Conference of the Prairie Grouse Technical Council, 1969*.

———. 1976. *The Sharp-tailed Grouse in Nebraska*. Lincoln: Nebraska Game and Parks Commission. 16 pp.

Smith, R. L. 1963. Some ecological notes on the grasshopper sparrow. *Wilson Bulletin* 75: 159–165.

Snow, C. 1973a. Golden Eagle (*Aquila chrysaetos*). Habitat Management Series for Unique or Endangered Species. Denver, CO: US Department of the Interior, Bureau of Land Management Technical Note 239.

———. 1973b. Southern Bald Eagle (*Haliaeetus leucocephalus leucocephalus*) and Northern Bald Eagle (*Haliaeetus leucocephalus alascanus*). Habitat Management Series for Endangered Species. Denver, CO: US Department of the Interior, Bureau of Land Management Technical Note T-N-171.

———. 1974a. Ferruginous Hawk (*Buteo regalis*). Habitat Management Series for Unique or Endangered Species. Report No. 13. Denver, CO: US Department of the Interior, Bureau of Land Management Technical Note T-N-255.

———. 1974b. Prairie Falcon (*Falco mexicanus*). Habitat Management Series for Endangered Species. Denver, CO: US Department of the Interior, Bureau of Land Management Technical Note 240.

Stout, G. D., ed. 1967. *The Shorebirds of North America*. New York: Viking Press.

Szczys, P. 2006. *Investigation of the Breeding Biology and Population Genetic Structure of the Black Tern, Chlidonias niger*. Nebraska Game and Parks Commission, All Bird Conservation, Playa Lakes Joint Venture, and Crescent Lake National Wildlife Refuge.

Tallman, D. A., D. L. Swanson, and J. S. Palmer. 2002. *Birds of South Dakota*. Aberdeen: South Dakota Ornithologists' Union.

Taylor, S. V., and V. M. Ashe. 1976. The flight display and other behavior of male lark buntings (*Calamospiza melanochorys*). *Bulletin of the Psychonomic Society* 7: 527–529.

Thompson, M. C., C. Ely, B. Gress, C. Otte, S. T. Patti, D. Seibel, and E. A. Young. 2011. *Birds of Kansas*. Lawrence: University Press of Kansas.

Tout, W. 1947. *Lincoln County Birds: Lincoln County, Nebraska*. North Platte, NE: Published by the author. 191 pp.

Twedt, C. M. 1974. Characteristics of sharp-tailed grouse display grounds in the Nebraska Sandhills. PhD dissertation. University of Nebraska–Lincoln.

Twedt, D. J., and R. D. Crawford. 1995. Yellow-headed blackbird (*Xanthocephalus xanthocephalus*). In: *The Birds of North America*, no. 192 (A. Poole and F. Gill, eds.). Philadelphia: Academy of Natural Sciences, and Washington, DC: American Ornithologists' Union. 28 pp.

US Fish and Wildlife Service (USFWS). 2008. *Birds of Conservation Concern 2008*. Arlington, VA: USFWS, Division of Migratory Bird Management. 85 pp.

———. 2019. *Waterfowl Population Status*. Washington, DC: US Department of the Interior. 68 pp.

Vodehnal, W. L. 1999. Status and management of the greater prairie chicken in Nebraska. Pp. 81–98, in: *The Greater Prairie Chicken: A National Look* (W. D. Svedarsky, R. H. Hier, and J. J. Silvy. eds.). Miscellaneous Publication 9-1999. St. Paul: University of Minnesota.

Vrtiska, M. P., and L. A. Powell. 2011. Estimates of duck breeding populations in the Nebraska Sandhills using double observer methodology. *Waterbirds* 34: 96–101.

Walker, J. A., Z. J. Cunningham, M. P. Vrtiska, S. E. Stephens, and L. A. Powell. 2008. Low reproductive success of mallards in a grassland-dominated landscape in the Sandhills of Nebraska. *Prairie Naturalist* 40: 1–13.

West, D. A. 1962. Hybridization in grosbeaks (*Pheucticus*) of the Great Plains. *Auk* 79: 399–424.

Wilcox, L. R. 1959. A twenty year banding study of the piping plover. *Auk* 76: 129–152.

Wilson, B. L., J. Minyard, and H. Minyard. 1986. Hybrid bluebird update. *Nebraska Bird Review* 54(1): 26–27. https://digitalcommons.unl.edu/nebbirdrev/944/

Yasukawa, K., and W. A. Searcy. 1995. Red-winged blackbird (*Agelaius phoeniceus*). In: *The Birds of North America*, no. 184 (A. Poole and F. Gill, eds.). Philadelphia: Academy of Natural Sciences, and Washington, DC: American Ornithologists' Union. 28 pp.

Zimmer, J. T. 1913. Birds of the Thomas County Forest Preserve. *Proceedings of the Nebraska Ornithologists' Union* 5: 51–104.

Index to Bird Species and Families

Acadian flycatcher, 119
Accipitridae, 101-106
acorn woodpecker, 113
Alaudidae, 127
Alcedinidae, 113
alder flycatcher, 119
American avocet, 10, 71, 72, 179, 181, 182, 184, 187
American bittern, 10, 33, 68, 94, 95, 175, 184, 187
American black duck, 43
American coot, 69
American crow, 127
American dipper, 135
American golden-plover, 73
American goldfinch, 143
American kestrel, 115
American pipit, 141
American redstart, 168, 180
American robin, 138
American tree sparrow, 150
American white pelican, 93, 179, 183, 184, 187
American wigeon, 10, 33, 42
Anatidae, 35-50
Apodidae, 63
Arctic tern, 90
Ardeidae, 94-98
avocet. *See* American avocet

Baird's sandpiper, 79, 80, 81
Baird's sparrow, 152
bald eagle, 101, 102-103, 179, 182, 183
Baltimore oriole, 159, 160, 180
bank swallow, 129, 130
barn owl, 17, 106-108, 182
barn swallow, 7, 33, 130, 184
barred owl, 112
Barrow's goldeneye, 48
bay-breasted warbler, 168
Bell's vireo, 123
belted kingfisher, 33, 113, 180
Bewick's wren, 135
black rail, 65
black scoter, 47
black tern, 10, 18, 33, 90, 187
black-and-white warbler, 164, 180
black-bellied plover, 73, 81
black-bellied whistling-duck, 35
black-billed cuckoo, 62
black-billed magpie, 127
blackbirds, 20, 155-163, 175, 184
Blackburnian warbler, 169
black-capped chickadee, 132, 150, 180

black-crowned night-heron, 10, 33, 98, 99, 175, 181, 184
black-headed grosbeak, 173
black-headed gull, 87
black-legged kittiwake, 87
black-necked stilt, 10, 33, 70-71, 179, 181, 184
blackpoll warbler, 169
black-throated blue warbler, 170
black-throated gray warbler, 171
black-throated green warbler,
black-throated sparrow, 171
blue grosbeak, 173
blue jay, 126
blue-gray gnatcatcher, 135
blue-headed vireo, 125
blue-winged teal, 33, 41, 43
blue-winged warbler, 164
bobolink, 33, 155, 158, 180, 182, 184
bobwhite. *See* northern bobwhite
Bohemian waxwing, 139
Bombycillidae, 139-140
Bonaparte's gull, 877
brant, 37
Brewer's blackbird, 161
Brewer's sparrow, 149
broad-tailed hummingbird, 64
broad-winged hawk, 103
brown creeper, 133
brown pelican, 94
brown thrasher, 139, 180
brown-headed cowbird, 161, 163, 173, 174
buff-breasted sandpiper, 80
bufflehead, 47-48
Bullock's oriole, 159, 160
burrowing owl, 7, 15-16, 110, 111, 184

cackling goose, 37
Calcariidae, 143-144
California gull, 88
calliope hummingbird, 65
Canada goose, 33, 37-38
Canada warbler, 171
canvasback, 10, 33, 45
Cape May warbler, 168
Caprimulgidae, 62-63
Cardinalidae, 172-174
cardinal. *See* northern cardinal
Carolina wren, 135
Caspian tern, 90, 183
Cassin's finch, 142
Cassin's kingbird, 121
Cassin's sparrow, 144
Cassin's vireo, 125
catbird. *See* gray catbird
Cathartidae, 100
cattle egret, 96-98, 178, 187
cave swallow, 132
cedar waxwing, 140
Certhiidae, 133
cerulean warbler, 168
Charadriidae, 73-75
chat. *See* yellow-breasted chat

chestnut-collared longspur, 144
chestnut-sided warbler, 169
chickadees, 114, 132. *See also* black-capped chickadee, mountain chickadee
chimney swift, 63
chipping sparrow, 149, 180
chuck-will's-widow, 63
chukar, 50
Cinclidae, 135
cinnamon teal, 10, 33, 41, 182, 184
clapper rail, 66
Clark's grebe, 10, 59, 182
Clark's nutcracker, 127
clay-colored sparrow, 149, 153
cliff swallow, 32, 130-132, 183
Columbidae, 59, 61
common (Eurasian) crane, 69
common eider, 47
common gallinule, 66
common goldeneye, 48
common grackle, 163
common loon, 92
common merganser, 48-49
common nighthawk, 62-63, 64
common poorwill, 63, 180
common raven, 127
common redpoll, 142
common tern, 90
common yellowthroat, 33, 166, 167, 180, 181
Connecticut warbler, 165
Cooper's hawk, 102
coot. *See* American coot
Cordilleran flycatcher, 120
cormorant. *See* double-crested cormorant, neotropic cormorant
Corvidae, 126-127
Costa's hummingbird, 64
crane. *See* common (Eurasian) crane, sandhill crane, whooping crane
creeper. *See* brown creeper
crow. *See* American crow
cuckoos, 29, 62. *See also* black-billed cuckoo, yellow-billed cuckoo
Cuculidae, 62
curve-billed thrasher, 139

dark-eyed junco, 150
dickcissel, 14, 161, 173, 174
dipper. *See* American dipper
double-crested cormorant, 33, 68, 93, 179, 181, 183, 184
dove. *See* Eurasian collared-dove, Inca dove, mourning dove, white-winged dove
downy woodpecker, 114, 115
dunlin, 79
dusky flycatcher, 120

eagles, 101-103, 183. *See also* bald eagle, golden eagle
eared grebe, 7, 10, 33, 57, 58, 179, 184, 187

Index to Bird Species and Families

eastern bluebird, 136
eastern kingbird, 122
eastern meadowlark, 157, 158
eastern phoebe, 120, 121
eastern screech-owl, 108
eastern towhee, 154, 155
eastern whip-poor-will, 63
eastern wood-pewee, 118
egrets, 94, 96-98. *See also* cattle egret, great egret, reddish egret, snowy egret
Eurasian collared-dove, 61
Eurasian wigeon, 42
European starling, 140
evening grosbeak, 141

falcons, 17, 115-117. *See also* American kestrel, gyrfalcon, merlin, peregrine falcon, prairie falcon
ferruginous hawk, 106, 107, 184
field sparrow, 149, 161
finches, 141-143. *See also* American goldfinch, Cassin's finch, gray-crowned rosy finch, house finch, lesser goldfinch, purple finch
flycatchers, 118-122. *See also* Acadian flycatcher, alder flycatcher, Cassin's kingbird, Cordilleran flycatcher, dusky flycatcher, eastern kingbird, eastern phoebe, eastern wood-pewee, great crested flycatcher, Hammond's flycatcher, least flycatcher, olive-sided flycatcher, Say's phoebe, scissor-tailed flycatcher, vermilion flycatcher, western kingbird, western wood-pewee, willow flycatcher, yellow-bellied flycatcher
Forster's tern, 10, 18, 33, 90, 178, 181
fox sparrow, 150
Franklin's gull, 33, 88
Fringillidae, 141-143

gadwall, 33, 41, 42, 43
Gaviidae, 92-93
glaucous gull, 89
glaucous-winged gull, 89
glossy ibis, 98-99
gnatcatcher. *See* blue-gray gnatcatcher
golden eagle, 101, 106
golden-crowned kinglet, 135-136
golden-winged warbler, 164
Grace's warbler, 170
grackles, 163. *See also* common grackle, great-tailed grackle
grasshopper sparrow, 145, 146, 147, 153, 184
gray catbird, 138-139
gray jay. *See* Canada jay
gray partridge, 50
gray-cheeked thrush, 137
gray-crowned rosy-finch, 141
great black-backed gull, 89
great blue heron, 33, 94, 97, 175, 179, 180, 181
great crested flycatcher, 121

great egret, 96
great horned owl,
greater prairie-chicken, 11, 12, 14, 33, 53-55
greater scaup, 46
greater white-fronted goose, 37,
greater yellowlegs, 83, 85
great-tailed grackle, 163
grebes, 57-60, 178, 179, 181, 183, 184. *See also* Clark's grebe, eared grebe, horned grebe, pied-billed grebe, red-necked grebe, western grebe
green heron, 98
green-tailed towhee, 154
green-winged teal, 33, 45, 117
grosbeaks, 172-173. *See also* black-headed grosbeak, blue grosbeak, evening grosbeak, rose-breasted grosbeak
grouse, 11, 13, 14, 21, 50-53. *See also* chukar, gray partridge, greater prairie-chicken, sharp-tailed grouse
Gruidae, 69-71
gulls, 87-92, 178, 183, 188. *See also* black-headed gull, black-legged kittiwake, Bonaparte's gull, California gull, Franklin's gull, glaucous gull, glaucous-winged gull, greater black-backed gull, herring gull, Iceland gull, laughing gull, lesser black-backed gull, little gull, mew gull, ring-billed gull, Ross's gull, Sabine's gull
gyrfalcon, 116

hairy woodpecker, 114-115
Hammond's flycatcher, 120
harlequin duck, 47
Harris's sparrow, 151
hawks, 17, 29, 101-107, 184, 187, 188. *See also* broad-winged hawk, Cooper's hawk, ferruginous hawk, sharp-shinned hawk, northern goshawk, northern harrier, red-shouldered hawk, red-tailed hawk, rough-legged hawk, Swainson's hawk, zone-tailed hawk
hermit thrush, 137-138
hermit warbler, 171
herons, 94-98. *See also* American bittern, black-crowned night-heron, great blue heron, green heron, least bittern, little blue heron, yellow-crowned night-heron
herring gull, 88-89
Hirundinidae, 129-132
hooded merganser, 48
hooded warbler, 166
horned grebe, 57
horned lark, 17, 21, 127-128, 153, 184
house finch, 140, 141-142, 150
house sparrow, 140
house wren, 134, 135
Hudsonian godwit, 77
hummingbirds, 64-65, 114. *See also* broad-tailed hummingbird,

calliope hummingbird, Costa's hummingbird, ruby-throated hummingbird, rufous hummingbird,

ibises, 98-100, 184, 187. *See also* glossy ibis, white ibis, white-faced ibis
Iceland gull, 89
Icteridae, 155-163
Icteriidae, 155
Inca dove, 61
indigo bunting, 161, 174

jaegers, 92. *See also* long-tailed jaeger, parasitic jaeger, pomarine jaeger
jays, 126-127. *See also* blue jay, Canada jay, pinyon jay, Steller's jay
junco. *See* dark-eyed junco

Kentucky warbler, 166
killdeer, 33, 73
kingfisher. *See* belted kingfisher
kinglet. *See* golden-crowned kinglet, ruby-crowned kinglet

Laniidae, 122-123
Lapland longspur, 143-144
Laridae, 87-92
lark bunting, 147, 153, 184
lark sparrow, 147, 148
lark. *See* horned lark
laughing gull, 88
lazuli bunting, 174
least bittern, 94, 178
least flycatcher, 119-120
least sandpiper, 80, 81
least tern, 89-90, 183, 188
LeConte's sparrow, 151, 152
lesser black-backed gull, 89
lesser goldfinch, 143
lesser scaup, 33, 46
lesser yellowlegs, 83
Lewis's woodpecker, 113
Lincoln's sparrow, 152-153
little blue heron, 96
little gull, 87
loggerhead shrike, 122, 123, 124
long-billed curlew, 6, 7, 10, 14, 20-21, 33, 74, 75-76, 78, 178, 180, 182, 184, 187
long-billed dowitcher, 81
long-eared owl, 112
longspurs, 143-144. *See also* chestnut-collared longspur, Lapland longspur, Smith's longspur, thick-billed longspur
long-tailed duck, 47
long-tailed jaeger, 92
loons, 92-93, 188. *See also* common loon, Pacific loon, red-throated loon, yellow-billed loon

MacGillivray's warbler, 166
magnolia warbler, 168
magpie. *See* black-billed magpie
mallard, 33, 41, 43
marbled godwit, 10, 77, 182

marsh hawk. *See* northern harrier
marsh wren, 20, 33, 134-135, 178, 181, 184
McCown's longspur. *See* thick-billed longspur
meadowlarks, 17, 157, 158, 184. *See also* eastern meadowlark, western meadowlark
merlin, 115
mew gull, 88
Mimidae, 138-139
Mississippi kite, 103
mockingbird. *See* northern mockingbird
Motacillidae, 141
mountain bluebird, 136
mountain chickadee, 132
mountain plover, 75
mourning dove, 61
mourning warbler, 166

Nashville warbler, 165
Nelson's sparrow, 151-152
neotropic cormorant, 93
nightjars, 63. *See also* chuck-will's-widow, common nighthawk, common poorwill, eastern whip-poor-will
northern bobwhite, 50
northern cardinal, 161, 172-173
northern flicker, 115
northern goshawk, 102
northern harrier, 16-18, 33, 101, 179, 182
northern mockingbird, 139
northern parula, 168
northern pintail, 33, 43, 44, 187
northern rough-winged swallow, 33, 129-130
northern saw-whet owl, 112
northern shoveler, 33, 41-42, 43
northern shrike, 122-123
northern waterthrush, 164
nuthatches, 114, 132-133. *See also* pygmy nuthatch, red-breasted nuthatch, white-breasted nuthatch

Odontophoridae, 50
olive-sided flycatcher, 118
orange-crowned warbler, 165
orchard oriole, 157-159
orioles, 157-159. *See also* Baltimore oriole, Bullock's oriole, orchard oriole
osprey, 100-101, 183
ovenbird, 164, 180
owls, 15, 17, 29, 106-112. *See also* barn owl, barred owl, burrowing owl, eastern screech-owl, great horned owl, long-eared owl, northern saw-whet owl, short-eared owl, snowy owl

Pacific loon, 92
painted bunting, 174
palm warbler, 170

Pandionidae, 100-101
parasitic jaeger, 92
Paridae, 132
Parulidae, 164-172
Passeridae, 140
pectoral sandpiper, 80
Pelecanidae, 93-94
peregrine falcon, 116
Phalacrocoracidae, 93
phalaropes, 19, 85-87, 181, 184. *See also* red phalarope, red-necked phalarope, Wilson's phalarope
pheasants, 50, 116. *See also* ring-necked pheasant
Philadelphia vireo, 126
Picidae, 113-115
pied-billed grebe, 33, 56, 57, 68
pigeons, 59, 116. *See also* rock pigeon
pine siskin, 143
pine warbler, 170
pinyon jay, 126
piping plover, 73-75
pipits, 141. *See also* American pipit, Sprague's pipit
plovers, 73-75, 81, 183, 188. *See also* American golden-plover, black-bellied plover, mountain plover, piping plover, killdeer, semipalmated plover, snowy plover
plumbeous vireo, 125
Podicipedidae, 56-59
Polioptilidae, 135
pomarine jaeger, 92
prairie falcon, 17, 116, 117
prairie warbler, 171
prothonotary warbler, 165
purple finch, 142
purple martin, 130
pygmy nuthatch, 133

quail. *See* northern bobwhite

rails, 65-67. *See also* black rail, clapper rail, king rail, sora, Virginia rail, yellow rail
Rallidae, 65-69
Recurvirostridae, 71-72
red crossbill, 142-143, 180
red knot, 79
red phalarope, 87
red-bellied woodpecker, 113-114
red-breasted merganser, 49
red-breasted nuthatch, 132
reddish egret, 96
red-eyed vireo, 126
redhead, 33, 45
red-headed woodpecker, 113
red-naped sapsucker, 114
red-necked grebe, 57
red-necked phalarope, 85-86
red-shouldered hawk, 103
red-tailed hawk, 104-106
red-throated loon, 92
red-winged blackbird, 19, 20, 33, 155, 159, 161, 162, 175
Regulidae, 135-136

ring-billed gull, 88
ring-necked duck, 46
ring-necked pheasant, 50
rock pigeon, 59
rock wren, 133, 183, 188
rose-breasted grosbeak, 173
Ross's goose, 37
Ross's gull, 87
rough-legged hawk, 106
ruby-crowned kinglet, 136
ruby-throated hummingbird, 64
ruddy duck, 7, 10, 33, 49, 182, 187
ruddy turnstone, 77
ruff, 79
rufous hummingbird, 65
rusty blackbird, 161, 163

Sabine's gull, 87
sage thrasher, 139
sanderling, 79
sandhill crane, 11, 14, 68, 69, 71, 180, 182
sandpipers, 75-87, 184, 187. *See also* Baird's sandpiper, buff-breasted sandpiper, dunlin, greater yellowlegs, Hudsonian godwit, least sandpiper, lesser yellowlegs, long-billed curlew, long-billed dowitcher, marbled godwit, pectoral sandpiper, red knot, ruddy turnstone, ruff, sanderling, semipalmated sandpiper, sharp-tailed sandpiper, short-billed dowitcher, solitary sandpiper, spotted sandpiper, stilt sandpiper, upland sandpiper, western sandpiper, whimbrel, white-rumped sandpiper, willet
savannah sparrow, 152, 153
Say's phoebe, 120-121
scarlet tanager, 172
scissor-tailed flycatcher, 122
Scolopacidae, 75-87
sedge wren, 134
semipalmated plover, 73
semipalmated sandpiper, 80-81
sharp-shinned hawk, 102
sharp-tailed grouse, 13, 14, 50-53, 116, 178, 180, 184
sharp-tailed sandpiper, 77
short-billed dowitcher, 81, 82-83
short-eared owl, 112
shrikes, 122-124. *See also* loggerhead shrike, northern shrike
Sittidae, 132-133
Smith's longspur, 144
snipes, 81, 84. *See also* Wilson's snipe
snow bunting, 144
snow goose, 35, 37
snowy egret, 96
snowy owl, 108
snowy plover, 75, 188
solitary sandpiper, 83
song sparrow, 33, 152, 161
sora, 33, 65, 66, 67, 175, 181, 184
sparrows, 140, 144-155. *See also* American tree sparrow, Baird's

sparrow, black-throated sparrow, Brewer's sparrow, Cassin's sparrow, chipping sparrow, clay-colored sparrow, dark-eyed junco, field sparrow, fox sparrow, grasshopper sparrow, Harris's sparrow, house sparrow (Old World sparrow), lark bunting, lark sparrow, LeConte's sparrow, Lincoln's sparrow, Nelson's sparrow, savannah sparrow, song sparrow, swamp sparrow, vesper sparrow, white-crowned sparrow, white-throated sparrow
spotted sandpiper, 33, 83, 182, 184
spotted towhee, 154, 155
Sprague's pipit, 21, 141
starling. *See* European starling
Steller's jay, 126, 127
Stercorariidae, 92
stilt sandpiper, 79
stilts, 71, 179, 181., 184 *See also* black-necked stilt
Strigidae, 108-112
Sturnidae, 140
summer tanager, 172
surf scoter, 47
Swainson's hawk, 103, 104, 105, 187, 188
Swainson's thrush, 137
swallows, 7, 114, 129-132, 183, 184. *See also* bank swallow, barn swallow, cave swallow, cliff swallow, northern rough-winged swallow, purple martin, tree swallow, violet-green swallow
swamp sparrow, 33, 154, 175, 178, 182
swifts, 63-64. *See also* chimney swift, white-throated swift

tanagers, 172. *See also* scarlet tanager, summer tanager, western tanager
Tennessee warbler, 165
terns, 18-19, 89-92. *See also* Arctic tern, black tern, Caspian tern, common tern, Forster's tern, least tern
thick-billed longspur, 144
thrashers, 139. *See also* brown thrasher, curve-billed thrasher, sage thrasher
Threskiornithidae, 98-100
thrushes, 136-138
titmice, 132
towhees, 154-155, 180. *See also* eastern towhee, green-tailed towhee, spotted towhee
Townsend's solitaire, 137
Townsend's warbler, 171
tree swallow, 114, 129
Trochilidae, 64-65
Troglodytidae, 133-135
trumpeter swan, 8, 10, 33, 38, 39, 178, 179, 187
tufted duck, 46
tufted titmouse, 132
tundra swan, 39

Turdidae, 136-138
turkey vulture, 17, 100
turkeys, 53, 178
Tyrannidae, 118-122
Tytonidae, 106

upland sandpiper, 33, 75, 76, 178, 184, 187

varied thrush, 138
veery, 137, 138
vesper sparrow, 151
violet-green swallow, 129
Vireonidae, 123, 125-126
Virginia rail, 33, 66, 175, 181
vultures, 17, 100. *See also* turkey vulture

warblers, 161, 164-172, 180, 184. *See also* American redstart, bay-breasted warbler, black-and-white warbler, Blackburnian warbler, blackpoll warbler, black-throated blue warbler, black-throated gray warbler, black-throated green warbler, blue-winged warbler, Canada warbler, Cape May warbler, cerulean warbler, chestnut-sided warbler, common yellowthroat, Connecticut warbler, golden-winged warbler, Grace's warbler, hermit warbler, hooded warbler, Kentucky warbler, MacGillivray's warbler, magnolia warbler, mourning warbler, Nashville warbler, northern parula, northern waterthrush, orange-crowned warbler, ovenbird, palm warbler, pine warbler, prairie warbler, prothonotary warbler, Tennessee warbler, Townsend's warbler, Wilson's warbler, worm-eating warbler, yellow-rumped warbler, yellow warbler
warbling vireo, 125
waterfowl, 7, 10, 18, 30, 103, 116, 178, 179, 181, 183, 187
waxwings, 139-140. *See also* Bohemian waxwing, cedar waxwing
western grebe, 10, 59
western kingbird, 121-122
western meadowlark, 157, 184
western sandpiper, 81
western tanager, 172
western wood-pewee, 118
whimbrel, 75
white ibis, 98
white-breasted nuthatch, 133
white-crowned sparrow, 150-151
white-eyed vireo, 123
white-faced ibis, 10, 100, 178, 181, 184, 187
white-rumped sandpiper, 80
white-tailed kite, 101
white-throated sparrow, 151
white-throated swift, 64
white-winged dove, 61
white-winged scoter, 47

whooping crane, 68, 71
wild turkey, 53, 178
willet, 10, 33, 83-84, 178, 187
willow flycatcher, 119
Wilson's phalarope, 10, 19, 33, 85, 86, 87, 181, 182
Wilson's snipe, 81, 84, 182, 184
Wilson's warbler, 171-172
winter wren, 134
wood duck, 33, 39-41, 179, 182, 187
wood thrush, 138, 161
woodpeckers, 29, 113-115, 133, 140, 180. *See also* acorn woodpecker, downy woodpecker, hairy woodpecker, Lewis's woodpecker, northern flicker, red-bellied woodpecker, red-headed woodpecker, red-naped sapsucker, yellow-bellied sapsucker
worm-eating warbler, 164
wrens, 20, 33, 133-135, 178, 181, 183, 184, 188. *See also* Bewick's wren, Carolina wren, house wren, marsh wren, rock wren, sedge wren, winter wren

yellow-bellied flycatcher, 118-119
yellow-bellied sapsucker, 114
yellow-billed cuckoo, 62
yellow-breasted chat, 155, 178, 180
yellow-crowned night-heron, 98
yellow-headed blackbird, 19-20, 33, 155, 156, 184
yellow rail, 65
yellow-rumped warbler, 170
yellow-throated vireo, 125
yellow warbler, 161, 169

zone-tailed hawk, 104

www.ingramcontent.com/pod-product-compliance
Lightning Source LLC
Chambersburg PA
CBHW080542170426
43195CB00016B/2654